ABOUT THE A

Travel writers DANA FACAROS and MICHAEL PAULS, their two children, and semi-cat Piggy have lived in a little Umbrian village for the past three years. When not writing, Michael plays the musical saw while Dana perfects her indescribable boar-mating call.

Their output is as prolific as the Umbrian truffle and includes Cadogan Guides to *Italy, Tuscany & Umbria, Spain, Greek Islands* and *Turkey*.

CADOGAN GUIDES

Other titles in the Cadogan Guide series:

AUSTRALIA
THE CARIBBEAN
GREEK ISLANDS
INDIA
IRELAND
ITALY
SCOTLAND
THE SOUTH OF FRANCE
SPAIN
THAILAND AND BURMA
TURKEY
TUSCANY & UMBRIA

Forthcoming:

BALI
GUATEMALA
MEXICO
MOROCCO
PORTUGAL

Forthcoming in the City Guide series:

ROME   NEW ORLEANS
VENICE   NEW YORK

CADOGAN GUIDES

ITALIAN ISLANDS

DANA FACAROS & MICHAEL PAULS
updated with the help of Michael Davidson & Brian Walsh

Illustrations by Pauline Pears

CADOGAN BOOKS

LONDON

Cadogan Books Ltd
(Holding Company – Metal Bulletin PLC)
16 Lower Marsh, London SE1

Cover design by Keith Pointing
Cover illustration by Povl Webb

Series Editors: Rachel Fielding and Paula Levey

First published in 1981
2nd revised edition 1986
This revised and updated edition published in 1989

British Library Cataloguing in Publication Data
Facaros, Dana
    Italian islands.—3rd ed.—(Cadogan guides)
    1. Italy. Islands,—Visitors' guides.
    I. Title   II. Pauls, Michael
    914.5′04928

ISBN 0–946313–82–2

Phototypeset in Ehrhardt on a Linotron 202
Printed and bound in Great Britain by Redwood Burn Limited
Trowbridge, Wiltshire

ACKNOWLEDGEMENTS

We gratefully acknowledge the assistance of the Ente Nazionale di Turismo in London; the staff of the provincial tourist offices and AASTs on the Italian islands, especially Maria Luisa Manca of Oristano, Giovanni Pais of Alghero, Dr Massimo Mance of Elba, Tommaso Mesolella of Ponza and Dr Solar of Nuoro, Sardinia.

To Jackson, who was a good boy

PLEASE NOTE

Every effort has been made to ensure the accuracy of the information in this book at the time of going to press. However, practical details such as opening hours, travel information, standards in hotels and restaurants and, in particular, prices are liable to change.

We will be delighted to receive any corrections and suggestions for improvement which can be incorporated into the next edition, but cannot accept any responsibility for consequences arising from the use of this guide.

We intend to keep this book as up-to-date as possible in the coming years, so please do write to us. Writers of the best letters will receive a free copy of the Cadogan Guide of their choice.

CONTENTS

LIST OF MAPS

INTRODUCTION

There are 32 islands off the coasts of Italy, ranging in size from Sicily and Sardinia—the largest in the Mediterranean—to little specks in the sea, where convicts get government-paid holidays for life. Some islands, Capri-fashion, have blossomed (or withered, depending on your point of view) into full-blown resorts, where you can count more signs in English and German than in Italian. Others, such as Ponza, Pantelleria and the Egadi Islands, are among Italy's best-kept secrets.

The Italians look upon their islands as very distinct characters and treasure them as their last refuges from the polluted sea that has sullied most of the choicest Riviera resorts on the mainland. The islands, particularly Sardinia and Sicily, have preserved many traditional customs long lost on the wealthier, industrialized mainland; their own dialects are alive and well. They are Italian but different, in many ways self-contained, each 'an epitome of the whole earth', as Bishop Berkeley described his own favourite island, Ischia.

Generally speaking, Italy's islands had their golden age in the centuries before Christ, when the Mediterranean was a busy highway instead of a deep blue barrier. The beautiful cave incisions on the island of Levanzo, stylistically similar to the prehistoric cave art of the Rhone, have been carbon-dated to 10,000 BC. Lipari, in the Aeolian archipelago, was an important Neolithic trading centre with samples of its prized obsidian (volcanic glass) found as far afield as Malta. On Sardinia, the fascinating Nuraghic civilization lasted from 1500 BC to Roman times, producing Europe's first castles and literally thousands of the sturdy stone towers known as *nuraghes*. A similar culture developed on distant Pantelleria, leaving the monumental *sesis* behind to confound us. And then of course there is the Sicily of the ancient Greeks, where great cities rivalled, and then surpassed, Athens itself in wealth and power. For most islands, their importance has been steadily declining ever since those heady days when Phoenician ships and triremes brought trade and prosperity to their shores.

Nowadays it's their very isolation from the world that is so alluring, and their often startling physical beauty: these islands have been sculpted by volcanoes and split by cataclysmic, prehistoric earthquakes into 'sheer, towering cliffs and mighty monoliths', but they also display a lush beauty, strewn as they are with wild flowers and cultivated with orchards and vines, almonds and capers, chestnuts and orange groves, olives and pine nuts. Add the charm and artistry of their Italian heritage and culture, and you have a mixture that's almost irresistible.

LIVORNO
TUSCAN
ISLANDS
Piombino
CORSICA
Porto S. Stefano
Civitavecchia
ROME
Anzio
ISCHIA
PONTINE
ISLANDS
CAPRI
NAPLES
SARDINIA
TYRRHENIAN
SEA
USTICA
EGADI
ISLANDS
PALERMO
SICILY
Agrigento
PANTELLERIA
CATANIA
PELAGIE
ISLANDS

YUGOSLAVIA
ADRIATIC
SEA
Ortona
TREMITI
ISLANDS
Vieste

AEOLIAN
ISLANDS

MEDITERRANEAN
SEA

miles   100   200
km   100   200   300

N

THE ITALIAN ISLANDS

Part I
GENERAL INFORMATION

A Town Market

Before You Go

Don't be a last-minute loser! The islands are a top destination for Italians on holiday, and the earlier you book, the better your chances of getting the flight/ferry/accommodation that you really want. A number of firms in Italy and abroad have begun to respond to demands of independent travellers for reasonably priced flights, flats, car hire, etc.; look over your travel agent's catalogues or write to your Italian State Tourist Office for their list of companies that deal with the islands. Their addresses are:

1 Princes Street, London W1R 8AY (tel (01) 408 1254; telex 22402).
47 Merrion Square, Dublin 2, Eire (tel (01) 766397; telex 31682).
630 Fifth Avenue, Suite 1565, New York, NY 10111 (tel (212) 245 4961; telex 236024).
500 N. Michigan Avenue, Suite 1046, Chicago, Ill. 60611 (tel (312) 644 0990/1; telex 0255160).
360 Post Street, Suite 801, San Francisco, California 94108 (tel (415) 392 5266; telex 67623).
Store 56, Plaza 3, Place Ville Marie, Montreal, Quebec (tel (514) 866 7667; telex 525607).

Getting to the Italian Islands

By Air

From Britain
Before shelling out for a regular fare, be sure to check the pages of *Time Out* and *The*

3

Times for bargain flights, as well as your local bucket shop. There are a number of weekly charter flights direct from London to Palermo and Sardinia; otherwise you'll have to aim for a city on the mainland (Rome, Pisa, Genoa, and Naples the most likely choices, served by regular British Air and Alitalia flights). Alitalia has the slight advantage in offering scheduled connecting flights from London to Alghero and Cagliari in Sardinia, and to Catania and Palermo (non-stop in the summer); also consider their economical fly–drive packages available on scheduled flights.

There are various deals where £200–£300 per person will cover the airfare, airport taxes and two weeks in a two-bedroomed apartment, and some travel companies offer perks such as car hire at greatly reduced rates. It's worth looking into the many combinations and possibilities with your travel agent. If you feel energetic enough to organize a party of 10–14 people, you can even get there and back free. **Global** is one firm which offers a number of attractive holiday centres in Sicily and Sardinia. Their London number is (01) 464 6666. **Magic of Italy** (tel (01) 743 9555) is another reputable company to bear in mind, and their offers include apartments in the glamorous Costa Smeralda.

From the USA and Canada
Alitalia offers non-stop flights to Rome and Milan from New York and Boston, and from Toronto and Montreal (for possible connections, see 'Domestic flights' below). TWA has a daily non-stop service between New York and Rome and Milan, and between Boston and Rome. Pan Am also flies from New York to Rome non-stop, while British Airways offers a daily service from New York to London to Pisa, which is the quickest way to reach Elba from Gotham. Again, Alitalia's car rental schemes may give them the edge if you mean to hire a car.

By Train

Most trains to Italy from London go via Paris, from where you have the choice of two trains leaving for Rome—one at 18.47, arriving 9.45 the following morning, or one at 20.56 arriving at 13.55 the following day (cost about £110). They stop at Genoa, Livorno and Civitavecchia for island connections. From Rome there are frequent trains south for Gaeta (Pontine Islands), Naples (Bay of Naples Islands and Aeolian Islands), and Palermo, Catania and Syracuse in Sicily.

Italian trains, known as the FS (*Ferrovie dello Stato*), are not expensive and run quite frequently up and down the 'boot' of Italy. In fact you can calculate approximately how much your fare will come to as Italian State Railway fares are based on distance travelled. For example (second-class fares):

1–5 km	L600
96–100 km	L5000
191–200 km	L10 000
501–525 km	L26 000
1000–1100 km	L45 000

In the larger towns of Italy, the stations have a *Prenotazione* counter, where you may, for a small fee, reserve a seat on a train of any class. This often proves to be a good exercise in the summer months, especially on long, tourist-crowded routes. If you don't make a reservation, particularly in season and on Friday evenings, to Sicily (when all the workers go home from their jobs in Rome and Naples), make sure you arrive at the station a good hour before your train departs or you'll never get a seat. You can also buy tickets and make reservations at authorized travel agencies. If you wait to buy your ticket on the train, there's a 20 per cent surcharge. Also note that domestic rail tickets are valid only for the day they're issued; if you're coming back the same way in three days or less, ask for a *ritorno* (a one-way ticket is an *andata*).

A good bargain for those planning extensive rail travel is the BTLC ticket, which can be purchased for periods of 8, 15, 21 or 30 days of unlimited travel on Italy's trains, with the special advantage of free seat reservations. Prices (second class) range from $170/£100 for eight days to $300/£170 for 30 days. Another ticket, the Italian Kilometric Ticket, is valid for 20 trips or 3000 km, whichever comes first (cost about $120/£69). One advantage of this ticket is that it can be used by up to five people, and is calculated by multiplying the distance travelled by the number of travellers. Thus five people going 10 km would count as 50 km on the ticket. For both of these, children under 12 pay half (or count half the distance travelled) and tots under 4 go free. There are also reductions for family groups of more than four people. These tickets may be purchased at **CIT offices** (which are good sources for precise schedules, etc.), whose foreign addresses are listed below.

New York: 666 5th Avenue, 6th Floor, New York, NY 10103
Chicago: 500 N. Michigan Avenue, Suite 1310 , Chicago, ILL 60611
Los Angeles: 15760 Ventura Blvd, Suite 819, Los Angeles, CA 91436
Montreal: 2055 Peel Street, Suite 102, Montreal, H3A 1V4, PQ
Toronto: 13 Balmuto Street, Toronto, ONT M4Y 1W4
London: 50 Conduit Street, London W1R 9FB

The perennial favourites, the Eurail Pass and the Eurail Youth Pass are available with unlimited mileage; the Eurail Pass ranges from $300 for 15 days to $800 for three months and the Eurail Youth Pass from $325 for one month to $430 for two months. However, if you are intending to spend all, or most of your holiday in Italy, you'll find the Eurail Pass is rarely worth the price.

By Coach

Euroways Express Coaches offer an economical service to Italy from London. An adult single to Rome is about £70 (£45 for students). In the summer the service continues down to Naples. For information, contact Wallace Arnold, 52 Grosvenor Gardens, London W1 (tel (01) 730 8235). Other companies include International Express (23 Crawley Road, Luton LU1 1HX, tel (0582) 404 511), Club Cantabrica (Holiday House, 146 London Road, St. Albans, tel (0727) 66177), or Miracle Bus (408 Strand, London WC2, tel (01) 379 6055).

By Car

To bring your car into Italy, you need your car registration (log book), valid driving licence with an Italian translation (provided by the AA or RAC), and valid insurance (a

Green Card is not necessary, but you'll need one if you go through Switzerland). US citizens will also require an International Driving Licence. Make sure everything is in excellent working order or your slightly bald tyre may enrich the coffers of the Swiss or Italian police—it's not uncommon to be stopped for no reason and have your car searched until the police find something to stick a fine on. Note that by law you are required to carry a portable triangular danger sign (available from ACI offices). Also beware that spare parts for non-Italian cars are difficult to come by.

Before leaving, you can save yourself about 15 per cent on expensive Italian petrol and motorway tolls by purchasing **Petrol Coupons**, issued to owners of GB-registered vehicles by London's CIT office (see p. 5), at Wastell Travel, 121 Wilton Rd, London SW1, tel (01) 834 7066, or at your local AA or RAC office, or at the frontier from Italian Auto Club offices. Coupons are sold only in person to the car-owner with his or her passport and car registration, and cannot be paid for in Italian lire. Along with the coupons and motorway vouchers, you get a *Carta Carburante* which entitles you to breakdown services provided by the Italian Auto Club (ACI). Unused coupons can be refunded at the place of purchase; prices are tagged to currency exchange rates.

Frontier Formalities

To enter Italy you need a passport, or if you're from a Common Market country, an identification card valid for foreign travel. Unless you have a special visa, you are allowed to stay in Italy for up to three months. If you're bringing along a cat or dog you'll need a veterinarian's certificate from home—the Italians are sticklers for forms, so get the proper international one (available from the ENIT). It must show that your pet is in good health and has been vaccinated for rabies in the past 11 months.

Italy restricts exportation of antiques and works of art, for which permission must be granted by the Ufficio Esportazione di Oggetti d'Arte e d'Antichita, Ministero della Pubblica Istruzione, Via Cernaia 1, Rome.

Currency

If you're carrying a lot of cash (more than the equivalent of 1 million lire) that you'll want to take with you when you leave Italy, you should declare the amount on form V2 when you arrive. You may take up to 400 000 lire in Italian currency in or out of the country (though really they hardly ever check). The best exchange rates for currency or traveller's cheques are given by the major banks and exchange bureaux licensed by the Bank of Italy. Hotels and FS-run exchanges at railway stations are usually not as good, but operate on Sundays. Currency exchanges usually stay open until 7 or 8 pm.

Climate

The Italian islands enjoy a typically Mediterranean climate, though Sicily can get particularly hot in the summer when the sirocco wind blows up from North Africa. In the spring, as the winter rains diminish, the weather is at its most pleasant, and hills which are dried out by late summer are a glorious green and covered with wild flowers. In the autumn it stays warm enough to swim in Sicily, usually until the end of October; the snow starts falling in the mountains of Sardinia in November.

Average monthly temperatures in ° Fahrenheit   *Sea temperatures*

	J	F	M	A	M	J	J	A	S	O	N	D		A	M	J	J	A	S	O
Cagliari	49	50	55	59	65	73	79	79	73	68	61	53		59	62	68	73	75	73	70
Capri	52	52	53	55	62	71	75	78	70	62	57	53		57	64	68	77	80	75	57
Palermo	50	51	55	61	65	73	78	76	73	68	62	55		62	68	73	82	80	77	73
Sassari	47	47	51	53	62	72	75	78	71	64	57	50		64	66	73	77	75	75	73
Taormina	52	51	55	61	68	75	80	80	75	68	61	55		64	66	73	75	77	75	66

Time
Italy is one hour ahead of Greenwich Mean Time. From the last weekend of March to the end of September, Italian Summer Time (daylight savings time) puts the country ahead another hour.

Getting Around the Islands

Domestic Flights

These are all on Alitalia, the national airline, or its subsidiaries ATI and Alisarda. Information on all of these lines can be had from Alitalia offices.

From Rome to: (Frequency/Duration)
Alghero (3 a day/50 min)
Bari (for Tremiti Islands) (5 a day/60 min)
Cagliari (9 a day/55 min)
Catania (8 a day/70 min)
Naples (4 a day/45 min)
Olbia (2 a day/45 min)
Palermo (7 a day/60 min)
Pisa (Tuscan Islands) (3 a day/45 min)
Reggio Calabria (for Messina) (4 a day/65 min)
Trapani/Marsala (2 a day/90 min)

From Milan to:
Alghero (4 a day/70 min)
Bari (5 a day/85 min)
Cagliari (5 a day/80 min)
Catania (5 a day/100 min)
Naples (5 a day/75 min)
Olbia (4 a day/65 min)
Palermo (3 a day/90 min)
Pisa (3 a day/45 min)
Reggio Calabria (1 a day/90 min)

From Naples to:
Palermo (2 a day/45 min)
Catania (2 a day/50 min)

From Pisa to:
Alghero (1 a day/55 min)
Cagliari (1 a day/65 min)
Olbia (1 a day/55 min)

Inter-island flights

From Palermo to:
Cagliari (1 a day/50 min)
Pantelleria (2 a day/45 min)
Lampedusa (1 a day/45 min)
Trapani (2 a day/25 min)

From Trapani to:
Pantelleria (2 a day/45 min)

From Cagliari to:
Alghero (4 a day/35 min)
Olbia (2 a day/35 min)
On domestic flights, children under 2 fly at a 90 per cent discount; between the ages of 2 and 12 they receive a 50 per cent discount, and between the ages of 12 and 21 they receive a 30 per cent discount. There are also a number of weekend discounts on domestic flights. Addresses of Alitalia offices on the islands are:

In Sicily
Agrigento: Akratur, Viaggie e Turismo, Via Cicerone 11 (tel (0992) 25566).
Augusta: G. Bozzanca & Figlio, Via C. Colombo 50 (tel (0931) 974106).
Caltanissetta: Kaltour, Viaggi e Turismo, Corso Umberto 1 (tel (0934) 21004).
Catania: Corso Sicilia 111/113 (tel (095) 252222 & 326419).
Marsala: Agenzia Ruggieri, Via Mazzini 111 (tel (0923) 951426).
Messina: A Meo & Figli, Via del Vespro 56 (tel (090) 719192).
Palermo: Via Mazzini 59 (tel (091) 6019200).
Ragusa: Ufficio Turistico Ibleo, Viale del Fante 4 (tel (0932) 22063).
Syracuse: Bozzanca & Figlio, Corso Matteotti 80/90 (tel (0931) 67122); Corso Gelone 91 (tel (0931) 60978).
Termini Imerese: F. Paolo Manzo, Viale Vittorio Amedeo 18 (tel (091) 8142080).
Trapani: Agenzia Nattale Salvo, Corso Italia 52/56 (tel (0923) 23819).

In Sardinia:
Cagliari: Via Caprera 12/14 (tel (070) 60107); Alisarda only Via Barone Rossi 27 (tel (070) 651381).
Nuoro: Agenzia Ancor, Via Manzoni (tel (0784) 30463); Alisarda, Via Lamarmora 117 (tel (0784) 37446).
Olbia: Alisarda, Corso Umberto 195/C (tel (0789) 693F00).
Sassari: Sarda Viaggi, Via Cagliari 30 (tel (079) 234498).

In Lampedusa:
Scalo Ati, at the airport (tel (0922) 970299).

In Pantelleria:
La Cossira, Via Borgo (tel (0923) 911078).

By Sea

There are several shipping lines serving all of Italy, apart from Tirrenia, the largest, which is government-subsidized. Their names are a typical continental alphabet soup— SNAV, SAS, NAVARMA, TOREMAR and the like. Their ticket offices are usually right on the quayside. For some of the most popular routes (especially to Sardinia) you must reserve car space in advance for the peak season (mid July–mid September). Long-distance Tirrenia tickets can be booked at a CIT office or one of their many agencies; the head offices of the other lines are listed below. Fares are moderate—it is almost always cheaper to go by sea than land. Note that in case of *mare brutto* (rough seas), the ship will remain in port until its next scheduled voyage.

On long, overnight trips (to Sardinia, Palermo–Naples, to Lampedusa, etc.) it is definitely worth your while to spend a few extra lire on a cabin. There are few things more excruciating than spending a night trying to sleep in an armchair, and if you're a woman, being pestered by frisky Italian youths.

Many islands are served by hydrofoils (*aliscafi*) as well as by ferryboats. Hydrofoils tend to be twice as fast and twice as expensive as the ships, and are even more choosy about the state of the sea.

Addresses of shipping lines

Alilauro Aliscafi, Via Caracciolo 13, 80122 Naples (tel (081) 681 041).
Aliscafi SNAV, Cortina del Porto, 98100 Messina (tel (090) 364 044).
CAREMAR, Molo Beverello, 80133 Naples (tel (081) 551 5FF384).
Caronte, Viale della Liberta 515, 98100 Messina (tel (090) 45 183).
Grandi Traghetti, Via Fieshi 17, 16128 Genoa (tel (010) 543 460).
  Via Mariano Stabile 179, 90139 Palermo (tel (091) 587 832).
Associated Oceanic Agencies, Eagle House, 109–110 Jermyn Street, London SW1 6ES (tel (01) 930 5683).
Libera Navigazione Lauro, Molo Beverello, 80133 Naples (tel (081) 322 838).
  Via Iasolino 21, Porto d'Ischia 80077 (tel (081) 991 889).
NAVARMA, Viale Elba 4, 57037 Portoferraio, Elba (tel (0565) 918 101).
  NAVARMA, Corso V. Emanuele 19, Porto Torres, Sardinia (tel (079) 516 151).
  Serena Holidays, 40/42 Kenway Road, London SW5 0RA (tel (01) 373 6548).
Navigazione Libera del Golfo, Molo Beverello, 80133 Naples (tel (081) 325 589).
SIREMAR, Via Francesco Crispi 120, Palermo (tel (091) 582 688).
  Carlo Genovese, Via Depretis 78, 80133 Naples (tel (081) 551 2112).
Società di Navigazione ARL Maregiglio, Giglio Porto, Isola di Giglio (tel (0564) 809 309).
Tirrenia, Stazione Marittima, Molo Angionino, Naples (tel (081) 720 1111).
TOREMAR, Via Calafati 4, 57100 Livorno (tel (0586) 24 113).

By Yacht

Almost all the islands have some sort of facilities for yachts, though they may not be equipped for a long stay. The harbourmaster (*capitaniera di porto*) at your first Italian port of call with give you a document called a *costituto*, which you will have to produce for subsequent harbourmasters; this permits the purchase of tax-free fuel. For further information write to either of these organizations:

Federazione Italiana Vela (Italian Sailing Federation), Porticciolo Duca degli Abruzzi, Genoa.

Federazione Italiana Motonautica (Italian Motorboat Federation), Via Cappuccio 19, Milan.

There are many UK yacht charter companies with bases in the Italian Islands. Look in magazines such as *Yachting World* for listings.

One Italian-based company with several bases in Sardinia is:

Charter and Charter, Piazza Municipio 84, 80133 Naples (tel (081) 551 0101).

Main Yacht Harbours on the Islands
Gulf of Naples—Capri: Procida. Ischia: Porto, Casamicciola, Lacco Ameno, Forio d'Ischia.
Tuscan Islands—Elba: Cavo, Rio Marina, Porto Azzurro, Marciana Marina, Portoferraio. Also: Giglio.
Sardinia—Santa Teresa di Gallura, La Maddalena, Porto Torres, Castelsardo, Porto Teulada, Ponteromano, Calasella, Portoscuso, Portovesme, Alghero, Basa Marina, Porto Conte, Palau, Porto Cervo, Porto Rotondo, Olbia, La Caletta, Arbatax, Poetto, Capo Carbonara, Cagliari.
Sicily—Palermo, Cefalu, Castellammare del Golfo, Capo d'Orlando, Milazzo, Messina, Termini Imerese, Augusta, Catania, Stazzo, Riposto, Syracuse, Marina di Ragusa, Marzameni, Gela, Scogliotto, Licata, Porto Empedocle, Sciacca, Mazara del Vallo, Marsala, Trapani, Giardini.
The islands off Sicily—Lipari, Vulcano, Panarea, Salina, Ustica, Favignana, Pantelleria, Lampedusa.
Port taxes—paid by the tonnage of your yacht—are reduced by two-thirds if you take out a subscription between June and September, by half for the four months June to September or for an entire 12-month period.

Helpful guides to the Italian coasts include *The Tyrrhenian Sea* by H. A. Denham and *Round the Italian Coast* by P. Bristow.

By Train

Sicily's trains pass through all the important centres (see the general map of Sicily for routes p. 91) and are almost invariably pokey, whether you take the *rapido* or *intercity* (the fastest), the *diretto* (which makes a few stops), or the *locale* (which stops at every one-mule village on the map). Sardinia, besides the FS, has its own narrow-gauge railway, the *Strada Ferrate Sarde*—scenic but slow. Anyone who travels the FS regularly may encounter the word *sciopero* which means 'strike'. The average *sciopero* lasts only an hour or two and comes without warning, but one train's stoppage causes delays in a domino effect throughout the system.

By Bus

On all the islands except for Sicily and Sardinia, which have a rail service (see above), buses provide the main means of public transport. Vehicles range from luxurious landyachts to minibuses, and all are run by private companies. Prices have gone up in recent years, and on routes where they compete with trains there isn't that much difference in fares. Often, however, the buses are faster, and the drivers will drop you off at destinations where trains don't stop.

First-timers to Sicily who want to take in the principal sights may want to consider the long-established Golden Ribbon, or *Nastro d'Oro* tour, which takes between 5 and 8 days and is available all year round. Tours include a guide, admission fees, hotel discounts and transport. Schedules, bookings and the latest fares are available at CIT offices (see p. 5).

For city buses you may have to purchase tickets from tobacconist shops or news-stands and validate them on the bus. Vendors of the tickets will know how many you need to reach your destination.

By Car

The reasons for bringing your own car to Italy (or renting one) are obvious, convenience being foremost, although putting up with Italian motorists may be something of a trial. On the small islands, however, a car can be a bit cumbersome. Also, it defeats one of the main reasons for getting away from it all—'it all' surely including the noise and pollution of motor cars. Of the larger islands, Sicily has an extensive public transport system, which is cheap and goes to all places of interest, although sometimes in a roundabout way. Unfortunately, the same cannot be said for Sardinia, where public transport to the provincial capitals is good, but difficult when you want to go anywhere else. The best 'sights'—the *nuraghes*, the Pisan churches and the beauties of nature—can only be reached by private transport. On Sardinia you'll wish you had a car.

The ACI (Automobile Club of Italy) is a good friend to the foreign motorist. For any motoring difficulty you may have, dial their assistance number 116; English-speaking operators are on duty 24 hours to answer your questions; if you need a tow, your car will be taken to the nearest ACI office:

In Sicily: Acireale (Via Mancinni 1, tel (095) 601 085); Agrigento (Via San Vito 23, tel (0922) 26 501), Caltanissetta (Contrada Sant'elia SS 122, tel (0934) 35 911); Catania (Via Sabotino 1, tel (095) 373 361); Enna (Via Roma 200, tel (0935) 21 823); Messina (Via L. Manara 23, tel (090) 293 3031); Palermo (Viale delle Alpi 6, tel (091) 266 295); Ragusa (Via Ercolano 22, tel (0971) 21 566); Syracuse (Foro Siracusano 27, tel (0931) 66 656); Trapani (Via Virgilio 71/81, tel (0923) 27 292).

In Sardinia: Cagliari (Via E. Carboni Boi 2, tel (070) 492 881); Nuoro (Via Sicilia 39, tel (0784) 30 034); Oristano (Via Cagliari 48, tel (0783) 212 453); Sassari (Viale Adua 32/b; tel (079) 271 462).

In the Tuscan Islands: Livorno (Via Verdi 32, tel (0586) 34 651).

In the Bay of Naples: Naples (Piazzale Tecchio 49/d, tel (081) 611 084).

In the Tremiti Islands: Foggia (Via Mastelloni, tel (0881) 36 833).

In the Pontine Islands: Latina (Via A. Saffi 23, tel (0773) 31 141).

Like their Roman forefathers, the Italians love to build roads. The biggest of these are the *autostrade*—super highways. In Sicily these autoducts are built on piers for miles on end. Tolls are charged on the *autostrade* (a foreign licence plate entitles you to a discount) but the Sicilian Catana–Palermo–Mazara del Vallo *autostrade* (A19 and A29) are free.

11

Other main roads are the *strade statali* (SS), which are always free. Motorists going to Sicily or Sardinia should purchase the excellent maps issued by the Italian Touring Club (obtainable in good Italian bookshops, or from Stanfords, 12–14 Long Acre, London WC2 (tel (01) 836 1321); or Rizzoli International Bookstore, 712 Fifth Avenue, New York).

Hiring a Car
Hiring a car is fairly simple if not particularly cheap. Italian car rental firms are called *Autonoleggi*. There are both large international firms through which you can reserve a car in advance, and local agencies, which often have lower prices. Air or train travellers should check out possible discount packages.

Most companies will require a deposit amounting to the estimated cost of the hire, and there's an 18 per cent VAT added to the final cost. At time of writing, a 5-seat Fiat Panda costs around L50 000 a day.

By Taxi
Unfortunately the taxi-drivers, especially in Sicily, see visitors as fair game and will invariably overcharge. Even when they have meters, as in Palermo, it's a fight to get them to turn them on. Always negotiate the price before you get in to avoid unpleasantness when you arrive. The average meter starts at L2500, and adds L600 per kilometre. There's an extra charge for luggage and night and holiday trips.

Hitch Hiking
It's legal to thumb a ride anywhere in Italy except on the *autostrade*. The problem is that in most places on the islands there isn't that much traffic, and you may have a long wait. Increase your chances by looking respectable and carrying a small suitcase instead of a huge backpack.

Tourist Information

There are two types of organization in Italy equipped to deal with any question a traveller may have: Ente Provinciale per il Turismo (EPT), or sometimes called Azienda Provinciale per il Turismo (APT), which has offices in every provincial capital and most main tourist resorts, and Azienda Autonoma di Soggiorno e Turismo (AAST), which can also be found in major centres but with more frequency. The EPTs are funded by the Italian government and sponsor annual summer events such as sports and theatres; the AASTs are supported by civic funds, and often have exchange facilities (open at odd hours), along with brochures about the rest of Italy. On small islands and in hopeful resorts, there are the Pro Loco tourist offices—generally one-room, one-employee seasonal operations, with a few brochures about the area. Although these information offices can provide up-to-the-minute lists of hotels and prices, they cannot make reservations for you. For hotel reservations, see a travel agent.

Consulates in Italy
British: Via XX Settembre 80a, Rome (tel (06) 475 5441).
Via Francesco Crispi 122, Naples (tel (081) 663 320).

Lungarno Corsini 2 (tel (055) 284 133).
Consulate in Cagliari: Via San Lucifero 87 (tel (070) 662 755).
Irish: Largo Nazareno 3, Rome (tel (06) 678 2541).
American: Via Veneto 121, Rome (tel (06) 46741).
   Via Vaccarini 1, Palermo (tel (091) 291 532)
   Lungarno Amerigo Vespucci 46, Florence (tel (055) 298 276)
   Piazza della Repubblica, Naples (tel (081) 660 966)
Canadian: Via Zara 30 (tel (06) 854 825).

Health

Citizens of Common Market countries should bring the E111 form with them to Italy, entitling them to free health care in Italy's National Health Service. Citizens of other countries would do well to take out a traveller's insurance policy.

If there's an emergency, dial 113 for ambulance, police or fire services. Less serious problems can be treated at a *Pronto Soccorso* (casualty department) at any hospital, or at a local health unit (*Unità Sanitaria Locale*).

Pharmacies are generally open 8.30–1 and 4–8. Any large town has a pharmacy that stays open 24 hours; its address will be in the windows of the other pharmacies.

Post Offices

These are usually open from 9 until 1, or until 6 or 7 in a large city. To have your mail sent poste restante (general delivery), have it addressed to the post office (*Fermo Posta*), but be prepared for long delays—the Italian postal system is notoriously bad. To pick up your mail you must present your passport and pay a nominal charge. Stamps may be purchased in post offices or at tobacconists (*tabbachi*, identified by their black signs with a white T). The rates for letters and postcards (depending how much of the card you write on!) are remarkably inconsistent—every tobacconist and postal clerk has his own idea on how many stamps you need.

You can also have money telegraphed to you through the post office which is one of the speedier ways of doing it. Italian banks, especially when money has to be transferred from a central branch in Rome, take their time, even if the money is sent by telex.

Telephones

Public telephones for international calls may be found in the offices of two of Italy's phone companies, SIP or AAST. They tend to be non-existent on the smaller islands, however, and you may have to call from your hotel. SIP offices are open 7 am–10 pm; rates are lower on Sundays and holidays, on Saturdays after 1 pm and from 10 pm to 8 am on weekdays. It is possible to make reverse-charge calls (collect calls) from a telephone office, but be prepared for a wait, as all these calls go through the operator in Rome. Direct calls may be made by dialling the international prefix, but even these may take a while if the international line is busy.

Local or long-distance calls can be made with *gettoni*, L200 tokens available in bars, from tobacconists or news-stands, or *gettone* machines (though these rarely work); for long-distance calls insert quite a few, since unused ones are returned after the call when you push the button. Other telephones will take L100, L200, or L500 coins. Others, run by the SIP company, take magnetic cards which may be purchased at their offices and come in handy for international calls.

Banking Hours and National Holidays

Banking hours in Italy are Monday to Friday 8.35–1.35 and 3–4, though these vary slightly from place to place. Most banks, shops and museums are closed on the following national holidays:

1 January (New Year's Day)
6 January (Epiphany)
Easter Monday
25 April (Liberation Day)
1 May (Labour Day)
15 August (Assumption, also known as *Ferragosto*, the official start of the Italian holiday season)
1 November (All Saints' Day)
8 December (Immaculate Conception)
25 December (Christmas Day)
26 December (*Santo Stefano*, St Stephen's Day)

Museums

National museums in Italy are generally open 9–1 and closed on Mondays and holidays. Most outdoor sites (archaeological excavations, castles, etc.) are open from 9 until sunset. Admission prices have gone up rapidly in recent years; in general the more visited and well known the site, the more you'll pay—usually between L1000 and L4000. Children under 12 are free. Privately-run museums and sites, of which there are few, have different hours and are more expensive on the whole (these will be referred to in the text).

Shopping

Italian shops are generally open 9–1 and 4–7. Measurements and sizes are the same as for the rest of Europe, but do try clothing and shoes on before making a purchase. Italians tend to have narrower feet for the length of the shoe, and their waists tend to be smaller than those of British and American women, so beware, especially since there are no refunds (although you may get an exchange). Men's shirts are sold by collar-size alone, so you may have trouble with the sleeves. Nevertheless, clothing, leather, and shoes are the most attractive buys in Italy these days. Apart from the fashionable shops, you may find some good bargains in the open-air markets, especially in Palermo. Popular items include lace, embroideries, and ceramics in Sicily, baskets and traditional masks in Sardinia, and wine and olive oil nearly everywhere.

Sizes

Women's Shirts/Dresses

						Sweaters					*Women's Shoes*					
UK	10	12	14	16	18	10	12	14	16		3	4	5	6	7	8
US	8	10	12	14	16	8	10	12	14		4	5	6	7	8	9
Italy	40	42	44	46	48	46	48	50	52		36	37	38	39	40	41

Men's shirts

UK/US	14	14$^{1}/_{2}$	15	15$^{1}/_{2}$	16	16$^{1}/_{2}$	17	17$^{1}/_{2}$
Italy	36	37	38	39	40	41	42	43

Men's suits

UK/US	36	38	40	42	44	46
Italy	46	48	50	52	54	56

Shoes

UK	2	3	4	5	6	7	8	9	10	11	12
US	5	6	7	7$^{1}/_{2}$	8	9	10	10$^{1}/_{2}$	11	12	13
Italy	34	36	37	38	39	40	41	42	43	44	45

Weights and Measures

1 kilogramme (1000 g)—2.2 lb
1 etto (100 g)—$\frac{1}{4}$ lb (approx)
1 litre—1.76 pints

1 lb—0.45 kg

1 pint—0.568 litres
1 quart—1.136 litres
1 Imperial gallon—4.546 litres
1 US gallon—3.785 litres

1 metre—39.37 inches
1 kilometre—0.621 miles

1 foot—0.3048 metres
1 mile—0.609 kilometres

Water Sports

It's no secret that Italy's coasts are no longer as inviting as they used to be—the dubious corollary of industrialization. However, the islands, with few exceptions, have at least one shore free of pollution. The only bad areas are around the major ports like Palermo, Catania and Cagliari; also watch the east coasts of the islands along the mainland, especially those in the Bay of Naples.

The islands are especially popular among underwater enthusiasts (although note that it's illegal to fish in Italian waters with an aqualung); the marine life is rich and colourful, and the sea a clear turquoise. Every province has information on fishing from boats and from the shore or with a snorkel, available from the local branch of the Federazione Italiana della Pesca Sportiva.

Festivals

The islands have maintained—or are in the process of reviving—ancient festivals and entertainments. Many of these have distinctly pagan pedigrees, with only a thin veneer of

Christianity applied to rites once devoted to Pan or Persephone. A special feature of Sicily are its traditional puppet shows, featuring battles between Charlemagne's knights (see 'Topics'); in Sardinia the festivals are occasions for Sard music, dancing, and choral songs. Palermo and Catania have regular opera seasons, and performances of all sorts are often staged in Sicily's ancient theatres in the summer.

Listed below are the festivals on the Italian islands; for detailed descriptions of the major events, see the individual towns or islands. Besides these, there are numerous small local *festas*, usually dedicated to a village's patron saint. If you hear of one, especially in rural Sardinia, don't miss the chance to attend—you may very well become the guest of honour.
(SI)=Sicily, (SA)=Sardinia.

January

1	Lively celebration with fireworks, **Capri**
6	Byzantine–Orthodox Epiphany celebrations, **Piano degli Albanesi (SI)**
17	Sant'Antonio, **Mamoiada (SA)** and **Sorgono (SA)**
20	St Sebastian, in **Syracuse (SI)**

February

Early	*Sagra del Mandorlo in Fiore* (Festival of Flowering Almonds) in **Agrigento (SI)**, with European folklore and marching bands
3	San Biagio, in **Salemi (SI)**, where tiny figures are made out of pasta for the children while the adults climb a slippery pole for the sausages and roast chickens hung on top
3–5	Sant' Agata, in **Catania (SI)** climaxing with the *Cannelore*, a procession of large wooden floats, some 5 m high, carried on the men's shoulders. On the floats are tableaux representing scenes from the life of Sant' Agata, elaborately decorated. The procession stops at various places in the city associated with the saint
Carnival	Carnival week, *Sa Sartiglia*, **Oristano (SA)**; 'The most beautiful carnival in Sicily' takes place in **Acireale**; also celebrations in **Trapani (SI)** and **Caltanissetta (SI)**; a very traditional carnival with parades and masks, in **Castellana Sicula (SI)**; also traditional festivities in **Mamoiada, Ottana, Bosa, Tempo Pausania, all in (SA)**
Last Sun	S. Silverio, **Ponza**

March

19	San Giuseppe, in **Salemi (SI)**, is marked by poetry recitals and figures of Mary, Joseph, and baby Jesus from 9-kg loaves of bread
25	Madonna of the Church of the Annunziata, **Trapani (SI)**

April

Holy Week celebrations on the islands often have a Spanish flavour, with their processions of floats carried by the robed and hooded members of local confraternities. Among the most fascinating are the celebrations in Spanish costumes of the medieval fraternities, in **Enna (SI)** and **Castelsardo (SA)**

Maundy Thursday	Procession, **Marsala (SI)**, with participants dressed as characters from the Passion; **Caltanissetta (SI)**, important medieval procession of the *Misteri* with musical bands from all over the province
Good Friday	Processions in traditional costumes, in **Acireale (SI)**, **Messina (SI)**, **Ragusa (SI)**, and **Vittoria (SI)**; procession of *Misteri* in **Erice (SI)**, **Agrigento (SI)** and **Trapani (SI)**; procession of the Lords of the City, **Caltanissetta (SI)**; famous processions of the *Misteri* figures from Christ's Passion, borne along by men in blue and white costumes, in **Procida**
Easter	*Abballu di li diavuli* (Dance of the Devils), in **Prizzi (SI)**, where masked figures of Death and Devils dance in pagan rhythms with a procession of the Madonna, until dispatched by avenging angels; Passion Play, in **Adrano (SI)**; *Festa di li Schetti*, in **Terrasini (SI)**, when young men lift and swing huge tree trunks, along with traditional music and dancing; processions in **Oliena (SA)**
Easter Monday	Pilgrimage to the Sanctuary of the Madonna del Monte, **Marciana (ELBA)**
Orthodox Easter	Traditional celebrations at **Piano degli Albanesi (SI)**
First Sun after Easter	Sant'Antioco, **S. Antioco (SA)**
15 days after Easter	Sant'Antioco, **Gavoi and Ulassai (SA)**
Mid-month	A week of sacred music at **Monreale (SI)**
25	S. Giorgio parade, in **Ragusa (SI)**
29	San Cristino, **Portoferraio (ELBA)**

May

1	Sant'Efisio, **Cagliari (SA)**
1–3	Madonna del Monte, **Marciana (ELBA)**
1–10	San Francesco, **Lula (SA)**
3	'The Third of May' festival, in **Piazza Armerina (SI)**, at the Sanctuario di Santa Maria delle Vittorie
4	Naked children in procession of St Sebastian, in **Mellili (SI)**
5	The Misericordia church commemorates the death of Napoleon with a procession (including a replica of his coffin), **Portoferraio (ELBA)**
7	Santa Restituta, **Bono (SA)**
8	Madonna delle Grazie, **Ierzu (SA)**
9	Race up to Trecastagni from **Catania (SI)** for the Three Holy Brothers
Early May	*Sagra del Lago*, **Pergusa (SI)**, with local folklore and fireworks

17

Throughout May	Film festival 'Angelo Rizzoli' at **Porto and Lacco Amero (ISCHIA)**
14	Patron saint San Costanzo, **Capri**
15	S. Simplicio, **Olbia (SA)**
17	Santa Restituta, patron saint of **Ischia**, is celebrated on Monte Vico and Lacco Ameno, with fireworks, etc.
Ascension Day	*Cavalcata Sarda*, **Sassari (SA)**; pilgrimage to the Shrine of Santa Lucia, **Portoferraio (ELBA)**
3rd Sun	S. Nicola, **Ottana (SA)**; S. Barbara, **Ulassai (SA)**
27–29	SS. Emiliano e Priamo, **Bosa (SA)**
Last 3 days	*Il Raduno del Costume e del Carretto*, **Taormina (SI)**
31	S. Restituta, **Bono (SA)**

June

All month	*La Mattanza*, the tuna fish massacre, in **Trapani (SI)** and **Favignana**
First week	S. Mauro, **San Mauro (near Sorgono, SA)**; S. Gavino, **Porto Torres (SA)**
First Sun	Madonna dei Martiri, **Fonni (SA)**; Sant'Anania, **Orgosolo (SA)**
3	Patron saint Madonna della Lettera, **Messina (SI)**
Early June	Sant'Antonio, **S. Teresa di Gallura (SA)**
Mid-month	*Sagra delle Ciliege* (the festival of cherries) in **Castelbuono (SI)**
19–21	The patron saint of **Alcamo (SI)**, Maria SS. dei Miracoli, with a pilgrimage to Monte Bonifato
20	San Silverio, **Ponza**
Last week	S. Giovanni, **Escalaplano, Fonni, Oliena and Isili, all (SA)**
29	San Paolo, **Osilo (SA)**; S. Pietro, **Bosa (SA)**; SS. Pietro and Paolo, **Pantelleria**
June–July	International Ballet Festival, in the Greek theatre (every other year), in **Syracuse (SI)**; International Festival of Underwater Activities; and mural-painting contest (even-numbered years only), **Ustica**
June–Aug	Musical, dance, and theatrical performances in Greek theatre, **Taormina (SI)**; handicraft exhibition in **Pantelleria**

July

All month	*Estate Ericina*, **Erice (SI)** summer festival with dances, exhibitions, and competitions, beginning with an auto race up Monte Erice; *Musicale Trapanese* at Villa Margherita, in **Trapani (SI)**
First week	Feast of Our Lady of Bonaria, **Cagliari (SA)**
First Sunday	Beginning of week-long celebration of Santa Venera, in **Acireale (SI)**; San Calogero Festival, with local folklore and exhibitions, **Agrigento (SI)**; Madonna della Neve, **Desulo (SA)**

18

5–7	Sant' Antine, in **Sedilo (SA)**; folk festival with horse race. The race, called the Ardilo, commemorates the battle of the Milvian Bridge, where the Emperor Constantine (Sant'Antine) defeated the pretender Maxentius in AD 312. Constantine is only one of many saints recognized by the Sards but not by the pope.
10–13	The Feast of the Three Maries, **Pantelleria**
13–16	The Feast of Santa Rosalia, in **Palermo (SI)**, is one of the most spectacular in the Mediterranean: parades, fireworks and other delights culminate in a torch-lit pilgrimage to the sanctuary of Santa Rosalia on Monte Pellegrino
15	SS. Giacomo and Quirico, at **Rio nell'Elba (ELBA)**.
21–22	S. Maria Maddalena, **Nuragus, near Isili (SA)**
25–26	S. Giacomo, **Ierzu (SA)**
26	Sant'Anna, **Oruferi (SA)**
27	San Pantaleo, **Macomer (SA)**
End of month	International film festival, **Taormina (SI)**; Sant'Anna, **Ischia Ponte**; wine-tasting festival, the *Rassegna dei Vini Elbani* at **Le Ghiaie (ELBA)**
Last Sunday	*Palio del Mare*, in **Syracuse (SI)**; Santa Venera, in **Avola (SI)**; Madonna di Sa Itria, **Gavoi (SA)**
July–Aug	*Estate Ennese*, operettas in the Castello di Lombardia, **Enna (SI)**; Pirandello performances, **Agrigento (SI)**

August

2	San Bartolomeo, **Alicudi**
All month	Cartoon festival, in **Erice (SI)**; 'The Iblean August', in **Ragusa (SI)** (folklore and sport festivities throughout the month, culminating in a celebration in honour of St John the Baptist on 29 August); lentil festival, **Ventotene** celebrating the island's main crop
First Sun	Santa Maria del Mare, **Bosa (SA)**
10	S. Lorenzo, **Silanus (SA)**
12	Santa Chiara, **Marciana Marina (ELBA)**
13–14	*Il Palio dei Normanni* (Norman Joust), in **Piazza Armerina (SI)**: the major medieval fête in Sicily, in which hundreds participate in medieval costume, re-enact Count Roger's taking of Piazza Armerina and the tournament presented before him between four teams representing the four quarters of the town. The winning team in the various competitions receive a standard from 'Roger' which they keep in their parish church for the year. The locals take their pageant very seriously, and the competition is fierce
13–15	*Assumption* and *Giganti* processions in **Messina (SI)**, with 6-m giants representing the legendary procreators Mata and Grifone; also the *Fiera di Messina* in August with folklore, sports and exhibitions; Feast of the Assumption, in **Trapani**, with

	puppet shows; Madonna dell'Alto, **Petralia Sotta (SI)**; pilgrimage grimage to Madonna del Monte, **Marciana (ELBA)**
14	*Li Candalieri*, **Sassari (SA)**;
Mid-month	Sant'Antonio, **Monti (SA)**; swimming marathon to Naples from **Capri**
15	'Ferragosto Fonnese', at **Fonni (SA)**; also Ferragosto at **Orgosolo and Ottana (SA)**; religious celebrations at **San Nicola (TREMITIS)**; Horse race around the lake, **Pantelleria**
16	San Rocco, **Rio nell'Elba (ELBA)**
20–23	S. Lussorio, **Oliena (SA)**
24	S. Bartolomeo, one of the most popular saints on the islands, with important festivities at **Ollolai (SA)**, **Ustica**, and **Lipari**
26–28	S. Bartolomeo, **Isili (SA)**
28–31	Sant'Ignazio, **Laconi (SA)**
29	*Festa del Redentore*, **Nuoro (SA)**; Misericordia procession, **Portoferraio (ELBA)**
29–3 Sept	*Madonnina delle Lacrime* pilgrimage, in **Syracuse (SI)**
Last Sunday	San Corrado, **Noto (SI)**
30	'Festival of the Grotto', **Dorgali (SA)**
31	S. Raimundo, **Bono (SA)**

September

1–8	*Nostra Signora di Montserrato*, **Oliena (SA)**
8–15	The 8th, the Nativity of Mary, in **Porto Azzurro (ELBA)**, followed by a week of pilgrimages to the Sanctuary of Monserrato
1st Sun	S. Basilio, **Aritzo (SA)**; S. Salvatore, **San Salvatore in Sinis (SA)**
8	Large pilgrimage to the Mother Church, followed by a sausage picnic, in **Altavilla Milicia (SI)**
Mid-Month	Festival of Hazelnuts, in **Polizzi Generosa (SI)**
12–14	S. Croce, **Oristano (SA)**
13–14	S. Basilio, **Desulo (SA)**
3rd Sun	Sant'Antonio, **Austis, near Sorgono (SA)**
20	Santa Candida, **Ventotene**, with a procession, music, and display of small, multicoloured hot-air balloons
22	*La Madonna di Porto Salvo*, with a pilgrimage to the Sanctuary, and a procession as well as other events in town, **Lampedusa**
25–28	SS. Cosmo e Damiano, **Mamoiada (SA)**; on the 27th, in **San Cosimo, near Mamoiada (SA)**
29	*Madonna del Miracolo*, **Bitti (SA)**; *Madonna del Remedio* **Ozieri (SA)**; S. Maria delle Grazie, **Nuoro (SA)**; St Michael's Fair, **Caltanissetta (SI)**; San Michele, **Procida**, where farmers deliver offerings to the saint at Terra Murata
Late Sept	Wine festivals, **Ischia**

October

2	Sant' Angelo, **Volcano**

20

14–16	Santa Teresa, **Santa Teresa di Gallura (SA)**
Last Sun	*Sagra delle Castagne e Nocciole* (feast of chestnuts and hazelnuts), **Aritzo (SA)**

November

1	All Souls', in **Palermo (SI)**, toy fair and sugar figurines for the children
25	Santa Caterina, **Abbasanta (SA)** and **Marciana (ELBA)**

December

All month	Display of *presepi*, or Christmas cribs, in **Acireale (SI)**
8	*Festa dell'Immacolata*, **Alghero (SA)** and **Capoliveri (ELBA)**
13	Santa Lucia, in **Syracuse (SI)**
24	Procession of characters from the Nativity, **Salemi (SI)**

Where to Stay

Like everywhere else in Europe, the hotels and pensions in Italy are classified and their prices accordingly regulated by the Provincial Tourist Boards. Price lists are posted on the door of every room, along with the prices of extras like continental breakfast or full or half board, and air conditioning if it is considered an 'extra'. Heating, if called for, is free of charge, although in modest establishments you may have to pay extra for a bath.

In Italy the hotel rates are annually adjusted (always upward) in March, although some places retain the right to boost prices during the tourist season and lower them after September. Reservations are indispensable in summer. The Italian Tourist Office annually publishes lists of hotels and pensions with their most recent rates and amenities, which are very helpful (although note that the Tourist Boards do not make reservations). **Throughout this book, prices listed are for a double room; it will be indicated whether or not this includes a private bath.** For a general guide, expect to pay on average (in lire) in 1989:

Category	Double with Bath
Luxury (*****)	L200–600 000
Class I (****)	L100–300 000
Class II (***)	L90–200 000
Class III (**)	L50–90 000
Class IV (*)	L30–50 000
Pension	L14–40 000

Similar to pensions are the inns known as *locande*, which can sometimes have comparatively high rates. Rooms in private houses can be had almost everywhere, although you have to pound the pavements to find them. Single travellers should be aware that, if a hotel has only double rooms left, the charge is legally supposed to be no more than ²/₃rds the price of a double. Many hoteliers will nevertheless try to charge you a double, and if the bed is a double, you'll probably have to pay it.

Note that many pensions and hotels in resort areas expect you to eat at least half your meals there (when they have restaurants, that is; some do not) and to stay a minimum of three days, especially in summer. Italian pensions are usually family-run establishments, so they are more relaxed (and noisier) than their hotel equivalents. In the south of Italy, especially in Sicily, a stay in a lowly pension or *locanda* may be an unforgettable adventure—do make the owners show you the room and WC before you commit yourself. Lavatory seats are a luxury in this part of the world; loo rolls are not always where you need them; hot water is rare much of the day; mysterious wall and wardrobe growths lend many a dingy room a nasty but natural texture. But even in the worst dive, the sheets will be spotless. Mosquito coils can handle the other major summertime nuisance. Beware, also, of assuming anything at all about a hotel by its classification, although 'Luxury' *is* luxury. The owners of the hotels are given enough discretion in rating their hotels to make guidelines useless. Some hotels are purposely classed lower to attract the bargain-minded traveller, although they may charge as much as a Class I hotel.

One of the biggest chains in Italy are the **Jolly Hotels**, always reliable if not all up to the same standard; these can generally be found near the centre of larger towns. **Motels** are operated by the ACI (the Italian Automobile Club) or by AGIP (the big oil company; usually located along major routes outside cities). These cater for motorists and are adequate, if nothing special. For AGIP motel reservations contact (in London) Quo Vadis Ltd, 243 Euston Road, London NW1 2BT (tel (01) 388 7512).

It is hard to make generalizations about the new crop of **Tourist Villages** (*Villaggio Turistico*) sprouting up along the coasts of Italy. Almost all of them consist of separate units (white Mediterranean tourist-style bungalows or Polynesian-style grass huts) near a beach, and offer a number of recreational facilities in Club Méditerranée style, which chiefly attract a youthful sun-and-fun crowd. Lists of these can be obtained from EPT offices.

Youth Hostels, unfortunately, are few and far between, especially on the islands. Students with valid student cards may, however, find inexpensive accommodation in university towns in summer by making inquiries to the person in charge of the *Casa dello Studente*. On the islands there are student houses at Casa del Goliardo in Palermo, and at the universities of Messina and Sassari. Further information can be had from the Associazione Italiana Alberghi per la Gioventù-A.I.G., Palazzo della Civiltà del Lavoro, Quadrato della Concordia, 00144 Rome, which maintains hostels in the following island locations:

Bola: Porto Torres, near Sassari in Sardinia.
Dei Giuliani, in Fertilia, near Alghero (April–Sept).
Delle Aquile, in Castoreale, Messina (June–Sept).
Eleonara d'Arborea, Torregrande-Oristano.
Lipari, Lipari Island. New ones have opened in Sardinia: Arzachena-Cannigione (Sassari), Bosa-Marina, Via Sardegna 1, (Nuoro), Tonara (Nuoro) and Oristano-Torregrande, Via dei Pescatori (Oristano), all open only July–Aug.

In Sicily, the Italian Alpine Club operates **refuges** on the main mountain trails. These offer simple accommodation, often with restaurants (listed along with the hotels in the sections on individual provinces). For up-to-date information on the refuges, write to the to the Club Alpino Italiano, Via Ugo Foscolo 3, Milano (tel (02) 802554) Charges average L10 000 a night, with a 20 per cent increase from December to April.

22

Note that for all overnight accommodation you will be asked for your passport for registration purposes. Contact the local Provincial Tourist Board (EPT or APT) if you feel you have any genuine grievance about your hotel.

Renting Accommodation

An agency known as Agriturist can arrange holiday rentals at farmhouses and country villas. For listings and other information, write to Corso Vittorio Emanuele 101, Rome (tel (06) 656 241). To rent a flat or villa, write to the local tourist office (AAST) for information a few months before you go. The ENIT offices have lists of agencies in the UK and the USA which specialize in rentals. The one with the widest selection on the islands is Interhome Ltd, 383 Richmond Road, Twickenham TW1 2EF (tel (01) 891 1294; telex 928539).

Camping

There are two forms of this increasingly popular way to spend a holiday. You can either pitch your tent where you please, which requires permission from the local authorities or landowner, or you can stay on an organized campsite—but don't expect any kind of 'communing with nature' here; Italians look upon camping as the cheap alternative to resort hotels, and it is especially popular with families. Most campsites have beaches nearby, and their facilities can include anything from basic toilets and showers to tennis courts and swimming pools. It is possible to book a place at any of these by writing to the Centro Internazionale Prenotazioni Campeggio, Casella Postale 23, 50041, Calenzano, Firenze, Italy: you can request a list of campsites with the booking form. At sites belonging to the Federcampeggio, expect to pay around not much more than L12 000 for a camper or tent. Some of the camping sites on the islands are very beautiful and well situated, and it's worth bearing in mind that the vast majority of Italians take their holidays during the same period, i.e. from 1–15 August, when the sites are bursting at the seams. If you can possibly go in September, do so, as you'll have the place to yourself. The Touring Club Italiano also publishes an annual guide to campsites and tourist villages. Write to: T.C.I., Corso Italia 10, Milan (tel (02) 85261). If you can't bring your own caravan (camper/trailer), you can hire one at a local firm: Sicilian ones include Happy Holiday, Via la Rocca 1, Catania (tel (095) 492 677); or Euroauto, Via Principe di Paternò 119/125 Palermo (tel (091) 201 529). In Sardinia there's Sarda Caravan, Viale Monastir, Cagliari (tel (070) 22 050), and Unimare, Via Principe Umberto 1, Olbia (tel (0789) 23 524).

Eating Out

There are people who return to different regions of Italy year after year just to eat and drink. It's no wonder: the average snack in a Sicilian railway station bar is better than the best of some entire national cuisines (and that's only a slight exaggeration). If this is your first trip to Italy, know that the lasagne at your local neighbourhood café or restaurant is but a pale shade of the beast in its native land. Even the smallest islands have their own culinary specialities.

Italian eating establishments open from noon to 3 or 4 pm and from 7 or 8 until 11 pm.

They come in many forms—the *ristorante, trattoria, rosticceria, tavola calda* and *pizzeria*. Although traditionally a *trattoria* is a cheaper, simpler place than a *ristorante*, in reality they are often exactly the same, both in quality and price, the only difference being that a *ristorante* has more pretensions. Most restaurants display a menu outside so that you know what to expect, at least as regards the price.

The *rosticceria, tavola calda*, or *gastronomia* are quite similar, the latter now the more popular name for the counters of prepared hot and cold food, where you choose what looks good, eat, pay and go. Some of these are quite elaborate, while the modest ones don't even have chairs or stools. If you're used to eating a light lunch instead of a major Italian midday feast, they're the answer.

You can tell a good *pizzeria* by the traditional Neapolitan pizza oven in the back. *Pizzerie* are often combined with *trattorie*, as many Italians like to eat pizza for the first course (the *primo*) of a large meal. In these places, the service charge may be 20 per cent if you order just a pizza and beer. Service in *ristoranti* and *trattorie* is generally 12 per cent, and there is also a *coperto e pane* (cover and bread) charge of L2000 or so. Tipping is discretionary, but customary. Tax law in Italy orders restaurants and bars to give patrons a receipt (*scontrino*) for everything they eat or drink, which you are supposed to take out of the restaurant with you and carry for 300 metres in case the receipt police intercept you. Only in Italy . . .

Many places offer *prezzo fisso* (set price) or *menu turistico* meals—often a real bargain. Posh joints with gourmet pretensions sometimes offer a *menu degustazione*, a fixed menu of the chef's specialities, which can be a real treat and usually good value as well. Of course you can always order *alla carta* from the menu, which is divided into the following categories (a fuller list of items on the menu can be found at the end of this book).

Antipasti (hors d'oeuvres). These are often sumptuously displayed to tempt you the minute you walk in; common starters are seafoods, vegetables, salami, ham, olives, etc. Depending on the restaurant, you can choose these yourself or order them from the menu.

Minestre. Broth or minestrone soups, or pasta dishes. The latter come under the sub-heading of *Pasta Asciutta*. Many Italians skip the antipasti, which are often as dear as they are good, and go straight for the spaghetti, before tackling the second course, or *secondo*. Note that you will be expected to have both a pasta and a main dish to follow, which can be a sharp surprise to one's digestive system if not used to it.

Pesce. Fish, often according to availability, since it is always fresh.

Carne. Meat, which includes chicken, beef, lamb, veal and pork. With meat or fish, you eat a *contorno* (side dish) of your choice—often salad, vegetables or potatoes.

Dolce o Frutta. Sweet or fruit, the latter being more popular after a big meal. Common sweets are the famous Italian ice cream, exotic cakes or pastries.

Wine of course is the most popular accompaniment to dinner. *Vino locale* (house wine) is the cheapest and usually quite good, and this is what you'll get unless you order a specific label. Mineral water (*acqua minerale*) comes under as many labels as the wine, with or without added or natural carbonization (or *gas*, as the Italians call those little bubbles). Italian beer, always served cold, is average, and of course you can always order the ubiquitous Coca-cola or Fanta. A small, black espresso coffee puts the final touch to an Italian meal.

First-timers to Italy will be pleasantly surprised by the depth and mastery of Italian cuisine—it certainly isn't all pasta, tomatoes and olive oil. Italian chefs do particularly good things to fish, the thick *zuppa di pesce* (fish soup) being a speciality on the coasts. The big secret of Italian cooking is the freshness of the ingredients, which will surely convert those who feel indifferent about the mass-market Italian-style food and restaurants that they experience at home.

Another curiosity that is immediately evident is the numbers which gather at a restaurant table. Italians do everything in groups of 10 to 25, instead of elsewhere in Europe where tables are booked for two. Witness the silence that falls when the pasta plates are served.

Bars have little in common with American bars or English pubs, and can be anything from luxurious open-air cafés to dingy back-alley meeting places for the boys. All serve primarily coffee in the form of *espresso* (small, stormy and black), *cappuccino* (with milk and a sprinkling of chocolate, and drunk only before noon), or simply *caffè con latte* (coffee with milk), often served in a glass. Many people have breakfast at a bar, where you can help yourself to *cornetti* (croissants) or whatever other pastries are available. Here the problems begin when you have to pay and haven't the slightest idea of what your pastry was called.

Of course you can also get alcohol, soft drinks, mineral water, juices, etc. at a bar, at any time of the day from 7 am to midnight. Alcohol is cheap, as long as it's not imported. Standing at the bar is about a third cheaper than sitting at a table to be served. The *scontrino* is the receipt, and you may be asked to collect one from the *cassa* (cashier) before being served, especially in the big cities.

Note: The prices quoted for restaurants in this book are average for one person going whole hog, with wine, antipasti, a fish dish, etc.; in each case you can order a fine meal for considerably less, depending on what you order, but beware of the extra charges—service, *coperto*, and tax—that can add up to 20 per cent to the bill.

Grocery Shopping

Italian groceries (*alimentari*) are open in the morning and after the siesta. They sell mainly canned and dried goods, milk, biscuits, wine and cheese, salami and olives. For fresh vegetables and fruit you will have to go to the market (*mercato*); for meat, to the butcher (*macelleria*); for bread, to the bakery (*panificio*); and for fish, to the fish market (*pesceria*). Besides normal metric weights, you may also purchase by the *etto* (100 grams, or a little less than a quarter pound). Prices are comparable to home except of course that wine is much cheaper. If you are doing your own cooking you'll have to do it from scratch; Italians disdain prepared foods, and the *alimentari* generally lack refrigeration for frozen foods, especially on the islands. Supermarkets in the larger towns are much like the ones at home, only they tend to be small and somehow only stock the ingredients for Italian dishes.

Part II

TOPICS

Castello di Gresti, Valguarera, Enna

Carts

'A cart is like a poem', wrote novelist René Bazin at the turn of the century—an odd statement unless like Bazin, you've been to Sicily where traditional carved and brightly painted carts are works of art. From Istanbul to the Philippines to New York City, the urge to tart up everyday transport is universal; in Sicily it began under the Bourbon government in 1830, when the first ruts dignified by the word 'road' were laid out across the island to better exploit its resources. The main means of transport also improved, from mule train to cart. These vehicles had to be sturdy, and were crafted with as much care as a Venetian takes constructing a gondola; different woods for the different parts, iron axles, all perfectly balanced to take extreme pre-autostrada conditions; each area of the island had its distinctive shape and structure.

The result was fairly costly, and it wasn't long before customers began to have painters embellish their investments with pictures from history and legend that were familiar to even the most rustic, uneducated Sicilian: scenes of Charlemagne and Orlando, famous operas, the battles of Napoleon and Garibaldi, Norman Crusaders and Saracens, New Testament stories, and so on, bordered by floral and geometric designs that dazzle the eye with their bright primary colours and can indeed be 'read' like a poem, even by the illiterate; the most lavish have spokes carved like intricate totem poles. Traditionally these are pulled by horses decked out in plumes, tassels, bells, and bright embroidered trappings.

26

Although the carts nowadays are rarely seen outside folklore parades and in tourist haunts, the painters have adapted to the times and the farmers' new vehicles, pick-up trucks and three-wheeled *Ape* delivery vans, some of which are as lyrical as the carts.

Emigration

Faced with a society of limited industrial growth, poverty and restrictions imposed by local corruption, many Sicilians have left their island to find better lives elsewhere. The latest wave of emigrants have headed to the industrial power centres of the north such as Milan and Turin, where in many cases they face the same problems as the German *gastarbeiter*, feeling no more at home in the 'European' north than a Turkish worker does in Frankfurt. With the advent of free movement of labour in the EEC, many Sicilians have also ended up in France, Belgium, Germany and Great Britain, often obtaining assisted passages, partially paid for by the recipient governments, and partially by the Italian State.

In the first quarter of the century, however, the vast majority took their chances on the other side of the Atlantic and formed their own pockets of Sicilian life in the USA. A native of Lipari island, for example, will almost certainly be able to trace a cousin or two in Brooklyn. Household names like Lucky Luciano and Al Capone are among the more disreputable, but with them go a good number of upright citizens such as Frank Capra, the Hollywood director who created celluloid fairy tales extolling democracy and the American dream. The fate of many emigrants who hang on too long in their adopted country has befallen a great number of Sicilian families. The dreams of the first immigrants who want to return home and buy a patch of land, a grocery store or restaurant to see them comfortably into old age, are shattered when the realization comes that their children have grown up as Americans and do not share their desire to go 'back'. Few Sicilians would leave their children and grandchildren to grow up thousands of miles away on another continent, and so unfortunately they find themselves in a situation with no solution. Because of this desire to return, as well as the economic investment represented by land, a Sicilian is loath to part with any he may own, with the result that tracts of wasteland with crumbling shuttered-up houses are part of the Sicilian land-scape. Presumably with the present increase in the standard of living in Italy, the wave of emigration which has lost Sicily not only labourers and farm workers, but also doctors, lawyers and businessmen, will give way in the face of more incentive to stay on home turf.

Goethe Takes a Holiday

In 1786, at the age of 38, Goethe suffered a severe mid-life crisis at the court in Weimar and bolted for Italy when no one was looking. Famous all over Europe as the author of *Werther*, he travelled under a false name, and did much to blaze The Grand Tour recounted in his *Italian Journey*, published from his letters and notes in 1816. Many have used it as their guide, following the great poet's steps from the Brenner Pass to Naples; but only a minority of Grand Tourists even now take up his challenge to sail on to Sicily.

'To me, Sicily implies Asia and Africa', he wrote, a sentiment that would make any Italian smile (the Milanese will tell you that 'Africa' really begins in Florence, while for the Florentines it begins in Rome; for the Romans, Naples, and so on). But Goethe's interests were historical and classical; he longs 'to stand at that miraculous centre upon which so many radii of world history converge'.

Goethe was one of the greatest poets who ever lived but *Italian Journey* could have been written by an insurance salesman; everything is *beautiful, important* or simply fills him with emotion. Much of it apparently hides what he was really thinking about—sex being near the top of the list; its easy availability in Italy did much to make it irresistible to 'Romantic' poets and artists of all nationalities.

Yet even described in stolid prose, Goethe's adventures would be the envy of the modern traveller, who may come home with only the tale of a rude waiter to jazz up his holiday tale. Two hundred years ago it took three or four days to sail from Naples to Palermo; Goethe was so seasick he couldn't stand up, though he still managed to compose an act or two of a play; on the return sail from Messina, his ship came within inches of crashing into the sheer cliffs of Capri; he mentions how advantageous it is to sail on a neutral ship flying a white flag, which offers protection from pirates. We take cameras to record our travels; Goethe took his own artist. In Naples he spent much of his time with Sir William and Lady Hamilton; in Palermo he impersonated an Englishman to meet the mother and relatives of the notorious swindler Cagliostro, who played a major role in the Diamond Necklace Affair. He was entertained by the viceroy, counts, and princes, and had an amusing encounter with the gruff governor of Messina, whose city had just been devastated by an earthquake. Inns, however, were few and far between, and in an especially poor one the beggars fought the dogs for the travellers' sausage skins and apple parings. Some towns had no accommodation at all, and Goethe and his artist companion had to rely on their Sicilian guide to buy a chicken from a peasant, and hire his pots, stove, dishes, and table; they were grateful for a pestilent mattress to sleep on in the barn. Think of them when deciding between the pasta with lobster or swordfish kebabs on your restaurant menu!

Goethe spent a month and a half in Sicily alone. Few modern travellers have the luxury to dawdle so. But a journey was far more serious in those days, a once-in-a-lifetime experience; not only did Goethe see the sights, but he studied minerals and agriculture, theorized on the 'primal plant', measured temples and ancient sculpture, read the *Odyssey* in the original Greek and began a new play. He travelled to learn about Sicily, and about himself; and his journey took on the weight of an archetype as old as the *Odyssey* itself: 'If I cannot come back reborn, it would be much better not to come back at all.'

Puppets and Mafiosi

The Crusades of the 11th century gave the century's hardiest warriors, the Normans, a taste not only for conquest but also for the new-fangled ideas of chivalry. The first appetite they gratified in Sicily and southern Italy, the second in a strict code of honour as recounted in the *Chansons de Geste*, singing the deeds of King Arthur, Charlemagne, and Roland (the famous 'Orlando'). Their new Sicilian subjects devoured the tales, and came to look upon Norman rule as a Golden Age; none of the subsequent Angevin, Spaniard, or Bourbon kings of Sicily cared so deeply for the island, or even bothered to visit, leaving the day-to-day corruption to viceroys and indifferent petty officials.

Dogged by centuries of injustice and misrule, the Sicilians preserved the Norman code of chivalry amongst themselves. Even the poorest illiterate could follow the adventures of *Carlomagno* and his paladins in the performances of the traditional *Teatro dei pupi*, or puppet theatre, where the moral of the story is always the same: a man's most important possession is his honour. And as the law of the land failed to defend their honour and property, landowners hired small companies of armed men, (*compagnie d'armi*), who took the law into their own hands. Secrecy was essential, and to maintain it, the penalty for any affront, large or trivial, was by necessity death. The fact that the landowners were nearly always absent from their estates, in their distant palaces in Palermo or Naples, left the *compagnie d'armi* free to cross over now and again into the brigandry they were organized to fight. The Mafia was only a step away.

The origins of the name 'Mafia' are lost in time; Sicilians traditionally prefer euphemisms like the *amici* (friends) or the **onorata società** (the 'honoured society'). Its base has always been limited to the western half of Sicily, between Palermo and Agrigento, where there were once large agricultural estates; in the east, and especially in Catania, the Mafia traditionally has little influence. For a long time Mafiosi preserved some of the rudiments of chivalry; even the most powerful dons led austere lives, donated large sums to charity, assisted the needy, granted favours, and came down heavily on freelance crime. But what useful purpose the Mafia may have served was always balanced by its sinister stranglehold over the areas it controlled; it has always been ruthlessly efficient, murderously vindictive, diverse in its activities, and hard to pin down. The Italians often compare it to the many-headed Hydra, who grew a new head whenever one was lopped off. The only person who came close to destroying the monster was Mussolini, who led a similar organization and didn't like the competition. The Mafia's hatred of the Fascists made it a strange bedfellow for the Allies. Whatever the truth of the story, the collaboration of the US Army and the famous gangster Lucky Luciano has already become a part of Italian folklore. Facing a surprise Sicilian independence movement led by the charismatic young bandit Giuliano, and strong Communist Party support for the oppressed farmers, the occupation forces took whatever allies they could find; unfortunately for western Sicily liberation meant a return to the protection and favours of 'the friends'.

Briefly, in the fifties and sixties, both the *teatro dei pupi* and the Mafia suffered a decline: both had become anachronisms. The old barriers of isolation and ignorance were crumbling; new roads, new money, and new jobs were rapidly changing the area, and no one cared any longer for the old code of honour; money, a scarcity in Sicily before, became the new criterion of respect. But while the knightly puppets are now benign folklore, the Mafia has nefariously adapted to the new order, forsaking austerity for flamboyant new riches, infiltrating the government and raking off building funds, expanding protection rackets, and like the American Mafia, delving into big money ventures like gambling, prostitution, and most notoriously, drugs—activities the old dons would have shunned.

The Mafia remains in the headlines, usually at the expense of the public prosecution and its rivals. Judges and police commanders continue to be murdered, and Palermo's courthouse has become an armoured bunker; a recent government report insists the Mafia has taken political control of entire provinces. ('Christian Democrats=Mafia' is a graffito you will see all over Italy.) What has changed are the attitudes of the Sicilians—now that the Mafia has devoted itself wholeheartedly to crime, its latent support has been replaced by a sense of revulsion; the 'friends' have irrevocably become the enemies of the just and honourable. Their poison threatens all of Italy despite the brave efforts of anti-Mafia squads, the paladins of our day, who thwack off one head of the monster after another, while the killings between rival clans continue in a nightmarish Punch and Judy show to the death.

Volcanoes

One of the world's most important schools of Volcanology is in Catania, but anyone who travels among the Italian islands can get a free extension course in the steamy science. Imagine, à la Disney's *Fantasia*, a time-lapse film of the islands shot over the past four millennia: between volcanoes, earthquakes, and other assorted cataclysms, it would have all the frenzy of a rock video. Three of Europe's most active volcanoes would provide the thumping, lurching rhythms to Stravinsky's *Rite of Spring*: mighty Etna, the bass, bursting forth with irregular but awesome thunder, accompanied by the boisterous choir of 300 minor craters ranked upon its flanks; the three craters of Vulcano like the Andrews sisters, erupting into song every hundred years or so; and Stromboli, a species of piccolo continuo sputtering with the reliable festival of fireworks that has earned it the nickname 'lighthouse of the Mediterranean'.

Many of the other islands are dead or dormant volcanoes. There are certain advantages to living with the big blisters: the rubbish they spew forth has a thousand and one uses: light airy pumice for soap and glass; obsidian and basalt, the 'steel' of prehistoric man; tufa for building houses; lava to make nearly indestructible paving stones; and especially, after a few centuries of mellowing, some of the most fertile soil in the world, perfect for vines, pistachios, citrus, almonds, and vegetables. Volcanic hot springs and mud pools soothe arthritis and a host of other ailments. The snows on Mount Etna cooled the sherbets of the emirs and chilled the ice cream before the advent of refrigeration.

Of course they occasionally make unruly neighbours. Vulcano is due to erupt any day now, keeping the population at a minimum; Etna has nearly destroyed Catania on more than one occasion, while the densely populated villages on its slopes have fared less well; each has an emergency supply of holy relics to ward off molten lava flows in their direction, and even today, despite all the study that's gone into volcanology, saintly intervention remains the best and often only civil defence available. Indeed, Etna scoffs at mere human attempts to make sense of its activities and predict its violence. In a recent fit of ill temper it destroyed the Volcanology school's observatory near the main crater, and about once a decade it spits out little lava bombs on the heads of tourists, just to keep them guessing.

Wastrels and Saints, Abandonment and Sorrow

We really have done our best to include every Italian island in this book, no matter how tiny—including even the islet of Meloria, a rock with a tower on it off Livorno's harbour near which the Genoese put an end to Pisa's maritime supremacy in a great sea battle of 1284. There are a few we just couldn't find: all the islands where Odysseus landed, for example, or the misty and elusive garden islet where Shakespeare imagined Prospero and Ariel (Ventotene, or one of the Aeolians perhaps?). Even now, no amount of motorscooters and shorefront trattorias, diving clubs and bottled gas can cure these minor landfalls of their ancient attachment to myth and shadow. Today, enjoying their greatest period of safety and prosperity since the emperors' navy enforced the *Pax Romana*, they continue to slide effortlessly, mischievously between legend and reality. They do so because we wish them to. Throughout history, men have been unable to treat Mediterranean islands as simple pieces of land, insisting on populating them with a cast of characters heavily weighted towards royal profligates and exiles, fictional characters (the Count of Montecristo, for one), holy monks and pirates. The first occupants on record tended to make the islands the homes of the gods—Pantelleria's Phoenician *femme fatale*, Tanit, Tyrrhenian Jove on Montecristo, or sturdy Aeolus, giving his bag of winds to Odysseus on Lipari. The Romans certainly enjoyed all these stories, and the emperors and their friends eventually bought up almost all the smaller islands for their summer playgrounds. Emperor Augustus packed his man-eating daughter Julia off to his villa on Ventotene, without noticeable improvement; her daughter, also named Julia, ended up on the distant Tremitis for similar indiscretions. Tiberius stocked girlfriends and boyfriends at his opulent retreat on Capri—not part of Capri, apparently, but the whole island. Tiberius exiled some of his predictably perverse children to Ponza, perhaps the birthplace of his grandson Nero. The juicy details come from the histories of Suetonius, the greatest tattler of antiquity. Other historians recommend caution with all this—the scholarly Tiberius may really have spent his time on Capri writing his lost histories and Etruscan grammar.

When things went wrong for the Roman Empire, they really went wrong for the islands. As soon as the Vandals passed through Italy in the 5th century, they settled in Africa and built a fleet, destroying the Roman naval monopoly forever. Soon, every small island was at the mercy of any raider and pirate that could learn to sail. At the same time, the wealthiest Roman families were bequeathing their now indefensible island possessions to the Church. Colonies of monks began to occupy many of the islands, variously praying humbly, accelerating into full-scale licentiousness, or getting carted off wholesale by African pirates. A disproportionate number of saint legends came out of these islands. St Mamilian slew a dragon on Montecristo in the 6th century, and his relics were scaring away pirates a thousand years later. St Michael did the same for Procida. Many of the island saints are still appreciated with unusual devotion—witness the grand pilgrimages to Santa Rosalia in Palermo. We hear the New York police still have trouble keeping down the noise each year when descendants of the Aeolian islanders celebrate St Bartholomew's Day in Brooklyn.

But neither San Domino's holy bones nor San Mamiliano's right arm could keep the islands from their eventual sad fate—endless pirate raids, as late as the 1800s, making it impossible for a permanent population ever to establish itself in many places. The end of the pirates brought no relief. Italian colonists and speculators descended on the islands in the 19th century, deforesting them as they did much of Calabria and the Basilicata, turning places like Lampedusa from pine-clad paradises into rocky wastelands. The new Italian kingdom contributed its share by grabbing up several islands whole, expelling the population and turning them into prison colonies. On many islands you may still sense the presence of the Homeric heroes or the saints, only because the intervening centuries have been a void, with a present population that has been around only for a few generations, without any real traditions or continuity. Little shadows of legend cannot help cropping up on such romantic backgrounds—Napoleon on Elba, the doomed, crooked banker Sindona's dreams for his native Lampedusa, or Roberto Rossellini and Ingrid Bergman having their affair on Stromboli. It isn't much, really, and one cannot help visiting some of these islands with the impression of being on a slate wiped clean by history, still haunted by the nymphs of the sea and the powers of the Mediterranean air, enjoying the quiet until real legends take form once more.

The Wonder of the World

Of all the long procession of heroes and rulers that have trodden Sicily's stage, from King Cocalus to General Patton, none perhaps would make a better movie subject than a medieval German lad, brought up in Sicily by Arab tutors, eventually showing a notable talent for poetry and an almost obsessive fascination for the art of hunting with falcons. At the age of three, little Friedrich von Hohenstaufen had already inherited the right to the Kingdom of Sicily and the Holy Roman Empire. When he claimed those rights in 1220 by winning the Battle of Bouvines, the new monarch—Frederick II—became the most powerful ruler medieval Europe had yet known.

Germany, for the moment, was quiet; this suited young Frederick perfectly, allowing him to spend nearly all his time in the much more culturally stimulating precincts of southern Italy, still in the afterglow of the remarkable Arab–Norman civilization founded by Roger de Hauteville. Change the scene to a dozen years later, and Frederick is at his court in Palermo, discussing philosophy with his circle of court scholars in Latin, Italian or Arabic, while Indian dancing girls swivel delicately atop crystal globes. (One wonders what his various wives thought of them; his third, and favourite, was Isabella of England, daughter of King John.) When he had a mind to travel, which was often, Frederick did it in style, in fairy-tale progresses of elephants and leopards, poets and astrologers, the Holy Roman Imperial bodyguard of a thousand scimitar-swinging Muslims; of course the dancing girls came along too. Medieval Europe had never seen anything like him; contemporary chroniclers called Frederick *Stupor Mundi*—the Wonder of the World.

Frederick wasn't all show. An active, intelligent ruler who worked for decades to weld the Italian part of his empire into a modern, centralized state, he founded cities (L'Aquila in the Abruzzo and Lucera in Apulia) and universities (Naples), and gave Sicily what may have been Europe's first written constitution, the famous *Constitutiones Melfitanes* of 1231. His long fight against the impostures and conspiracies of the popes earned him the unprecedented honour of being excommunicated two and a half times. His big mistake, attempting to infringe the liberties of the north Italian free cities, got him nothing but trouble, and eventually scotched whatever chance he had of realizing his political ambitions.

For all the war and strife, Frederick still found time to preside over the most brilliant court in Europe; his poets made the greatest contribution, creating some of the first and finest Italian vernacular poetry—only two generations or so before Dante. His government encouraged advances in art and architecture everywhere, and itself built palaces and castles all over the Italian south. Not many of them survived the papal reaction and Angevin invasion that followed Frederick's death in 1250, but two extremely intriguing buildings remain, reminders of a strain of Frederician mysticism that no one since has been able to adequately explain. One is the bizarre, octagonal Castel del Monte in Apulia—almost a Great Pyramid of Italy, for all the speculation and theorizing that has gone on about its purpose and its arcane geometry. The other, set at the very centre of Sicily, is the similarly octagonal Tower of the Winds; it has some considerable mysteries of its own, which you may explore if you ever make it to Enna.

Part III
ISLANDS ALONG THE COAST OF ITALY

Madonna di Monserrato, Elba

Elba and the Tuscan Archipelago

Thanks to Napoleon, everyone has heard of Elba. What is not so well known, however, is that Elba is only the largest of a group of islands, ranged in a semicircle off the coast of Tuscany. These smaller islands—there are six of them—have truly earned their obscurity. Three are penal colonies, and two others have no permanent residents. Here is a brief introduction to them, from north to south.

Gorgona, the tiniest, is a prison, **Capraia** is too, but only one-quarter of it. The rest has a small population and is beginning to attract tourists. **Pianosa**, the flat island, like Gorgona has only crooks and guards. **Montecristo** no longer has a Count, only a custodian; it is now a nature reserve. **Giglio**, the largest and most populated, is full of tourists. Finally there is **Giannutri**, a summer paradise for a select few.

Geographically the islands have much in common with nearby Corsica. There's lots of pink granite and Laricio pines. All of the group except Pianosa are mountainous—the archipelago is really only the summits of a submerged mountain range. Historically, they have moved in the orbit of Italy since the days of the Etruscans. While perhaps lacking in 'sights' and tourist attractions, the six smaller islands each have their share of natural beauty. Elba itself, surprisingly, is one of the more popular holiday spots in the western Mediterranean, and by no means lacking in diversions.

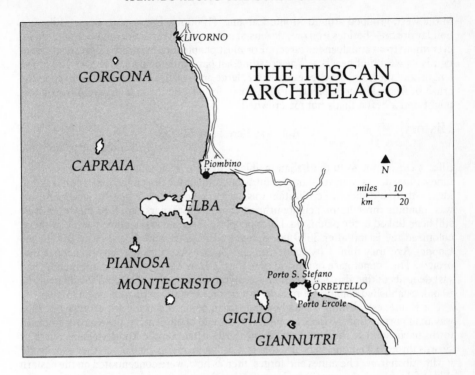

LIVORNO

GORGONA

THE TUSCAN
ARCHIPELAGO

CAPRAIA   Piombino

▲
N

miles   10
km   20

ELBA

PIANOSA
MONTECRISTO   Porto S. Stefano
                              ORBETELLO
                         Porto Ercole

GIGLIO

GIANNUTRI

ELBA

When the government closed the steel mills on Elba after the war, the national and local governments sought to make up the lost income by promoting tourism on the island. They have been singularly successful; Elba has become one of Europe's holiday playgrounds, and with tourists approaching some two million every year, prosperity has returned to its 30,000 inhabitants.

Tourist Elba, however, is no glamour puss. It is a comfortable place that attracts mainly families. Germans in particular are fond of the island; they have bought up most of the southern coast, and many of them come back every year. There is no single, big, crowded, tourist ghetto, as is true on some other Mediterranean islands, but a number of quiet, small resorts all around the coast. The lives of the Elbans themselves have adjusted to the cyclical rhythms of tourist migrations. In winter the island seems empty; much of the population stays only to work during the season. Other activities do exist to supplement tourism, such as fishing and mining, but the old iron mines, after thousands of years, have finally given out. The last of them closed in 1984.

In an unspectacular way, Elba is beautiful. Pink and green predominate—pink for the granite outcrops and houses, green because the island is heavily forested. Like its neighbour Corsica, it is a chain of mountains rising out of the sea, the tallest of which are

35

to the west, grouped around Monte Capanne (1000 m). For a mineralogist, Elba is a holiday dream—besides iron ore, dozens of common and rare minerals are found there, everything from andalusite to zircon. For most people, however, Elba's greatest attraction is its wealth of beaches. The coastline, all bays and peninsulas, is over 150 km in length, and there are beaches everywhere, large and small, sand or pebbles. Even in the crush of August, there's plenty of Elba-room for all, and if you look carefully, you just might find a beach that's not too crowded.

History

Able was I ere I saw Elba
—the Napoleonic palindrome

Elba is close enough to the Italian mainland to have been inhabited from the earliest times. Indeed, it is so near—both for invasions and for the dissemination of cultures and ideas—that no distinctive civilization was ever founded there. When Neanderthal Man was tramping through the neighbourhood about 50,000 years ago, Elba may even have still been linked to the peninsula. Later peoples, a seemingly unending parade of them, colonized the island after 3000 BC, drawn by Elba's treasure hoard of metals. In the Copper Age they mined its copper; in the Bronze Age they alloyed the copper into bronze. The copper gave out just in time for the Iron Age, and Elba, conveniently, had vast deposits of this also. Competition was fierce: Etruscans and Greeks fought over the island, established colonies of miners, but neither left any permanent settlements.

For Rome, establishing its hold on the Italian peninsula in the 4th century BC, Elba was an important prize. After its conquest at the end of the century, the Romans founded towns to consolidate their hold, and thenceforth, whenever the Roman legions ran their swords through Teutons, Persians, Gauls, Carthaginians, or each other, they usually did it with Elban iron. The mines and forges, then as now, were concentrated on the eastern third of the island; the remainder became a holiday spot for the wealthy, as witnessed by the remains of large villas discovered near Portoferraio.

The fall of Rome brought invasions, disorder, depopulation, and pirates to Elba; the Lombards in the 6th century, under the murderous Gummarith, subjugated the island with their usual bloodshed; Saracens and adventurous barons from Italy fought for the scraps. By the 11th century Pisa, as the island lay across its most important trade route, had assumed complete control. It held the island for almost 500 years, constructing fortresses at Luceri and Volterraio and exploiting the mineral resources. At the time the capital was called *Ferraia*, of which the modern capital of Portoferraio was only the port. Not a trace remains of the medieval city, and archaeologists are still trying to discover its site.

From the 13th century on, Genoa contested Pisa's possession of the island. In the 16th century Duke Cosimo I saw his opportunity and seized it for Florence. He built Portoferraio and the walls around it, but soon had to contend with the growing power of Spain in the western Mediterranean, and after some inconclusive skirmishes Elba was partitioned between Tuscany and Spain. Spain built the town and fortress of Porto Azzurro as a counter to Portoferraio, an arrangement that lasted throughout the 18th century, despite French efforts to grab the island.

NAPOLEON

During the Napoleonic wars, Elba was occupied for a time by the English, and

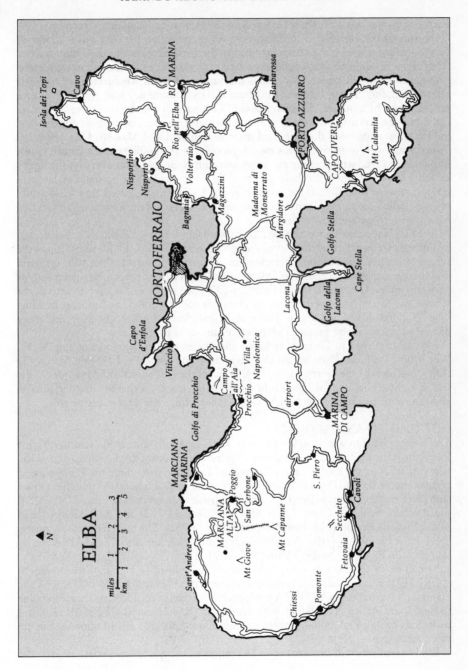

ELBA

N

miles 1 2 3
km 1 2 3 4 5

Isola dei Topi
Cavo
RIO MARINA
Barbarossa
PORTO AZZURRO
Nisportino
Nisporto
Rio nell'Elba
Volterraio
Magazzini
Madonna di
Monserrato
Margidore
Mt Calamita
CAPOLIVERI
Golfo Stella
Cape Stella
Bagnaia
PORTOFERRAIO
Capo
d'Enfola
Viticcio
Campo
all'Aia
Villa
Napoleonica
Procchio
Golfo di Procchio
airport
Lacona
Golfo della
Lacona
MARCIANA
MARINA
MARINA
DI CAMPO
Poggio
MARCIANA
ALTA
San Cerbone
S. Piero
Seccheto
Cavoli
Sant'Andrea
Mt Giove
Mt Capanne
Fetovaia
Pomonte
Chiessi

Portoferraio was unsuccessfully besieged for over a year by Napoleon's troops in 1799. Napoleon finally annexed it in 1802, with no premonition that the 1814 Treaty of Fontainebleau would put a temporary end to the First Empire and send him to Elba. After all these centuries, Elba suddenly found itself on the centre stage of world history.

Napoleon himself chose Elba, from the variety of small Mediterranean outposts offered him, for 'the gentleness of its climate and its inhabitants'. Also, perhaps because on clear days he could see his own island of Corsica. No one, however, seems to have consulted the Elbans themselves on the matter, and they can be excused for the cold indifference with which they received their new ruler. On 4 May 1814, he arrived at Portoferraio with some 500 of his most loyal officers and soldiers and a British Commissioner charged with keeping an eye on him. But Napoleon soon won over the hearts of the Elbans by being the best governor they ever had. New systems of law and education were established, the last vestiges of feudalism abolished, and what would today be called economic planning was begun; he reorganized the iron mines and started Elba's modern network of roads.

Not that Napoleon ever really took his stewardship seriously. Remaking nations and institutions was a reflex by then, after doing it all across Europe for 20 years. It was the return to France that occupied his attention. The atmosphere was thick with intrigues and rumours, and secret communications flowed incessantly between Napoleon and his partisans on the Continent. On 20 February 1815, just nine months after his arrival, the Elbans and the embarrassed British watchdog awakened to find the Emperor missing. The 'Hundred Days' had begun. Later, after Waterloo, a smaller, gloomier, and more distant island would be found to keep Napoleon out of trouble.

Elba was returned to Tuscany, and soon after joined the new Kingdom of Italy. World War II hit Elba hard; Portoferraio and environs were bombed in 1943–44, first by the Allies, and then by the Germans. In 1944, in one of the more disgraceful episodes of the war, Elba was 'liberated' by Free French and African troops, with more murder, pillage, and rape than had been seen in the Mediterranean since the days of the pirates.

GETTING TO AND AROUND

You'll never have to wait long for a ferry to Elba, especially during the summer. Gritty Piombino is the major point of departure. Any train going down the Tyrrhenian coast will take you as far as the station called Campiglia Marittima; from there the FS operates a regular shuttle train to Piombino (don't get off at the central station; the train has a short stop there and continues to the port). Two companies run services to Elba, TOREMAR (head office: Scali del Corso 5, Livorno, tel (0586) 22 772) and NAVARMA (head office: Piazzale Premuda 13, Piombino, tel (0565) 33 032). The most frequent passage is the 1-hour Piombino–Cavo–Portoferraio trip, and there are also TOREMAR ferries that go from Piombino to Rio Marina and then to Porto Azzurro (2 hours). Services to Elba can be as frequent as every half-hour in July, down to two or three in winter. TOREMAR also has a daily Livorno–Portoferraio run (5 hours) by way of Gorgona and Capraia. Note that the NAVARMA service is really a part of the ferry trip from Piombino to Bastia, in Corsica. To keep up with demand in the summer, TOREMAR also runs hydrofoils on the Piombino–Portoferraio run; these only take 30–40 minutes, but are more expensive.

Elba has an efficient bus service to all corners of the island, and buses depart with some frequency. The hub of the system is Portoferraio, with buses leaving and returning to the terminal by the Grattacielo, facing the harbour. There are a couple of **car hire** agencies on the island: Maggiore, Calata Italia 8, Portoferraio (tel (0565) 915 368); or Avis, Via IV Novembre, in Porto Azzurro (tel (0565) 95 000).

TOURIST INFORMATION

The office for the island is the Grattacielo, Calata Italia 26 in Portoferraio, just across from the ferry dock (tel (0565) 92 671). During the summer the Livorno EPT runs a booth in Piombino, just across from the ferry dock (tel (0565) 36 432).

Portoferraio

Portoferraio, with 11,000 souls, is the capital and only city of Elba. The massive walls built by Duke Cosimo remain, though Portoferraio has spilled out westwards along the bay. Here the ferries dock at the Calata Italia, where the visitor's introduction to Elba is the **Grattacielo** ('skyscraper'), a 10-storey pile of peeling paint built in the 1950s that is one of the most endearingly hideous buildings in the Mediterranean. It is also the most important building for tourists, since it contains the tourist information office, most of the ferryboat offices, and the Portoferraio bus terminal at the back, with connections to all of Elba's towns and resorts.

Follow Calata Italia and its various pseudonyms under the walls, next the old U-shaped harbour. On the far side rises the **Torre del Martello**, from which in the old days a chain was stretched across the harbour in times of danger. The main gate of the city is the **Porta a Mare** at the base of the U, over which can be seen the inscription of Duke Cosimo reminding us with the accustomed Medicean vanity how he built the whole town 'from the foundations upwards'; the new town had originally been dubbed Cosmopolis.

Directly inside the Porta a Mare is **Piazza Cavour**. Portoferraio is a big natural amphitheatre; from the piazza the town slopes upwards in all directions towards the walls on the high cliffs. North of the Piazza, Via Garibaldi leads up to the main attraction, Napoleon's house, the **Palazzo dei Mulini** (9–2, Sun 9–1, closed Mon, adm). Napoleon had the house built according to his own simple tastes; inside can be seen his furnishings, books and other paraphernalia, including the flag with three golden bees that he bestowed on the Elbans. It's worth the trip just to see the contemporary political cartoons mocking the emperor. The gardens around the house offer fine views over the city walls. On either side you can see the two Medici fortresses dominating the highest points in the city: **Forte Falcone** to the west and **Forte Stella** to the east, the former still used by the Italian navy, the latter used as housing.

On the way down Via Garibaldi, you may want to stop at one of the parish churches, the **Misericordia** or the **Holy Sacrament**, both of which have copies of Napoleon's death mask; on 5 May the Misericordia holds a procession with a replica of Napoleon's coffin to commemorate his death. The **Town Hall**, originally a bakery for Cosimo's troops, was the boyhood home of Victor Hugo, whose father was the French military commander in Elba. There's a Roman altar displayed in the courtyard, and inside, the **Biblioteca Foresiana** has a collection of books about Elba and a small picture collection. Two blocks west is the **Teatro dei Vigilanti**, built by Napoleon around an abandoned church, while east of Via Garibaldi lies the **Piazza della Repubblica**, the throbbing heart of Portoferraio, with its crowded cafés, 18th-century **Cathedral**, not really a cathedral at all these days, and the nearby market.

Around Portoferraio

Most of Portoferraio's hotels and restaurants are in the modern extension outside the city walls. There's a pebble beach, **Le Ghiaie** on the north side, and another called **Le Viste** under the walls near Forte Falcone. Two roads lead from the capital, one along the northern coast to the small resorts of **Acquaviva** and **Vitaccio**, and to **Capo d'Enfola**, a lovely headland rising sheer out of the sea, barely connected to the rest of the island.

The second road runs south to the junction of **Bivio Boni**, where it branches to the east and west. Nearby there is the thermal spa at **San Giovanni**, and the ruins of a Roman villa at **Le Grotte**, on the south shore of the Gulf of Portoferraio, more interesting for the view than the little that remains. There are beaches here at Ottone, Magazzini, and **Bagnaia**, the latter the site of the simple, beautiful 12th-century **Church of Santo Stefano**, the best Pisan monument in the archipelago. At **Acquabona** you can shoot some bogies at Elba's only golf course (9 holes), or continue west from Bivio Boni to the resort at **Biodola Bay** and the **Villa Napoleonica di San Martino**. The emperor soon tired of life in Portoferraio and built this house as his country retreat. In later years the husband of his niece (daughter of Jerome) purchased the place and added a pretentious Neoclassical façade with big Ns pasted everywhere; it's now another Napoleonic museum (9–2, Sun 9–1, closed Mon).

Eastern Elba

Rio nell'Elba is the old mining centre, though it's not at all what one would expect a mining town to look like—it's as pleasant and pastel as any other Elban town, set in the hills overlooking the eastern coast. Archaeological sites, the scanty remains of mines and Etruscan mining camps dot the neighbourhood. There are many undeveloped beaches on the western side of Rio's peninsula, including Nisporto and Nisportino. The road between Portoferraio and Rio passes the steep hill of **Volterraio**, where you can make the long climb to the 11th-century Pisan castle on the summit.

Rio Marina, as its name implies, is the port for Rio nell'Elba. Here, the **Mineralogical Museum** (open Sat mornings, call ahead tel 962 001) in the Palazzo Comunale has displays of all the island's unusual rocks and minerals. Rio Marina has a busy harbour, its many small fishing boats under the vigilant eye of an octagonal Pisan watchtower. The eastern side of this peninsula, like the western side, has some fine beaches where you can sometimes escape the crowds—Ortano, Porticciolo, Barbarossa, and many others. On the northern tip stands **Cavo**, an older resort town on a tiny port.

Porto Azzurro and Capoliveri

South of Rio, the road passes through some difficult terrain towards **Porto Azzurro**, built by the Spaniards and now a large holiday town. Until 1947 it was called *Porto Longone*. The fortress, built in 1603 to withstand the Austrians and French, was later converted into a famous Italian calaboose that hosted many political prisoners and criminal celebrities. Besides the town beach, there are several others nearby, including a bizarre one at **Terrenere**, where a yellow-green sulphurous pond festers near the blue sea in a landscape of pebble beach and ancient mine debris—for those jaded travellers seeking something beyond Elba's mass tourism. During the season, day excursions run from Porto Azzurro to the island of Montecristo.

Just north of Porto Azzurro is the **Sanctuary of Monserrato**, a famous shrine with an icon known as the 'Black Madonna'. The Spanish governor built this here in 1606 because the mountain (Monte Castello) reminded him of the peculiar mountain of Monserrat near Barcelona. Similar Black Madonnas are revered from Portugal to Poland; over the centuries the oxidation of yellow paint has darkened them (just as it threatens Van Gogh's *Sunflowers*). South of Porto Azzurro is another Spanish fortress at **Capo Focardo**, on a large oval-shaped peninsula consisting of Monte Calamita and the rough hill country around it.

On this peninsula is **Capoliveri**, one of the oldest inhabited sites on the island. The town takes its name from the Roman *Caput Liberi*, which may refer either to the worship of Liber, an Italian equivalent of Dionysus (this has always been a wine-growing area) or to the free men (*liberi*) who lived there. In Roman times Capoliveri was an 'Alsatia', a refuge for any man who could escape to it. It has had a reputation for independence ever since, giving a bad time to the Pisans, the Spanish, and even Napoleon. Today it is a peaceful place, with fine views from its hilltop over the surrounding countryside and sea. Although Capoliveri is very scenic and surrounded by beaches, much of its coast is privately owned. South of Capoliveri, near the coast, is the **Sanctuary of the Madonna delle Grazie**, with a painting of the Madonna and Child by the school of Raphael, miraculously saved from a shipwreck. The coast west of Capoliveri is marked by two lovely broad gulfs, **Golfo Stella** and **Golfo della Lacona**, separated by a steep, narrow tongue of land. Both are developed resort areas, with centres at Lacona and Lido Margidore.

Western Elba

Beyond Biodola, the scenic corniche road west from Portoferraio passes through the adjacent resort towns of **Procchio** and **Campo all'Aia**, the former larger and one of the more expensive resorts on Elba. Seven km west is **Marciana Marina**, another popular resort, with a 15th-century Pisan watchtower, the **Torre Saracena**. This is the port for Marciana, the oldest continuously inhabited town on Elba.

In the 14th and 15th centuries, when life near the coast wasn't safe, Marciana was the 'capital' of the feudal Appiani barons, the most powerful family on the island. Today, high in the mountain forests on the slopes of Monte Capanne, it is a surprisingly beautiful town of narrow streets, stone stairs, archways, and belvederes. Sections of the old city wall and gate are still intact, and the old Pisan **fortress** hangs over the town (not open to visitors). The palace of the Appiani may be seen on a narrow *vicolo* in the oldest part of town. Marciana's **Archaeology Museum** (10–12.30 and 4–7.30, closed Wed and from Oct–Mar) has a small collection of prehistoric and Roman objects found in the area. From Marciana a cable lift climbs to the summit of Elba's highest peak, **Monte**

Torre di San Giovanni

Capanne, with stupendous views over Corsica, the Tuscan archipelago, and the mountains of Tuscany itself.

Three churches outside of Marciana are of interest: the ruined Pisan **San Lorenzo**, the **Sanctuary of San Cerbone**, who escaped here from the troublesome Lombards (later his body was buried in a miraculous rainstorm, so the Lombards wouldn't see), and the **Sanctuary of the Madonna del Monte**, dating from the 11th century and one of the most important shrines on the island. Pagan Elbans may have worshipped on this site as well, as did Napoleon for two weeks, after a fashion, with his Polish mistress, Maria Walewska. Another mountain village, almost a twin of Marciana, is **Poggio**, just to the east. Poggio has a natural spring where the Elbans bottle their local *acqua minerale*—called Napoleone, of course. It's very good, but the Elbans keep it all to themselves.

On the rugged coast to the west and south of Marciana, there are yet more beaches and resorts: **Sant'Andrea, Patresi, Chiessi, Pomonte, Fetovaia** (a lovely stretch, protected by a rocky promontory), **Seccheto** and **Cavoli**. Seccheto has ancient granite quarries from which the stone was cut for the Pantheon in Rome.

Seven km east of Marciana stretches Elba's pocket-sized plain, the **Campo nell'-Elba**, extending across the island from Procchio to Marina di Campo, separating the western mountains from the central range. Elba's small airport is here—it is the only place they could put it. Two old, pretty towns lie on the edge of the plain: **Sant'Ilario in Campo** and **San Piero in Campo**. San Piero's parish church of San Niccolò has interesting frescoes; it was built on the ruins of an ancient temple to Glaucus. Halfway between the two towns are the ruins of the Pisan church of **San Giovanni**, along with a Pisan watchtower. On the coast is **Marina di Campo**, Elba's first and perhaps largest resort, with the largest beach. The watchtower in the harbour was built by the Medici.

WHERE TO STAY (tel prefix 0565)

With more than 150 hotels around the island, Elba has something for everyone. The emphasis is on the not-too-expensive resort, attractive to family holiday-makers. Many hotels stay open all the year round, with substantial off-season discounts. Beware, however, that Elba is a big package-tour destination, and despite its scores of lodgings, book ahead to avoid disappointment.

If you want to stay in Portoferraio, an interesting possibility is the **Ape Elbana**, Via de'Medici 2, tel 92 245. The 'Elban Bee' is the oldest hotel on the island; it entertained Napoleon's guests (L30–52 000, all with bath). For something a little more up-to-date, ****Villa Ottone**, at Ottone, tel 966 042, is in a 19th-century villa right on the beach, with a shady garden and tennis, open all year (L105–185 000). Some of the city's hotels are near the beach of Le Ghiaie and the city park; one that is quite pleasant is the ***Villa Ombrosa**, Via de Gasperi, tel 92 363 (L55–75 000, depending on the plumbing). The resorts begin where Portoferraio's suburbs end. Some areas within a few kilometres offer good value in lovely settings, such as the ***Mare**, at Magazzini, tel 966 069 (L53–74 000); and **Tirrena**, also at Magazzini, tel 966 002 (L44–53 000, all with bath). Further out in peaceful Bagnaia, **Clare**, tel 961 077, a little hotel with a garden (L42–54 000, all with bath). South of Portoferraio at Acquabona is the ***Acquabona Golf Hotel**, tel 940 064, with Elba's only golf course—sorry, there's only room for 9 holes—as well as a swimming pool and tennis and comfortable, well-equipped rooms (L60–90 000).

At Cavo, on the east coast, prices tend to be slightly lower, and as Porto Azzurro tends to be crowded, there are plenty of campsites and holiday apartments there. The same is true of most of the beaches on the southeastern peninsula around Capoliveri, although many pleasant hotels are right on the beach like **La Voce del Mare**, at Naregno beach, tel 968 455 (L37–46 000 without bath, L42–52 000 with). The best beach on Elba may be at Cavoli, west of Campo nell'Elba; there you'll find **La Conchiglia**, tel 987 010, small and air-conditioned (L42–55 000, all rooms with bath). Of the resorts on the west end of the island, there are some smart establishments around Procchio, more modest hotels at Santa Andre and Pomonte, and some which are blissfully out of the way, like the **Andreina** at La Cala, west of Marciana Marina, tel 908 150 (L44–54 000 without bath, L42–52 000 with).

EATING OUT

In the long list of restaurants on the island, few really stand out. What do stand out are Elba's DOC wines; both *Elba rosso* and *Elba bianco* can hold their own with any in Tuscany. To start with, while you're waiting for the ferry at Piombino you might try the **Ristorante Terrazza**, above the bar in the port area, with delicious *spaghetti alle vongole* and a big picture window with a panoramic view of Piombino's steel mills (L20 000).

One of the most popular places to eat in Portoferraio, right in Piazza della Repubblica, is **La Ferrigna** (tel 92 129) offering some extravagant sorts of seafood antipasti, stuffed roast fish, and an Elban version of Livornese *cacciucco*; there are tables on the convivial piazza (L40–50 000). **La Bussola**, in Portoferraio at Le Ghiaie (the pebble beach north of town), tel 915 091, does tasty swordfish, and every other sort of grilled fish you can pronounce in Italian for a bargain L30 000 or so. **Chiasso**, in Capoliveri's Via Nazario Sauro, tel 968 709, offers sole stuffed with shrimp and an Elban favourite that rarely travels to the mainland, *risotto al nero di seppia* (with cuttlefish in its own ink), L50 000. In Portoferraio, **Arsa** is a good, honest, inexpensive trattoria by the port, at Via Manzoni 8, L24–32 000. Pizzerias and seafood places abound in answer to demand, and one place where you can have both is the **Garden**, Via Vittorio Emanuele 14 (L40 000). In Porto

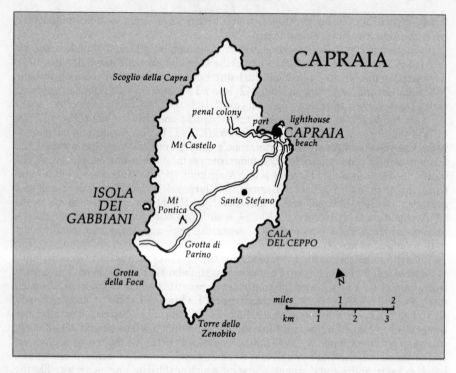

Azzurro, among the many seafood restaurants on the beach, is the **Delfino Verde**, built over the sea for a fine view (L45 000 and up). At Poggio, 3 km from Marciana, **Publius**, Piazza XX Settembre 13, tel 99 208, is as worth visiting for its lovely views as for its menu, with items you won't find elsewhere on the island: *pappardelle* in boar sauce, *fagioli al fiasco* (Tuscan beans), and game in season—as well as good fish dishes (L40 000).

CAPRAIA

Capraia, 65 km from Livorno, is the third largest of the islands, after Elba and Giglio. It measures about 10 km by 5, and has some 400 inhabitants. Like Elba, it is mountainous, but has fewer trees; most of the island is covered with scrubby *macchia*.

History
In Roman times Capraia seems to have been a private estate, and the ruins of an extensive villa can be seen. In the days of the Empire, the island was occupied by a colony of Christian monks. Such an island was perfect for the Christian ideal of withdrawal and contemplation, but it also prevented the Church authorities from keeping a close watch on the colony, and the monks slipped into unorthodoxy and loose behaviour; an armed mission from Pope Gregory the Great was needed to force them back in line in the late 6th century.

44

When Saracen pirates began to infest the Tyrrhenian Sea, Capraia, like most of the group, became deserted. The Pisans thought it important enough to repopulate and fortify in the 11th century. Genoa eventually gained control, as she did in Corsica only 32 km away. The proximity gave Capraia its one big moment in history; in 1767 the revolutionary forces of the Corsican nationalist leader, Pasquale Paoli, and the weakness of the Genoese, resulted in, of all things, an independent Capraia, which soon learned to support itself by piracy. French occupation put an end to that four years later.

WHAT TO SEE
Seven years ago tourist accommodation on Capraia consisted of one hotel and two tiny pensions. Today, by a miracle of 20th-century Eurotourism, these have all grown into three-star hotels, and two more have sprouted to join them. It helps that Capraia is an island, and a pretty one, but its real attraction is its natural setting, its deep-sea diving and marine grottoes. In the last century the northern quarter of the island was put to use as an agricultural penal colony, which is what it still is today. The civilian population is almost entirely concentrated in the port and only town, **Capraia Isola**. The port is actually half a kilometre away from the town, connected by the island's only paved road. In the town are the Baroque church and convent of **Sant'Antonio**. Used as a barracks in the last century it is now crumbling and abandoned. On the outskirts are the ruins of the **Roman villa**, apocryphally the abode of Augustus' profligate daughter Julia, and an 11th-century Pisan chapel dedicated to the **Vergine Assunta**. Overlooking it all is the large and impressive fortress of **San Giorgio**, begun by the Pisans and completed by the Genoese. The well-preserved **watchtower** at the port was built by the Genoese Bank of St George.

On the eastern side of town there is a beach under the cliffs with an interesting tower, built by the Pisans, and connected to the cliff by a natural bridge. A visiting Californian at the turn of the century was so struck by it that he built a copy of it on a beach near San Diego.

From Capraia Isola a road leads southwest across the island, passing another Pisan church, that of **Santo Stefano**, built on the ruins of a 5th-century church used by the early monks, destroyed by the Saracen pirates. Near Monte Pontica is a cave, the **Grotta di Parino**, a sacred spot used as a place of meditation by the monks. The road ends at a lighthouse on the western coast. Just south of here is a sea cave, the **Grotta della Foca**, where some Mediterranean seals are still reported to live. At the southern tip of the island is another Genoese watchtower, the **Torre dello Zenobito**.

GORGONA

To see **Gorgona**, 37 km from Livorno, you'll either have to get permission from the Ministero di Grazia e Giustizia in Rome (quite difficult) or else punch a *carabiniere*! Gorgona, a hilly, rectangular square mile, was first used as a prison by Pope Gregory the Great. A Carthusian monastery lasted until the new Italian state expropriated the entire island in 1869; in the beginning, it was to be a 'model prison' with workshops and vineyards, but it wasn't long before it deteriorated into just another lock-up. There's nothing to see on Gorgona, except maquis and a handful of olive trees, and you'll have to be content with the view from the boat, which stops daily on the way to Capraia to drop off new cons and supplies. Ambitious plans are afoot to close the prison and turn Gorgona into a wildlife preserve, but so far nothing has been decided.

PIANOSA

Pianosa is the black sheep of the family of Tuscan islands—its name, taken from the Roman *Planasia*, explains why: it's as flat as a pool table, broken only by a few tiny conical mounds, and about 18 square kilometres in area. Its only port is the Cala Giovanna, near the entrance of the prison. The island has had a troubled history in modern times. The Genoese sacked and depopulated it, as did Dragut's pirates in the 1550s. Even so, it managed to support a sizeable population of farmers and fishermen until it was taken over as a penal colony in 1856.

The prison occupies the entire island, and as with Gorgona, you will need to get special permission to gain admittance. Also like Gorgona, the early dreams of a modern progressive prison with rehabilitation through farm labour have been allowed to die, and most of Pianosa is just wasteland. There are substantial Roman ruins on the island. It was the property of Augustus' famous general Cornelius Agrippa, who left behind his big villa, complete with theatre, and some remnants of the ancient port of Cala Giovanna.

MONTECRISTO

Montecristo, administratively a part of the *comune* of Portoferraio, in Elba, has recently been declared a nature reserve. It has a population of three: the guard and his family. The island (7¹⁄₂ square kilometres) is roughly round in shape and very mountainous. Its summit, Monte della Fortezza (639 m), is the highest in the archipelago outside western Elba. There is little vegetation on most of Montecristo, and it is generally so rocky and inaccessible—there are no roads and few level places to build them—that it has never been deemed worth settling by anyone except monks.

The island has had religious importance since ancient times. Under the Romans, both the island and its peak were called *Mons Jovis*, and an important temple of Jupiter was built on the summit. Of this not a trace remains; unless the Christian monks themselves destroyed it, its fate is a mystery. These monks, living as hermits, occupied Montecristo in the last stages of Roman decline. The most famous of them was San Mamiliano, a 6th-century bishop of Palermo who fled here, via Elba, from the Arian heretic Vandals. He was reputed to have killed a dragon upon arrival. When he died, a divine signal was seen by fishermen from Elba, Giglio and Genoa, who all made haste to the island. Realizing that he was a suitable subject for canonization, they began to fight over the remains. In the true tradition of Christian brotherhood, they struck a deal and cut Mamiliano up in three pieces. Giglio got an arm, which proved its worth by repulsing the

Turks in an 18th-century pirate raid. Charity might have bade them leave some bones behind for Montecristo, for without any relics to protect them the last colony of monks was carried off by pirates in 1553.

More recently Montecristo became a household word, thanks to Alexander Dumas' novel, even though none of the action of the book takes place there. The island served as a hunting retreat for the pathetic fool Vittorio Emanuele III, penultimate king of Italy, until his death in 1945.

Montecristo today might as well be a prison, like Pianosa or Gorgona: so seriously does the Portoferraio government take its status as a nature reserve that it won't let anyone see it. Private boats, and day excursions from Giglio Porto and Porto Azzurro in Elba, are allowed to dock at Cala Maestra, one of the many coves around the island's coast, and visitors are allowed on the fine beach in the cove, but no further. The mountains, the ruins of the old monastery and the royal villa (now the custodian's house)—all are out of bounds. Incidentally, the trees and exotic plants you'll see at Cala Maestra don't really belong there. They are not native to the island, but were planted when Montecristo was a royal playground.

GIGLIO

Giglio is the largest of the Tuscan islands after Elba, measuring about 20 km by 8. It is villages, Giglio Porto, Giglio Castello and Campese. Like so many of the Italian islands, Giglio suffered grievously from deforestation and abandonment of the land in the last two centuries. Though much of it is still green and pretty, large sections have become almost barren. A remarkable change in the environmental consciousness of the Giglians seems to have taken place over the last few years; if the big signs posted all over the harbour are any indication, they've gone to the opposite extreme—no camping, no noise, no riding over the wildflowers (and no collecting rocks—they're part of the island too!)

The word *Giglio* means lily, and the lily has become the island's symbol, although it has in fact nothing to do with the island's name. The Romans called it *Aegilium* or *Gilium*. Under them, Giglio like most of the other Italian islands was a resort for the very wealthy. Pisa, Aragon, and various feudal families held the island in the Middle Ages. Duke Cosimo seized it for Tuscany in the 16th century, but did little to protect it against its greatest danger, pirates. Fortunately, the Giglians had the holy right arm of San Mamiliano to protect them (see p. 46).

GETTING AROUND
Porto Santo Stefano is the main port for Giglio, a one-hour run twice daily, and more frequently in the summer on the Toremar line. The railway station for Porto S. Stefano, along the main Livorno–Rome line, is Orbetello Scalo; buses meet the trains to carry passengers to the port. Giannutri can be reached on a regular basis only in July and August, on a daily boat from Porto S. Stefano (Società Maregiglio, tel 812 920). On Giglio, buses run fairly regularly from the ferry dock to Giglio Castello and Campese.

TOURIST INFORMATION
In Giglio Porto at Via Umberto I 48 (tel 809 265).

WHAT TO SEE
Giglio Porto, the island's metropolis, is a colourful place, with red and green light-

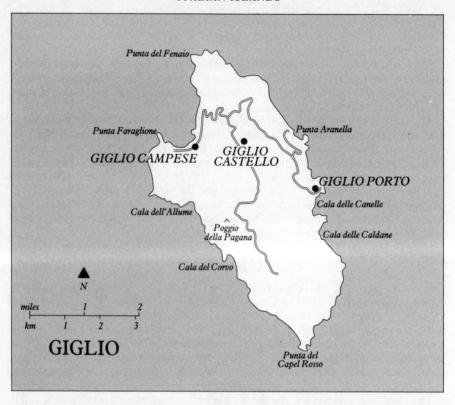

Punta del Fenaio

Punta Faraglione

Punta Aranella

GIGLIO CAMPESE

GIGLIO
CASTELLO

GIGLIO PORTO

Cala dell'Allume

Cala delle Canelle

Poggio
della Pagana

Cala delle Caldane

Cala del Corvo

N

miles   1   2

km   1   2   3

GIGLIO

Punta del
Capel Rosso

houses to welcome the ferries in, and pink and beige houses straggling up the hills. There are two beaches south of the town, at **Cala delle Canelle** and **Cala delle Caldane,** one to the north at **Punta Aranella**, all more or less developed, and in the town itself, the world's smallest beach, tucked behind the houses on the left side of the port. From Giglio Porto a difficult mountain road leads up to **Giglio Castello**, the only secure refuge in pirate days, and until recently the only real town. The fortress itself was begun by the Pisans and completed under the Grand Dukes. The picturesque town inside, all medieval alleys and overhanging arches, has plenty of gulls and swallows, a few lazy German tourists, and a small Baroque church with an odd tower where you can see the famous arm of S. Mamiliano.

From Giglio Castello, a road leads southwards past **Poggio della Pagana**, the island's highest peak (530 m), through land largely reforested with pines to Punta del Capel Rosso, at the southern tip, then back along the coast to Giglio Porto. The main road from Giglio Castello continues on to **Campese**, a growing resort area with an old watchtower and a large sandy beach.

WHERE TO STAY AND EAT   (tel prefix 0564)
The number of tourists, and of hotels (13) on Giglio seems to have stabilized in the last

few years, leaving it not entirely overcrowded even in the summer months. Right in the port there's ***Demo's, a little flash in the sixties Miami Beach style (tel 809 235, L48–70 000) and the smaller, cosier **La Pergola next door (tel 809 051, L45–50 000). But persevere until you leave the Porto and you can enjoy the more serene ***Arenella, very close to the beach at Punta Arenella, with a pretty garden and a good restaurant (tel 809 340, L48–72 000). And if you really want to get away from it all, your best chance on the entire Tuscan coast is **Pardini's Hermitage. Located at a quiet cove called Cala degli Alberi, this place can only be reached by boat (ask at the Giglio Sub shop on the port, but it's better to book as there are only ten rooms). They'll keep you busy with sports and nature activities if you want, or you can just enjoy the sea and mountains by yourself (tel 809 034; prices for full board per person can range from 62–105 000; basic double room is L39–55 000). A good, modern beach hotel off in Campese is the **Campese (tel 804 003, L60–72 000).

Giglio Porto has its share of seafood restaurants around the harbour. La Margherita (tel 809 237) is probably the most popular; good fish and a terrace right on the beach (L30–40 000). The real find on the island, however, is up in Giglio Castello: Da Maria, on Via Casamatta (tel 806 062); not only good seafood (like stuffed squid or lobster flambé) but game dishes like the house speciality, wild rabbit *alla cacciatora* (L30–35 000).

GIANNUTRI

Among the Tuscan islands, only Gorgona is smaller than Giannutri. Because the island is small, lacks water and has little level ground for agriculture, it has never been continuously inhabited. With no population to attract the pirates, Giannutri has little history to speak of, although it has been known since ancient times. The Greeks called the island *Artemesia*, after the goddess, and the Romans converted it to *Diamium*. Perhaps the island acquired these associations from its crescent-moon shape. Like Gorgona and Pianosa, Giannutri was a private estate; there are remains of a Roman villa on the northern coast, near Cala Maestra.

Until recently the island's ownership was shared by a few families who had holiday cottages near Cala Maestra. Now, a tourist village has been built on the other side of the island, at Cala Spalmatoio, which is where you'll have to stay if you want a holiday on Giannutri—there are no hotels. There is no permanent population either, only the workers in the tourist village.

The island is about 5 km around the crescent and never more than 500 m wide. It is hilly, with many trees, and surrounded by a rocky coast broken only by beaches at Cala Maestra and Cala Spalmatoio. Besides the Roman villa, there are interesting caves near Spalmatoio and near the lighthouse at the southern tip.

WHERE TO STAY AND EAT (tel prefix 0564)
To arrange accommodation in the Villaggio Residenziale, the only place to stay on Giannutri (tel 896 039). There are two restaurants, the summer-only La Torre at Cala Spalmatoio (tel 896 039), with simple meals for around L25 000, and the Taverna del

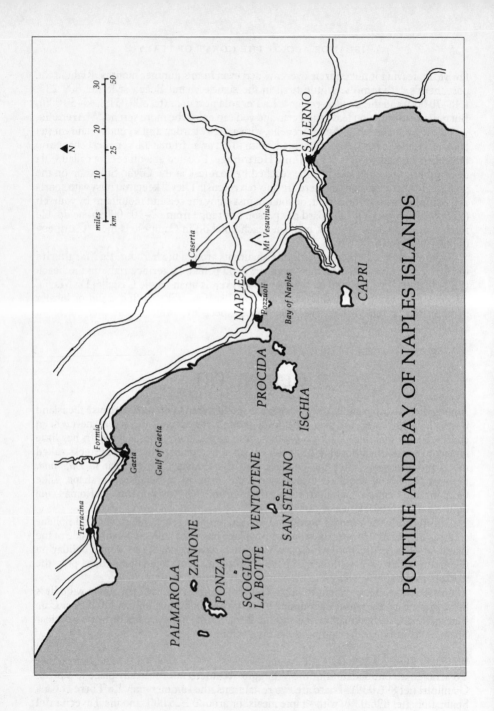

PONTINE AND BAY OF NAPLES ISLANDS

SALERNO

Mt Vesuvius

CAPRI

CASERTA

NAPLES

Pozzuoli

Bay of Naples

PROCIDA

ISCHIA

Formia

Gaeta

Gulf of Gaeta

VENTOTENE

SAN STEFANO

Terracina

PALMAROLA

ZANONE

PONZA

SCOGLIO
LA BOTTE

N

miles   10   20   30
km   25   50

Granduca at Cala Maestra (tel 896 035), open all year, with pizza in the summer and a tasty, filling *zuppa di pesce* on the menu anytime; also around L25 000.

The Pontine Islands

Scattered across the Gulf of Gaeta, there are five Pontine (or Ponziane) islands: two are inhabited (Ponza and Ventotene) and three are now abandoned (Palmarola, Zanone and Santo Stefano). Although all are volcanic in origin, they belong to two different chains: Ventotene and Santo Stefano are part of the same formation as Ischia and Procida in the Bay of Naples, while Ponza, Palmarola and Zanone belong to the volcanic substructure of the mainland, near Anzio. Accordingly, the islands are quite fertile, producing wine and lentils.

All are dramatically beautiful, and until recently all were almost unknown to the flood of tourists which swept down on the nearby Bay of Naples. This changed noticeably in the 1980s, when Ponza enjoyed (or endured) a veritable stampede of visitors in the summer months, fleeing the denser crowds on Capri and Ischia. Outside the high season, however, you'll find an island as peaceful, charming and unspoiled as Capri was 50 years ago.

PONZA

The 3-hour sail from Formia to Ponza has two lovely highlights. The first is the vision of the old walled town of Gaeta on the rocks just off Formia, and the second is the most unusual sight of Ponza in the distance. At first it appears large and mountainous; then you realize that, as in a child's drawing, the mountains are all a single narrow chain, with no other mountains to back them up. After sailing past the uninhabited island of Zanone and the islet of Gavi, the rough-cut nature of the coast, untidy with numerous *scogli* and *faraglioni* (standing sea rocks and islets), sheer cliffs, grottoes and beaches, adds to the delightful first impression of Ponza.

History

Inhabited in the Paleolithic era, Ponza later became an exporter of that most valuable Stone Age commodity, obsidian, used to make tools. This hard volcanic glass was mined on the island of Palmarola, worked at Fieno on Ponza and then shipped to Cuma, an important centre on the mainland.

The Volscians, one of the early tribes near Rome, were the first historic inhabitants of Ponza, and they used it as a naval yard. The increasing power of Rome forced the Volscians out in 313 BC; at first favouring the island, the Romans built temples to the Dioscuri and later to Mithras, an aqueduct, and the two Imperial villas owned by Augustus. In the later years of Tiberius, however, Ponza became a place of political exile, hosting such notables as Caligula's brothers, his wife Orestilia, and his sister Agrippina

GAVI

Punta Incenso

Piano d'Incenso

Cala Schiavone

Punta Beppe Antonio

Cala Gaetano

Punta Forte Papa

S. EVANGELISTA

Cala Fontana

Le Forna

Cala Feola

Cala Inferno

Spiaggia del Core

N

PONZA

Punta Bianca

Spiaggia di Lucia Rosa

miles   ½   1

km   1   2

Spiaggia di Frontone

Santa Maria

Punta Madonna

Sant'Antonio

PONZA

LE FORMICHE

Capo Bianco   Chiaia di Luna

Mt Guardia

CALZONE MUTO

Punta Fieno

Faro della Guardia

the Younger, who was accused of plotting against him. Liberated after his assassination, she returned to Rome with baby Nero, who may have been born on Ponza.

After the fall of Rome, Ponza was deserted by all but a group of monks at Santa Maria, where the exiled Pope, San Silverio, was lodged in 537. The monks, however, were no match for the pirates, who forced them to flee shortly thereafter. Little of note marked the passing of centuries on Ponza; the island was ignored even by its owners, the Farnese family, who had it for many years, although they occasionally sent expeditions to see what they could exploit. The last of the dynasty, Elisabetta, Queen of Spain, gave the island to her son Charles III of Naples in 1731.

When Charles became King of Spain, he left the islands to his son, Ferdinand IV of Naples. The Bourbons, for all their faults, tried to promote colonies on abandoned islands like Ponza, where the settlers, sponsored by the king, received generous tax incentives to develop the island. They fished, planted the first vineyards, and made a good living from the abundant coral along the coasts. These early Ponzese colonists must have wondered what they had got themselves into when an earthquake knocked a whole peninsula into the sea in 1821, and when a fierce hailstorm in 1835 destroyed all the crops, and even some of the houses.

But they persevered, and by the time of the Unification of Italy (1860) there were enough Ponzese to export. Some migrated to South America, and a large colony settled outside New York city, where they still celebrate the island's festivals. Under the Fascists, Ponza once more became an island of exile, first for anti-Fascists and, after the liberation, for Il Duce himself, for six days. More recently, Fellini filmed the last scenes of his classic *Satyricon* on Ponza, and other directors have since followed, attracted by the unspoilt charm of the island.

GETTING AROUND
The main year-round port for Ponza is Formia, halfway between Rome and Naples. Trains run along that route every half-hour on average, but note that not all stop at Formia, so make sure you board the right one. Caremar sells tickets at the quayside both for its morning ferry and for the hydrofoil; the ferry takes 3 hours and costs L12 500 (return). In the summer additional services out of Formia for both Ponza and Ventotene are offered by Basso Lazio, whose office in Formia is at Via Vitruvio 60. There is also a daily boat (Mazzella Line) from Terracina (tel (0773) 74840) which departs at 8.15 am and arrives at 10.45, with an additional service in August departing at 7.45 am. In the summer Aliscafi SNAV offers a hydrofoil service from Anzio to Ponza (4 a day, 1 hour), continuing to Capri and Ischia, and there's one hydrofoil a day from San Felice Circeo; a single to Ponza costs around L24 000. SNAV offices in Anzio are at Via Porto Innocen-ziano 18 (tel (06) 984 5085). Caremar also operates a summer ferry from Anzio to Ponza and Ventotene; the office is at Via Porto Innocenziano 51 (tel (06) 983 1231) in Anzio. On Ponza itself small buses run between Sant'Antonio and Piano d'Incenso every 20 minutes. They tend to be packed, so try to make your cross-island excursions early in the day.

TOURIST INFORMATION
In the summer there's a Pro Loco office open near the Municipio, Via Roma 3. The very helpful AAST in Formia, just up the road from the port, also has plenty of information about the Pontine islands (tel (0771) 21490).

The Beach of the Chiaia di Luna, Ponza

The Port

All boats arrive in the principal town and port, known variously as Ponza or simply Porto. For many this is the archetypical Tyrrhenian town, its pretty pastel-and-whitewashed houses arranged artistically around the amphitheatre of the busy fishing port, over-looking the sea and its stately assortment of monolithic *scoglios*. One side of the town is dominated by the **Torre dei Borboni**, now a hotel, and the lighthouse at Punta Madonna. The parish **church**, dating back to the 17th century, has recently been restored with funds from the Ponzese in America and contains the statue of San Silverio, the island's patron saint. Dominating the town is the **Municipio**, with its yellow arcades surrounded by cafés, restaurants, and a monument known as the Mamozio. It's a very pretty town, but no longer undiscovered. It seems destined to share the same fate as Capri—upmarket shops are beginning to creep in where previously there were basic grocery stores, and the port area is choc-a-bloc with boats of all shape, size and colour.

Tunnels link the port with its suburbs of **Sant'Antonio** (with a small but not very clean beach) and **Santa Maria**. According to local tradition, Santa Maria was once the residence of Circe, seductress of Odysseus, at a time when Ponza was known as *Eea*. Such traditions are never total fabrications; it is quite possible that a local but similar sorceress–goddess was once worshipped at Santa Maria and her identity was confused with Circe under the Romans. A sea cave known as the **Grotto di Circe** nearby may be visited by boat. In the vicinity of Santa Maria are numerous Roman cisterns and an underground aqueduct called the **Grotta del Serpente** which once supplied a popu-lation of 20,000; the water was stored in a great reservoir, the *Piscinae Limariae*. Unfortunately all these features are hard to find on your own, and you'll have to inquire locally for exact directions. It's rather easier to find the small pension that housed Mussolini during his six-day exile on Ponza.

Besides waterworks, the Romans dug several tunnels on Ponza. One leads from the port area to the loveliest of the island's many small bays, **Chiaia di Luna** ('moonlight bay'), a luminescent crescent of beach beneath a steep, pale, 90-m cliff that amply

deserves its romantic name. Although across the island, it's within walking distance—
Ponza is a long, thin sickle, following the shape of an ancient crater.

Around the Island

The main attractions on the rest of Ponza are most easily seen by boat. Small motor
launches are readily available for hire at the port and at Santa Maria, as are the rubber
rafts, popular with underwater enthusiasts. Scuba-diving is very popular in the clean
waters around Ponza, with their sunken ships, coral, odd rock formations and big eels.
Beginners can apply at the Nautilus sub-aqua school at Le Forna. In the summer there
are organized sea excursions around the island.

Outside the port area, white houses are scattered along the island's single road, which
twists and turns through the vineyard-clad hills with frequent panoramas of cliff and sea.
The only real settlement along the way is **Le Forna**, named after the kilns that line the
bottom of Capo Bosca hill. From here the houses and farms extend to **Punta Forte
Papa**, many of them built in the North African *domus* style (with low domes), a style more
flamboyantly expressed on another Italian island, Pantelleria, close to Tunis. Particularly
impressive at Le Forna, however, are the *case di tufa*—elaborate cisterns dug in the rock
designed to collect the maximum amount of rainwater. The centre of Le Forna is the
church **Maria Assunta**, begun in 1770. A pension and various restaurants open here in
the summer.

A narrow lane and steps descend from Le Forna to the **Piscina Naturale**, a
volcanically-created pool separated from the sea by a narrow strip of land pierced by a
tunnel-grotto that permits small boats to enter. Many people come here to swim. Other
beaches near Le Forna are **Cala Feola** and **Cala Fontana**, which derives its name from
a natural spring utilized by the Romans. A pretty stairway takes you down to the small
beach. From here you can see the jetty of the company that mines the white bentonite of
Ponza, reputedly unique to the island. On the promontory of Forte Papa to the northwest
is a 16th-century watchtower built by the Farnese family, named after Pope Paul III, a
member of the clan. In 1944 an English cargo ship carrying German prisoners foundered on the rocks, with few survivors.

Cala Inferno, on the eastern side of the island (within easy walking distance), derives
its name from the 'infernal' whiteness of its cliffs. Here you can see the fragmentary
remains of the Roman aqueduct which transported water to Santa Maria.

East of Le Forna, towards the end of the road, is the district known as **La Piana**,
followed by **Calacaparra** with the sole Ponzese football field and a restaurant. The
trans-Ponza highway stops at **Cala Gaetano**, from where some of the best views of the
island may be had, including the turquoise sea and Ventotene. On a clear day you can
make out Gaeta on the mainland.

Around Ponza by boat: Grotte di Pilato

Many of the island's wonders are accessible only (or at least most easily) by sea. Most
interesting from a scholarly viewpoint is the **Grotte di Pilato**, not far from the port. Its
name has nothing to do with Pontius Pilate and everything to do with an imaginative
Neapolitan compiler centuries ago, who associated Ponza with Pontius.

The Grotte di Pilato is a natural grotto containing a rock-cut pool, with something resembling an apse carved in the back and four corridors leading into the rock. In ancient times this cave was used by augurers who would dissect the entrails not of birds or goats but of sea eels, in order to discern the future. On the right side of the cave a hole bored in the wall opens up towards the constellations of the Great Bear and Draco, thought to have had some magical significance in auguries. Even today the grotto is a mysterious place, especially at night, should you have the good fortune to visit it then.

Cliffs and Beaches
On the same eastern side of Ponza are two fine beaches, **Frontone** and **Core**, with the magnificent cliffs of Punta Bianca in between. From Core you can take a small boat into the **Grotta degli Smeralda**, where the water lives up to its emeraldy name. Due east of Cala Inferno many amphorae from ancient shipwrecks have been found. Passing the small islet of **Sant'Evangelista**, the enormous **Natural Arch** comes into view, and the beach of Schiavone.

Round the islet of Gavi and continuing down the west coast of Ponza you come to **Punta Beppe Antonio**, with another grotto and beach. From there you come to the cliffs and beaches of Le Forna, and from there to the **Spiaggia di Lucia Rosa**. Lucia Rosa was the daughter of one of the early colonists who had an unfortunate infatuation with a man of beautiful moustaches. Father said no, and so the lovelorn Lucia Rosa flung herself over the cliff near the tiny islets or *faraglioni* that still bear her name. South of here stretch two long beaches of white pebbles, a perlite mine and Capo Bianco Grotto. The beautiful Chiaia di Luna follows, and then the major wine-producing district of Ponza, **Punta Fieno**. Here a German father-and-son team, the archaeologists Schneider, found the remains of the Neolithic obsidian works, where the obsidian of Palmarola was worked. A lighthouse commands the southern tip of the island, on a leg of the island's tallest mountain, **Monte Guardia**. The remainder of the trip to the port, around the Punta Madonna and Le Grotte di Pilato, takes you past a pair of rocks with the odd name **Calzone Muto**—'Silent Pants'.

SAN SILVERIO
San Silverio di Frosinone, the beloved patron saint of Ponza, is honoured with two festivals, on the last Sunday in February, and on 20 June. The good and humble Silverius was one of the Dark Ages' numerous Popes-for-a year (536) until Theodora, imperious wife of the Byzantine Emperor Justinian, had him unjustly accused of conspiring with the Goths—after he himself had personally opened the gates of Rome for the Byzantine General Belisarius—and stripped him of his robes and exiled him from Rome, installing in his place her friend Vigilius. Silverius wandered in the Peloponnese and Naples, before ending up on Ponza, where he became the islanders' spiritual leader. A council of bishops gathered then on Ponza and inveighed against Theodora's anti-Pope. Realizing that a schism was in the making, the Empress sent assassins after Silverio, and he was murdered on 20 June 537 as he attempted to flee to Palmarola. Belisarius, hearing of his death, repented for the role he played in the affair, and founded the church of Santa Maria de' Crociferi in Rome, near the Trevi fountain; a plaque still in the church tells of his remorse.

The *festa* on 20 June is the island's event of the year. Houses are given a new coat of whitewash, and the port and Santa Maria are brightly decorated with streamers and lights. On the big day itself, San Silverio's statue, adorned with coral and gold, is carried from the church to Santa Maria, with the entire population of Ponza in procession either by land or in small boats. Later in the day the 'Gallina' takes place at Punta Bianca: a pole is extended out over the sea with a chicken at one end, and the young gallants of Ponza vie to see who can walk along the pole, pluck a feather from the chicken and return without mishap. The day ends with a concert in front of the Municipio.

WHERE TO STAY   (tel prefix 0771)

The most picturesque place to stay on Ponza is the ***La Torre dei Borboni in the port (Via Madonna; tel 80 109), with a third of its rooms and apartments in the 18th-century castle, affording wonderful views over the town and port. The hotel's restaurant has won many awards, and steps lead down to a small private beach—as similar ones may have done in the days of Augustus, who had a villa on the same commanding site. Prices begin at L80 000 with bath. In the same price range is the ***Bellavista, Via Parata (tel 80 036), which sits at the top of its own little secluded cove. For something less pricey and right on the sea, try **Gennarino a Mare on the Via Dante (tel 80 071), with balconies overlooking the sea, and a restaurant (L60 000). There are also many rooms to let in private homes, but they tend to be a little expensive—inquire at the Pro Loco for a list.

EATING OUT

Specialities of Ponza include *lenticchie alla ponzese* (lentil soup), *coniglio alla cacciatora* (rabbit with onions, tomatoes, etc.) and lobster dishes. The best wines of Ponza are *Forna Grande, del Fieno* and *delle Grottelle*. Of the restaurants along the waterfront, L'Ancora has a good name, with dinner at around L30 000. La Lanterna, on the road above the port is a straightforward family-run trattoria with simple good food—L20 000. Next to the Municipio the Ippocambo serves fish but its prices are high—you're paying for the prime viewing spot. Il Gambero, in Via Comandante, specializes in fish and lobster dishes and is open all year, with prices for a complete meal around L30 000 (much more for lobster). The specialities at Le Querce in Santa Maria are local dishes and *zuppa di pesce* (L22 000). Outside the port area there's the Ristorante alle Piscine, with moderately priced local dishes and a fine view of the sea, and in Le Forna, on the Via Forna Chiesa, is the Zi Arcangelo with a similar cuisine and views over Palmarola (L20 000).

PALMAROLA

West of Ponza and most easily reached from that island by hired or excursion boat is the small island of Palmarola which is uninhabited but not without charm. The mountains of Palmarola have an Alpine dignity, and like Ponza the island is surrounded by all sorts of picturesque volcanic debris, most spectacularly a rock known as the 'Cathedral' on the west side of the island. Also on the coast are the beach, located beneath a rugged cliff of white and gold, and its small port.

Striking and beautiful as it is, Palmarola has been bad luck to many: here in 303 the

Romans abandoned a group of 300 Christians to die of thirst and hunger; in 537 the ex-Pope San Silverio was murdered here when he escaped from Ponza to Palmarola; the boilers of the English cargo ship that sank at Forte Papa blew up at Palmarola, initiating that disaster; and even more recently an aeroplane crashed on the island. The deserted fields and terraces of the farmers who once lived here add another touch of melancholy. Nevertheless, a lot of people own property on the island, and have constructed summer houses there. At Cala del Porto, the best place for landing on the island, there are at present two *abusive* (meaning 'illegal') beach trattorias, fighting with the authorities to stay open.

ZANONE

An hour-and-a-half northeast of Ponza lies Zanone. Unlike Ponza and Palmarola, this island has never been cultivated or deforested, and remains splendidly pristine today. The last human inhabitants were the monks of Santo Spirito; part of the Circeo 'National Park', today the island is the natural reserve of the shy, curved-horn *mouflons* (rare wild sheep), and over a hundred species of birds and rare plants. The only sometime human resident is the island's warden. The main attraction of the island, though, is its rich fishing grounds, which beckon the scuba-divers from Ponza. Although there are no organized excursions to Zanone, it is easy to hire a motor boat and visit this ecological island paradise on your own.

VENTOTENE

Tiny, rural Ventotene resembles a table from many angles, a flat, green land on a platform of tufa, carved into curious shapes by the wind. The island, along with tiny Santo Stefano, belongs to the cone of the great underwater volcano, Campano, and locals say their home will never erode away (an obvious concern on such a small piece of real estate) because San Paolo della Croce anchored it down with basalt. With no hills or forests to shelter it, Ventotene deserves its name, and it has acquired two interesting scientific phenomena: the highest part of the island, Montagnozzo (138 m), is covered with sand carried there from Africa and elsewhere by the wind; the sand is particularly deep around Cala Nave and Parata Grande, where roots of ancient trees have chemically petrified in the fine, loose layers of sand.

History

Called Pandataria by the Romans, the little island, less than one square mile in area, saw a disproportionate number of Imperial celebrities come and go—on holiday, in disgrace, or in pieces. The first to come was Julia, only child of Caesar Augustus and the most famous adultress of her day. In 25 BC she had a grand summer villa built at Punta Eolo and brought the cult of Venus–Isis to Ventotene, building a temple near the modern lighthouse. The second of her three husbands, Agrippa, Augustus' admiral, was probably the guiding light behind the artificial port, still in use today.

Julia's villa was her pleasure palace far from the wagging tongues of Rome, and such was the respect she—or her father—commanded that even 200 years later the fishermen of Gaeta wouldn't divulge the names of the men their great-grandfathers had ferried in the night to her villa. Detested by her third husband, Tiberius, whom Augustus had forced to divorce his wife in order to wed her, Julia found her escapades eventually catching up with her and she was exiled to Ventotene by her own father. Here she suffered for five years without men or wine, and with only the company of her mother Scribonia (first wife of Augustus) to comfort her. Although the Roman people several times interceded for Julia's return, Augustus was adamant that she should never enter Rome again, although he eventually sent her to more comfortable surroundings at Reggio Calabria.

The presence of Julia's villa on tiny Ventotene, close to yet so far from Rome, made it an ideal place for exiles of noble blood. Julia's daughter Agrippina, one of the few decent characters in the bloody soap opera of the Imperial family, was framed in a conspiracy against Tiberius, her dead husband's uncle, and exiled by him to Ventotene. When she protested, Tiberius had her beaten; realizing that her rage was futile, she starved herself to death. Later Tiberius passed a bill in the Senate praising himself for not having had the poor woman strangled! When her son Caligula became emperor, he retrieved her ashes from Ventotene and gave them a proper burial (this was before he went mad).

Agrippina's grandson Nero (son of her no-good daughter Agrippina the Younger)

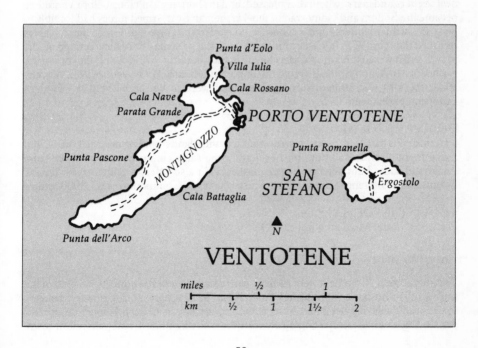

59

perpetuated the cruelties on the island when he had his wife Octavia exiled there to pacify his new mistress, the cunning Poppea Sabina. When the people of Rome clamoured for 20-year-old Octavia's return, felling the recently erected statues of Poppea, the latter persuaded Nero to have her rival permanently removed. Nero sent his henchmen to the villa, where they slit the veins of the young Empress, and when through sheer terror she took too long to die, they scalded her in a hot bath, after which they cut off her head and gave it to Poppea.

The last member of the Imperial family to languish on Ventotene was Flavia Domitilla, the daughter of Diocletion who was banished after the Emperor's death for harbouring Christian sentiments.

During the Middle Ages Pandataria gradually became known as Ventotene, from the many winds that sweep across the unprotected island. For a while the only inhabitants were Benedictine monks; in 1249 Pope Innocent IV ceded their monastery to that of Santo Spirito on Zanone, then five years later he transferred all the monks to Salerno. Ventotene was then left to the mercy of pirates, who made it a base, and to the Farnese, who owned the island for many years, exploiting the coral and minerals and stealing the ancient statues (a job finished off by an 18th-century Englishman, Sir George Hamilton).

The first colony sent to Ventotene under the Bourbons was an experiment à la Rousseau. In 1768 some 300 thieves, prostitutes and other evildoers from the prisons and gutters of Naples were brought to the island to demonstrate that, once removed from the evils of society, they would become models of virtue. They were left free to build their own shelters and marry whom they pleased; and in short, it wasn't long before Ventotene became the Sodom and Gomorrah of the Tyrrhenian Sea. Armed forces had forcibly to evict the wild islanders, and an honest colony from Torre del Greco near Naples replaced them in 1772. In Fascist times 800 political prisoners were incarcerated on the island, and it was in this anti-Fascist climate in the middle of World War II that two of the prisoners, Rossi and Spinelli, wrote the important *Manifesto di Ventotene* (1942) formulating the idea of a united Europe—ideas that were to be the basis of the modern European parliament.

GETTING AROUND
Caremar runs a daily ferry service year-round to the island from Formia (see Ponza), and a less frequent hydrofoil link. In the summer the same company runs a service from Anzio and links Ventotene to Ponza. Basso Lazio also offers a daily service linking Formia and Ventotene in the summer. The trip takes 2 ½ hours and costs L8000 return.

TOURIST INFORMATION
Pro Loco, in the Municipio (tel (0771) 85 132).

Porto Ventotene

The single town, Porto Ventotene, is piled over the old **Porto Romano**, carved out of the tufa by Julia's husband, Agrippa. It forms a basin (6670 square metres, now used mainly by the island's fishing fleet) and is considered something of an engineering feat, its dark sides neatly cut and contrasting nicely with the white lighthouse and pale yellow town.

Equally impressive are the two subterranean aqueducts, or *condotti*, dug out by the Romans, one extending inland to the piazza Castello. This supplied not only the people of the port, but also the sacred fishpond by the temple of Venus–Isis near the modern lighthouse. Here a small head of the goddess was discovered (now in the museum of Naples).

The centre of activity in the village is **La Piazzetta**, where the simple, pink Baroque church of **Santa Candida**, patron saint of Ventotene, has recently been restored inside with bright colours. According to tradition Candida suffered martyrdom with iron combs in North Africa, after which her body was placed in a small boat which miraculously drifted to Ventotene, and lay hidden in the Grotto di Santa Candida. The statue of the saint by the altar was donated by a father and son who were abducted by Algerian pirates while cutting wood on the island. When ransomed by the king, they thus offered their thanks to Santa Candida for promoting their safe return. Notice the little figures of woodcarvers beside her.

Julia's Villa

There's a small museum in the Municipio, open in the mornings, displaying items found on Ventotene. You can also see the bleak prison, and can walk along beyond the rocky beach at Cala Rossano to the northernmost point of Ventotene, Punta d'Eolo, where **Julia's villa** once stood. Clambering over the rocks you soon discover that it was truly enormous—scattered all over the promontory are ruined walls, sections of mosaic floor, archways and steps leading down to the sea. Unfortunately the Bourbon colony on the island quarried the site thoroughly, and it takes an effort of imagination to conjure up the Imperial villa. A local engineer and architect, Luigi Jacono, made detailed drawings and studies of the site, and if you can find copies they are helpful in sorting out where the odeon, baths, grand entrance, reservoirs, guardhouse and courts once stood.

Walking Around Ventotene

You can stroll around the rest of the island in less than an hour, past little farms of lentils and barbed-wire gardens of twisted metal. In the autumn, hunters come from the mainland to shoot migratory birds, so if you come then take care. Here and there you'll find little paths winding towards the sea, the cliffs and beaches. With so many cliffs and small grottoes, the island is perhaps best circumnavigated by sea, and in the summer there are several small boats in the Porto Romano offering such an excursion, as well as to the islet of San Stefano nearby, to the east.

WHERE TO STAY (tel prefix 0771)

Although there are plans to build a large hotel on the island—a subject of hot debate between the island purists and those wanting to encourage tourism—there are only one small hotel, three small pensions and rooms to let in private houses. The hotel ****Cala-battaglia**, Via Olivi (tel 85195), provides the most luxury, if you can call it that (L55 000 with bath). The three pensions are ***Il Cacciatore**, Loc. Montagnozzo (tel 85 055), ***Isolabella**, Via Calarossano (tel 85 027) and ***La Vela**, Via Olivi (tel 85185).

EATING OUT

The few restaurants on Ventotene are stretched to the limit serving the summer visitors. One that stays open all year, specializing in lentil soup and fresh fish, is **Zi Amalia** in

Piazza Castello (around L25 000 for fish). Down by the port **L'Aragosta** serves, naturally, lobster amongst its other fish dishes, and near the beach of Cala Nave **La Lampara** has mostly fish, but occasionally some meat offerings (L22–35 000).

SANTO STEFANO

Just east of Ventotene lies the islet of Santo Stefano, not much more than a cliff in the sea. In 1795 the Bourbons built a penitentiary here, originally used to house political enemies, generally those advocating the Unification of Italy. The most famous in this respect was Luigi Settembrini, founder of the 'Sons of Young Italy' and father of a character in Thomas Mann's *Magic Mountain*. Settembrini gives an account of his uncomfortable stay on Santo Stefano in his memoirs (*Le Ricordanze*).

La Citadella, as the prison is known, was built in the form of a semicircle, with all the cells facing inwards. It was designed by Francesco Carpi, who himself became one of the first inmates and later died on the island.

During World War II, the prisoners almost caused La Citadella to be blown to smithereens by the Allies when they took over the prison. The chaplain, however, finally persuaded them to lay down their arms and raise the white flag. Since 1965 the prison has been closed; a developer wanted to turn it into a hotel, but nothing has come of it. Today Santo Stefano is used for grazing livestock, and may be visited from Ventotene.

Islands in the Bay of Naples: Ischia, Procida and Capri

Without a doubt, the islands in the Bay of Naples—Capri, Ischia, and to a far lesser extent Procida—are the holiday queens of the Italian islands. Every schoolchild has heard of Capri, made so notorious by the antics of Emperor Tiberius and Norman Douglas' 'gentlemanly freaks'. Ischia, fifty years ago, was the favourite island of jet-setters jaded by Capri. Renowned in ancient times for its mud baths, it has become a home-from-home for the German bourgeoisie. If anyone tries to tell you it's still 'unspoiled', take this into consideration: Ischia is Italy's biggest buyer of spaghetti-flavoured icecream. Still, the smart set can't get there fast enough; both Ischia and Capri are connected to Naples' Capodichino Airport by helicopter. Procida, on the other hand, has hardly been developed at all, though not through any lack of charm. For many Italians, the very name of the island conjures up the same associations that Alcatraz does for Americans, which has managed to keep the developers away until very recently.

Despite their location, the three islands are of very different geological origins. Ischia and Procida are a part of the enormous submerged volcano of Campano, which stretches from Ventotene in the Pontine Islands down to Stromboli and the Aeolian Islands. In not too ancient times, the two islands were connected to each other and, if the Greek geographer Strabo is to be believed, also to the Phlegrean Fields on the mainland.

Phlegrean means 'fiery' in Greek, and Strabo records how, during an eruption of the now dormant volcano Epomeo on Ischia, an earthquake split Ischia–Procida from the mainland, then, in another upheaval, jolted the once united island in twain. In this same geological cataclysm, Capri broke off from the Sorrentine peninsula, a blow that shattered its coasts to form the island's famous cliffs.

ISCHIA

Ischia is a remarkably lovely island, able to hold its own even with Capri. The sea of vineyards encircling the island's highest peak, volcanic Monte Epomeo (793 m) produces the excellent wine named after the mountain, and the villages high on its slopes, like Fontana and Buonapane, remain untouched by the international onslaught of tourists at the resorts of Casamicciola, Forio, Lacco Ameno and Ischia town.

Unlike Capri, Ischia has many long, first-class beaches, on one of which, Maronti, the volcanic nature of the island is very evident. The hot mineral springs that gush all year round have attracted cure-seekers since Roman times, and are still recommended today for people suffering from rheumatism, arthritis, neuralgia and obesity. Because many of the springs are radioactive, a doctor's permission is often required before you take a soak (there are physicians on the island who specialize in prescribing such treatments, and they charge a pretty penny). The hottest spring on the island is Terme Rita, at Casamicciola, which belches from the earth at around 180°F. For a lark try the Terme Comunali at the port, or the unique baths at Cavascura above Sant'Angelo.

History

Inhabited by 2000 BC, Ischia became an important stop along one of the earliest trade routes in the Mediterranean, from Mycenean Greece to the Etruscans of northern Italy and the mineral wealth of Elba. The prevailing currents and winds made it natural for the Greek ships sailing west to circumvent Sicily and land in the Bay of Naples—as did that most famous sailor, Odysseus himself. As an island along the sea lane, Ischia was the perfect place to found an outpost to secure the route and trade, and here in 756 BC Chalcidians and Eretrians from the Greek island of Euboea settled the first Greek colony in western Europe.

They called the island *Pithekoussai*, referring to its abundant clay (*pithos*). However, when Montagnone (a now extinct volcano on Ischia) erupted, the colonists fled to the mainland, establishing themselves at Cumae, where they prospered. Roman writers later refer to the island as *Eneria*, deriving from Aeneas' supposed stop on the island to repair his ships, or **Inarime**, a name of unknown origin. The name Ischia is believed to be a corruption of *insula*, or just plain island.

In the year AD 6, Augustus traded the larger, more fertile island of Ischia for Capri, which then belonged to Naples. For most of its history Ischia and its famous castle remained attached to that great city, sheltering many of its nobles from political adversity; but during one period, in the early 16th century, the island outshone Naples as a

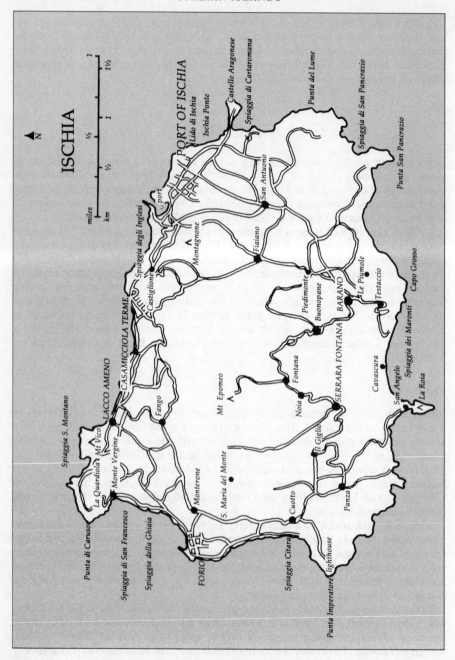

ISCHIA

N

miles
km

½   ½   1   1
½   1   1½

Spiaggia S. Montano
Punta di Caruso
La Quardiola
Mt Vico
Monte Vergine
LACCO AMENO
Spiaggia di San Francesco
Spiaggia della Ghiaia
CASAMICCIOLA TERME
Fango
Monterone
S. Maria del Monte
Mt Epomeo
Cuotto
FORIO
Spiaggia Citara
Punta Imperatore lighthouse
Il Giglio
Panza
Spiaggia degli Inglesi
Castiglione
Montagnone
Noia
Fontana
SERRARA FONTANA
San Angelo
La Roia
Spiaggia dei Maronti
Cavascura
Piedimonte
Buonopane
BARANO
Le Piumole
Testaccio
Capo Grosso
Fiaiano
San Antuono
PORT OF ISCHIA
port
Lido di Ischia
Ischia Ponte
Castello Aragonese
Spiaggia di Cartaromana
Punta del Lume
Spiaggia di San Pancrazio
Punta San Pancrazio

cultural centre. This was due to one woman, Vittoria Colonna, who lived much of her childhood in the castle of Ischia, when her father's estates were confiscated by Pope Alexander VI. She was betrothed in the castle at the age of 6 to another leading personage of the era, Francesco Ferrante, nephew of Constanza d'Avolas, the duchess who ruled Ischia for 50 years. On 27 December 1509, Vittoria and Francesco were married at the castle of Ischia in the celebrity wedding of the decade, but two years later Francesco was drawn away by the wars in the north and only once returned to Vittoria and Ischia before he died.

Vittoria was one of the greatest poets of her day, and is particularly known through her spiritual friendship with Michelangelo, who wrote sonnets to her. Few poets of the time were untouched by her graciousness. She was on close terms with the most brilliant men of Rome, her opinions were sought after, and her behaviour was always perfectly proper amidst the intrigues that surrounded her belligerent family. The contrast between the elegant court that surrounded her during her years on Ischia and the ravages and slave-taking wrought on the island by the corsairs Barbarossa and Dragut, a few years after her departure for Rome, illustrates the extremities of the period.

Another writer of far-reaching influence to find inspiration on Ischia was Giambattista Vico. In the mid-17th century he was offered an easy tutoring job on the island, giving him the leisure to formulate his murky and celebrated *New Science*, a work that had a profound influence on James Joyce. George Bishop Berkeley, the Irish philosopher, visited the island at the beginning of the 18th century and wrote of it extensively in his Journals; Henrik Ibsen spent the summer of 1867 at Casamicciola and wrote much of *Peer Gynt* during his stay.

In the 19th century, Ischia, like so many islands, was a political prison. During the Napoleonic Wars it suffered in the battles between French and English, and for a brief period was Nelson's base.

GETTING AROUND

The boats from Naples are all clustered around the Molo Beverello in the centre of the port. You can simply look at the timetables of the various companies and board the next ferry. They go so often, especially in the summer, that the wait is never long. The ferryboats take about 1½ hours to reach Ischia; the numerous hydrofoils take 30 to 40 minutes. Caremar hydrofoils depart from the Molo Beverello, others from the Mergellina (Via Caracciolo) a few miles away. Steamer fares from Naples are around L6000; hydrofoil L12 000. Caremar also offers 4 daily connections between Procida and Pozzuoli and Ischia (but not between Capri and Ischia); in the summer Aliscafi SNAV runs a hydrofoil service between Anzio, Ponza, Ischia and Capri, and Lauro Lines have an extensive ferry and hydrofoil service, linking Ischia with Naples, Sorrento, Capri, and the Pontine islands.

Buses to the various towns on the island depart from the square next to Santa Maria di Portosalvo, near the beginning of SS260 which encircles Ischia. The service (SEPSA) is very good to all parts, but be prepared to put up with crowded buses from June onwards. Another form of transport, three-wheeled, canopied mini-taxis, queue near the baths.

TOURIST INFORMATION
Via Iasolino (tel (081) 991146).

Ischia Porto

The first hint you receive of Ischia's volcanic origins comes when you enter the almost perfectly round harbour of Ischia Porto, formed by a sister crater of Monte Epomeo. Only in 1854 was it connected to the sea, the narrow strip of land carved out by the engineers of Ferdinand II. Full of yachts, lined with restaurants, and a step away from the tourist information office, it is everything a Mediterranean port should be. Note that while ships to Naples and Capri dock at one side, by the neo-classical church of **Santa Maria di Portosalvo**, and the hydrofoils near the newly modernized **Terme Comunali** (built in 1845), ships to Procida and Pozzuoli call at the other side of the lighthouse.

Via Roma, the main shopping street of Porto, with cafés and boutiques, passes the **Chiesa dell'Assunta**, built in 1300 and since remodelled in the Baroque style. Further on, when Via Roma becomes the more fashionable Corso Vittoria Colonna, turn down Via V. F. d'Avalos for the numerous seaside hotels and pensions, or in the other direction, Via V. E. Cortese for the **Pineta** (pinewood), and lovely shady divider between Ischia Porto and Ischia Ponte.

Ischia Ponte

Ischia Ponte, once a separate fishing village, is slowly being gobbled up by tourist sprawl. 'Ponte' refers to the causeway built by Alfonso (il Magnifico) of Aragon in 1438 to the **Castello d'Ischia** on its offshore rock. With the large dome of its abandoned church in the centre, the fortress where Vittoria Colonna spent so many years looks from the distance like a fairytale illustration. As King Alfonso also financed most of the walls around the islet, which can be visited, it is sometimes called the Castello Aragonese. Not only are the narrow streets and 500-year-old houses interesting; the views from the walls are superb. During the festival of Sant'Anna (end July), near the castle, you can see the island's traditional dance, the *'ndrezzata*, a ritualistic dagger dance dating from the time of Vittoria Colonna, accompanied by clarinets and tambours.

Even better views can be had from the summit of the extinct volcano, **Montagnone** (255 m); a cablecar goes from Via Baldassarre Cossa at Ischia Porto (only 5 minutes from the station). Views from the top take in the Phlegrean Fields on the mainland, Ischia's little sister island Procida, and the rest of Ischia as well.

Popular beaches line much of the town's shore. Some are organized, like Ciro, Medusa, Lauro and Starace; others, like the Spiaggia degli Inglesi (named after the English occupation at the beginning of the 18th century) and Dei Pini, are free. The public tennis courts are on the Lido C. Colombo (tel 991 013).

WHERE TO STAY   (tel prefix 081)
The finest hotel in Ischia Porto is the ******Excelsior Belvedere** on Via E. Gianturco 19 (tel 991 522), open from April until October. Not only is it quieter than most, but guests can enjoy the fine pool and garden; rates are L150–230 000. You can also indulge in luxury at the ******Mare Blu**, Via Pontano 40 (tel 982555; L95–120 000), in a charming position on the waterfront with a view of the Aragonese castle and the isle of Vivara. Also

by the sea, with lovely balconies, a pleasant garden and a large therapeutic pool is the ***Nuovo Lido**, Via R. Gianturco 31 (tel 991550; L62–80 000). In the same street, the **Villa Paradiso**, Via R. Gian Turco 3 (tel 991 501; L50–65 000) is more intimate. A pleasant, moderately priced small hotel with a thermal bath is the ***Felix Hotel Terme**, Via A. de Luca 60 (tel 991 201), situated in a pinewood with its own pool, and only a few minutes' walk from the beach and the port (open from May to Oct, L55–65 000). The ***Continental Terme**, Via L. Mazella 74 (tel 991588) is a pretty bungalow complex surrounded by flowers and greenery, It has four thermal pools and a staff of specialized doctors (L90–120 000). On the same street is ***Hermitage & Park Terme**, Via L. Mazella 68 (tel 992 395; L120–150 000). Most of the rooms have a sea view as does the restaurant, which serves excellent food. The least expensive place to stay is near the Castello Aragonese and is open all year: *Il Monasterio** (tel 992 435; L19–23 000); and the showers are usually hot.

EATING OUT

Ischians are very fond of rabbit stew, but on the whole the island is better known for its vino than its cucina; at least once treat yourself to a bottle of *Epomeo* (red or white), *Ischia* (red or white) and *Biancolella*.

Prices on Ischia tend to be high, and many people eat in their hotels. For fish the best place to look is along the Via Porto; one that's exceptionally good here is **Portucciullo**, which is fairly expensive (L50 000 a meal). Less costly, at Via Porto 66, is **Gennaro**, open from April until October, and **Da Ciccio**, at Via Porto I, specializing in *risotto alla pescatore* (L30 000). Another reasonable place to eat is **La Cantina**, Via Nitrodi 6 (tel 99071), serving typical Ischian dishes, local wine and homemade bread (L25 000, closed Oct–Mar). Near the Aragonese Castle stands the lovely and tranquil **Giardini Eden**, Via Nuova Cartaromana 50 (tel 993909). You couldn't find fresher fish or lobster, as they pluck it out of the water in front of you. The place is also well known for its good pasta dishes (L50–80 000, closed evenings and from Oct–Apr). There are also many snack bars and pizzerias that save the pocket of budget travellers—but again, you'll pay more at these than almost anywhere else in Italy. One is the **Pizzeria Romana** at Via Alfredo da Luca 6.

Around Ischia: Casamicciola

Besides the state highway (SS270) there are many scenic secondary roads zigzagging across the island that you will be able to enjoy if you have a car or a sturdy constitution and a good pair of shoes. A few miles west of Ischia Porto (bus every half-hour) is the popular resort of **Casamicciola Terme**, the oldest spa on the island and the probable location of a Greek settlement. All remains of this, however, were obliterated in the 1883 earthquake in which 7000 people were killed. Henrik Ibsen spent a summer in a nearby villa (a medallion minted in his honour can be seen in the Piazza). The mineral springs of Casamicciola are particularly potent—Rita and Gurgitello rate as the hottest—and contain large quantities of iodine.

Casamicciola, spread out under its pines, is more a conglomeration of hotels than a proper town, although there is a centre at **Piazza Marina** with shops, car-hire firms, banks and the AVET tourist information office (tel 994 441). Besides the Lido, there are beaches at Suorangela and Castagna. The heliport lies just west of the town. From Piazza Marina, an hour's walk will take you to the **Geophysical Observatory**, built in 1891.

Lacco Ameno

A half-hour's walk along the coast from Casamicciola leads to the more fashionable **Lacco Ameno**, another large resort, where the local landmark is the **Fungho**, a mushroom-shaped rock that dominates the beach. In the centre of town you can pay your respects at the bright pink **Sanctuary of Santa Restituta**, patron saint of Ischia. Martyred in the 3rd century, her body was thrown into the sea, then floated ashore at Lacco Ameno. The oldest part of the Sanctuary dates from 1036, and was constructed on the site of an early Christian basilica. Excavations in the church crypt have produced evidence of Roman baths. Greek and Roman tools and vases have also been discovered west of Lacco Ameno at Monte Vico and behind the town on Fundera plain. Some of these may be seen in the local **Museum** (open mornings only) near the church and the neo-Pompeian **Terme Regina Isabella**, connected to the luxury hotel in Piazza Santa Restituta.

For the hardy, there is a charming country path, the **Calata Sant'Antonio** leading from Lacco Ameno (off Via Roma) to the Chiesa dell'Immacolata in Casamicciola; the local milkmen, after delivering their wares udder-fresh from door to door, would herd their goats home along this path every evening.

Forio

Forio, the wine-producing centre of Ischia and a growing resort, is one of the prettiest towns on the island and supports a small art colony. Forio has three outstanding landmarks, the first of which is the huge tower known as the **Torrione**, built by King Ferrante in 1480 on the site of an even older tower. It did little, however, to defend the island from pirate raids and was later converted to a prison, and nowadays, a gallery of local art. Near it rises the dome of **Santa Maria di Loreto**, a fine Baroque church begun in the 14th century; the two towers are decorated with majolica tiles. On the point furthest west stands the white **Church of the Soccorso**, to whom the local fishermen pray for help, as can be seen from the numerous votive offerings inside.

Behind Forio there are several paths leading up into the hills, towards Monterone, Sant'Antuono and Santa Maria del Monte, below Monte Epomeo. There are beaches on either side of Forio, along with the very popular Citara and Cava dell'Isola to the south, and at Ghiaia and San Francesco to the north. Near Citara are the **Gardens of Poseidon**, a recently-built complex of swimming pools set in a Mediterranean formal garden.

Sant'Angelo

From Forio, continuing counterclockwise, SS270 passes through the hill village of **Oanza** and on to **Serrara Fontana**, both of which have roads leading down to

Sant'Angelo. The buses to this lovely fishing port stop at the top of the hill because there isn't enough room for them to turn around in Sant'Angelo itself. The walk down at the edge of the cliff is quite lovely, with numerous views of **Punta Sant'Angelo**, a small islet connected to Ischia by a narrow isthmus of sand. Only a stump remains of the **Torre Sant'Angelo** which once stood on top.

East of the village stretches the lovely beach of **Maronti**, which you can reach either by taking the path or by hiring a boat. The path runs past numerous fumaroles, hissing and steaming, and the beach itself has patches of scalding hot sand where you can wrap your picnic lunch in foil and cook it, if you so wish. Above the beach are the hot springs of **Cavascura**, at the mouth of an old river canyon; the sheer sides of the canyon, the little wooden bridges and the individual baths carved in the rock—each named after a mythological deity—make it an unusual place indeed.

Monte Epomeo

From Serrara Fontana the road towards Barano is most picturesque, winding its way around the inner valleys of Monte Epomeo (790 m). If you're going by bus, stop off at Fontana, where you can start your climb up to the old volcano itself—it hasn't erupted since 1302. Mules may be hired if you're not up to the climb yourself, and there's a hermitage where you can spend the night, located in the very crater itself. Watching the sun rise or set from such vantage points is always memorable, but with the entire Bay of Naples spread out below you, it is sublime.

The next village along the route is **Buonopane** ('good bread'), followed by **Barano**, an oasis of tranquillity on exuberant Ischia. In Piazza San Rocco, in the centre of town, the church of the same name has a characteristic campanile. The road from here to Ischia Ponte passes scattered homes and summer villas, half-hidden in the lush vegetation and pine trees.

WHERE TO STAY AND EAT   (tel prefix 081)

It would take pages to list all the hotels on Ischia; most of those outside Ischia Porto are in Forio, Lacco Ameno, Casamicciola, Barano and Sant'Angelo, and almost all close in the winter months. Many hotels in Forio are connected to thermal establishments, like the modern *****Punta del Sole** on Piazza Maltese (tel 998 208), with a pool and garden (L55 000). For something less expensive, ****San Francesco** on Via T. Cigliano 9 (tel 987 397) in nearby San Francesco, has similar facilities but no thermal baths (L35–45 000, all with shower). On San Francesco Beach near Forio, **La Meridiana** specializes in various lobster dishes at around L45 000 for an average meal. Less expensive is **La Giara** at 40 Via Marina, also serving fish (L35 000). Two other good places here are **Da Peppina**, on Via Bocca, and **La Pagliarella**, on Via Coste, where you can eat well for around L30 000.

In Lacco Ameno: ******San Montano**, on Via Monte Vico, is a hotel that offers—in addition to thermal baths—a pool, tennis courts and many other comforts (tel 994 033; L160–190 000). A bargain, by Ischia standards, is the ****Bristol**, at Via Fundera 72 (tel 994 566), with a small garden and swimming pool (L40 000 with shower). Lacco Ameno's **Padrone d'o Mare**, open all year round, specializes in various fish dishes for around L27 000; here too is the **Pizzeria da Vito Marie**, on Il Tenne, which is good, and less expensive.

In Casamicciola: prices tend to be a little lower. There's the *****Ibsen** with a pool and thermal bath on the Corso V. Emanuele 35 (tel 994 588; L42–60 000) with special facilities for the handicapped. Less expensive **Delle Rose**, Via Casa Mennella 9 (tel 994 082) has charm, a swimming pool and rooms with bath for L35–45 000. At trattoria **Nizzola** on Via Piccola Sentinelle, you can eat well for around L25 000.

In Barano: Most of the hotels in Barano are on Maronti beach, like the moderately priced *****Helios**, Via Maronti (tel 990 001; L50 000). ****La Luna**, Via Testaccio 2, is about the least expensive (tel 990 299; L35 000 with bath). One of the prettiest spots to dine is **Franceshino**, at Belvedere di Barano (tel 990 396). The sound of the waves and the sight of the moon on the water help to set the atmosphere as you decide between their delicious meat dishes and excellent fish. Their home-made pasta is a bonus (L30–35 000, closed Oct–Mar).

In Sant'Angelo: **Romantica Terme** on Via Ruffano (tel 999 216 is good value, near the sea, with a pool, tennis courts and spa for L25–42 000. The best eating place here is **Dal Pescatore** on the Piazza Troia (open from Mar to Oct), with good fish, as its name suggests, for around L25 000.

PROCIDA

Lovely, uncomplicated, and tiny, Procida is in many ways the archetypal image of all that an 'Italian island' evokes in any holiday dreamer's mind. Scented by lemon groves, said to produce the finest lemons in Italy, embellished with colourful houses as original as they are beautiful, a setting for two famous love stories, Procida is an island where most people still earn a living from the sea, as fishermen or sailors, and also from carving exquisite models of historic ships. Its very proximity to the glamour, chaos and more celebrated charms of Naples, Capri, and Ischia has saved it from the worst ravages of touristic excess. The pace of life is delightfully slow, and when there's talk of closing the penitentiary and converting it into a Grand Hotel, the locals shudder—they prefer the cons to any Capri-like transformation of their idyllic life. Connected to Procida by a modern bridge is the minute islet of Vivara—officially, though it sounds bizarre, a natural park of Naples. It teems with wild rabbits, an important ingredient in Procida's cuisine, along with the more obvious fruits of the sea.

History

Only a few miles from the mainland and Monte Procida itself, Procida the island was near enough to Naples to have a minor or at least a spectator's role in many of the turbulent events that transpired there, but far enough away to stay out of trouble. Like Ischia, to which it was once connected, Procida (ancient *Prochyo*, or 'deep', in some way connected with Aeneas' wet-nurse) was inhabited in the Neolithic period. The Romans used the island as a hunting reserve, and there was at least an agricultural settlement there in the Dark Ages—Pope Gregory the Great wrote a letter in the 6th century praising the wine of Procida. Shortly thereafter the first chapel of San Michele

70

Arcangelo was erected on Punta Lingua, on the site where a statue of the saint stood; according to legend, during a pirate attack the people prayed fervently to the statue for deliverance, and the saint responded and saved his beloved Procida at least this once.

In the 11th century a Benedictine abbey was founded by the chapel, and the fortifications of the Terra Murata ('the walled land') were begun. These proved insufficient against the ravages of first Barbarossa (1544), then Dragut (1562) and Bolla (1572). After Barbarossa burned the church, the fishermen had to donate a third of their income to reconstruct it—Pope Julius III generously decreed they could fish on Sundays and holidays as well for ten years to make ends meet, permission which was extended for

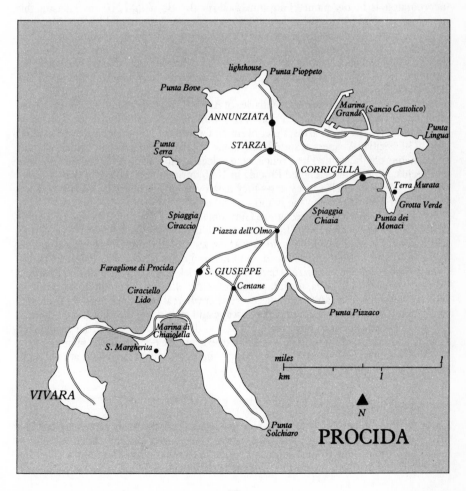

fifteen more years after Dragut. By then, however, the Benedictines had long abandoned Procida.

The Bourbon kings, like the Romans before them, often came to Procida to hunt; Ferdinand IV made the island and its town a royal domain, but turned its fortress into a prison. Procida prefers to recall another event of the period: the visit in 1811–12 by the wandering French poet Alphonse Lamartine. A beautiful daughter of a fisherman fell in love with him and gave up an advantageous marriage for his sake, only to be jilted by the fickle Frenchman. Inconsolate, she died two months later, and at least received the dubious compensation of immortality in his novel *Graziella*, a spectacular best-seller in its day. Procida, for its part, pays homage to her memory with an annual end-of-summer Miss Graziella beauty pageant.

Another famous personage connected with the island was so fond of it that he incorporated it in his name, Giovanni da Procida. Born in 1210 in Salerno, this nobleman, a good friend of Emperor Frederick 'Stupor Mundi' and his son Manfred, owned a castle on the island which he visited often on tours of his domains. When Charles of Anjou, a Guelph, took Naples, he confiscated all the property of Ghibellines like Giovanni da Procida, and the latter was forced to flee to Spain. Here Constance, the last of the Swabians and wife of King Peter of Aragon, received him well and made him Baron of Valencia.

But Giovanni got his revenge on Charles of Anjou. When the proud Sicilians began to chafe under the harsh rule of the French, Giovanni acted as a middleman to assure them that should they rise up in arms, Peter of Aragon would support their cause and be their king. The Sicilian Vespers resulted, and some 8000 Frenchmen died in that island's spontaneous combustion. The French were at least symbolically revenged on Giovanni da Procida. When they occupied Procida in 1806 during the Napoleonic Wars—about 650 years after the Sicilian Vespers—they destroyed his marble coat-of-arms, the last reminder of his presence on the island.

Readers of Boccaccio may recognize Giovanni's nephew, Gianni da Procida, from the Sixth Tale of the Fifth Day of the *Decameron*. Gianni so loved a girl of Ischia named Restituta that he sailed over daily, to look at the walls of her house if nothing else. One foul day a band of Sicilians pounced upon her and carried her off to Palermo, determined to give such a lovely prize to their king, Frederick of Aragon, who stowed Restituta in his garden villa, La Cuba, for future pleasures. Meanwhile Gianni in despair went in search of his sweetheart and finally discovered her whereabouts; he contrived to enter La Cuba with the aid of Restituta to plot an escape and make love; the king caught them *in flagrante*, and was about to burn them publicly at the stake when a courtier recognized Gianni, and informed the king he was about to execute the nephew of the man who gave him the throne of Sicily, and there's a happy ending. A good story—and according to scholars, a true one.

GETTING AROUND

Caremar runs 4 ferries daily from Naples to Procida from the Molo Beverello, taking a little over 1 hour; other connections are between Ischia and Pozzuoli. There are also at least 4 hydrofoils daily from Naples to Procida, a trip that takes 30 minutes. The one public bus departs from the port to Chiaiolella to coincide with the arrival of each ferry.

TOURIST INFORMATION
Via Rodia (tel (081) 896 9624).

The Port and Corricella

Ships and hydrofoils call at the port, the **Marina Grande**, also called Sancio Cattolico, or known locally as Sent'Co. The church near the landing, **Santa Maria della Pietà** (1760), immediately gives you a taste of Procida's delightful architecture—wide arches in random rhythms and exterior rampant stairs crisscrossing the façades, all in softly moulded lines in colour either faded pastel or more racy deep pinks, blues, and yellows. The style reaches its epiphany over the hill at **Corricella**, the oldest village on the island, built on a protected cove by fishermen, under the citadel of the Terra Murata. Steep stone stairways cascade down amongst the rounded arches; from the little port they're like a hundred watchful eyes, scanning the sea for the return. Some have been so remodelled over the centuries according to the needs of its inhabitants as to give immediate proof of an old island saying, that 'a house isn't only a house. A house is a story.' The same could be said of Corricella's simple church, **San Rocco**, restored numerous times throughout the centuries. From here Via San Rocco leads to the Piazza dei Martiri where twelve Procidanese were executed in 1799 by the Bourbons for plotting a revolt. Near the piazza is the domed **Madonna delle Grazie** (1700), containing a much-loved statue of the Virgin.

The Terra Murata

Via Madonna delle Grazie leads up to the **Terra Murata** (91 m, Procida's highest point), passing on the right the romantic if roofless ruins of **Santa Margherita Nuova**, built in 1586 at the edge of the Punta dei Monaci. The fortifications of the citadel belong to different dates, the latest portions from 1521; the oldest section of the medieval walls can be seen near the Porta Mezz'Olmo, at the beginning of the Via San Michele. Rising above the walls, houses and prison of the Terra Murata are the three domes of **San Michele Arcangelo**, which, despite its exotic, almost Saracen appearance from a distance, wears a simple unadorned façade, rebuilt after the various pirates' depredations. The domes are untiled—Procida receives so little rain that tiles aren't strictly necessary, or at least worth the cost. Of the original pre-16th-century structure, only part of the ceiling in the Sala del Capitolo remains. Many rich works of art in the three-naved church itself attest to the former splendour of the monastery; the ceiling frescoes date from the 17th century, as do the apse paintings by Nicola Rosso, the most interesting of which shows the God's aide-de-camp Michael and his troop of *putti* swooping down to save Procida from the Turks. Pride of place goes to a splashy canvas by Neapolitan Luca Giordano.

In Piazza d'Armi is the Cardinal of Aragon's 1563 **Castello d'Aragona**, a fancy name for the clink (pop. 90, who wish they could catch the next boat to Naples); here, too, you can see parts of the walls, in which are crammed tortuous alleyways and steep narrow houses. Other old palaces may be seen along the escarpment over **Chiaia beach**—including the **Palazzo Minichini**, on Via Marcello Scotti, adjacent to the fine old church of **San Tommaso d'Aquino**. Over the south side of the beach is the so-called 'Casa di Graziella'.

Across Procida

North of Marina Grande is the quarter known as Annunziata, after the old **Chiesa dell'Annunziata**, reconstructed in 1600 and containing a miraculous Madonna, to whom are given the many, varied votive offerings that adorn the interior of the church. There are pretty views from here of Punta Pioppeto and the **faro**, or lighthouse where people often come for a swim. Nearby stands the only remaining watchtower of the original three constructed in the 16th century. From Punta Cottimo you can see the island of Ventotene, geologically related to Procida.

The rest of the island has many rural beauty spots, shaded walkways and narrow roads, old farmhouses and crumbling small palazzi, such as that of Giovanni da Procida on Via Giovanni da Procida. The area around **Centane**, especially Punta Solchiaro, is most typical, and has the most striking belvedere, with views over the entire east coast of the island.

On the west end of the island, the long stretch of sand between Punta Serra and the peninsula of Santa Margherita Vecchia has been divided into three beaches—**Spiaggia Ciraccio**, where two Roman tombs were discovered; **Spiaggia Ciraciello**, on the other side of the pyramid-shaped rock, Il Faraglione di Procida; and towards the peninsula, the **Lido**. The hillock on the peninsula is capped by the tower-like ruin of the church of **Santa Margherita Vecchia**, once a Benedictine abbey abandoned in 1586; on the other side of it lies the small fishing port and beach **Marina di Chiaiolella**, on a rounded cove that long ago was a volcanic crater.

From here you can cross the new pedestrian-only bridge to the islet of **Vivara**, where the birds are protected these days but the rabbits are fair game. Here were discovered the Neolithic implements (at Capitello and Punta de Mezzodi) now in Ischia's museum. A narrow road leads towards the summit of Vivara, through the crumbling arch of an old hunting lodge, to the Belvedere, with fine panoramas of Procida and Pozzuoli on the mainland.

WHERE TO STAY
(tel prefix 081)

The only hotel open all year round on Procida is ****L'Oasi** at Via Elleri 16 (tel 896 7499; L60–70 000), a villa with a restaurant and garden. Others include ****Arcate**, Via Marcello Scotti 10 (open April–Oct) on the beach in Chiaia (tel 896 7120; L65–75 000) and the ****Riviera**, in Chiaiolella, which has fine views (tel 896 7197; L42 000 with bath, L32 000 without). If these hotels are full, inquire at the tourist office about a room in a private house, or resort to the campsite at Punta Serra.

EATING OUT

There are several fairly inexpensive restaurants along the port at Marina Grande, like **La Medusa**, (tel 896 7481, around L15–20 000). Also good bargains are **Da Michele** (tel 896 7602), **Il Cantino**, where they have a very good *pesce fritto* for around L25–35 000 (Via Nitrodi 6, tel 99 071) **Crescenzo** (tel 896 7255), at 28 Via Marina in Chiaiolella, where you mustn't miss the *spaghetti ai frutti di mare* (L30 000; it also has a few rooms to let) and the **Lido Conchigla** on the beach at Chiaia, both specializing in seafood for around L30 000. Another good one is **Mariano** (tel 896 7350), where again the speciality is seafood.

CAPRI

Capri is pure enchantment, and can lay fair claim to being the most beautiful island in the Mediterranean; it is also the most overrun and exploited to the hilt; in 1988 so many tourists tried to jam on it that there was danger of some falling off, and the government moved to restrict the number of sailings. With more than 800 species of plant, it is very much a garden perched on a rugged chunk of limestone. Unlike Ischia and other, more recent, tourist haunts, Capri has the relaxed air of having seen it all. No room remains for property speculators. Everything has been built and planted; the tourists come and go every day and night, and they seem to be invisible to the Capriots and other residents who have learned to turn a blind eye to them, since the space they occupy will be filled next day by other anonymous camera-clutching tourists. Between June and September you begin to understand why the word 'trash' is inscribed on the bins in 30 different languages. However, if you don't mind all the trendy shops being closed, try going in November or February, when you may be lucky to arrive for a few brilliant days between the rains, and have this Garden of Eden practically to yourself. It's worth the risk of a soaking or two.

There are various schools of thought on the etymology of the island's name. The belief that it came from the Latin word for goat (*capra*) is now in disfavour; those who think it derived from the Greek *kapros* (boar) have fossils to back them up. Yet another group maintains that it comes from an ancient Tyrrhenian (Etruscan) word meaning 'rocky' (*capr-*) as evidenced by the many other places that begin with this prefix, such as Caprera (an island off Sardinia), Cabrera (off Majorca) and Caprara in the Tremiti Islands, to name just a few. It is the first syllable that is emphasized in the pronunciation of Capri—CAPri, not CapRI, like the Ford.

History

Some time in the Quaternary period Capri broke away from the Sorrentine peninsula, taking with it elephants and tigers, as we have learnt from the remains discovered by Ignazio Cerio at the beginning of this century. Other finds have dated the first inhabitants back to the Palaeolithic era. A strong tradition associates the island with the Sirens of the *Odyssey*, and with the mysterious Teleboeans from the Greek island of Kephalonia, led by their King Telon. Neolithic ceramic-ware decorated with red bands, first found on the island, has since been designated the 'Capri style'.

Little is known of Capri at the time when Augustus arrived, except that it was still very Greek and that a dying ilex (holm oak) suddenly revived and sprouted new leaves. The Emperor thought this was a good portent, and he traded Ischia to Naples for Capri and made the island one of his retreats, reputedly building as many as twelve sumptuous palaces. Life must have been good on Capri; at one point Augustus called it *Apragopolis*, or 'Lubberland', as Robert Graves translates Suetonius' 'land of layabouts'.

Augustus was succeeded by his stepson Tiberius, whose exploits reported by the same Suetonius gave Capri much of its early notoriety. The Roman writer turned the island into a dirty old man's dream come true, with Tiberius hurling his victims off the cliffs to add a touch of reality. Although scholars have now discredited much of Suetonius' yellow journalism, that imaginative writer's images of sexual acrobats dressing up as

75

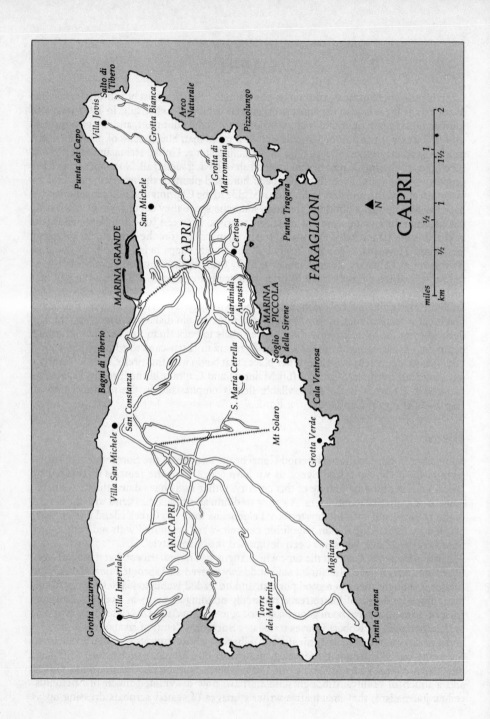

nymphs and frolicking in Tiberius' gardens, along with the anthropophagous Sirens singing seductive songs on the seashore, have permeated the Capri legends.

In reality, Tiberius made Capri the capital of the Roman Empire between AD 27 and 37. The sheer cliffs made it into a natural citadel, from where the ageing Emperor could conduct (or neglect) the affairs of state as he pleased. Here he nurtured at his bosom his bomb of a successor, Caligula.

After the death of Tiberius, Capri is occasionally mentioned as a place of exile. Then the Benedictine friars arrived and built chapels on the island, and of course it suffered the usual ravages of Saracens and pirates. In 1371 a Carthusian monastery (La Certosa) was founded on Capri, on land granted by the Angevins, whom the Capriots favoured over the Aragonese until 1442 when they rather capriciously changed sides. A plague in 1656 left the island all but abandoned; only the Carthusians stayed behind, safe inside the walls of La Certosa, picking up the titles to land that had no owners and becoming quite wealthy (and unpopular) in the process.

In 1806 Hudson Lowe was commander of the English garrison on Capri. Lowe was a man of strange coincidences—he was quartered in Napoleon's house in Ajaccio when the English occupied Corsica and later became Napoleon's jailer on St Helena. He took his job on Capri seriously indeed, fortifying the island until it became 'a little Gibraltar', but for all that still managed to lose it to the French in 1808—a 'discreditable Lowe business' according to Norman Douglas, longtime resident and writer on things Capricious.

The last chapter of the island's history began with the 'discovery' of the Blue Grotto by a German artist called Kopisch in 1826; he swam into it 'by accident'. Perhaps it was just a coincidence that Kopisch's discovery followed the landslide that had covered the entrance of another, even lovelier cave. Anyway, the magic of the name, Blue Grotto of Capri, proved irresistible, and the Capriots converted their fishing boats into excursion boats to take tourists to the cave while farmers sold their land and built hotels.

GETTING AROUND

Glitterati may fly into Anacapri's heliport from Naples; the rest of us must rely on the ferries and hydrofoils. Minimum year-round service: 6 Caremar or NLG ferries daily from Naples (1½ hrs); 5 a day from Sorrento (35 min); 1 (NLG) from Castellammare (1¾ hrs). From Naples, L3000; from Sorrento, L2000. Hydrofoils: 8 a day on the Aliscafi SNAV line from Molo Mergellina in Naples; 4 from Molo Beverello on Aliscafi Caremar (L7000); from Sorrento, Aliscafi Alivit has 4 services daily.

In the summer you can catch a steamer or hydrofoil to Capri nearly every hour, from Naples or Sorrento. There are also daily hydrofoils from Amalfi and from Anzio, via Ponza and Ischia (3½ hours on Aliscafi SNAV).

Arriving in Marina Grande, you can ascend to either Capri or Anacapri by bus; after 10 pm they run every half-hour. The funicular ascends to Capri town every 15 minutes from 6.35 am until 10 pm; the chairlift from Anacapri to Monte Solaro (a 12-minute trip) runs continuously from 9 am to sunset. There are also buses from Anacapri to the Blue Grotto, Faro and Marina Piccola; and buses from Capri town to Damecuta and Marina Piccola. From June until September, there are daily tours of Capri by motor launch starting at 9 am from Marina Grande.

TOURIST INFORMATION

AAST Main office: Piazza I. Cerio 11, Capri, tel (081) 837 0424, with information offices on the quay, at Marina Grande (tel 837 0634); Piazza Umberto I, Capri (tel 837 0686), and Via G. Orlandi 19/A, Anacapri (tel 837 1524).

Marina Grande and the Grotta Azzurra

All the ferries and hydrofoils from the mainland call at **Marina Grande** (most pleasure boats anchor in the Marina Piccola on the other side of the island). Here Capri's dependence on tourism is at its most evident; Marina Grande is little more than a commercialized station platform, but as such does its best to get you off to your destination; the *funivia* (cablecar) will lift you to the town of Capri every 15 minutes, buses will wind you up to Anacapri, glorious old bath-tub convertible taxis hope to trundle you off to your hotel, boats for the Grotta Azzurra and other excursions around the island bob up and down at their landings.

The **Blue Grotto** is well named if nothing else—its shimmering, irridescent blueness is caused by the reflection of light on the water in the morning. Similar caverns are fairly common in the Mediterranean, but Capri's is the yardstick by which they are measured. In summer (1 June–30 Sept), boats for the Blue Grotto leave at 9 am—when the sea is calm. The entrance to the cave is quite low, and if there's any swell on the sea at all someone is sure to get a nasty knock on the head.

The **sea excursion around the island** is a rare experience, but again possible only in good weather. Besides visiting other lovely grottoes, such as the **Grotta Bianca** and the **Grotta Verde** (the White Cave and the Green Cave), there are breathtaking views of the cliffs and Capri's uncanny rock formations.

Capri Town

Haunted by the smiling shade of Gracie Fields, the charming white town of Capri is daily worn down by the tread of thousands of her less ectoplasmic followers. The **megalithic walls** supporting some of the houses have seen at least 3000 years of similar comings and goings, although certainly on a much smaller scale than what you'll find here in August. Its architecture complements the island's natural beauty—much of what is typical and 'homemade' in Mediterranean architecture can be seen here in the older quarters: the moulded arches and domes, the narrow streets and stairways crossed by buttresses supporting the buildings, the ubiquitous whitewash, the play of light and shadow, and sudden little squares, just large enough for a few children to improvise a game of football. Most of the island's hotels are scattered throughout the town, generally very tasteful and surrounded by gardens. The supreme example is the famous Quisisana, a hotel whose register over the years is like a veritable *Who's Who* of the famous and pampered.

If you go up to Capri by *funivia*, you'll surface right next to the Piazza Umberto and the much photographed **Cathedral**, with its joyful campanile and clock. Built in the 17th century in the local Baroque style, the Cathedral has a charming buttressed roof. In a little square in the church's shadow, known as **La Piazzetta**, are the outdoor cafés frequented by such a variety of past eccentrics, dilettantes and celebrities that each chair should have a historical plaque on it. The other side of the piazza is a sheer drop down to Marina Grande.

Walks from the Town

For the post office and for buses to Anacapri, take the Via Roma from the piazza; for the exclusive boutiques, head towards the Via Vittoria Emanuele to Via Camarelle and Via Tragara. The latter street eventually leads to the **Faraglioni**, the three enormous sheer-sided limestone pinnacles towering straight up in the ever-blue green sea. These rocks are home to the rare blue lizard (*Lacerta caerulea Faraglionensis*) and a rare species of seagull that supposedly guffaws. From Via Tragara a stairway descends to the point and the **Porto di Tragara**, where you can take a swim from the platforms beneath the vertical rocks.

Nearby is the **Tragara Terrace**, with magnificent views, and the tall skinny rock called **Pizzolungo**. Still following the main track along the coast and up the stairway, you'll come upon the **Grotta di Matromania** (always open). The Romans worshipped the fertility goddess Cybele, or *Mater Magna*, in this cave. Part of Capri's reputation as an island of orgies may derive from this ancient Eastern cult's noisy hypnotic rituals, which culminated rather abruptly with the self-castration of the priest-for-a-day. Only vestiges now remain of the once elaborate décor inside the cave.

From the Grotta di Matromania a stepped path leads down to yet another famous eroded rock: the **Arco Naturale**, where dark pines—as everywhere else on Capri— cling to every tiny ledge they can sink their roots into. On the way back to town you'll pass some of the island's vineyards that produce the rare and famous *Lachrimae Tiberii*, and, in the Piazza Cerio, the **Centro Caprense Ignazio Cerio**, with fossils and archaeological finds from Capri (open 10–12, Mon– Fri).

La Certosa and Gardens of Augustus

A shorter but equally enjoyable walk starting from the Piazza Umberto (take Via Vittorio Emanuele, which becomes Via F. Serena, then Via Matteotti) leads you to **La Certosa**, the Carthusian charterhouse founded in 1371 by Giacomo Arcucci (a member of a famous Capri family) and suppressed in 1808. Built over one of Tiberius' villas, the golden-hued church and cloisters are very pleasing, topped by a Baroque tower added in

La Piazzetta, Capri

79

the 17th century. La Certosa, with its collection of paintings from the 17th to 19th centuries, is open daily from 9 until 2 (closed Mon).

A few minutes away from La Certosa are the **Gardens of Augustus,** founded by Caesar himself. A wide variety of trees and plants grow on the fertile terraces and belvederes overlooking one of the most striking views in the world. A narrow road (Via Krupp, built by the studious arms manufacturer, who spent his leisure hours studying lamprey larvae off the Salto di Tiberio) takes you down the cliffs in a hundred hairpin turns to the **Marina Piccola,** the charming little port with most of Capri's bathing establishments—Da Maria, La Canzione del Mare, Le Sirene and Internazionale (all but the last connected to restaurants). On one side are the ruins of a Saracen tower; on the other is the **Scoglio delle Sirene** (Sirens' Rock); if you read the books of Norman Douglas and Edwin Cerio, son of Ignazio Cerio the archaeologist, they will convince you that this really was the home of the Sirens. There is a bus, fortunately, that makes the steep climb back up the cliffs to Capri town.

A much longer but equally rewarding walk or drive is to the **Villa Jovis** (Via Botteghe to Via Tiberio) passing the church of **Monte San Michele,** a fine example of local architecture, built in the 14th century. The Villa Jovis on Punta Lo Capo (310 m) was the most important of the twelve villas on Capri: from here Tiberius governed the Roman Empire for his last ten years. Although much has been sacked through the centuries, the extent of the remaining walls and foundations gives a fair idea of the grandeur of the former Imperial Palace. Near here, the **Faro,** or lighthouse, was believed to have been part of a system of semaphores through which messages were sent to Rome. The great sheer cliff beside the villa, the **Salto di Tiberio,** is always pointed out as the precipice from which the emperor hurled the lovers who bored him, according to Suetonius. The view of the Bays of Salerno and Naples is as spectacular as any.

Towards Anacapri

On the north coast between Capri and Anacapri, the only other town of the island, are the so-called **Baths of Tiberius** and the meagre remains of Augustus' sea palace, the **Palazzo a Mare.** You can swim here at the establishment Bagni di Tiberio. Above here, carved into the escarpment of Anacapri, is the **Scala Fenicia,** in truth Greco-Roman in origin and for thousands of years the only way to reach the upper part of the island. Originally 800 in number, these steps have crumbled over the years and are impassable today. Near here, on the road from Marina Grande to Anacapri, lies the first Christian church on the island, dedicated to patron saint **San Costanzo.** According to legend Costanzo was a bishop of Constantinople whose body, packed in a barrel, floated to Capri during the Iconoclasm in Greece. A church, with a reputation for defending the island from Saracens, was built for him over one of the Roman villas. Four ancient columns support the Byzantine dome of this 11th-century church, designed in the form of a Greek cross.

Anacapri

On top of the green plateau spreads the town of Anacapri (300 m), once a fierce rival to Capri below, but since the building of the roads connecting them in 1874, the two towns have learned to reconcile their differences. Although it has its share of hotels, Anacapri retains a rustic air, with its many olive trees and vineyards surrounding it on all sides, and its simple style of architecture, rather Moorish in style with cubic, flat-roofed houses. In Anacapri's Piazza San Nicola, the 18th-century church of **San Michele** (open 10–6 April–Oct, 10–2 Sun, adm) contains a magnificent mosaic floor of majolica tiles, by the Abruzzese artist Leonardo Chiaiese. The design itself, showing Adam and Eve in the Garden of Eden, and their Expulsion, is by D. A. Vaccano. The church of **Santa Sofia** very near it, on the Piazza Diaz, was built in the Middle Ages, but later Baroqued.

From Piazza Vittoria a chairlift travels to the summit of **Monte Solaro**, the highest point on the island at 585 m. Also from Piazza Vittoria, take Via Orlandi to Via Capodimonte and the **Villa San Michele** of Axel Munthe (1857–1949), one of the greatest physicians of his day, and a leader in the field of psychiatry. Extremely generous, donating his services to the victims of plagues, earthquakes and World War I, he also found time to establish bird sanctuaries on Capri and elsewhere; in 1929 he wrote his best-selling autobiography *The Story of San Michele* to which his villa owes most of its fame. The house contains Roman artefacts discovered on Capri (open daily, 9 until sunset; adm). Near here is the so-called **Castello di Barbarossa**, after the pirate captain who plagued the Mediterranean for so many years. These ruins date from the 8th and 9th centuries. Via Capodimonte continues through the valley of **Santa Maria a Cetrella**, another white church of local design. From the church the road goes to the top of Monte Solaro.

Another path from Piazza Vittoria (Via Caposcuro to Via Maigliara) skirts Monte Solaro, passing through the vineyards to the **Belvedere della Migliara**, from where you can see the Faraglioni and the entrance of the **Green Grotto**. A bus leaves Anacapri every hour in the summer for Punta Carena and its lighthouse at the southernmost tip of the island. The unusual arched doorways on the left belonged to the **Torre di Materita**; further on, overlooking the **Cala del Tombosiello**, is a ruined watchtower. **Punta Carena** is the most out-of-the-way place on the island for a quiet swim.

Another bus leaves from the piazza for the Grotta Azzurra and the bathing area adjacent to it, passing by way of the old windmill and the **Villa Imperiale**, another of the summer residences built by Augustus, known also as the 'Damecuta', from the tower next to it. After the Villa Jovis, this villa is the best-preserved, and has recently been further excavated (open from 9 am until one hour before sunset; closed Mon).

WHERE TO STAY   (tel prefix 081)
If you have the money, the smart place to stay on Capri is the sumptuous *******Quisisana** in the middle of town on Via Camarelle (tel 837 0788; open April–1 Jan), where a room in the high season will set you back L370 000. For something less pricey and boasting a wonderful view, there's ******La Scalinatella**, on Via Tragara (tel 837 0633; L250 000). Open all year, *****La Floridana**, Via Campo di Teste (tel 837 0101) also has fine panoramas of the sea and rooms from L100–140 000. Less expensive, the ****Villa Krupp** (Via Matteoti, tel 837 0362) is also open all year round (L55–65 000 with bath). For the record, the **Faraglioni**, Via Camerelle (tel 837 0320), opens from April to Oct, and is the cheapest place to stay on Capri, at L22 000, without bath.

In Anacapri, *****San Michele**, Via G. Orlandi (tel 837 1427), is an elegant villa with wonderful views. Open all year round, rates are L65–100 000 (all rooms with bath). The

81

Bellavista, Via G. Orlandi (tel 837 1463), has a fine view as well, and many facilities, for L50 000 without bath, L70 000 with; open all year.

EATING OUT
Fish makes an all-too-frequent appearance on menus, but you'll find a healthy and varied selection of meat recipes. Capri's specialities are its wine (delicious and rare) and Certosina liqueur distilled from herbs. Restaurant prices can be equally rare, and if you want to eat reasonably you'll have to go down to Marina Grande, where there are a number of pizzerias and trattorias. If money is no object, there's **La Pigna**, Via Roma 8 (tel 837 0280; closed Tues), with its huge pine trees, splendid views, a shimmering clientele and elegant cuisine for around L50 000 a meal. One of their many dishes is *fettucine alla Sofia Loren*, presumably so-called because it's plentiful and raunchy. Also in the ozone layer, but with even loftier prices, is **I Faraglioni** on pretty Via Camerelle 75, with delectable house specialities like *crepe al formaggio, risotto ai frutti di mare* and a succulent Chateaubriand (L60 000). **La Capannina**, Via delle Botteghe 14 (tel 837 0732), has long been a popular spot among visiting celebrities, with seafood specialities such as *gnocchetti al salmone* and many dishes with mussels and clams (around L50 000). **Bagni Tiberio**, in Marina Grande, is more moderately priced but very good, with dinners for around L35 000. If you have your heart set on tasting Capri's famous wine, try **Da Paolino** on Via Palazzo a Mare 11, which has some unusual offerings like peppers stuffed with spaghetti, rabbit from the oven and some very good desserts (L45 000 at least).

In Anacapri, **Da Gelsomina la Migliera**, on Via Migliera 6, offers not only home-made wine, but true homecooked island specialities, including mushrooms collected on Monte Solaro, for around L40 000 a person (closed Tues). For something less costly, **Materita**, on Via G. Orlandi 140, has pizza and other trattoria specialities for about L25 000.

The Tremiti Islands

Along the dreary east coast of the Italian peninsula, where the Adriatic is a stolid, polluted grey and the flat beaches are little better, the spur of the Gargano peninsula is a delightful surprise, dramatically rocky and rugged, where plunging cliffs alternate with nooky little beaches. Some 30 km offshore are the four Tremiti Islands—San Domino, San Nicola, Caprara and Pianosa—their charming but measly acreage comprising the sole Italian territory in the Adriatic Sea; the uninhabited Pelagose Islands to the northeast now belong to Yugoslavia.

'Tremiti' is thought to be derived from *Tre Monti*, the 'three mountains' of the central islands of San Nicola, San Domino, and Caprara. They are called the islands of Diomedes, the Achaean hero who fought so bravely at Troy while Achilles sulked in his tent. After the war, Diomedes discovered that his enemy Aphrodite, the goddess of love and supporter of the Trojans, had made his wife Aegialea fall in love with another man and conspire against his life. Diomedes and his followers escaped in the nick of time; they sailed to the Gargano coast, where he founded a new kingdom, Daunia, and marked its frontiers by hurling limestone boulders out into the sea, thus creating the Tremiti Islands.

Venus, however, would not let Diomedes off so easily, and abruptly put all his followers to death. Their spirits were transformed into birds, who still lament the cruelty of the goddess of love. The most common species of these still on the islands are the greater and lesser Berta (*Procellaria diomedea*), or puffins, whose cry is indeed very much like an infant's wail.

The picture-postcard beauty of this tiny Adriatic archipelago is its main attraction— the bluest, cleanest sea in the Adriatic, shady pine trees and unusual calcareous cliffs. The only beach on the islands, Cala delle Arene (on San Domino), becomes as crowded as a Japanese subway at rush hour in the summer; many visitors prefer to bake on the rocks.

History

The Tremiti Islands were inhabited in the Neolithic era, around 4000 BC, leaving us clay pots and tools and evidence of a cemetery at Cala Tramontana, on San Domino. In Roman times, when that island was called *Teutria*, Caesar Augustus exiled his grand-daughter Julia there for her adultery and promiscuity, just as he had had her mother Julia banished to Ventotene (Pontine Islands). Julia bore a child on San Domino, which the

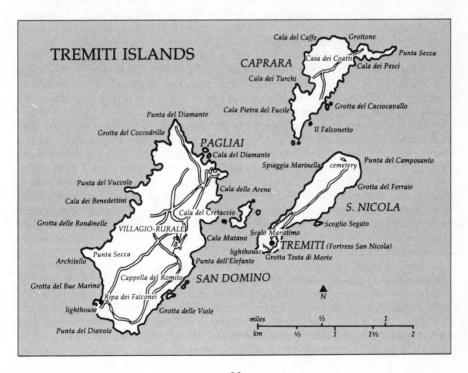

Emperor ordered to be exposed to the elements until it died, and 20 years later she herself died without ever seeing the mainland again. Popular legend has it, however, that she took advantage of her Nubian guard's infatuation for her, persuading him to build a raft and sail with her to a love-nest on the Italian shore. Mother Nature intervened and sank the boat, drowning the two of them off the coast at Vieste.

Another, stronger tradition tells of a hermit, perhaps named Nicola, who lived on San Nicola in the 4th century, when the island was deserted. In a vision, the Madonna showed Nicola where a great treasure lay and advised him to build a church with the money. He dilly-dallied so long that the Mother of God had to reappear and admonish him, but eventually he found the treasure and built the first chapel of Santa Maria a Mare.

In 786, Charlemagne's father-in-law Paolo Vinifrido was accused of conspiracy and exiled to the Tremiti Islands, minus his hands and eyes. He somehow managed to escape to Montecassino, the monastery founded by St Benedict. Perhaps he told them tales of his short stay, for in 1010 monks of this order founded a monastery on San Domino. When this larger island proved indefensible, they moved in 1045 to nearby San Nicola and built their abbey near Nicola's humble church, which they rebuilt.

When the Normans invaded southern Italy and Sicily shortly afterwards, the feudal lords of the mainland stored their treasures in the monastery of San Nicola, increasing its already growing reputation of power and wealth. The monks owned vast tracts of land in Italy, not to mention rivers, castles, ports, salt mines and so on, with numerous rights and jurisdictions. They became quite independent of Montecassino, and acquired notoriety for their licentious living. The popes and Benedictine headquarters attempted to assert their authority over the monks (who were in league with the pirates) but failed; in the end it was the monks themselves who caused their own demise: when the debts from their high living came due, they were forced to sell their property and smuggle just to make ends meet. In 1194 leaders of the Fourth Crusade sacked the monastery, supposedly to punish the monks for their wickedness, and finally, after several Inquisitions into the monks' depravity, the monastery was dissolved in 1236.

The following year they were replaced by the Cistercians, a reformed order founded by Bernardo di Chiaravalle in 1112. The Benedictines had left enough behind for the Cistercians to prosper, and the 400 monks were self-sufficient. Among their works are many of the monastery's fortifications, as its fabulous reputation attracted pirates with some regularity. Eventually, in the mid-14th century, these corsairs forced the abandonment of San Nicola, either because the monks had had enough and left for the mainland, or, in another version, because they were all massacred when a pirate captain tricked them into believing he was dead and desired a Christian burial. The Cistercians dutifully complied, and during the night the captain rose from the grave and let in his men through the gate.

In 1412 another monastic order, little known outside Italy—the Lateranesi (or Lateran Canons), founded by San Frediano di Lucca and obeying the Mystic Rules of St Augustine—was sent by Pope Gregory XII to restore the monastery of San Nicola Tremiti. The few monks were not enthusiastic about their task, fearful of the pirates, but they obeyed and repaired the church and monastery. Although the Lateranesi started on a pious and humble path, like the monks before them they were soon cursed with riches donated by pilgrims and nobles attracted by their very saintliness. By 1465, however, the

Abbot had requested and received the title of prince of Tremiti; in 1535 Pope Paul III allowed them to administer justice and use torture if necessary to promote it. Nevertheless the monks did well by the lay population, building a school and a hospital, as well as more fortifications, new cloisters, cisterns, and a watchtower on the then uninhabited San Domino.

The requirements of defending San Nicola put the monks into perpetual debt, although it must have seemed worthwhile when in 1567 the Sultan's fleet besieged the island for three days without success. The Lateranesi emerged victorious, but their fortunes rapidly declined. The monks took to smuggling, and their affairs were in such disorder that they lost many privileges. Things became so bad that they tried to sell their islands to Spain in 1574 and 1610 to pay back their debts. When they did succeed in selling them to a Florentine cardinal, the Spanish viceroys of Naples quickly stepped in with soldiers and imprisoned the Abbot. This, in turn, displeased the Republic of Venice, which didn't want the Spanish in the Adriatic, and the Spaniards were diplomatically persuaded to go home, leaving the monks back where they started—in deep debt.

In 1737 Charles III of Naples claimed the Tremiti Islands as his inheritance and garrisoned them. King Ferdinand IV went a step further in 1781, claiming for the crown all of the islands' property, thus ending the rule of the monastic orders on the islands. Instead Ferdinand initiated—what else?—a penal colony in the fortress, used to confine mainly political prisoners until the 1860 unification of Italy. In 1912, during the war in Libya, prisoners of war were brought to the islands, along with an epidemic of smallpox. The Fascists also sent their undesirables to San Nicola and San Domino.

People are no longer condemned for life on the little islands—they pay good money to go there, at least in the months of July and August. In the past decade over 100,000 people annually have visited San Domino and San Nicola, mostly on day trips. During the summer the native population of the islands rises to some 400, nearly all of whom make a living from tourism; in winter a mere 40 people hold the fort, and ships from Manfredonia are infrequent.

GETTING AROUND

To reach the numerous small ports that serve the Tremiti Islands is no mean task. The quickest way is to catch one of the infrequent flights to Pescara, then take the bus or train to Ortona, Vasto or Termoli for the hydrofoil. Or you can catch a more regular flight to Bari (from Milan or Rome), then take the bus or train to Manfredonia for the ferry. Trains to the Adriatic coast leave Venice, Milan and Rome several times a day.

Adriatica Lines runs most of the steamers and hydrofoils to the Tremiti Islands; the islands themselves are linked by sea taxis. In the winter Manfredonia is the main port (5 hours), the steamer departing several times a week; there are also connections from Rodi Garganico which take only 1½ hours. In the summer these departures are daily, and there are additional ones from the ports of Vieste (3 hours), Pugnochiuso (4 hours) and Peschici (2 hours). In the summer you can take a hydrofoil from Ortona (2 hours), Vasto (1 hour) and Termoli (45 minutes).

TOURIST INFORMATION

Information can be found at the Municipio (tel 663009). While there are a post office, telephones (in Belvedere Bar), church and tourist office on San Nicola, the Tremiti Islands' only bank branch (open in summer) is on San Domino, in the Villagio Rurale.

SAN NICOLA

Unlike the verdant paradise of its sister island, the third of a square mile that comprises San Nicola is covered with *macchia*, and green as it may be in the spring, without trees it seems desolate, like a wilder part of the Irish coast. The famous fortress–monastery dominates it from all sides, from its most impressive angle, below the Torrione del Cavaliere it looks like a gaping-mouthed cyclops with antennae. Ships call at the port directly beneath it.

The Citadel and Town

To visit the monastery—and the town—enter the **Porta Marina**, the gate in the outer series of walls, where the statue of Santa Maria a Mare once stood, and climb to the **Torre del Cavaliere del Crocefisso**. From the window over the gate here the monks and their defenders would pour boiling oil on the heads of their enemies. An inscription on the gate reads *Conteret et Confringet*, ('Crush and Kill'), a hardly Christian sentiment referring to the rights granted to the Abbot of Tremiti by Pope Paul III to torture and kill heretics and other trouble-makers in the area.

A ramp from this tower leads up to another, the square **Torre del Pennello**, and to the main streets of San Nicola town, Via Diomede and Via Roma. Within the walls here you can see the small houses once inhabited by prisoners. Via Diomede ends in front of the 14th-century Cistercian fortifications; to the right is the **Torrione Angioino**, near the restaurant of the same name. Charles II of Anjou, married to the Queen of Naples, ordered it to be built in 1294 to defend the kingdom's east coast from pirates.

The stairway continues up from here to another portico and the lovely octagonal **Cisterna della Meridiana**, which got its name from its orientation towards the four cardinal points. It is still used today to collect precious rainwater. The date on the stairs from here recalls the Bourbon reconstruction of the castle.

Santa Maria a Mare and the Monastery

Further up stands the church of **Santa Maria a Mare**, built on the site of the 4th-century chapel of the hermit Nicola by the Benedictines in 1045 and later restored by the Lateranesi. Four statues, two of them headless, adorn the rather severe façade, and between them is an interesting relief of the Coronation of the Virgin. Note the walls of the church, pockmarked by cannon fire. Inside, the floor of the church still retains its original mosaics of birds and a griffon, along with a wooden ceiling. On the altar stands the wooden statue of Santa Maria a Mare brought to the island by the Benedictines, but more interesting is the large Byzantine crucifix, *Il Cristo Grande*, in the right-hand chapel. This, according to legend, floated ashore from Greece in the 9th century. When the faithful attempted to carry it inside the church, they found that the door was too small and left it outside. When they returned the next day, they found that the crucifix had miraculously entered the church of its own accord, without enlarging the door. Whenever the monks tried to move it from the right-hand chapel, it always returned to its chosen place in the night, so they left it where it stands today.

On the right as you leave the church are the old cloisters, a finely made **cistern** restored by the Bourbons, and the rather grand **Dormitorio Nuovo**, built by the then wealthy Lateranesi monks. The huge tower near here, the **Torrione del Cavaliere di San Nicola**, is the highest, overlooking the rest of the island, its flat plain and one road.

Directly below it is **La Tagliata,** a ditch dug by the monks, initiated by the Benedictines as a defensive fosse dividing the island in two. Near, the Torrione the **Prigione** with its partially blocked windows, is where prisoners were held in solitary confinement. Some of their graffiti can still be seen on the walls.

From a gate in the Torrione the island's road passes across the **Prato Asinaro** (asses' meadow) to the decrepit cemetery at the far end of San Nicola. There is little of note along this lonely highway: a few pieces of an ancient sepulchre said to have contained the bones of Diomedes, cisterns, and a modern, rather powerful iron crucifix with a little roof.

WHERE TO STAY
There are no hotels on San Nicola; the Municipio has a list of rooms to let in private houses.

EATING OUT
Look for *troccoli* (homemade pasta dish), eggs with sea urchins, fish dishes, and *spaghetti alla pirata* (with lobster). San Nicola's restaurants cater mainly for the influx of trippers from San Domino; there are good moderately priced meals at **La Conchiglia** on Via Roma, **Al Torrione** at Via Marconi 74, and **Bella Ida** on Via Roma. Average prices are L18–25 000.

SAN DOMINO

San Domino's name is believed to derive from a misspelling of San Doimo, a saint from Spalato (modern Split). Although it is the largest, most luxuriant island in the group, its indefensible position condemned it to be uninhabited throughout most of history. In 1935 the government built the little rose-coloured Villagio Rurale to encourage agriculture on the island, and these houses are the oldest buildings on San Domino apart from the dilapidated ruins of Cappella del Romito, built by a 13th-century hermit, Pietro Polono.

Around the Island

The tourist brochures don't exaggerate too much when they call San Domino 'the pearl of the Adriatic'. With its marvellous coastline of cliffs and jutting rocks, penetrated by grottoes, the island is covered with lush greenery and pine bosques, a far cry from the rugged, sparsely vegetated isles surrounding it, such as the Isola Cretaccio stuck between San Domino and San Nicola.

Perhaps unfortunately for San Domino, its small size and compact beauties make it ideal for day trippers to explore, either by boat or on foot (there are also little 'buses' that go up and down the one-mile-long stretch of road). **Punta del Diamante**, the northernmost tip, may perhaps have acquired its name from its hard shiny rocks. An unhappily sited electricity plant sits at the end of the point, overlooking a group of pyramid-shaped rocks in the sea, known as the *Pagliai*, or hayricks.

To the southeast, many of the island's tourist facilities and restaurants are concentrated around its one beach, **Cala delle Arene**, and the shady rocks that serve as an alternative at **Cala Matano**, just to the south by the Eden Hotel and the Villaggio Rurale. From here you can take the Strada Comunale past the lighthouse, then find your own way up to the **Cappella del Romito**, the highest point of the island (85 m).

Continuing generally south along the coast are the **Punta dell' Elefante** which vaguely resembles an elephant drinking the sea; the violet-coloured **Grotta delle Ciole**; and the **Grotta delle Murene** where sea eels are said to breed. The often devilish sea off the Punta del Diavolo earned it its name.

The Ripa dei Falconei and Grotta del Bue Marino

The most spectacular feature on the island, the 75-m crag known as the **Ripa dei Falconei**, and the deep Grotta del Bue Marino beneath it, may seem vaguely familiar if you've seen *The Guns of Navarone*. In the Middle Ages San Domino was famous for its peregrine and Eleonora falcons, which brave souls would steal from the nests on top of the crag to train for the genteel sport of falconry. Now rare and protected by the government, the falcons continue to nest on top of the Ripa.

The **Grotta del Bue Marino**, named after another rare, almost extinct creature, the Mediterranean seal, is the largest cave on San Domino, more than 45 m long. If you go in by boat, be sure to take a torch to see all the rock formations and the entrance to a narrow passageway, said to lead to the Cappella del Romito, perhaps used by pirates when the monks occupied the island.

North along the coast are the unusually barren **Punta Secca** and a natural arch, the **Architello**. Above the **Cala dei Benedettini** is a cistern built by the monks during their brief stay on San Domino in the 11th century. But you'll have to look hard at the **Grotta del Coccodrillo** to see the crocodile.

WHERE TO STAY   tel prefix 0882

The plushest place to stay on San Domino is the ***Kyrie**, at Vuccolo (tel 603 055), with showers in every room for L110–160 000; facilities include a pool, tennis courts and sailing. Far more reasonable and with shower in every room is *Gabbiano**, at Belvedere (tel 663 044), with pleasant rooms L35–44 000, open all year. In between, there's the comfortable ***San Domino** at Cameroni (tel 663 027; 25 rooms, L60–90 000). The last two hotels are open all year round, but for all accommodation reserve early for the summer months.

There is one campsite, near Punta del Diamante, with room for 800 tents (tel 663 034). It is connected to the **Tourist Village Internazionale**, and rents out tents if you don't bring your own.

EATING OUT

La Livornese in the Cala delle Arene and **Trattoria del Pesce** on Via Diomede (the former more expensive at L25–35 000 per person) are very good, specializing in local fish dishes. Less expensive is the **Rosticceria Martella**, with good pizzas for L8000. Near the Villagio is the restaurant **Da Carlucetta**, which specializes in *linguine al sugo di aragosta*, a pasta dish with a lobster-based sauce (L25–40 000). Of the other places to eat, **Il Pirata** has a garden, and **Belmare** a terrace with lovely views.

PIANOSA AND CAPRARA

Of the other two Tremiti Islands, **Pianosa** is a low, very flat island 17 km northeast of San Nicola. Uninhabited, the few shelters on its coast are used by Italian and Yugoslav fishermen on overnight trips. **Caprara**, north of San Nicola and the same area as that island, is inhabited mainly by wild rabbits, who live in the brush. Near the lighthouse are an enormous natural arch, the **Architiello**, grander than the one on San Domino, and the lovely **Grottone**, almost 30 m high at its mouth. Small boats can anchor in the **Cala dei Turchi**, as the Sultan's fleet did during its unsuccessful siege of San Nicola. From here a path leads up to the pretty lighthouse and the long-abandoned Casa dei Coatti, a building used when Caprara was cultivated. Caprara's name comes from the capers (*capperaia*) which still grow wild there.

Part IV
SICILY

Archaeological Ruins at Tindari, Sicily

Sicily is the schoolroom model of Italy for beginners, with every Italian quality and defect magnified, exasperated, and brightly coloured. . . . Everywhere in Italy life is more or less slowed down by the exuberant intelligence of the inhabitants: in Sicily it is practically paralysed by it.

—Luigi Barzini, *The Italians*

On the map, the triangle of intensity and excess that is Sicily lies vulnerably at the tip of the Italian 'toe' which at any moment could give it a smart kick up to Sardinia. The largest island in the Mediterranean sea, square at the crossroads of Europe, Asia, and Africa, it is separated from the big boot only by the 4-km wide Straits of Messina; since its ancient monsters Scylla and Charybdis were long ago defeated by an earthquake, a strong swimmer could paddle there. Despite this proximity Sicily has had its own history, civilizations, kings and language. The Sicilians and their customs are so distinct that mainland Italians speak of them as another race—as indeed the Sicilians consider themselves to be, their blood a mix of the Greeks, Carthaginians, Arabs, and Normans who settled the island. Rome, Spain, and Italy have ruled it but never colonized; Sicilians are Latins only by adoption.

Tourism is only a sideline on this rich and colourful island; few people outside hotels speak English, although they are always ready to interpret your sign language and pidgin Italian. If you go to a small, seldom-frequented village, you will be the event of the day. Resorts and sights that attract an international crowd have very distinct boundaries— easy to find and easy to miss, whatever your preference.

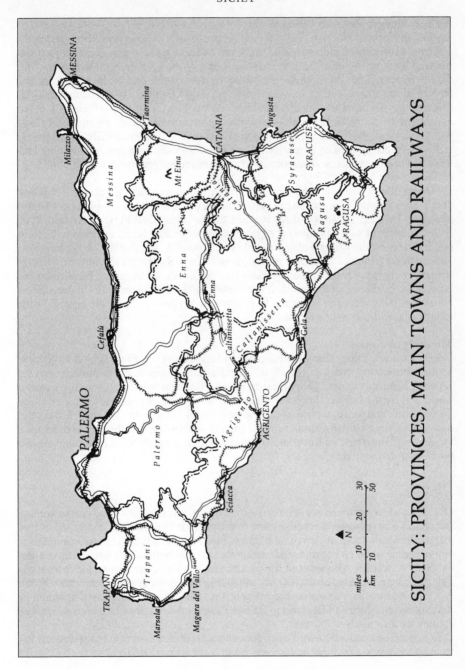

SICILY: PROVINCES, MAIN TOWNS AND RAILWAYS

A Little Geography, and When to Go

One of the names given to Sicily by the Greeks was *Trinacria* (the 'three-pointed', referring to the three headlands), and the island's symbol remains a head sprouting three running legs. Its modern name derives from one of the island's earliest peoples, the Sikels. Mount Etna, the highest volcano in Europe, is the outstanding geographical feature of the island, and its lava has made the soil of Sicily rich—inexhaustibly rich, thought the Arabs, who called it Paradise. Along with Etna, most of Sicily's other mountains are in the eastern half—Nebrodi, Peloritani and Iblean, the main ranges—with the highest, the Madonie, in the north central part of the island. Sicily's main rivers, some navigable in ancient times, have since filled with silt from careless farming and irrigation practices. Forests that once covered the island fell prey to ancient shipbuilders, and now cover less than 75 per cent of the total land area.

Despite the ravages over the centuries, Sicily is still incredibly fertile; any building over 100 years old is likely to have plants sprouting out of it. The best months to visit the island are February, March and April, when the spring goddess Persephone returns to Sicily, strewing it with wild flowers of every imaginable hue. Summers tend to be long and hot, leaving the wheatfields on the plains as brown as the tourists on the beaches; Africa is only 80 miles away and in foul moods blasts Sicily with the hot, suffocating sirocco. In September the grapes are harvested and crushed into wine. The olives come later, at the beginning of the mild but wet winter; snow coats the summits of the highest mountains but melts early in spring. In February many parts of Sicily are adorned with the frilly lace of almond blossoms.

The Best of Sicily

There are a few things that the first-timer to Sicily won't want to miss—smouldering **Mount Etna**, with views of the entire island and of Malta from its summit, and its superbly beautiful resort, **Taormina**; **Syracuse**, once the greatest city in the western world; **Palermo**, with its Norman churches full of magnificent mosaics; the Valley of the Temples in **Agrigento**, with some of the best Greek temples in existence; **Erice**, the holy city of Venus; the romantic ruins of ancient **Selinunte**; and **Piazza Armerina**, a medieval hill town near an Imperial Roman villa with some of the most incredible mosaic floors ever discovered.

History

Old as the Mediterranean is in human history, in geological terms it was born yesterday, the earth's birth pangs still reverberating in the volcanic eruptions and earthquakes that plague the whole south of Italy. The island of Sicily was once connected to North Africa on the mainland, but it became separated in the Tertiary period, long before the coming of the first peoples, who crossed the Straits of Messina in the Upper (or Advanced) Palaeolithic period, around 20,000 BC. Inhabiting mostly the coastal areas, these Stone Age peoples have left us not only their simple tools but also beautiful incised drawings in the grottoes of **Monte Pellegrino** in Palermo and on the island of **Levanzo** which was connected with Sicily at the time.

Sometime around 4000–3000 BC, influences from the eastern Mediterranean introduced the first Neolithic culture on Sicily called **Stentinello** after the village in

Syracuse province where Sicily's great archaeologist Paolo Orsi first identified the culture. The Stentinello people lived in settlements instead of caves, made weapons of obsidian, and decorated their pottery with incisions or seashell impressions. They were farmers, sailors and merchants.

After 3000 BC copper and rock-cut oven tombs were the new fashion, brought over to Sicily from the Aegean, although metal as a material for weapons and tools didn't become important until the **Bronze Age** (1400 BC). This was a period of turmoil and immigration in the Mediterranean, and Sicily received people and ideas not only from the east but also from the **Iberians** in the west, who worked in metal and made the bell beakers found on the island.

The Arrival of the Greeks and Carthaginians

Troy fell sometime around 1200 BC, and from this and other Bronze Age holocausts in Asia Minor, survivors migrated to the safer shores of Sicily, beginning with the **Elymnians**, who settled Segesta and Erice. Various references to Sicily in the *Odyssey* confirm this early connection between Sicily and the Mycenean world of Greece. The other ancient 'indigenous' peoples of Sicily divided the island east/west between them: the **Sikans**, believed to be of Iberian descent, and the **Sikels**, who may have come from the Italian peninsula, although other scholars suggest they were a cadet branch of the Sikans. Both Sikans and Sikels were apparently agreeable, accommodating races—which made their lands easily accessible for others.

Sometime during the 8th century BC, **Greeks** from Chalcis and Eretria began to colonize Italy—first Ischia and Cumae in the Bay of Naples, and then the eastern coast of Sicily, at Naxos, Leontini and Catania. The reasons behind the Greeks' western expansion are probably twofold: the pressures of a growing population and exhausted soil at home, and the need to protect their growing trade routes in the west. The colonies thrived and like amoebas began to split and create new colonies, spreading Greek culture throughout eastern Sicily, much to the alarm of the **Phoenicians** who felt their own sea-trading livelihood threatened by the newcomers. From their centre at Carthage the Phoenicians established outposts in western Sicily at Palermo and Motya, and were generally allied with the Elymnians.

The rivalry between Carthage and the Greeks in Sicily came to a head in 480 BC, when the combined Greek armies of Syracuse, Gela and Akragas (Agrigento) defeated the Carthaginians in the great **Battle of Himera**. According to the Greeks, it took place on the very day that the Athenians defeated the Persians in the Battle of Salamis. True or not, these two major victories over the 'barbarians' initiated a long period of relative peace, which saw the most amazing achievements of the ancient Greeks, many of which happened in the New World of Magna Graecia.

If Sicily was the America of its day, always trying to upstage the rest of the world in its architecture and luxuries, the city of Syracuse was its New York. Athens became jealous, and on various pretexts launched its **Great Expedition** to capture the city, which failed miserably (see 'Syracuse'). But the Greek colonies were in no position to benefit from the Athenian humiliation; petty tyrants, inter-city rivalries and democracy eroded their power and ability to unify.

The Romans

In the **First Punic War** (mid-3rd century BC) most of Sicily fell fairly comfortably under

Roman rule, but in the **Second Punic War** Hannibal's victories encouraged the Sicilian Greeks to ally themselves with their ancient rivals—a fatal mistake, since the Romans defeated Carthage, then came south to exact revenge. One of the Praetors sent to govern the island, **Verres**, systematically stole its treasures and works of art. Sicily was to remain a grain-producing backwater for the next 1000 years, and like many islands its history was reduced to a list of subsequent invaders—**Vandals, Ostrogoths, Byzantines and Saracens**.

The Saracen–Norman Civilization

The Saracens, the first post-Roman invaders to stick around long enough to settle down, founded a splendid civilization in Sicily. They built their capital Palermo into one of the most splendid cities of the 10th century. They grew the first orange and lemon trees, date palms and sugar cane in Sicily. They tolerated the Christian faith of the native population, founded by St Paul himself, though partly because non-Muslims had to pay more taxes. By 1060, however, Arab Sicily was divided against itself and square in the path of Norman ambitions in southern Italy. Several factions invited the **Normans** to Sicily to put down their rivals, only to realize too late that the Normans had come to stay.

The adventurous Normans were led by the twelve sons of a modest landowner in Normandy, Tancred de Hauteville. After serving as mercenaries for and against the Pope in northern Italy, they were authorized by Pope Nicholas II to rule whatever pieces of southern Italy they could capture, probably in the hope that these powerful nuisances would self-destruct. But by the time the brothers were through, one of them, **Robert Guiscard** (1015–85), controlled nearly all of southern Italy as the Duke of Apulia, leaving the conquest of Sicily to the youngest brother, **Roger** (1031–1101), whose remarkable success, through a combination of fighting skill and diplomacy, won him all of Sicily by 1091, and the title Count of Sicily.

Because Roger wasn't followed by a wave of Norman immigrants, necessity dictated reconciliation with the native Byzantine and Arab population. Their religions were tolerated, and their languages. Arabic and Greek, and to a much lesser extent Latin, were the official languages of Sicily, while Count Roger spoke Norman French. Both Arabs and Greeks served in the government and armies of Roger, and built—especially under Roger's capable son, **King Roger II** (ruled 1112–54)—the magnificent churches and palaces that are still one of the wonders of Sicily today. Roger II's rule was a glorious time for Sicily, and although his son and grandson **William I**, 'the Bad' (ruled 1154–66), and **William II**, 'the Good'(1166–89, married to Joan of England, sister of Richard the Lionheart), could not match him in intelligence and strength, the island thrived, perfecting its unique mixture of culture that brought a second Golden Age to Sicily, which lasted 100 years.

Dissensions followed the early death of William II, who left no heirs. Many Sicilian barons preferred **Tancred**, Count of Lecce, William II's bastard nephew, but William had willed the crown to his aunt **Constance**, a posthumous daughter of Roger II and to her husband, the Swabian **Henry of Hohenstaufen**, son of Emperor Frederick Barbarossa. In the end, Henry became King of Sicily only after Tancred's death—by which time he was the Holy Roman Emperor Henry VI, and had only three years to live (he died of dysentery in Messina in 1197).

Frederick II 'Stupor Mundi'

At the age of 44, Henry's wife Constance became regent for their 3-year-old son Frederick (1194–1250). Crowned in 1198, he was left totally orphaned six months later. Although the mightiest of the medieval popes, Innocent III, was his appointed guardian, the Swabian barons took control of Frederick, and it was their grasping influences Frederick had to shake off to establish himself as King and later as Emperor. Called *Stupor Mundi* ('the Wonder of the World') in his lifetime, he made his court one of the most brilliant in Europe. The seeds of modern Italian literature and poetry were nurtured in Palermo, Greek and Arabic classics were translated, new scientific theories propounded and mathematicians congregated under Frederick's patronage. Politically, Sicily felt the power of his awe-inspiring personality and benefited from his rule while he lived, although the island was constantly called upon to assist him in his never-ending quarrels with the Pope. In his later years Frederick all but abandoned Palermo and Sicily for the mainland. Now that the island was firmly in the sphere of Europe, with few of its old connections to Africa or the East, it began its long decline. Realizing where their future destiny lay, the Sicilians during Frederick's reign began to leave off speaking Greek and Arabic, and evolve their own unique version of Italian.

The Sicilian Vespers

Not long after Frederick's death in 1250, his powerful central administration began to crumble. His son, Emperor **Conrad IV** suddenly followed his father to the grave in 1254, during his campaign to claim the crown of Sicily; his son **Conradin** was too young to act for himself, and the throne was claimed by Frederick's illegitimate son **Manfred**, crowned in Palermo in 1258 in the face of papal hostility, Manfred quickly consolidated his power, and by 1261 controlled all of Italy. The newly elected Pope Urban IV, hastily hunting about for an alternative candidate to support, hit upon **Charles of Anjou**, ruthless younger brother of the King of France. Charles managed to capture back northern Italy, and in Benevento in 1266 slew Manfred in battle. The last hurrah of the Hohenstaufen came in the person of the young Conradin, who was enthusiastically received by the Ghibellines in Rome but was soon captured by Charles and beheaded in Naples (1268), an unpopular act that tainted the Angevins from the start. Charles, as the Pope's man, introduced religious intolerance, heavy taxes and unpopular French customs. He visited Sicily only once, preferring to stay in Naples, which was an unforgivable insult to the proud Sicilians. In 1282 their hatred exploded in the **War of the Vespers**, named after the incident at a Palermitan church that triggered the rebellion. All the French in Sicily were massacred (they were summarily identified by their inability to pronounce *ci*, evidence of how quickly the Sicilian language had become universal); the Sicilian barons quickly convened a parliament and invited **Peter III of Aragon**, husband of Manfred's daughter Constance, to wear the crown of Sicily; he duly accepted, but he and his Spaniards had to defend their new holding against the French for 21 years.

The Spaniards

Under Peter and his sons Alfonso and James, Sicily was treated as a mere appendage, a granary for Aragon. **James** (1291–8) eventually tried to return the island to the Pope and the Angevins for political reasons. The Sicilian barons and James' younger brother, the Viceroy Frederick, reacted to this by holding a parliament in Enna and crowning

Frederick 'King of Trinacria', though he has gone down in history as **Frederick II of Aragon**.

Frederick II's manoeuvrings kept Sicily politically independent but backwardly feudal. He died in 1337, and the Black Death arrived ten years later—two factors contributing greatly to the disintegration of Sicilian society. Power existed primarily in the hands of two wealthy families, the **Ventimiglia** who sided with the Spaniards, and the **Chiaramonte** who tried to bring the Angevins back. Civil war and anarchy were the order of the day.

Aragonese kings, and after the marriage of Ferdinand and Isabella, Spanish kings, ruled Sicily indifferently through their viceroys. In the 15th century Sicily became a joint Spanish possession with Naples, and the island suffered by comparison. The Spanish Inquisition arrived in 1487, and Sicily remained an intolerant backwater throughout the Renaissance. Barbary pirates attacked the coasts, and the viceroys had great difficulty recruiting Sicilians to defend themselves. At the end of the War of the Spanish Succession, the Treaty of The Hague (1720) gave Sicily to the house of Savoy, then to Austria.

The Bourbons

The Sicilians liked neither the Piedmontese nor the Austrians and were relieved when in 1734 the Spanish Infante, **Charles of Bourbon**, came and took this southern headache away from Austria, meeting little resistance. Charles stayed a week before moving to Naples. When he became King of Spain, he left Sicily and Naples to his third son Ferdinand, then 8 years old. With his Austrian wife, Maria Caroline, **Ferdinand IV** (1750–1825) lived a merry life in Naples and only made two trips to Sicily—once to avoid Napoleon and again when Joseph Bonaparte was proclaimed King of Naples in 1805.

Ferdinand managed to regain Naples in 1815, and celebrated by crowning himself **Ferdinand I of the Two Sicilies**. He was succeeded by Francis I, and in turn by **Ferdinand II**, who earned himself the nickname Re Bomba ('King Bomb') for the ferocity with which he put down a Sicilian revolt in 1848.

Union with Italy

In 1860, defying the wishes of Prime Minister Cavour (whose concept of 'Italy' ended somewhere to the north of Naples) **Garibaldi** with his long-haired Thousand landed in Sicily at Marsala and, after meeting initial indifference, soon joined by the Sicilians in his efforts to join their island to the new kingdom of Italy under the king of Savoy **Vittorio Emanuele II**. Within the year he had succeeded, and the island's political history has been the same as the rest of Italy ever since. Yet the new Italian government did little to make Sicily, or the rest of the south, very welcome in the new nation; without the impetuous Garibaldi the Savoys would have left the poor, troublesome island to the Bourbons. Poverty grew worse than ever; tens of thousands of Sicilians migrated to America and elsewhere in search of jobs. Fascism, on the whole, was good to Sicily; not only did Mussolini put more money into roads and building programmes, but he appointed a prefect named Mori to destroy the Mafia, and using the Mafia's own calculating methods, he all but succeeded when interrupted by the war.

During **World War II**, Sicily was the first territory in Europe to be successfully retaken by the Allies (Operation Husky, July 1943). The Americans under Patton stormed the beach at Gela, and the British under Montgomery took the beaches at Pozzallo, then advanced on the German fastnesses entrenched around Mount Etna. The Nazis were finally forced to abandon Sicily on 18 August. Ironically, the vacuum they left was quickly filled by Mafiosi, who helped the Allies against the Fascists who had tried to destroy them.

During and after the war, Sicilian separatists, disillusioned with 80 years of Italian rule, were clamouring for independence. The peasants, intellectuals and landowners who supported the separatist cause (which was also promoted by famous bandit **Salvatore (Turiddu) Giuliano**, the modern Sicilian Robin Hood) hoped to achieve independence at the end of the war, with a little help from the Allies. However, in 1943 the Italian army, the Communists and the Mafia, each for their own reasons fearing an independent Sicily, joined forces against the separatists. When the United Nations was founded in 1945, the Sicilians could not obtain recognition, and the United States wasn't interested when Giuliano proposed Sicily as the 49th State. But such was the power of the separatist movement that Italy had to grant Sicily regional autonomy, although the Sicilians will be the first to tell you that it is superficial and ineffective against their many problems. When the popular Giuliano was assassinated in 1950, at the age of 27, the spirit of Free Sicily died with him.

Sicily Today

Sicily's population has now stabilized at about 5 million. Smaller families are beginning to alleviate the need to emigrate, although many Sicilians still have to look for jobs in the north; unfortunately even now those who leave are the best and brightest. A surprising number become administrators or policemen.

In a game attempt to make up for the neglect of the past, major economic reforms initiated in the post-war years—the *Cassa per il Mezzogiorno* (Fund for the South), supported by the World Bank and Common Market; agricultural reforms (50 per cent of the arable land had been owned by 1 per cent of the population); and industrial programmes—are bearing fruit, both sweet and bitter. Baroque shop fronts are now crammed with smart new video recorders and electric toasters, and the narrow medieval streets in some towns have become permanent traffic jams of new shiny cars. The huge refineries and chemical plants at Augusta, one of the biggest projects, is a hideous scar on a once lovely shore. Even more devastating is the amount of development money diverting into the pockets of the *mafiosi*, who remain the plague of Sicily.

The sums and effort spent by governmental attempts at reform seem pathetic when placed next to the work of a single individual—Danilo Dolci. Born in the north of Italy in 1924, Dolci left a promising architectural career soon after the war to help the poor. In 1950 he arrived in western Sicily. One of the first things he saw was a child starve to death. Like Gandhi, Dolci began a series of fasts to change policies towards the poor and their housing conditions that brought him international recognition. Since then he has built a modern residential and educational village at Trappeto on the Gulf of Castellammare, offering training and cultural events; he has worked hard for the construction of Sicily's largest dam on the Iato, delayed by the government and opposed by the Mafia, which greatly enhanced the fertility of the Iato valley; his long-range plans are for the development of all rural western Sicily to improve the living conditions and offer new jobs for its inhabitants. Although supported and funded by groups in Northern Italy and

97

Northern Europe, he has fought long hard battles against the regional and national governments, the Church, and Mafia; his commitment and real accomplishments make him Sicily's brightest hope.

Painting and Sculpture

Great Sicilian painters can be counted on one finger. It's sad but true—the Renaissance, with its attempts to revive ancient Greek culture and arts, and which should have bloomed in Sicily, was so utterly blighted by the Spanish Inquisition that the 15th–16th centuries could be called the island's Dark Ages. The one exception, the one universal artist Sicily produced but soon lost to the rest of Europe, was **Antonello da Messina** (1430–79), who learned the new Flemish techniques of oil painting from a pupil of Jan van Eyck and introduced it to the Venetians in the 1470s. His exquisite subtlety of colour and the understatement of his simple compositions make him one of the great masters of Renaissance art. Four of his paintings may be seen in Sicily, two damaged by earth-quakes at Messina and Syracuse, a third at Cefalù, and the fourth, one of his master-pieces, at Palermo.

Other Sicilian painters include the 14th-century 'Master of the Polittico of Trapani'; the 'Master of the Triumph of Death Palermo', who may well have been a 15th-century Catalan instead of Sicilian; and **Pietro Novelli** of Monreale (1603–47), one of the fathers of Baroque painting, who broke away from the *tenebroso* influence of Caravaggio mid-career for a lighter, more classical style. Both the museums at Palermo and Syracuse contain a fine array of local 13th–16th-century paintings by unknown or unheralded artists.

In sculpture Sicily fares somewhat better. Besides the beautiful statues and reliefs left by the ancient Greeks (now in the archaeology museums of Syracuse and Palermo), every other church in Sicily seems to have a work by the prolific if rarely brilliant **Gagini** family, who originally came from Lombardy and then found their fortune embellishing altars and choirs in the 15th and 16th centuries. Artistically the head of the clan was Antonello, whose many Madonnas and Annunciations are often tender and moving. Other family members specialized in architectural details, and still others worked in silver. Another fine Renaissance sculptor, **Francesco Laurana**, left some beautiful samples of his art on the island, the best being a Madonna in Palermo Cathedral. **Fra Umile of Petralia**, high in the mountains, is renowned for his rare wooden crucifixes. Most brilliant of all are the works of a native Palermitan, **Giacomo Serpotta** (1656–1732), who decorated a number of chapel and church interiors around Palermo with charming, refined stuccoes; of all Italian sculptors, Serpotta is considered the truest Rococo spirit, cheerful and with a grace none of more drama-prone contemporaries on the peninsula could equal.

Architecture

The ancients bequeathed many fine buildings to Sicily—among them the beautiful lone **Temple of Segesta** and the Doric **temples of ancient Akragas** (Agrigento), including one that is the largest Greek temple in the world, and another that is one of the best-preserved. One huge theatre in **Syracuse** was carved in the living rock. The stage of the theatre at **Taormina** is well preserved, and it enjoys the magnificent backdrop of Mount Etna. In the middle of Sicily, the Roman **Villa of Casale** has floor after floor of wondrous lifelike mosaics, a few surely done by Michelangelo during an earlier incarnation.

Somewhere between art and architecture are the **Norman cathedrals**, the masterpieces born of Sicily's three distinct cultures. When the rather severe architectural concepts of the northern French of the 12th century were combined with the imaginative intricate masonry of the Arabs and embellished by Byzantine mosaicists, the results left us with one of the most beautiful churches in the world—**Monreale**. Other prime examples of the lovely hybrid style may be seen in **Cefalù and Palermo Cathedrals**, and in Palermo's magnificent **Cappella Palatina** and **Martorana Church**. The so-called *Chiaramonte* style, often seen in 14th-century palaces, was also a hybrid of sorts, put together by the powerful family of the same name when they commissioned yet another palazzo. It is an exuberant but delicate style, best seen in the arched mullioned windows.

While the Inquisition nipped the Sicilian Renaissance in the bud, the Baroque blossomed, even more fantastically in Sicily than elsewhere. The 18th-century saw two exceptional local architects on the scene to rebuild the island's eastern cities decimated in the earthquake of 1693. **Rosario Gagliardi** (1700?–70), a priest from the southeastern corner of the island, designed churches that express the ideal best in Noto, Ragusa and Modica—places few foreigners visit, so that Gagliardi remains undeservedly unknown. **Giovan Battista Vaccarini** (1702–70) remade Catania into a pageant of Sicilian Rococo, one of Europe's most stunning 18th-century cities. In the west, Trapani-native **Giovanni Biagio Amico** (1684–1754) decorated the western cities with dynamic church façades. Extreme, even by a Baroque yardstick, are the dreamy, often playful extravagances in the villas of Bagheria, once a fashionable suburb of Palermo, where the Villa Palagonia, built in 1713 by **Tomaso Napoli** (1655–1725), takes the prize for folly.

Of post-Baroque architecture in Sicily, there is little to say, though Palermo has worthy examples of neo-classical architecture (the Teatro Massimo), the Chinese (the Villa La Favorita), and a handful of Liberty-Style (Art Nouveau) cafés. Mussolini meant well when he constructed a large number of public buildings on the island, but unfortunately they won't go away. Usually made of cheap travertine, with ambiguous slogans about mystic power engraved on their façades, these Fascist monuments stick out like sore thumbs in every large town.

Music and Literature

Quite a few Sicilians have made names for themselves in the other arts. Among the ancient Sicilians there's the bucolic poet **Theocritus**, father of the pastoral, **Diodorus Siculus**, the first to attempt a history of the world, and the ancient philosopher **Empedocles**. In the 12th century, **Frederick II**, no mean poet himself, encouraged the first poetry in the Italian language, of which **Ciullo d'Alcamo** produced the earliest known verse, almost a century before *The Divine Comedy*. **Alessandro Scarlatti** and **Vincenzo Bellini** (composer of *Norma*) are the island's most notable musicians. **Luigi Pirandello**, the 1934 Nobel Prize-winning playwright who revolutionized modern drama, was born near Agrigento. In literature, the poetic **Giuseppe di Lampedusa** (*The Leopard*), and **Giovanni Verga** (*Maestro Don Gesualdo*), were also sons of Sicily. Both books offer rare visions of Sicilian life in the past; Verga's short stories, written in a succinct, objective style, are like modern slices of Greek tragedy (*Cavaliere Rusticana, La Lupa*). *Report from Palermo* (in English *Poverty in Sicily*), by **Danilo Dolci**, offers a more contemporary, journalistic view of the island's problems, as does his recent compilation of interviews with Sicilians from every walk of life, *Sicilian Lives*.

Religion and Festivals

Giuseppe Pitrè, Sicily's great student of folklore, wrote: 'In Sicily the past is not dead, but rather accompanies one from cradle to grave, in festivals and games, in spectacles and in church, in rites and in traditions; everywhere it lives and speaks . . .'. Most Sicilians, of course, belong at least nominally to the Roman Catholic faith, although descendants of Greek immigrants of the 18th and 19th centuries still practise the Orthodox rite. Whether or not the Church exerts much control over the lives of the people any more is debatable; older women, as usual, are the only ones to attend mass regularly, and they keep the roadside shrines supplied with flowers and candles or lightbulbs. The sacraments of the Church, however, are practised with enthusiasm by all. Parents buy elaborate gowns for their baby's baptism and throw great parties. Little white suits and miniature nun's habits or wedding gowns, palm branches, flowers, and corny photographs are called for at First Communions. Weddings are sumptuous occasions, often after long engagements. Perhaps because of the Spanish influence (or was it vice versa?) death calls for the most Baroque and elaborate rituals; gilt funeral procession, groaning under the weight of flowers, followed by a long file of mourners solemnly making their way to the hilltop cemetery, are moving scenes that make passersby cross themselves and sigh. Horseshoe-shaped wreaths as big as a man are bought in remembrance of 'Uncle' or 'Colleague', and black-bordered obituaries are posted all over town; houses and businesses often have signs on the doors saying 'Per mia Mama' (or whoever), advising visitors that the occupant is in mourning. Cemeteries are palatial and often the main tourist attraction in a small town; at night the red candles in the *Campo Santo* flicker eerily on every hillside outside every village.

Nearly every festival in Sicily is religious in origin. Feast days may be marked with a simple extra mass, or with exuberant fireworks as at the *Festa di Santa Rosalia* in Palermo. During the *festa* of a town's patron saint, the streets around the church are decorated with coloured lights and bunting; stalls offer plastic toys, sticky candy and other local delicacies. After mass, the saint's statue or relics are carried in a procession and there may be dances and fireworks in the evening. Pilgrimages to mountain sanctuaries are common, and many towns have lavish carnival celebrations (the most traditional, with masks and parades, is at Acireale). Holy Week is the climax of the Sicilians' religious calendar, when the influence of centuries of Spanish occupation can be observed. In many towns, beautiful (or sometimes maudlin) scenes from Christ's Passion—known as the Misteri—are borne in solemn procession through the streets by men dressed in hooded robes or Spanish costumes of the various medieval guilds. The most authentic of these processions are in the interior of the island (Caltanissetta and Enna Provinces) where the Middle Ages seem like yesterday. Another popular holiday is All Souls' Day (1

November), especially in Palermo. On All Souls' Eve, presents are given to children, supposedly from the dead, and cemeteries are adorned and illuminated for the many visitors who come to commune with the bones of their ancestors.

Unfortunately, unless you go to a special folk festival you are unlikely to find any traditional Sicilian music, dances or costumes. Sicilian music, with its eerie quarter tones more reminiscent of Greek music than anything like 'O Sole Mio', is played on instruments like the *guartara* (a terracotta wind instrument), the *ciaramedda* (the shepherd's goatskin bagpipe), the *friscalettu* (reed flute) and the *tambureddu* (skin drum). The women's costumes favour red and black with wide skirts, though they vary widely from town to town. Traditional male costumes feature baggy black caps, white shirts, vests and dark breeches. Their Spanish-period attire which you can see at some *festas* is more colourful with its doublets and wide hats.

The *Opera dei Pupi* or puppet theatres have been enjoying a small revival ever since Sicilians realized that the art is in danger of dying out. Although souvenir shops everywhere peddle cheap versions of the marionettes, regular performances are to be found only in Palermo, Acireale, Taormina, Catania and Messina. Many festivals often feature puppet shows as well. Sicilian puppeteers perform only one play, the story of Orlando (Roland) and his Christian Paladins fighting the Saracens (see 'Topics'), performed in incomprehensible dialect. Some of the puppets stand 4 or 5 feet high and wear real metal armour and swords, which are banged around for a good part of the show. Like a soap opera, a performance always ends in the air, tempting audiences back for the next evening's entertainment.

Cuisine

Generally Sicilian food comes hotter, spicier or sweeter than in the rest of Italy. With its rich seas brimming with tunny and swordfish, its abundant fresh produce, its citrus and almonds, the island has always been an inspiration to its conquerors' chefs from the classical Greeks to the modern Sicilian exponents of *la nuova cucina*. The longest lasting gastronomical influence has been Arabic, with a decided leaning towards aubergines (introduced by the Saracens), olives, pine nuts, anchovies, and especially capers whenever feasible. *Pasta con le sarde*, the most typical dish on the island, was said to have been invented by the first Saracen chefs to feed the conquering army; when properly prepared, it combines sardines, wild fennel, peppers, olive oil, currants, pine nuts, and saffron—an unusual but tasty concoction, but beware some of the cheaper versions. Other popular first courses are *pasta con le fave* (with fava beans, tomatoes, and fennel seed) and the pungent *pasta ca'anciova e muddica*, with anchovies in tomato paste. Western Sicilians wholeheartedly adopted the semolina couscous of the Saracens, here called *cùscusu* and served with fish; *pesto trapanese* is another western dish, made from fresh tomatoes, almonds, garlic, and basil, ground together with a mortar. In eastern Sicily the favourite pasta dish is named after Bellini's opera *pasta alla Norma*, and features fried aubergine, fresh tomato sauce, basil and ricotta cheese.

Not surprisingly, seafood dominates the list of Sicilian *secondi*. The humble sardine is dressed up to perform a starring role in *sarde a beccofico*, filled with breadcrumbs and currants and baked in the oven with orange juice. In late spring, fresh tuna (*tonno*) , and their deep red flesh is prepared in a wide variety of ways, often cooked with mint or its roe sprinkled over pasta. The real denizen of local seafood, however, is the swordfish (*pescespada*) with its mighty blade, usually grilled with lemon, olive oil and oregano, a sauce called *salmorigano* or as *involtini* (flat slices rolled with a breadcrumb filling). *Involtini* are also the most popular way to serve beef, pounded thin and filled with breadcrumbs, cheese and ham, on a spit). The larger gourmet version, *farsumagru*, includes hard-boiled eggs.

Sicily has a thriving snack culture, and instead of a full meal you can indulge in *arancine* (deep fried breaded rice balls with a meat, cheese, tomato or vegetable filling, so named from their resemblance to oranges), or *sfincione*, thick pizza with warm onions and anchovies, or chickpea fritters called *pannelle*.

Sicilians save most of their artistry for sweets and desserts. Most famous of these are *cannoli*, pastry tubes filled with fresh ricotta, bits of chocolate, and candied fruit, and the rich *cassata* made with icecream, almonds, and candied fruit. In the summer delicious ices, lemon or coffee *granitas*, homemade icecream with fresh fruits, and fruit sorbets help keep the temperature down. The most prominent displays in any pastry shop window are of candied fruit and *frutta alla Martorana*, which is marzipan shaped and coloured expertly to look like figs, fennel, tomatoes, bananas, clams, or even spaghetti or fried eggs, and was once the secret of the monks at La Martorana in Palermo. For festivals little manikins of pure sugar are made with exquisite skill; for St Joseph's Day (March 19) elaborate biscuits in fantastical shapes are used as ornaments; at Christmas the ring pastry *buccellato* with almonds, walnuts, and dried figs. A year-round treat are the *biscotti regina* rolled in sesame seeds.

Sicilian Wines

Sicilian vintners have worked hard to improve their product and earn a respectable place on Italy's dense wine maps, and appreciative imbibers will want to try *Corvo* (a dry, fruity white or very respectable red); *Etna* (a dry white, and excellent, lusty red); *Regaleali* (dry white or red, among Sicily's best); *Alcamo*, a dry white to complement any seafood; the various Marsalas, from the sickening sweet to a dry wine that you can drink as an aperitif; the wines of Linguaglossa; sweet, amber *Moscato* from Syracuse; *Mamertino* from Messina, a favourite of the ancient Romans. Sicily also has its own brewery, which produces Messina beer.

GETTING TO SICILY

By Air
There are frequent domestic flights to the airports of Palermo, Catania, and Trapani–Marsala from domestic airports, and occasional non-stop scheduled flights from London. Many charters go directly from London to Palermo all year round, and if they have any extra seats you may find this the most economical route.

By Train
Numerous trains travel southwards along the mainland, timed to coincide with the frequent ferry services across the Straits from Villa S. Giovanni to Messina, and from there trains continue to either Palermo or Catania. If Palermo is your goal, you may want

to consider taking the overnight ferry there from Naples, which runs daily, and is inexpensive and far more pleasant than the lengthy train journey (see below).

By Sea

Tirrenia links Sicily with the rest of the Mediterranean. Its ferries depart from Naples daily at 8.30 pm for Palermo, arriving at 6.30 the next morning. Fares in the high season (June–September) are around L37 000 per passenger in a second-class cabin; the charge for a small car will be around L45 000. There are 4 services a week between Genoa and Palermo, departing at 3 pm and arriving at 2 pm the following day, and a weekly service between Cagliari and Palermo, departing from Cagliari at 7 pm and arriving in Palermo at 7.30 am the next day. Once a week there's a ferry from Tunis, leaving at 8 pm and arriving the next day at 6 am in Palermo. Three times a week there is also a ferry from Reggio Calabria to Catania, Syracuse and Malta.

There is a regular hydrofoil run by Aliscafi SNAV from Reggio Calabria to Messina 19 times a day (15 minutes). Caronte Lines ferries vehicles over the strait every 30 minutes or so. Siremar (Sicilia Regionale Marittima) operates nearly all the services to the outlying Sicilian islands (see the individual islands for more details).

By Car

It's a long drive from Britain to Sicily, and you may well save money flying to Palermo and hiring a car on the spot. Consider the overnight ferry from Naples to cut a day of travelling time, although book well in advance if you're coming in the summer.

GETTING AROUND IN SICILY

Trains within Sicily (see map) are either frequent and fast or poky and irregular. Some routes that look possible on the map, for example from Syracuse to Agrigento, actually take a whole day to complete (if you're lucky). Between Palermo and Messina and Messina and Syracuse the FS runs comfortable, regular trains; elsewhere expect *locales* that may make half-hour stops in the middle of nowhere. Often you'll find **coach** services on Sicily more frequent, convenient, and just as reasonably priced.

Sicily has its share of autostrade: one almost encircles the island (except between Gela and Campobelle del Mazara), and several crisscross the interior. Unlike those on the mainland, Sicilian autostrade are free of tolls and are rarely crowded. The state roads are almost invariably in an excellent state of repair. However, driving in the large cities and in nearly every provincial capital can be highly exasperating, and in many cases you'd get to your destination faster by walking—especially when you include the headache of finding a place to park; you're better off leaving the car in a hotel garage.

The Ionian Coast

To have seen Italy without having seen Sicily
is not to have seen Italy at all, for Sicily is
the clue to everything.
—Goethe, *Italian Journey*

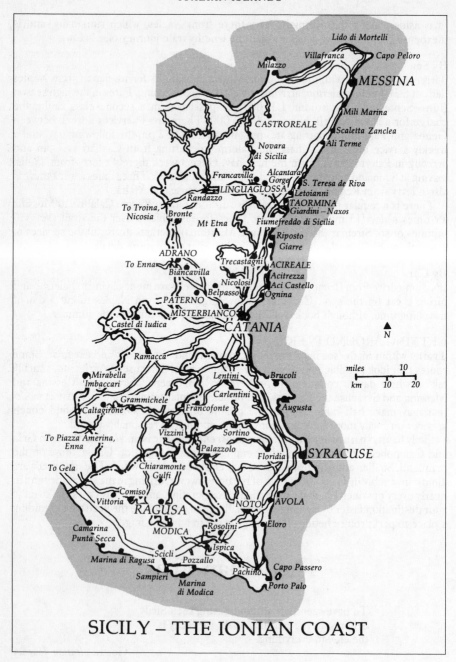

SICILY – THE IONIAN COAST

The east coast of Sicily, facing the Ionian Sea, is the most stunning and the most visited: Mt Etna and its fertile fingers of lava form a unique backdrop to the palms and citrus trees in the celebrated resort of Taormina, a dense array of hill towns, and the metropolis of eastern Sicily, strange, crumbling, Baroque Catania. Syracuse contains some of the island's most remarkable ancient remains: Noto stands out as a unique planned town of the late 17th century.

Messina

Founded by two giants named Mata and Grifone on a strait plagued by the monsters Scylla and Charybdis and land rocked by earthquakes, Sicily's third city Messina (pop. 273,810) is the island's most modern town, but not oppressively so, despite its tragic history. Today's architects could learn a lesson here (but beware the somewhat Byzantine street plan). Messina's pleasant position at the foot of the Peloritani Mountains, on an unindustrialized coast, adds to its charm, and its importance as 'the Gateway to Sicily' remains undiminished.

History

With its harbour and strategic situation on the Straits, Messina has been important since ancient times. Initially colonized by the Cumaeans and Chalcidians in the 8th century BC, Messina was then known as 'Zancle' (sickle) after the shape of its harbour. In 493 BC, Zancle was captured by Anaxilas, tyrant of Rhegium across the Straits, who renamed it Messana after his native Messenia in Greece. The Carthaginian Himilco destroyed the town in 397, then Syracuse rebuilt it, only to see it occupied by the belligerent mercenaries of the tyrant Agathocles, the Marmertines (sons of Mars). The Marmertines controlled large areas of Sicily and Calabria until conquered by Hieron II. From then on the city, described by Cicero as 'great and wealthy', was an ally of Rome.

The Normans, who arrived in 1061, brought a new prosperity. During the Crusades, Messina became an important port, famous for its monastery of St Salvador of the Greeks. Richard the Lionheart spent a winter here in 1190–1, sacked the town and rebuilt the Castle of Matefriffon. Messina stubbornly resisted the grasping Charles of Anjou in 1282, but had less luck against the Spaniards, under whom the population was decimated in the 17th century. This began a series of hard knocks for Messina. In 1743, the plague killed 40,000, then in 1783 an earthquake demolished the city, and in 1848 the Bourbons, under 'Re Bomba' (Ferdinand II), bombarded the city fiercely from the sea to quell Sicilian cries for independence. There was a cholera epidemic in 1854, another earthquake in 1894, and then, on 28 December 1908, the most devastating tremor of all, which killed 84,000 inhabitants in the small hours of the morning, caused the coast to sink 2 feet into the sea, and altered the dreaded whirlpool Charybdis so that it no longer posed a threat to sailors. Organizations all over the world contributed to the rebuilding of Messina, but before the great work was complete the Americans bombed it, destroying much that had been built.

GETTING AROUND

By air: the nearest airport is at Reggio di Calabria. Buses leave for the airport from Piazza del Duomo.

By train: all trains going to Sicily stop at Messina via the FS ferries, which also take cars and passengers.

By ferry: frequent crossings from Villa San Giovanni, less frequently from Reggio di Calabria, both of which lie at the end of the Autostrada del Sole, a mere 1395 km from Milan. In Messina the port is off Via della Libertà.

By hydrofoil (SNAV): these depart every half-hour or so from Reggio di Calabria (15-minute trip) and Villa San Giovanni (8-minute trip). In the summer (June to September) hydrofoils leave Messina for the Aeolian Islands on the SNAV line. Tickets and information from Cortina del Porto (tel (090) 364 044); departures are from Via Garibaldi.

By coach: buses that leave Messina for the rest of the province and Sicily all depart from the vicinity of the railway station, from Via Primo Settembre. The SAIS line takes the popular Taormina–Catania route from here. For Milazzo, take the Giunta bus from Via Terranova.

TOURIST INFORMATION
EPT, Via Calabria Isolato 301 bis (tel (090) 775 356).
AAST Piazza Cairoli 45 (tel (090) 293 3541).
Touring Club Italiano, c/o Lisciotto Viaggi, Piazza Cairoli 221.
Post Office: Piazza Antonello.
Telephones: Via Consulato del Mare, Via Cavour & Stazione Centrale.

The Cathedral
The centre of the city is the Piazza del Duomo, with Messina's most important building, the Cathedral. Built by Roger II in 1160, it was shattered by the 1908 earthquake, rebuilt, and destroyed again by World War II bombs, after which it burned for three days. Again the Messinians rebuilt their duomo on the old Norman model, incorporating pieces of the original that had survived the destruction—including the charming reliefs of farming peasants and part of the Norman portal. In the campanile, a fascinating **astronomical clock** built in Strasbourg in 1933 and reputedly the largest in the world, tells the year, the date, the phase of the moon and the location of the planets. As if that weren't enough, the clock also provides a display of bronze mechanical figures. Every day at noon, a crowd gathers to watch: the lion waves his banner and roars three times, the cock flaps his wings and crows, Jesus pops out of the tomb, the dove circles around as a model of the church of Montalto rises from the ground (the real one can be seen on the hill to the left), and Mary is saluted by various dignitaries to the tune of Schubert's 'Ave Maria' on the loudspeaker. Inside the cathedral are its restored treasures, including Antonello Gagini's *John the Baptist* and part of the tomb of the English Archbishop of Messina, Palmer, who died in 1195. Also on the Piazza del Duomo is the beautifully restored 16th-century **Orion Fountain** by Angelo Montorsoli, a pupil of Michelangelo.

Nearby, on the broad Via Garibaldi, is another reconstruction, the pretty Arab–Norman church of **Annunziata dei Catalani**. From the Via Garibaldi you can see why the Greeks named the port the Sickle, the very tip of which is marked by one of the Italians' beloved Madonnas on a Pillar and the Spanish fort of **San Salvatore**, built in 1546. At the crossroads of Via Garibaldi and Via della Libertà the public garden of **Villa Mazzini** has a charming little **Aquarium** of Mediterranean sea creatures (open Tues, Thurs, Sat and Sun, 9–1). Across the street stands the church **San Giovanni di Malta** and in the Piazza Unità d'Italia splashes another fine fountain by Montorsoli, the **Fontana di Nettuno**.

Museo Nazionale

Continuing along Via della Libertà (bus 8 from the railway station) are the buildings where the big Messina Fair takes place each August, and at the end of the street, the Museo Nazionale (open 9–2, Sun 9–1, also Tues, Thurs & Sat 4–7 pm; closed Mon). This contains objects removed from the earthquake-shattered churches, most important- ly two works by Caravaggio, both painted in 1609, the year before his wretched death on a Roman beach: the *Adoration of the Shepherds*, a deceptively simple triangular composition, and the powerful *Raising of Lazarus*, one of his most disturbing works, where Lazarus' hand rises stiffly in the unrelieved dark void that occupies the entire upper half of the large canvas. Also look for the earthquake-damaged but still lovely triptych of the *Annunciation* by native son Antonello da Messina.

North 11 km of Messina is the very popular beach, the **Lido Mortelle** (frequent bus from Messina), right by the Capo Peloro or Punto del Faro, the northeasternmost corner of Sicily. From here a huge power cable stretches over the Straits, supported by two monster pylons to permit ships to pass beneath.

The Straits of Messina

The *Fretum Siculum*, as the Romans knew it, has been on the map since the dawn of Western civilization, when Odysseus' ships were almost wrecked by the two monsters, Scylla (the rock) and Charybdis (the whirlpool). In summer they sometimes produce the mirage called 'Fata Morgana' which distorts the coast of Calabria, caused by the enchantments of Morgan la Faye. And what is she doing in this sunny clime? When the Normans brought the tales of Roland with them to Sicily, they also brought the legends of King Arthur and transplanted them in the fertile Sicilian imagination. Mt Etna became the fairy kingdom of Mongibel, where Morgan lived and where her sprites entrapped Arthur. Nowadays the Straits swarm with swordfish, the quarry of fishermen from the small villages that dot the headland. If you are lucky you'll see the fishing boats with enormously long prows, the harpoonist perched precariously on the end, in hot pursuit of the swordfish.

Crossing the Straits has posed an interesting challenge since the Second Punic War, when the Romans, having captured Hannibal's war elephants in Palermo, lacked the ships to send the heavy pachyderms across, and ended up floating them on rafts built over large, empty jars. There has been a lot of talk lately about building the world's longest suspension bridge over the Straits, or a tunnel, or most interestingly, a sus- pended underwater tunnel called the Archimedes Bridge, proposed by British engineer Alan Grant, that would be anchored to the seabed with adjustable steel cables. A major hurdle to building any link is the fact that it has to be able to withstand a major earthquake; at present those interested in the venture are keeping a close eye on the progress of the Channel Tunnel.

A Jaunt to Reggio

There is one compelling reason to cross the Straits and visit the dusty, ugly city of Règgio

Calabria: the **Museo Nazionale della Magna Grecia,** north of the centre on Corso Garibaldi in a chuky piece of Fascisti travertine (daily except Mon, 9–1.30 and 3.30–7, Sun 9–12.30; adm). Even if there were nothing else, the trip to Règgio would be worthwhile just for the *Warriors of Riace,* two bronze masterpieces that rank among the greatest productions of antiquity to come down to us. If you haven't heard of them, it is because they were only found in 1972, by divers exploring an ancient shipwreck off Riace on Calabria's Ionian coast. The museum keeps the pair down in the basement, in a room all their own next to a big exhibition detailing the tremendously complex—and excellently done—restoration job. These fellows, both about 6 ft 7 in and indecently virile, may perhaps have come from a temple at Delphi; no one knows why they were being shipped to Magna Graecia. One of them has been attributed to the great sculptor Phidias.

The warriors share the basement with a few other rare works of Greek sculpture, notably the unknown subject called 'The Philosopher', as well as anchors and ship fittings, and amphorae that once held wine or oil—all recovered from the shipwreck, in mud well over a metre deep. Other rooms contain beautiful terracotta **ex-voto plaques,** recovered from the temples of Magna Graecia. Most of these offerings show goddesses in the magical archaic Greek style—usually Persephone, who has influence with Death, being abducted by Hades, receiving propitiatory gifts, or accepting soils into the underworld. Chickens are a recurring motif, not too surprisingly, since to the ancient Greeks a soul rises out of its burial urn the same way a chicken hatches from an egg. Other works help complete the picture of life and art in Magna Graecia: Greek painted ceramics from Locris and Attica, bits of architectural decoration from various temples, some still with bits of their original paint, records of city finances on bronze tablets, and a rare early Hellenistic mosaic of a dragon, made in Calabria.

WHERE TO STAY

(tel prefix 090)

The ******Jolly Hotel Dello Stretto,** Via Garibaldi 126 (tel 43 401) is Messina's favourite and most expensive place to stay (L85–115 000). Another choice, the ******Riviera Grand Hotel,** Viale della Libertà 516 (tel 57 101; L95 000 with bath), is air-conditioned and large, and is not far from the centre; it has a good restaurant with a view. For comfort and Art Nouveau furnishings, check in at the less expensive ****Monza,** Viale San Martino 63 (tel 773 755), where a room with a bath is L45–60 000. For something clean, cheap, and within hearing distance of the clock, there's the ***Roma,** Piazza Duomo 3 (tel 775 566; L17 000 without bath). There are a number of pleasant camping sites, a list of which can be obtained from one of the tourist office; a night for two (plus car and tent) will come out at around L10 000.

EATING OUT

Swordfish dishes and cassata made from almond paste are the specialities of Messina. Try also *spaghetti en papillotte* or *ghiotta di pescestocco,* the Easter *sciuscello* made of chicken stock, curd and meatballs, and *'ncaciata,* a local pasta dish. Especially famous among local wines are the *Capo Bianco, Cariddi* and *Mamertino.* For a first-rate introduction to the island's cuisine, try **Pippo Nunnari,** Via Ugo Bassi 157 (tel 293 8584), but expect to pay around L40 000 for a full meal. **Alberto's,** Via Ghibellina 95 (tel 710 711), serves as many as 44 different types of antipasta, which won a place in Ernest Hemingway's heart, whom Alberto used to serve in Cuba. The constantly varied menu here guarantees freshness and originality. Try the *linguine alla ghiotta di ventrete pescestocco, spaghetti alla samba dello Stretto, panzerottini di scampi in salsa di granchio*—full meal with wine at least L50 000. For a fine range of local wines and wonderful pasta **Antonio's**, Via Maddalena 156 (tel 293 9853), is hard to beat; full meal L25–35 000. In the same price bracket the trattoria **Piero**, Via Ghibellina 121 (tel 718 365), serves excellent *antipasta di mare* accompanied by local wines. For something inexpensive, a good place to look is around the university (Piazza Maurolico).

South to Taormina

The Ionian coast south of Messina is fringed with small towns and beaches wedged between the Peloritani Mountains, the handmaidens of Queen Etna. The closer you get to Taormina, the more spectacular the scenery, whether you go by car or train; the latter, even the *rapidos*, seems to stop at every little town along the way.

Mili Marina, directly across the Straits from Règgio di Calabria, has a lovely old Basilian monastery church, **Santa Maria** founded in 1082 by Count Roger, whose son Jordanus was buried there ten years later. **Giampilieri Marina** is an old resort nearby. In the mountains above the beach in **Scaletta Zanclea** moulder the melancholy ruins of a 13th-century castle. Medicinal treatments may be had at the spa of **Ali Terme** with its mineral springs and mud baths, located on a wide stretch of beach. Above Santa Teresa di Riva, the next town on the coast, **Sàvoca** was once the haunt of cut-throat *banditti* who lived in the ruined castle; today you can visit the small **catacombs** with mummified bodies, a tidier miniature of the macabre galleries in Palermo. Sàvoca's church of **San Michele** has a good Gothic porch.

Forza d'Agro

South of Santa Teresa, a kilometre or so inland but at 427 m altitude, **Forza d'Agro** is a pretty, medieval village, dominated by a 16th-century castle; its main church, 16th-century **Sant'Agostino**, contains a beautiful painting by Antonio Giuffré of *Three Angels visiting Abraham*, and a medieval gonfalon. From here you can visit the exquisite Norman church, **SS. Pietro e Paolo**, built by a certain Master Gerard the Frank in 1172 for the Orthodox Basilian monks. Situated on the banks of the Fiumara d'Agro, the building reflects the lavish Norman–Byzantine decorative ideal, with local lava added for multi-coloured effect. Just before Taormina, **Capo Sant' Alessio**, with its castle perched on the 120-m cliffs, offers a striking view from the window of your train or car. Below it lie the budding resorts of **Letoianni** and **Sant'Alessio Siculo**, both with wide beaches.

Taormina

Enchanting and unique, with the dreamlike scenery honeymooners love, Taormina is Sicily's resort *extraordinaire*, discovered by Europe's leisured classes who began to winter there at the turn of the century, among them D. H. Lawrence who lived in a villa in Taormina during 1920–3 (a plaque in Via Fontana Vecchia commemorates his stay).

This lovely town is filled with fine medieval buildings, gorgeous bougainvillea spilling into charming little squares, and bustling cafés and boutiques. The absence of traffic in the heart of the town enables the visitor to wander unhindered, or sit in the shade of the lemon and orange trees. Noted for its mild climate, Taormina enjoys a year-round season, and its spectacular situation is enhanced by the looming eminence of blue snow-capped Mt Etna. The view from the Greek theatre is one of the most impressive to be found in all of Sicily.

History
Taormina was founded in 358 BC, after Dionysius of Syracuse destroyed the ancient colony of Naxos below. Andromachus, father of Timaeus the historian, took the refugees of Naxos to *Tauromenium*, as it was then known; later Andromachus was the only tyrant to join Timoleon, the new ruler of Syracuse, in his efforts to restore democracy in Sicily. During this time the town prospered (the Romans made it a privileged *civitas foedecata*) but later it erred in supporting Pompey against Octavian, who as Augustus turned it into a strategic military colony. The Saracens destroyed Taormina in 902 but then had a change of heart and rebuilt it. In 1410 the Sicilian parliament deliberated here in electing a new king for the island when the Aragonese line died out with Martin II. During World War II Marshal Kesselring made Taormina his headquarters, and the town consequently suffered bomb damage.

GETTING AROUND
Two roads lead up to Taormina, both branching off SS 114. Via Luigi Pirandello, the most picturesque, is also the route of the buses from the railway station Taormina–Giardini. The main beach of Taormina, Mazzarco, can be reached by the cablecar, or *funivia* (frequent departures from Via Pirandello all year round—a one-way ticket costs L1000). A tourist card may be purchased to make a number of trips at a discount. There are frequent buses down to Capo Taormina, Letoianni, and up to Castelmola; for the daily coach excursions to Mt Etna, see a local travel agent.

TOURIST INFORMATION
AAST, Palazzo Corvaja, Piazza Santa Katerina (tel (0942) 23 243).

To Piazza Vittorio Emanuele

From sea level, Via Pirandello winds up past villas, hotels, the Anglican **Church of St George** and the *funivia* station before finally flowing into Taormino's main street, Corso Umberto. To the right is the **Church of San Pancrazio** built on the site of a temple to Serapidean Zeus, where you can make out the *cella* foundations. Through the **Porta Messina**, the main entrance of the town, the Corso leads to the central **Piazza Vittorio Emanuele**, site of the magnificent **Palazzo Corvaia**, once the seat of the Sicilian parliament and today an art gallery. Built in the 14th century and recently restored, the palace is typically decorated with black lava and white pumice stone. Behind Santa Caterina, also in Piazza Vittorio Emanuele, are a few vestiges of the ancient **Odeon**. Some Imperial **Roman baths** have been excavated towards the beginning of Via Teatro Greco.

The Greek Theatre

Via Teatro Greco, naturally enough, leads to Taormina's great Greek theatre. The ancient Greeks, modern scholars argue, had little thought for views, but dug their theatres out of the hills and mountains wherever it was most convenient. Yet here in Taormina it's hard to imagine that they didn't give the backdrop at least a thought—indeed, one wonders how the drama could ever compete against such a spectacular panorama of sea, jutting coastline, rolling hills and a smouldering volcano. The theatre itself (open daily 9 am to sunset; adm) was originally constructed in the 3rd century BC and rebuilt in their characteristic brick by the Romans in the 2nd century AD; it was used exclusively for gladiatorial bouts. Some 110 m in diameter, it is the second largest in Sicily, after the theatre in Syracuse, and although the *cavea* has fallen somewhat into disrepair, the *scena* is very well preserved. The columns above the theatre belonged to a portico which once encircled the *cavea*. By the entrance to the theatre, a small **antiquarium** contains a few tablets from ancient Tauromenium.

Down the Corso

Back to the Corso, in the main shopping area of town, steps descend to the so-called **Naumachia** (perhaps the ancient cistern) with a barrel-vaulted roof. At the top of the steps in lively Piazza Nove Aprile is the 17th-century church of **San Guiseppe**. In the square itself, another church, **Sant' Agostino** built in 1488, has been converted into a library. The **Belvedere** and its fabulous views, however, attract most attention. Passing beneath the **Torre dell' Orologio** (12th century, restored in the 17th) you enter the **Borgo Medioevale**, the oldest and most charming quarter of Taormina, still retaining an Arabic touch or two.

The **Cathedral**, on the Piazza del Duomo, is a simple structure from the 13th century, with a later rose window and some fine paintings inside, including a 15th-century triptych by Giuffré. In front of the cathedral is a small fountain (1635) by the Montorsoli school. Below this square, the 16th-century **San Domenico Convent**, used as Nazi headquarters during the war, has been turned into a luxury hotel. The end of

The Theatre at Taormina

Umberto is closed by the 1440 **Porto del Tocco**. Down the steps, just off Piazza Sant'
Antonio, is the **Palazzo del Duca di Santo Stefano**, one of the last palaces built by the
Normans in Sicily, and recently restored; note the elegant windows. Above the Corso, on
Via Dionisio Primo, stands the battlemented tower of the **Badia Vecchia** (the old
convent), with its wide, pointed window. Belonging to the 15th century, this is the
loveliest monument in Taormina. Below the town, on Via Bagnoli Croce, are the
beautiful **public gardens**, with unusual wooden toy palaces scattered throughout, and
spectacular views over the town and sea.

Castelmola
For a superb view of the surrounding region, you can go on foot (Via Circonvallazione to
the Mulattiera Castel Taormina) or by car (Via Castelmola) to the **Sanctuario Madonna della Rocca** and the **Castle of Taormina**—of little interest in themselves, but
commanding unforgettable panoramas. For an even better view, ascend to the village of
Castelmola and its medieval castle. The village is also famous for its almond wine.

ACTIVITIES
Taormina's main beach, **Mazzarco**, has every facility, including restaurants—as have
other beaches in the area, such as Lido Spisone and Lido Mazzeo and the coves around
pretty Isola Bella and Capo Taormina. One of the most important displays of Sicilian
folklore takes place annually on the last three days of May in Taormina—*Il Raduno del
Costume e del Carretto Siciliano*. Traditional puppet shows are performed, as well as
folksongs and dances, and painted carts trundle around in a spectacularly colourful
parade. Every Friday there's a puppet show in the Teatro S. Nicola.

WHERE TO STAY   (tel prefix 0942)
Taormina is packed with luxurious accommodation of every description, most elegantly
the *****San Domenico Palace** on the Piazza San Domenico (tel 23 701), many of its
rooms occupying a 15th-century monastery; its pool is the loveliest in Taormina and its
rates by far the steepest at L350 000 (open all year). The ****Excelsior Palace**, Via
Toselli 8 (tel 23 975), is one of many with a spectacular location (and pool): L115 000.
Smaller and quieter, but also affording great views, are the ***Bel Soggiorno** (open all
year), Via Luigi Pirandello 60 (tel 23 342, L60–75 000 with bath); the ***Villa Belvedere**, Via Bagnoli Croce 79 (tel 23 791), with a garden terrace and pool (L75 000); and,
perhaps most famous of all, the ****Timeo**, on Via Teatro Greco 59 (tel 23 801), with
panoramic views and a lovely garden (L90 000 to 120 000).

Less expensive is the castle-like **Villa Carlotta**, below town on Via Luigi Pirandello
81 (tel 23 732; L55 000, with bath). Further up the same street, at No. 26, the **Pensione
Svizzera** (tel 23 790) also has fine views (L40 000). For something rockbottom that's not
a pit of contagious disease, try **Diane** at Via Giovanni 6 (tel 23 898), where one of four
rooms costs L16 000.

There are many other places by the sea, like the elegant old ***Lido Mediterraneo** at
Spisone (tel 24 422), where a double room with bath is L100,000 and the more cosy,
bright pink **Villino Gallodoro**, Via Nazionale 151 (tel 23 860, L38 000).

EATING OUT
Not surprisingly there are many places to choose from, although many are spoilt by
having to cater for too many tourists. The **Ciclope**, Corso Umberto, is the place to find

typical Sicilian cooking with excellent antipasta (L35–45 000; closed Wed). Further along Corso Umberto is the fashionable **Granduca**, considered to be one of the best restaurants in Taormina (Sicilian specialities, for at least L50 000). To eat with a charming view over the Greek theatre, try the **Giova Rosy Senior** at 38 Corso Umberto (tel 24 411). The risotto dishes are a speciality and the restaurant also serves shrimp and lobster cooked with vodka (L35–45 000). Head for **Il Pescatore** to sample locally caught fish. On the Via Nazionale Isolabella (tel 23 460), this is one of the most attractive trattorias in the area, and a full meal will run to L35 000. For beautiful al fresco dining by the sea, **Oliviera** is highly recommended for its excellent seafood and pasta (L50 000). There are less expensive places to eat in the town. **L'Anfora**, Salita Dente 5, is a family run trattoria which serves authentic Sicilian dishes for around L20–25 000. For good deals, check out the 'menu turistico' posted on many of the little places along the side streets, like **Mama Rosa** (around L18 000) and the **Nuova Grotta di Ulisse** (around L22 000).

Giardini–Naxos

TOURIST INFORMATION
Via Tysandros 76/E (tel (0942) 51 010).

South of Taormina, on the south side of the station, **Giardini–Naxos** is Sicily's newest and fastest growing resort, with its beach of golden sand, modern hotels, swimming pools, garden district of Contrada Recanati, and convention centre. Yet while the Giardini half is as new as anything in Sicily, **Naxos** (signposted from Giardini, on Capo Schisò) was nothing less than the first Greek colony on the island. Founded *c.*750 BC, its name derives from the Cycladian island of Naxos, but most of the original colonists are thought to have been from Euboea and Ionia, who came in search of land to farm and found the native Sikels easy to encroach on. Giardini's beach was attractive to these pioneers as it is to modern sun worshippers, as ancient Greeks beached their ships rather than anchor them in deep harbours. The colony prospered so well that before long the Naxians were founding their own colonies, including Leontini and Catana (Catania); troubles, however, were never far, and came in the form of the newer, but more powerful Dorian settlements. With few defences, Naxos was attacked in turn by Hippocrates of Gela (495 BC) and Hieron of Syracuse (476 BC) and survived, only to choose the wrong side in the battle between Athens and Syracuse. In retaliation the Syracusan tyrant Dionysius the Elder besieged and razed Naxos in 403 BC, selling its citizens into slavery; he gave the territory back to the Sikels, though they preferred the heights of Taormina, and eventually the Naxians who escaped bondage settled there as well, and the city by the sea was heard from no more.

The Excavations
The well-ordered site of ancient Naxos (open 9 am to sunset, Sun 9–12), built on the ancient, level stream of lava that forms the Capo Schisò, enjoys a beautiful setting, with both the sea and Mt Etna for a backdrop. Archaeologists so far have uncovered the polygonal city **walls**, the remains of two **temples** believed to have been part of a

The Crater of Mt Etna

celebrated sanctuary of Aphrodite, and two kilns; the street plan (a new one super-imposed on the more ancient one), along with some Hellenistic tombs, suggests that at one time settlers returned to Naxos. An old Bourbon fort on the cape has been converted into an **Archaeology Museum**, chronicling the history of the site into the Byzantine era; among the exhibits are terracotta ex-votos from the temple of Aphrodite, coins from the 5th century BC, and *antefixes*, or architectural ornaments with more female figurines and the head of fertility-wine god Silenus, who was especially associated with the colony for the heady wines it produced.

The Alcantara Gorge
From Giardini you can take a walk on the wild side: through the dramatic, volcanic wonderland of the **Gole dell'Alcantara**, or Alcantara Gorge, carved by the river of the same name through the hardened basalt of one of Etna's ancient eruptions, 20 m deep and a mere 3 m wide in some places. Like a multi-layered Russian torte, the basalt of the steep walls has revealed a variety of colours when sliced; along the way are unusual stone formations sculpted by the elements. To enter the gorge, head up 17 km on SS185 to the parking area, where a lift awaits to lower you into the scenic abyss. Wear your bathing suit and rubber shoes.

A couple of kilometres beyond the parking area, still on SS185, lies **Francavilla di Sicilia** with a medieval castle and bridge spanning the Alcantara; the ruins near the bridge belong to a domed Byzantine church.

WHERE TO STAY AND EAT   (tel prefix 0942)
There's a wealth of hotels along this stretch of the coast, which is the popular riviera for many Italian families. The ***Naxos Beach Hotel** on Via Recanati 26 (tel 51551) is large and conveniently situated on the shore with its own pool and tennis court (L75 000 with bath). The hotel restaurant **La Casa del Massaro** produces some marvellous examples of Sicilian cooking—excellent pasta, seafood, grilled meats and some of the highest quality Sicilian wines (L35–50 000). A slightly more personal hotel is the

***Tritone**, Via Tsyandros 22 (tel 51 468), with a good restaurant and reasonable rates for its rooms—L45 000. There's no shortage of pensioni either—among them *La Sirena, Via Schiso 36, which has rooms with bath for L32 000. The restaurant here has the old favourite pasta with aubergine (eggplant) and a small selection of fish and meat dishes for L25 000. There are a number of pizzerias along the front, where a meal will cost in the region of L10 000.

Mt Etna

I do not think I shall ever forget the sight of Etna at sunset; the mountain almost invisible in a blur of pastel grey, glowing on the top and then repeating its shape, as though reflected, in a wisp of grey smoke, with the whole horizon behind radiant with pink light, fading gently into a grey pastel sky. Nothing I have ever seen in Art or Nature was quite so revolting.

—Evelyn Waugh

Awesome smouldering Mt Etna (in Arabic 'Gibel Utlamat'—hence the Sicilian name 'Mongibello') at 3269 m has little to do with the rest of Sicily's geology. Vulcanologists believe its career began under the sea from where it pushed its way up to become part of the island. More than 135 eruptions have been recorded, beginning in 475 BC, when both Pindar and Aeschylus wrote about a great volcanic explosion. Some 30 or 40 years later the pre-Socratic philosopher Empedocles, from Agrigento, committed a strange suicide by leaping into Etna's 40-km-diameter crater, either to seek divine consciousness in death or to prove that hot air rises; only his slippers remained on the rim to tell the tale. Several eruptions in the Middle Ages reached the sea. The worst eruption on record was in 1669, when a wide gap opened up from the summit to the town of Nicolosi, and lava overwhelmed most of Catania. The volcano has continued to be quite active since then, if not as ruinously, and tourist excursions to the summit may occasionally be cancelled owing to uncertain volcanic conditions. An observatory at the summit monitors Etna's activity.

GETTING AROUND
For many, the ascent up the mountain is the highlight of a visit to Sicily. The main route up on wheels is from the south, the Strada dell'Etna, beginning in Catania. If you do not have a car, there is a daily bus (Etna Trasporti) from Catania's Stazione Centrale at 7 am, and various tour excursions from Catania and Taormina, which have the advantage of supplying the necessary outer wear for the top of the volcano (it's freezing up there, even in August). The trip takes an entire day. You can pick up the secondary approach, **Etna Nord**, by following the signs south of Taormina, but watch carefully for those signs; otherwise you may end up on an unplanned safari of the lower slopes. The very beautiful small towns and villages at the foot of Etna can easily be visited on the Circumetnea railway, departing from Catania; to see everything take the 8.45 am train.

TOURIST INFORMATION
Linguaglossa (tel (095) 643 094).

Strada dell'Etna
The Strada dell' Etna from Catania passes through **Gravina** where the craters Pomiciari

115

di Santa Maria were formed in 1381; **Mascalucia,** a wine centre; and, above it, **Massa Annunziata** where pistachio trees flourish on the cooled lava of 1669. **Nicolosi** at 698 m, lies east of the smoking Monti Rossi craters, also formed in 1669, and one can walk up it in an hour. Nicolosi has become a popular ski resort with two ski lifts and a chairlift. From here, you cross fields of more recent lava to the Serra la Nave ski slopes, overlooked by the fine old Grand Hotel dell' Etna, and to the Casa Cantoniera which has wonderful views. The Strada dell' Etna ends at the Rifugio G. Sapienza, a hostel operated by the Italian Alpine Club at 1910 m. Here you can sleep and eat, but to ascend to the crater you need to find a guide or take the cablecar to the **Observatory** (2942 m), and a jeep or coach to the crater from there. Working on the veteran partygoer's premise that ash is good for the plants, if not the carpet, the same applies to Etna; the volcanic deposits on the lower slopes have made the soil extremely fertile, producing belts of orange groves, olive trees and vines, above which are scattered orchards of fruit and pistacchio trees. Forests grow up to 2100 m; above that height the only plant is the Spino Santo (*Astigalus aetnensis*) amid the barren lunar landscape of volcanic matter, smoking and reeking of sulphur. Peering into the multiple depths of the crater is a remarkable, sublime, and perhaps even revolting experience, depending on your temperament—as is the view of Sicily, Calabria, the Aeolian Islands and, on a clear day, Malta far in the distance. While on top you can take in the **Torre del Filosofo** celebrating Hadrian's ascent of the volcano, and the chasm known as the **Valle del Bove** whose sides are sheer 914 m cliffs.

The **Ascent of Etna North**, commencing off the SS114 at Mangano, ascends up to **Zafferana Etnea** a summer resort with many hotels, and **Fornazzo–Milo** with views of the Valle del Bove. Here a road branches off to the alpine refuges Citelli (1741 m) and Sucai (1589 m) while the main road goes to **Linguaglossa**, a newer ski resort amid tall trees, with a National Ski School on the Piano Provenzana, a few kilometres further up the slope, which has four ski lifts. In Linguaglossa you can pop into the tourist office, which has a showcase room of Etna's minerals, flora and fauna, and the **Chiesa Madre** church has some exquisitely carved 18th-century wood panels and stalls.

Villages around Mt Etna: on the Circumetnea Railway

Paternò is the first important stop along the tracks, 20 km west of Catania, with a 13th-century restored **Norman castle** at the top of the town. Here Frederick II of Aragon died on his way to his beloved Enna. There are some good frescoes in the chapel of Santa Barbara, and the convent of **San Francesco** is a French gothic affair from the 15th century. **Biancavilla,** 15 km from Paternò, glistens with its orange groves; **Adrano,** the next station a few kilometres further on, was founded in 400 BC by Dionysius I of Syracuse as 'Adranon', named after the god whose temple was near the site. The **Castello,** founded by Count Roger in the 11th century, has been turned into a prehistory museum and art gallery (open 9–1 and 3–6; winter 9–4; Sun 9–1; closed Mon). Near here are a few vestiges of the **Greek wall**, and the **Chiesa Madre**, also Norman, incorporating columns from an ancient Greek temple. The harsh cold stone of the 18th-century church of **Santa Lucia** is softened by the spacious palmed **Vittoria gardens**, which it overlooks, and the tableau gives a vague atmosphere of Spain. At Easter, Adrano presents a passion play, one of the most famous in Sicily. Near Adrano is the recently excavated Sikel town of **Mendolito** (8th–6th centuries BC), where a long, as yet untranslatable, inscription in Sikel was discovered, along with a treasure-trove of bronze artefacts.

Bronte, also on the Circumetnea route, is a small town named after the dukedom that Ferdinand III of Sicily (perhaps better known as Ferdinand III of Naples) bestowed on Lord Nelson for services rendered in 1799, not the least of which was shipping the king away to Palermo when the French were knocking on Naples' gate; it brought the admiral a cool £3000 a year. His seat in Bronte, the **Castello Maniace** (formerly owned by the Bridport family, now the property of the municipality and currently undergoing extensive restoration), was founded by Margaret of Navarre in 1173 as a convent, marking the site where the Byzantine George Maniakes defeated the Saracens in 1040. In 1905, the Scottish poet 'Fiona Macleod' (a pseudonym adopted by the writer William Sharp) died here, and he is buried under an Ionic cross. For permission to visit the castle, you have to apply in advance, in writing. Anyone, however, can drop in at the **Museo dell'antica civiltà locale**, 5 km out of Bronte, an agrotourist reconstruction of a typical rural settlement of bygone days, centred around an Arab–Norman building dating from around AD 1000, which was for centuries inhabited by monks skilled in making paper and curing animal skins. On display are the tools of their craft, together with the tools and utensils used over the centuries by local artisans, a mini zoo where Tibetan goats are cross-bred, and of all things, a chastity belt.

Randazzo, under the north slopes of the volcano, is perhaps the most interesting village of Mt Etna. Although built out of lava, it has never succumbed to an eruption, and has preserved its medieval atmosphere, although it suffered Allied bombardments when the Nazis made it one of their last strongholds in Sicily. The private **Museo Vagliasindi** (on the Corso No. 265), houses a good collection of finds from a nearby Greek necropolis (to see it, ask the owner). The town's **Cathedral of Santa Maria** dates from the 13th century. The church of **San Nicolo** is of the 14th century with later additions and has a few Gagini works. **San Martino** has a lovely campanile, although the church itself was damaged in the war. Next to the church the restored 13th-century castle-prison bears bullet holes which commemorate the final German defeat in August 1943. From here the Circumetnea continues to the winter resort of Linguaglossa (see above).

The Coast from Taormina to Catania

The coast here is loaded with campsites, castles and beaches. Starting from the north, **Calatabiano** has a lofty medieval castle, north of which are steps descending into the Alcantara Gorge (see above, Giardini–Naxos). **Giarre** further south, is a major wine-producing centre.

TOURIST INFORMATION
Acireale: Corso Umberto 179 (tel (095) 604 521).
Via delle Terme 61 (tel (095) 601 508).

Acireale

Acireale is built on streams of lava, and has become an attractive tourist centre for its sandy beach, the sulphur baths at Santa Venera, and the 'most beautiful carnival in Sicily'. The town itself, 152 m above the sea, was rebuilt after the 1693 earthquake and has a pleasant Baroque character. In the **Biblioteca Zelantea** (open 10–1 and 4–6) in Via Marchese di Siciliano, there is a library, museum and art gallery, including some beautiful drawings and a painting attributed to Rubens. The **Puppet Theatre** on Via Alessi gives performances in the summer; there are lovely views of Etna from the park **Villa Belvedere**. The **Palazzo Comunale** (1659) is a good example of bizarre Spanish–Sicilian Baroque, as is the genuinely Baroque **Basilica San Sebastiano** on Piazza Vigo, finished in 1705.

Just inland from Acireale is **Trecastagni** ('the three chestnut trees') with the most beautiful Renaissance church in Sicily, the **Chiesa Madre** built by the sculptor Antonello Gagini. Here also, on the night of 9 May, thousands pay tribute to the Three Saintly Brothers (Cirino, Alfio and Filadelfo); barefoot pilgrims dressed all in red run up from Catania to the Sanctuary of Trecastagni, where they light candles to the three saints. Traditional carts pulled by bedecked horses and mules, and Catanians on bicycles, accompany the valiant runners.

Aci Castello

Many other towns on the coast have names prefixed with 'Aci'—after the River Aci, which according to the ancient Greeks sprang out of the earth where the shepherd Acis died, murdered by Polythemus, the Cyclops, for jealousy of the maiden Galatea. Some rocks off the coast are known as 'Il Ciclopi', the rocks thrown by Polythemus after Odysseus' ships when the Greeks made their escape from his cave. The fiery cauldron of Etna, of course, was the Forge of Hesphestus (Vulcan), or the monster Typhon, conceived by Mother Earth to do battle with the Olympian gods.

Aci Castello, facing the islets of the Cyclops, derives its name both from Aci and from the castle built in 1297 by Roger di Lauria, who rebelled against Frederick II of Aragon. So impregnable was this fortress that only by building a wooden castle the same height right next to it could Frederick reduce it. The castle is still well preserved today, its splendid gaunt structure resembling the prow of a beached ship, overlooking the sea, the strange rocks of the Cyclops, and the holidaymakers from Catania who have made the 'Riviera dei Ciclopi' the most popular resort in the province. Nearby is **Aci Trezza**, a lively offshoot of Aci Castello, with streets jammed with cars and bars and people in summer.

WHERE TO STAY AND EAT   (tel prefix 095)

The ***Aloha d'Oro**, Strada Panoramica (tel 604 344), is the best bet, with a pool, proximity to the sea, and the best restaurant in the area, featuring superb fish soup, meat grilled over an open fire and irresistible icecream. Apart from the fine Sicilian specialities there are very satisfying pizzas at L8000 (rooms L85 000; meals L25 000). The ***Park Hotel**, at Capo Mulini (tel 877 511), is a great favourite mainly because of its pleasant setting (L60 000) but if you want to be right on the beach make for the ***Santa Tecla**, Via Balestrate (tel 247 602; L100 000). The most reasonably priced hotel in the 3-star category is the ***Delle Terme**, Via Alcide De Gasperi (tel 601 166) where rooms go for L50 000.

Highly recommended for its delicious seafood, stuffed pancakes and excellent wines is the **Barbarossa**, Strada Provinciale (L30 000). Two other worthy places are the **Panoramica**, Viale Ionio 12, with pork stew a speciality (L22 000) and the **Bettola** at

Santa Maria La Scala, where apart, once again, from good seafood you can sample some fine white Sicilian wines (L30 000).
In Aci Castello: the sumptuous ****Catania Sheraton, Via A. da Messina 45 (tel 631 557), with luxury rooms at L170–200 000 and some sumptuous things on offer in its restaurant too (L30–45 000). Throughout the summer and at weekends the trattoria Villa delle Rose, Via Nazionale 15, is packed with Catanese, enjoying the view from the saloon and the seafood from the Gulf of Catania. Very good *pasta alla Norma* followed by grilled fish comes out at about L35 000 (closed Mon and Nov). The pizzeria which sits at the foot of the Norman castle has a view of the bay and is an ideal place to sit and witness the evening *passegiata* in full swing. On the menu are a wide selection of antipasti and pizza, and mussels are a regular feature (pizza meal L10 000).
In Aci Trezza: ****I Faraglioni, Lungomare dei Ciclopi 115 (tel 536), has the advantage of its own beach and excellent restaurant (L 95 000), and the ***Eden Riviera, Via Litteri 57 (tel 636 577), is in a pleasant green setting with its own pool (L60 000).

Catania

Catania is Sicily's second largest city, the island's industrial and business centre. Its very prosperity has caused great neglect of its marvellous Baroque quarter, as people desert it for the anonymous apartment buildings on the outskirts of the town, leaving the piles of crumbling terracotta to fend for themselves. The oldest areas are in bad shape even by Sicilian standards, and a modern 'urban redevelopment' area east of the Giardino Bellini adds nothing to the city's prestige. And yet, at least in one respect, change is evident. Five years ago it was impossible to find any kind of restaurant in Baroque Catania. Today there's one on every block.

History

Chalcidians from Naxos founded Catania in 729 BC, on its fertile plain (known as the Laestrygonian Fields in ancient times, after the cannibalistic Laestrygones in Book 10 of the *Odyssey*), and it prospered from the first. Catania's tyrant drew up a code of laws in the 7th century BC which were adopted by all the Ionian colonies of Magna Graecia. The Syracusans under Hieron I took the city in 476 BC and exiled its inhabitants, but in 461 the Catanians triumphantly returned and sent Hieron's Doric colonists packing. An ally of Athens, Catania was the Athenians' base in the ill-starred Great Expedition and suffered the consequences when Dionysius of Syracuse sold the inhabitants into slavery in 403 BC. Himilco the Carthaginian, Timoleon and Pyrrhus, followed by the inevitable Romans, trace the domination of the city up until Christian times. Augustus rewarded Catania for having supported him in the civil war against Pompey. In 253 Catania's patron St Agatha, suffered martyrdom apparently by having her breasts lopped off.
    In the early Middle Ages, Catania itself suffered a series of terrible disasters. A major earthquake devastated the city in 1169, and it was sacked twice, first by Henry IV, then by Frederick II. In 1669, the worst eruption in Etna's history buried it in lava, and before it could recover the 1693 earthquake destroyed almost everything else. However, with their usual resilience the Catanians rebuilt the city, better than ever under the direction

of great Sicilian architect Vaccarini, who made Catania into a showcase of Sicilian Baroque.

GETTING AROUND
By air: to Palermo, Venice, Bologna, Rome, Milan and Naples. The airport is at Fontanarossa, 4¹/₂ miles from the town. The terminal is at Corso Sicilia 105; buses leave from here and Piazza Stesicoro for the airport. A Giunta bus links the airport to Milazzo (for the Aeolian Islands).
By train: to Messina and the south; also to Enna, Caltanissetta, Palermo and all major tourist centres. Ditto for buses. Catania is the hub of all transport in eastern Sicily and you may have to back-track to Catania from Syracuse, for example, to get to your destination. Buses depart from the Stazione Centrale. The narrow-gauge Circumetnea (see Mt Etna, above), which calls at all the major villages around Mt Etna, leaves from the Corso Italia Station.

TOURIST INFORMATION
Largo Paisiello 5 (tel (095) 312 124); Fontana Rossa Airport (tel 341 900); Stazione Centrale (tel 322 440). For information on Mt Etna call in at the 'Italian Alpine Club', Via Napoli 116 (guides available for climbers).
Police: Piazza G. Verga (tel (095) 316817).
Post Office: Via Etnea 215.

The Piazza del Duomo
In the centre of the Piazza del Duomo, the Baroque showcase at the heart of the city, stands a fountain, with an elephant made of lava supporting an obelisk on its back—Catania's symbol—the obelisk originally having served as a turning-post in the Roman circus. Vaccarini turned the statue into a fountain. Bernini built a similar one in Piazza Minerva in Rome; Napoleon was so struck with the symbol that he incorporated the elephant-obelisk emblem into several buildings in Paris.

The elephant smiles benignly towards the **Cathedral of St Agatha**. Count Rosa founded the church in 1094, but following the eruption and the earthquake it had to be rebuilt, only the two apses of lava having survived from the original Norman structure. The façade was designed by Vaccarini, and the columns he placed in the lower front of this came from the Roman amphitheatre. Inside are the tombs of Bellini and the Aragonese Viceroy Fernandez d'Acuna (1494), which is in the chapel of Sant' Agata. The saint's relics are only displayed on high feast days—Agatha's veil is accredited with halting the lava flow in 1669, when the inhabitants waved it in front of the molten matter. A fresco in the sacristy, painted in 1675, portrays Etna's attack on Catania.

Also in the Piazza del Duomo are the 1741 **Municipio** with fine windows, another work of Vaccarini; an 18th-century **Palazzo** by Di Benedetto on the south side; and next to it the **Porta Uzeda**, an 18th-century archway through which you will find a small park where old men sun themselves and suspiciously eye all foreigners.

Around Piazza Mazzini
Two main streets, Via Garibaldi and Via Vittorio Emanuele, run west from the Piazza del Duomo. Via Garibaldi leads to the elegant **Piazza Mazzini** with its arcades of Roman

columns from a nearby basilica. The effect of this little piazza, as with all of old Catania's numerous squares, is somewhat tarnished by its use as a parking lot. Just beyond, to the left, the Via Castello Ursino leads directly up to the **Castello Ursino** in the Piazza Federico di Svevia (Swabia). Built by Emperor Frederick II to intimidate local hotheads, the castle was restored in the 19th century after being damaged by the 1669 eruption. Only the keep remains, but it is still impressive and contains the **Museo Civico**, which has undergone restoration and is due to open in 1989; it houses Prince Biscari's archaeological collection, objects from San Nicolo Monastery, and an example of the Sicilian carved and painted carts.

On the other side of Piazza Mazzini, at the intersection of Via Vittorio Emanuele, is Piazza San Francesco where you'll find **Bellini's house and museum** (open 9–1.30; Tues and Thurs also 4–7; Sun 8.30–1) with mementoes of the composer's life, some of his original scores, and models of scenes from his operas. Next to it, passing beneath an archway, is the famous **Via Crociferi**, one of the prettiest streets in Sicily, with its Baroque palazzi and small churches—the best of these being **San Benedetto** with an elegant façade.

The Greek Theatre and San Nicolo d'Arena

Continuing down Via Vittorio Emanuele, the **Greek Theatre** can be seen on the right; to enter, walk up Via Tineo to Via Teatro Greco (no. 47; open daily from 9–1 and 4 to dusk). The present structure actually belongs to the Roman era, built in the 2nd century AD, on the site of the Greek theatre where Alcibiades spoke to gain support for the Athenian cause. Next to it are the ruins of the **Odeon**. Both are made of lava, which was originally covered with a refined layer of marble stucco.

A few blocks west on Via Teatro stands **Piazza Dante**, a beautifully laid-out Baroque square much deteriorated through lack of care. Facing it is the gigantic church and monastery of **San Nicolo d'Arena**—surely one of the oddest, spookiest monuments in Sicily. The Italians say it has a 'mastodonic aspect'. The largest church on the island and the second largest convent in Europe (after the Mafra in Portugal), it was begun in the 16th century but never finished, then restored in 1735 after an earthquake destroyed it. Still unfinished, its façade is dominated by stumps of columns, like the bottom teeth of a gaping mouth. The vast interior is undergoing badly needed renovation, but if the door is open you can peep in and see the huge organ, of 2916 pipes—its builder, Donato del Piano, was buried underneath it—and the meridian line on the transept floor. To visit the dome for its view, apply to the sacristan. The Convent of San Nicolo now houses the library—and a few bulldozers and asphalt spreaders; it's a maintenance yard for the city road crews. There is also an astrophysical observatory in the San Nicolo complex, but it too has suffered from Catanese indifference.

Via Etnea
Back at Piazza del Duomo, Via Etnea, the main street of Catania, cuts straight across the city, with a view of Mt Etna at its very end. Every evening the most enthusiastic *passegiata* in Sicily takes place on this long street, the pavements crammed with icecream-eating Catanese peering in the windows of the many shoe, silver, jewellery and baby-clothes shops. At the end of the street, near Piazza del Duomo, is the **Università** with the pretty

Collegiata church, a royal chapel built by the Bourbons in 1768 (open 8–11 and 5–7.30). The University itself, Sicily's first, was founded by Alfonso V in 1434 and rebuilt after the earthquake (Vaccarini worked on the courtyard in 1752).

Further up, Via Etnea gives on to the Piazza Stesicoro (named after a Greek poet from Sicily), site of a major urban bus stop, the Bellini monument, and the remains of the 2nd-century **Roman amphitheatre**. This was once one of the world's second largest amphitheatres—a painting on the site shows the amphitheatre in its glory, before the Ostrogoths started using it as a quarry. Here, according to tradition, St Agatha suffered martyrdom. All the marble facing has worn away to expose the lava foundation. From here, Via dei Cappuccini leads past the **church of Santo Carcere**, built on the supposed site of Agatha's prison. It has a beautiful 13th-century door and the old church of **Sant' Agata la Vetere**, the ancient cathedral. Beneath the ruined church of **St Euplio**, also in Piazza Stesicoro, was the Roman Hypogeum.

Via Etnea continues north to the elaborate main post office and the **Giardino Bellini**, one of the prettiest public gardens in Sicily, meticulously maintained (unlike most of Catania's public places). The flower clock and calendar on the hillside are unique in Italy.

East Catania

Along the east end of the park runs the main street of many names—Viale Regina Margherita here, Viale Venti Settembre and Corso Italia further east. **Santa Maria di Gesù** stands to the northwest of the park; Antonello Gagini designed the chapel doorway and sculpted the *Madonna with the Angels* inside. At Corso Italia 21 is the Palazzo delle Scienze (by the modern Piazza Giovanni Verga). There are three museums nearby (all open 10–12, closed Sun): the **Geology Museum** and the **Mineralogy and Vulcanology Museums** (Corso Italia 55). Not surprisingly Catania has one of the best schools of vulcanology anywhere. In the untidy quarter east of Piazza del Duomo, in Piazza Bellini, is the beautiful **Teatro Massimo** where operas are performed in winter and spring. The Stazione Centrale is by the sea, near a fountain of the Rape of Persephone, floodlit at night to suggest the underworld.

The nearest beaches to the city are **Ognina**, a pretty place with lava cliffs to the north of town, and **Lido di Plaia** in the south (bus D in the summer from Piazza Giovanni Verga and Via Etnea). Near Lido di Plaia there's the airport at Fontanarossa and, at the mouth of the River Simeto, the necropolis of ancient **Symaethus**.

WHERE TO STAY   (tel prefix 095)
****Excelsior, on the Piazza G. Verga (tel 325 733), is the most comfortable hotel in Catania; open all year round (L160 000). The ****Centrale Palace, as the name suggests, is conveniently situated on Via Etnea, no. 218 (tel 325 344; L150 000) and not far away from that is the ****Jolly Trinacria, Piazza Trento 13 (tel 316 820), which blends comfort with a relaxed atmosphere (L140–160 000). The *Savona, on Vittorio Emanuele 210 (tel 326 982), has good clean rooms with bath for L40 000 (less without bath). There are a host of less expensive hotels to choose from. Among them the **San Domenico, Via Etnea 270 (tel 438 527; L45 000), and the ** Torino, Via P. Toselli 43 (tel 320 909; L40 000). At the lower end of the price and comfort scale, there are a

number of Locande—the **Elite** on Via Etnea 263 (tel 327 948) charges L13 000 a night, but all you'll get for that is a bed. The Locanda **Tosta** on Via Macallè 18 charges slightly less (tel 327 637).

EATING OUT

Catania's specialities include *scacciata*, made at Christmas, with anchovies, fresh cheese, pepper and sauces, stuffed in a pastry envelope; *cannelloni alla Catanese*; and the ever popular *pasta alla Norma*, with fresh basil, eggplant and tomato sauce. The Arab, French and Spanish influences have had a marked effect on the cuisine, making it distinct from that of mainland Italy. Favourite wines are *Trecastagni* and *Il Sparviero dell' Etna* (reds), *Castelriccio* (rosé) and *Ciclope-Mazzullo* (white).

La Siciliana, Viale Marco Polo 52, tel 376 400 (closed Sun eve and Mon), is considered by many to be one of Sicily's finest restaurants, serving true local cuisine (outside dining in the summer). In the age of fast food this restaurant will restore your faith in establishments where care and pride go into the preparation of every dish. Apart from the wonderful array of seafood, the roast lamb and breaded cutlets deserve mention, as do the vegetables and salads. Some very decent white wines are available, as well as the special red *Cerasuolo di Vittoria*. Full meals in the range of L30–40 000. **Pagano**, Via De Roberto 37 (tel 322 730), takes great pains to produce authentic Catanese food—of particular note are their pastas, stews and rice dishes, helped down with a bottle of *Torrepalino dell'Etna* (L30 000). **Costa Azzurra**, Località Ognina, Via de Cristoforo 4 (tel 494 920), has achieved a wide reputation for its adventurous cooking, using truffles, clams and the freshest of vegetables, especially eggplant, in a number of original and delicious ways. To complete the meal they always have a good choice of cheeses and icecream (L35–40 000). Since 1830 **Stella Antica Friggitoria Catanese**, Via Ventimiglia 66 (tel 325 429), has become an institution in Catania and wondrous concoctions appear from the frying pan; you can eat very well for L15 000 (closed Mon).

Catania to Syracuse: Augusta

The Plain of Catania, south of the city, is drained by the rivers Simeto and Pittano, but there's little to tempt the traveller to stop. In between Catania and Syracuse, below the honey-producing Iblean Hills that inspired Theocritus' bucolic poetry, lies **Augusta**, Italy's main oil port, a naval base, chemical works, and in general a thoroughly awful place; the road from Augusta to Syracuse is almost surreal with its mesh of coloured pipes and tubes and industrial geegaws. You could be forgiven for thinking the only exciting thing about Augusta is the 'Norwegian' café advertising live Greek music, but even that turns out to be a sham—no Scandinavians in sight and the music blares out of the juke-box to attract the occasional Greek sailor, who must wonder what on earth he's doing there.

Like Syracuse, Augusta is built on an islet connected by bridge to the mainland. Frederick II founded the city on the site of the ancient Xiphonia in 1232 for refugees from Centuripe and Montalbano. Most of the original buildings were destroyed in the 1693 earthquake and again in the 1943 air raids, although the **cathedral** still stands (dating from the 17th century) and two 16th-century towers along the **Porto Megarese**. The **Municipio** still sports Stupor Mundi's imperial eagle over the door. Augusta's main interest for the tourist, however, is its proximity to the excavations of **Megara Hyblaea** (see below) and the beach resorts at **Brucoli** and **Agnone**.

Carlentini

Inland from Augusta is Carlentini, founded in 1551 by Charles V as a summer town for the inhabitants of Lentini. From here one can visit **Lentini** itself (ancient Leontinoi), the second oldest Greek colony in Sicily after Naxos. Founded by the Chalcidians on the site of an early Sikel town, it soon became important as an agricultural centre. Syracuse ruled over the city for most of its existence, though in the mid-5th century BC, in a brief interlude of independence, it became allied with Athens and sent the renowned orator Gorgias to the Athenian assembly to plead for protection from its old master. When Syracuse attacked Leontinoi in 427 BC, the Athenians jumped at the chance to send aid. Although the Syracusans eventually made a treaty with them, the Athenians used the Leontinoi conflict as one of their major reasons for the disastrous Great Expedition a few years later. Leontinoi, like Syracuse, sided with Carthage in the Second Punic War, and was also attacked by the vengeance-seeking Romans; however, unlike Syracuse, Leontinoi was granted no mercy, and the Romans beheaded 2000 citizens for desertion, in accordance with ancient law.

The medieval town of Lentini fell flat in the 1693 earthquake although you can still see the ruins of **Frederick II's castle**. The **Chiesa Madre**'s right-hand nave was a 3rd-century Christian hypogeum; also note the beloved 9th-century Byzantine icon of the Madonna Odigistria. At the **Museum** in Piazza del Liceo (open 9.30–1; closed Mon) are items from various stages of the town's history. The remains of **ancient Leontinoi** lie between Lentini and Carlentini, spread over two hills, Metapiccola and San Mauro. Traces of the early Sikel town may be seen on Metapiccola, while around San Mauro are remains of Leontinoi's defences, a Hellenistic necropolis and part of the south gate to the city.

A Plunge inland: Francofonte, Vizzini, Grammichele

From Lentini, SS194 leads up 13 km to **Francofonte**, which disputes with Vizzini the claim to be the setting for Verga's story and Mascagni's opera, *Cavalleria Rusticana* as well as Verga's *Mastro Don Gesualdo*. In the church **Santa Maria di Gesù** the altarpiece of the Madonna and Child (1527) is by Antonello Gagini. **Vizzini**, just off SS194, 618 m up in the Iblean Mountains, stands on the site of ancient Bidis, mentioned by Cicero.

To the east, **Grammichele** often receives special mention in books on urban design. The modern town is built on the site of Occialà, which was destroyed in the earthquake of 1693. The new town was designed in a strict hexagonal form by Nicola Branci Forte, after a book by Tommaso Campornella (*Civitas Solis*), reviving the 8th-century BC Babylonian idea of radioconcentric city planning. From the air it is a perfect geometric symbol; the completely paved central square, equally hexagonal, lacks only a few De Chirico mannequins in heroic poses for total Metaphysical weirdness. Grammichele is also renowned for its dried figs.

Along the coast: Megara Hyblaea

Across the bay from Augusta (signposted on SS114 on the Augusta–Syracuse bus route) is Megara Hyblaea, founded in 730 BC by the ancient Megarians. This site, at the mouth of the River Cantera, was originally inhabited in the Neolithic period. Pantalica, the Sikel king of Hybla, offered it to the Greek colonists, whose manufacture of ceramics brought it considerable prosperity. Gelon of Syracuse destroyed the city in 483 BC, Timoleon had the site resettled, but the Consul Marcellus delivered its coup de grâce in 214 when the new town defied the Romans. A part of the ruins has been covered by the sea; those visible on land include a **Doric temple**, possibly dedicated to Aphrodite; the monumental **agora**; Archaic tombs; and some Hellenistic houses on a regular plan. In the **Antiquarium** on the site are a few of the finds. The archaeological digs, led by the Ecole Française, have been particularly interesting in recent years, especially regarding Archaic urban planning projects. Both the digs and the Antiquarium are open from 9 am–dusk; closed Mon.

Melilli, Thapsos and Pantalica

Melilli, 5 km inland from Megara Hyblaea, is famous for the festival of St Sebastian which takes place every 4 May. Here, in return for a favour from the saint, parents promise that their children will take part in the procession of St Sebastian—as stark naked as the saint himself, when Roman archers made him a vertical pincushion. The discarded clothing is later given to the poor children of the town. At **Cava Secchiera**, near Melilli, are some prehistoric rock-cut tombs.

East of Melilli, out on the Magnisi peninsula, are the ruins of **Thapsos**, the largest Bronze Age town in Sicily (nearest town is Priolo, and the excavations are 2¹/₂ km away, by the lighthouse). Dating from the 14th century BC, the settlement consists of circular and multi-roomed huts, only recently discovered. Most interesting are the tombs carved out of the rock with little cupolas, where vases imported from Mycenae and Malta have been found. Thapsos gave its name to the Bronze Age culture on Sicily, and is known for its vases on pedestals. Around the beginning of the first millennium BC the inhabitants of Thapsos were forced inland, perhaps to Pantalica.

West of Melilli the road leads through the Anapo valley to **Sortino** which has an impressive church. A new road (from SS124, turn off at Ferla) takes you to the vast Bronze Age **necropolis of Pantalica** in the deep valleys of the Anapo and Calcinara rivers. The settlement of Pantalica, dating from 1200 BC when invaders forced the coastal residents to move inland, is now believed to be the legendary Sikel town of Hybla. Few traces remain of this: one building, perhaps the *anactoron* or palace, along with signs of a wall. In the surrounding cliffs, however, are some 5000 family tombs carved in the rock like a honeycomb, attesting to the large size of ancient Hybla. In the 8th century BC, Pantalica was abandoned for reasons unknown. Later, threatened like the Sikels by invaders on the coast, the Byzantines sought shelter at Pantalica and expanded the tombs for dwellings. Two small chapels remain from this period.

Syracuse

The fabulous New York of the ancient world, the thriving metropolis of Magna Graecia—not terribly much has happened in Syracuse since Plato imparted philosophy to its tyrant and Archimedes invented his brilliant machines to defend the city from the Romans and the dull Latin urge to mediocrity. Yet if Syracuse retains only splendid ruins of its Golden Age, it has found a far more comfortable, less troublesome role as a pleasant, often lovely small city, a civilized place rarely in the headlines, a town in which to raise a family and live a normal life. The light is sharp and brilliant—that, perhaps more than anything, reminds one of its Greek founders.

Although the spiritual heart of the city still rests in the narrow lanes of Ortygia island, the inexorable urge towards modernization has pushed the commercial centre deep into the adjacent mainland. Even so the city (pop. 120,000) is small compared to ancient Syracuse; you can easily walk to all the main points of interest, and usually without an umbrella—Syracuse is renowned for its dry and healthy climate. Perhaps the only real blemish in Syracuse is a result of its persistence in making a living in the modern world—the oil rig erected in the centre of the bay, an ungainly robot from outer space.

History

According to Thucydides, ancient Syracuse (from 'Suraka', the Phoenician name of a nearby marsh) was founded in 733 BC by colonists from Corinth, who usurped the native Sikels and soon established a thriving town. The location was ideal; the small offshore island of Ortygia could easily be defended, the plains facing it were fertile, and the natural harbour offered immense possibilities for maritime activities. It wasn't long before the oligarchs of Syracuse were founding colonies of their own on Sicily, at Akrae and Camarina, increasing the city's sphere of influence to the borders of powerful Gela and Megara Hyblaea.

In 485 BC political turmoil within Syracuse caused the oligarchs to invite **Gelon**, the tyrant of Gela, to take control of the city. Gelon realized the potential of the Grand Harbour and made Syracuse a sea power; on land he annexed Megara Hyblaea and moved much of the population of his native Gela and that of Camarina to Syracuse. It was Gelon, in alliance with Theron of Akragas, who defeated the massive Carthaginian attack on Himera in 480.

Hieron, and the Great Expedition
Two years later Gelon was succeeded by his brother **Hieron**, a precursor of the archetypical Renaissance tyrant—cruel yet cultured, a passionate lover of poetry, patronizing and surrounding himself with the greatest talents of his time—**Simonides, Pindar** and **Aeschylus**. Pindar praised Hieron's victories in the chariot race, and Aeschylus is thought to have written *Prometheus Bound* and *Prometheus Unbound* in Syracuse, where they had their debut. Militarily, Hieron aided the Greek navy in defeating the Etruscans at Cumae (474 BC), ending another barbarian threat to Greek holdings.

Shortly after Hieron's death in 466, Syracuse turned democratic, but remained nonetheless powerful. Athens grew jealous of this new rival, and feared for its own allies and interests in western Greece. As Syracuse was allied with Sparta, Athens' arch-enemy, in the Peloponnesian War, Athens had the excuse it needed for an attack on Syracuse—with the eventual goal of adding all of Sicily to its mighty empire. Thucydides described this haughty **Great Expedition** from Athens in detail, how the 134 Athenian triremes led by the indecisive Admiral Nicias, set sail in 415 BC and almost succeeded in taking Syracuse, blockading it by land from Eurayalus. The Spartans sent reinforcements to Syracuse, under Gylippos, who in turn blockaded the Athenian fleet in the Grand Harbour. When the Athenians attempted to escape, Syracuse attacked and sank half their ships, and completely routed the soldiers who tried to flee south by land. 'This was the greatest Hellenic achievement of any war, at once most glorious to the victors and most calamitous to the conquered', commented Thucydides. Indeed, this surprise victory over the most powerful city of its day could do nothing but give a mighty boost to Syracuse' prestige; within the next few years it overtook Athens as the leader of the Western world. On the other side of the coin, the miserable Athenians captured at Syracuse were kept in the quarries (*latomiae*) under inhuman conditions. Few ever returned to Athens; the story goes that only those who were able to recite passages of Aeschylus or Euripides, the two favourite poets of the Syracusans, were ever let out again.

Dionysius
The next tyrant of Syracuse, the ambitious **Dionysius**, was also a poet, and wrote numerous tragedies which he entered year after year in the festivals of his near-namesake, only to be begrudged a prize by the Athenians (still no doubt miffed by their humiliation at Syracuse). However, in 368, when Athens sought an alliance with Syracuse, the festival judges suddenly found Dionysius' entry a work of genius, whereupon Dionysius celebrated his long-sought victory so lavishly that it killed him.

Unfortunately—or perhaps fortunately—none of Dionysius' poetry has come down to us, and history remembers him instead for his military genius. He built the fortress and walls on the strategic Epipolae Ridge west of Syracuse which proved so crucial to the city's defence during his campaign to rid Sicily of the Carthaginians. In this, however, he never quite succeeded, despite his gathering of engineers from all over Greece and Italy to design new weapons. Most spectacular of these was the catapult, which was instrumental in the Greeks' victory over the Carthaginians at Motya in western Sicily (see the 'Stagnone Islands').

Plato to Pyrrhus
Dionysius made Syracuse a powerful empire, but his son and successor **Dionysius II** was rather ineffectual, despite **Plato**'s efforts to make him a philosopher king according to the ideals of *The Republic*. When **Dion**, uncle of Dionysius II and friend of Plato, grew tired of his nephew's tyranny, he rose to overthrow him, and was in turn assassinated for acting the tyrant. The year 343 BC found Syracuse in a bad way through the neglect of its despots. Fearing a new Carthaginian offensive, the citizens appealed to mother Corinth for aid and were sent **Timoleon**, a man of justice and peace who, after overthrowing all the petty tyrants of Sicily, established democracy and made a peace treaty with Carthage.

Timoleon's good works lasted through his lifetime, but when he died in 336 BC the internecine bickering among the Greeks began again, eventually bringing the bellicose adventurer **Agathocles** to power in 317 BC. Throughout his rule, Syracuse was at war, conquering most of Greek Sicily except for Akragas. When Agathocles died in 289 without an heir, his fragile empire crumbled. In the confusion that followed, the Carthaginians saw their chance and sailed into the Grand Harbour—this time deterred by **Pyrrhus of Epirus**, who came to the rescue at the request of Syracuse and Akragas. Once again, the barbarian threat temporarily served to unite the Greek factions.

Hieron II

The Syracusans elected **Hieron II** (ruled 275–216 BC), one of Pyrrhus' officers, as their new ruler. As wise as he was long-lived, Hieron II was a blessing to the city. Besides making a treaty with the Romans and supporting them in the First Punic War, he improved the laws and life of Syracuse, redesigning the Neopolis quarter and building the mammoth altar to Zeus the Giver of Freedom (or 'Zeus Eleftherios'). **Theocritus**, the first writer of idyllic poetry, frequented the court of Hieron II, who also patronized his talented and scientific cousin, **Archimedes**.

Hieron II was succeeded by his grandson **Hieronymus**, who made the mistake of pledging allegiance to Hannibal in 215, when that Carthaginian was at the height of his power. This brought the wrath of **Rome** down upon Syracuse in the form of the Consul Marcellus, who laid siege to Syracuse. Here the Romans faced not so much the defending army of a city as the genius of one man—Archimedes. In his role as General of Ordnance, Archimedes had for some time been busy designing ingenious war machinery to defend the city. His contraptions dropped 600-lb lead weights onto the Roman scaling engines and his grapnels were lowered to snatch the Roman ships in the harbour, lift them up by their hulls and spill their crews into the sea. According to legend, Archimedes even reflected the sun's rays with mirrors to ignite the more distant Roman ships.

After the Romans

Despite all his tricks, the Romans prevailed, surprising the Syracusans during a festival in which Archimedes was slain despite express orders to capture the genius. From then on, Syracuse dwindled in importance, although always admired by the Romans for its beauty. Christianity found Syracuse a fertile field in its early days, especially after **St Paul** stopped for three days en route from Malta to Rome.

Late in the 3rd century AD, the first of the tribes of ransacking barbarians passed through, and in 535 Belisarius captured Syracuse from the Ostrogoths in the name of Byzantium. One of the Eastern emperors, **Constans**, moved his capital from Constantinople to Syracuse in 663, but he died five years later when a homesick servant clipped him over the head with a soap dish; nor did the court lose any time in returning to Constantinople. A key Byzantine port, Syracuse was besieged and destroyed by the Arabs in 878. Liberated again by the Byzantines in 1040, this time under George Maniakes, Syracuse regained some of its former prosperity under the Normans. From 1361 to 1536 the Camera Regionale sat at Syracuse, though many of the fine palaces of that period were felled in the 1693 earthquake. The city also suffered from both Allied and Luftwaffe bombings 250 years later.

GETTING AROUND

By rail: frequent service to and from Messina and Catania, less frequent to Ragusa and Licata and stops in between.

By bus: hourly coach service to and from Catania (nearest airport), less often to Palermo, Agrigento, Gela, Caltanissetta, Piazza Armerina, Ragusa, Palazzolo Acreide, Noto and all other towns in the province, departing from the Piazza della Posta. To get to the Archaeology Zone, take the city bus from the Corsobelone.

By sea: there are ferries 3 times a week from the Foro Italico to Reggio Calabria, Catania and Malta via Tirrenia Lines whose office is at Viale Mazzini 4 (tel 66 956/65 684).

TOURIST INFORMATION
EPT: Via S. Sebastiano 43/45 (tel (0931) 67 710); information office in the Archaeological Zone (tel 60 510). AAST: Via Maestranza 33 (tel (0931) 66 932). Railway Station (tel 66 932, summer only).

Ortygia Island

Ortygia (Greek for 'quail'), a name associated with the goddess Artemis, originally referred to the whole of Syracuse, but later became sole property of the island. Two bridges connect it to the mainland; the main one, **Ponte Nuovo**, leads on to the large Piazza della Poste (main post office, stops for provincial buses) and the adjacent Piazza Pancali, which boasts the ruins of the Doric **Temple of Apollo** excavated in 1943. Dating back to the mid-6th century BC, this temple was the first large structure built by the Greek colonists in Sicily. Two of its columns and part of the *cella* walls have been reconstructed, though it is still hard to imagine what the temple originally looked like. Painted terracotta fragments from the cornice are in the Archaeology Museum.

From here the narrow Via Cavour leads up to **Piazza Archimede**, the old heart of Ortygia. The 19th-century fountain in its centre has been confusingly dubbed 'the Fountain of Arethusa', but this isn't the real one. Note the **Palazzo Lanza** (15th century) and the Banco d'Italia housed in a medieval Catalan building. Just off the piazza, on Via Montalto, the 1397 **Palazzo Montalto** offers an inspired example of the Chiaramonte style, with its delicately mullioned triple windows.

Piazza del Duomo
Via Cavour continues to Piazza del Duomo, one of Sicily's most elegant squares. The site was sacred even in Sikel times; here the 5th-century Greeks dedicated a temple to Athena in thanksgiving for their victory at Himera. This temple was adapted by the Christians and became the **Cathedral** in 640, under Bishop Zosimus. Further remodelling took place under the Normans, and when the façade toppled in the earthquake, Andrea Palma designed the lovely Baroque front (finished 1754) that one sees today. Inside, the ancient Doric columns trace the skeleton of Athena's temple, the excellent proportions of which are felt throughout the building. To the immediate left is the **baptistry**, containing an ancient Greek marble font resting on Norman bronze lions. This is followed by the **Chapel of Santa Lucia**, patroness of Syracuse. At the far end of the same aisle is the Cappella del Crocifisso with a painting of *St Zosimus* by Antonello da Messina, and one of St Marcian attributed to the school of Antonello, which also painted the thirteen panels in the sacristy (door in the chapel).

Other buildings in Piazza del Duomo include the **Palazzo Arcivescovile**, housing the Biblioteca Alagoniana with its 13th-century manuscripts; the church of **Santa Lucia alla Badia** begun in 1695 after the earthquake; and the **Municipio**, a 17th-century palace built over the ruins of an 8th-century BC settlement, which houses the models of the small **Ionic Temple Antiquarium** (usually open in office hours).

The Fountain of Arethusa
> In Xanadu did Kubla Khan
> A stately pleasure-dome decree:
> Where Alph, the sacred river, ran
> Through caverns measureless to man
> Down to a sunless sea.
>
> — S. T. Coleridge, 'Kubla Khan'

The river is said to bubble up in the **Fountain of Arethusa,** just west of the Piazza del Duomo. This beautiful freshwater spring so close to the sea fascinated the ancient Greeks; according to them, the nymph Arethusa was being pursued by the river god Alpheus through Arcadia in Greece, when she begged Artemis, the goddess of virginity, to save her from the god's embrace. Artemis obliged by turning her into a fountain, in which form she fled under the sea to Sicily, with Alpheus in hot pursuit, rising up in Ortygia where their waters were mixed. Strabo records in this connection that a cup thrown in the River Alpheus in Arcadia would turn up in Arethusa's fountain in Syracuse. The potent symbolism of an underground river was highly significant in the esoteric circles of the Renaissance; learned academies were known as 'Arcadian'; in England, Sir Philip Sidney wrote his masterpiece, *Arcadia*, long before Coleridge's opium dream. On a more mundane level Nelson replenished his fleet from the fountain in preparation for the Battle of the Nile; perhaps the luxuriant papyrus along its edges brought him luck. Recently the fountain has been lovingly restored and a small **Tropical Aquarium** installed nearby (9–1; closed Fri and Sun) along with the tree-lined promenade called the **Foro Italico** whence the steamers depart for Malta. At the far end of the promenade is the 15th-century **Porta Marina** with Gothic inscriptions.

On the southernmost tip of Ortygia rises the **Castello Maniace**, named after George Maniakes, the Byzantine liberator of the city. Built by Frederick II in 1239, the keep is 50 m square but only two-thirds of its original height. Now a barracks, it can be visited only with permission from the military authority on the Longomare Ortygia. Beneath the castle one can also visit the imaginatively named **Bagno della Regina** (the Queen's Bath), actually an ancient underground reservoir.

Museum of Medieval and Modern Art
The only other example of Swabian architecture on Ortygia is the **Palazzo Bellomo** (Via Capodieci), although later additions almost overwhelm the original building. The Palazzo now contains the Museum of Medieval and Modern Art (open 9–2; closed Mon), an interesting collection with some fine medieval paintings, including the partly damaged *Annunciation* of Antonello da Messina. On the other side of the street is the 14th-century church of **San Martino** with a fine interior and a 15th-century triptych of the Madonna and Child. Two other churches of interest lie at the opposite end of Ortygia: **San Filippo** in Via Vittorio Veneto, a fine street of 17th-century Spanish mansions, is also from the 17th century, and **San Pietro** around the corner, in Via San Pietro, was founded in the 4th century by St Germanus. Its original form as a Roman basilica can still be discerned despite later alterations.

The Mainland

In the ancient quarter of **Achradina**, facing Ortygia, is the large square called **Foro**

Siracusano, the site of the Greek *agora*, now dominated by the Fascist-built Pantheon to the Fallen. Towards the railway station (Via Elorina) are the ruins known as the **Ginnasio Romano** although they actually encompass a small 1st-century theatre, its *cavea* picturesquely flooded. Archaeologists believe it was constructed for the minority who still appreciated drama after gladiatorial contests became the fare at the far larger Greek Theatre.

Borgo Santa Lucia

The quarter Borgo Santa Lucia to the east is named after the saint who suffered martyrdom in 304 on the site where the church of **Santa Lucia** now stands, built in 1629. A few elements remain of the original Norman structure, including the doorway and rose window. Hanging in the apse are two ancient crucifixes and one of Caravaggio's masterpieces, the *Burial of St Lucy* (1608) where the artist greatly distorted the size of the gravediggers to create a memorable vision of mindless brutality. Until the Venetian relic pirates swiped her remains in 1038, St Lucia lay in the octagonal Sepolcro Chapel built by Giovanni 'The Lizard' Vermexio. Although usually portrayed with her eyes on a platter like a waitress bringing a customer a couple of fried eggs, Lucia is really more concerned with light, or *luce*; her festival on 13 December is most enthusiastically celebrated in Sweden, where she brings the hope of light to the land of the midday moon. Beneath the church is a vast series of **catacombs**, the oldest in Sicily—used by the Christians since the 2nd century—and the second largest in Italy, after those in Rome. A small underground chapel has traces of Byzantine paintings.

Also in Borgo Santa Lucia, on Via dell'Arsenale, are the rather scanty remains of the ancient **Arsenal** and next to it a **Byzantine bath-house**. In the summer a boat leaves from St Lucia for **Capo Santa Panagia**, the Athenian base in the Great Expedition. Fossils have been found in the caves there, along with signs of Neolithic habitation. Inquire at the quay for departure times.

Latomia and the Catacombs

To the north and west of St Lucia is the ancient quarter of Tyche. Where the Riviera Dionisio il Grande and the Via Bassa meet is the entrance to the **Latomia dei Cappuccini**, the quarries begun in the 6th century BC. Once the horrible prison of the captured Athenian soldiers, the quarries are now the lovely peaceful gardens of the Capuchin friars (open 9–1). To the west, on Via August von Platen, are the **Catacombs of Vigna Cassia** (open 9–12.30 and 4–6) from the 3rd century BC, with a few traces of paintings, and the **Protestant Cemetery of Villa Landolina**, located in a small *latomia*, where the refined and soulful German Romantic poet August von Platen is buried.

In the same vicinity (Via San Giovanni) is the beautiful ruined church of **San Giovanni** built on the site of the first cathedral of Syracuse, rebuilt by the Normans, then destroyed by the 1693 earthquake—though the fine rose window somehow managed to escape intact. The main point of interest here is the crypt (open 9–12.30 and 3.30–6.30) where the first Bishop of Syracuse, San Marcian, was martyred in the 3rd century. The symbols of the four Evangelists are carved on the columns of the small chapel, which also contains an altar on the site where St Paul is said to have preached to the Syracusans, the pillar where St Marcian was martyred, and what is believed to be the first painting of St Lucia on the wall, dating back to the 4th century—a fine work of art. The friar on duty will conduct you through the **catacombs** used into the 6th century,

The Landolina Venus, Museum of Archaeology, Syracuse

which still retain traces of early Christian paintings. Back outside, numerous yellow signs show the way to the as yet unfinished **Sanctuary of the Madonnina delle Lacrime**, built to house a small factory-made statue of the Madonna which wept for five days in 1953. When finished, the sanctuary will resemble a grotesque, giant Christmas tree.

Archaeology Museum

Across Viale Teocrito from the sanctuary is the equally new Archaeology Museum, which finally opened its doors in 1988, housing perhaps the greatest hoard of Greek art between Athens and London; the collection's star exhibit is the notoriously voluptuous **Landolina Venus** (Landolina was the name of the archaeologist who found her); just as remarkable are the more maternal statue of an unknown fertility goddess suckling twins, and the sarcophagus of Valerius and Adelphia with its quaint biblical scenes. Also on exhibit are animal remains of prehistoric Sicily, finds from the Ionic and Doric periods of the Greek colonization, with some marvellous terracotta masks, beautiful painted vases and statues from the 5th century BC. Another section is devoted to the three sub-colonies of Syracuse—Akra, Kasmena and Kamarina, including some remarkable seated figures from the 6th century BC.

Archaeological Zone

The Archaeological Zone (open from 9 am until one hour before sunset, closed Mon and major holidays; adm) is in the quarter of Neopolis, that part of Syracuse built by Hieron II. The Spaniards in the 16th century rifled Neopolis for stone to build their walls, but the ruins are still very impressive, even the much-pilfered **Altar of Hieron II** (241–215 BC), over 180 m long, dedicated to Zeus Eleftherios. Hieron II built this altar in honour of Timoleon's expulsion of tyrants, which the ancient Syracusans commemorated annually with a great sacrifice. Although only the base of the altar remains, it does give one some idea of the magnitude of the public monuments built by the western Greeks.

This grandeur is also evident in the **Greek Theatre** carved out of the living rock. One of the largest in the world, it measures 138 m in diameter and seats 15,000. The original theatre, built by Timoleon, which saw the début of *The Persians* by Aeschylus, was enlarged by Hieron II and later partially reconstructed by the Romans, who staged gladiatorial matches there and, by flooding the orchestra, mock naval engagements (*naumachiae*). Along the top of the seats are inscriptions dedicating various parts of the theatre to Zeus and the family of Hieron II. As in ancient times, Greek dramas are still performed here in even-numbered years (apply to the Tourist Board for details).

Above the theatre runs a long terrace called the **Street of Tombs**, of mostly Byzantine graves. The largest niche is a *nymphaeum* built by Hieron II, where the waters of an ancient aqueduct still cascade. West of the theatre, the very ancient **Sanctuary of Apollo Temenites**, sacred since the 7th century BC, may be visited, along with the equally primitive **Linear Theatre** where the seats consist of 17 steps carved into the hillside.

East of the Greek Theatre is the luxuriant **Latomia del Paradiso** where the main attraction lies in the odd **Ear of Dionysius**, an artificial cavern 65 m long and 21 m high, of uncertain purpose, but known for its excellent acoustics. Caravaggio christened it after its ear-shaped entrance, although some have speculated that the tyrant Dionysius incarcerated political prisoners in here so that he could secretly listen to their conversations. Next to the cavern is the **Grotta dei Cordari**, the Ropemakers' Cave, where for centuries Syracusans made their ropes.

One enters through another gate (but with the same ticket) to the **Roman Amphitheatre** built in the 3rd century AD. Like the Greek Theatre, it is one of the largest of its kind, measuring 140 m across. From the corridor below the front seats, the wild beasts and gladiators would enter the arena, in the centre of which is a mysterious pit. The names of their wealthy owners can be seen inscribed on some of the seats.

Euryalus Castle and the Olympieion

One interesting short excursion from Syracuse (city bus 8 or 10) is to the **Euryalus Castle**; get off the bus in front of the Albergo della Gioventù (the youth hostel). The castle (open from 9 am until dusk; closed Mon), built on the Epipolae Ridge, was begun by Dionysius the Elder in the early 4th century BC, and later modified by Archimedes. Euryalus means 'broad nail' in Greek, and the castle defended the crucial inland supply route to Syracuse in times of siege. Three great trenches, connected by underground passages, were constructed to repulse the rapidly evolving machines of war. The castle with its five huge towers was only part of the vast 27-km-long system of defence designed by Dionysius; mysteriously, however, the defenders surrendered without a fight to the Roman Marcellus in 212 BC. The castle is the best preserved and most intriguing example of Greek defensive works in the world; it also affords an excellent view of the Syracusan plain below.

The **Olympieion**, the scant but picturesque ruins of a Doric temple of Olympian Zeus, can also be reached by buses 8 or 10. Still standing on the right bank of the River Cyane are two columns and part of the stylobate. From here one can walk to the source of the **Cyane** ('blue' in Greek), the river named after Persephone's nymph who wept so much at the goddess's abduction that she turned into a spring. Along the banks of the Cyane grows the exotic papyrus, reputedly a gift to Syracuse from the Hellenistic ruler

Ptolemy Philadelphus of Egypt. It grows wild nowhere else outside North Africa. If one has the time, a more leisurely way to visit the Olympieion and the Cyane is by punt (inquire at the Tourist Office or at the Marina for availability and price).

And when you've had your fill of ruins, consider a dip at one of many beaches to the south—**Pantanelli** being the closest, with the more organized **Lido Arenella, Fontane Bianche** and **Lido Sayonara** further on. Be warned, though—this is about as distant from 'getting away from it all' as you could manage. Fonte Bianche is a horrible, huge, noisy over-organized resort such as only the Italian seaside can produce: self-service cafés, lines of umbrellas, and above all a constant and deafening racket from pop music and people. You'll pay to park, swim, shower, use the loo and so on.

WHERE TO STAY   (tel prefix 0931)
Despite its role as one of the leading tourist centres in Sicily, Syracuse is not well endowed with good hotels. In Ortygia, the ***Grand Hotel**, Viale Mazzini 12 (tel 65 101), is the most comfortable, a fine old establishment with rooms for L55 000 with bath, less expensive without. Also pleasant, in a quiet garden setting, is the ***Grand Hotel Villa Politi**, Via M. Politi 2 (tel 32 100; L75 000). Best among the less expensive choices is the *Gran Bretagne**, near the Tirrenia dock at Via Savoia 21 (tel 68 765), where rooms are L36 000 without bath. There's a pleasant **youth hostel** by the Euryalus Castle on Via Epipoli 45 (tel 711 118), open all year, and a campsite (open April–Oct) at Fontane Bianche (tel 790 356). There are also two tourist villages: **Il Minareto** at Faro Castelluccio (tel 721 210, open Mar–Oct) and **Capo Passero** in Via Tagliamento (tel 842 030, open all year)

EATING OUT
Syracuse chefs boast of their *pasta fritta* (sweet balls of pasta covered with honey), *tonno alla marinara* (tuna fish with onions and spices), and stuffed artichokes. These dishes occasionally show up in the city's good selection of restaurants. For a taste of real Syracuse and Sicilian cooking try **Jonico a Rutta e Ciale**, Riviera Dionisio il Grande 194 (tel 66 639), where apart from traditional Sicilian pasta dishes they also have smoked pork belly and a choice of cheeses from Ragusa. This, with a lovely view from the terrace, and a mini ethnographic museum, at L45–60 000 (closed Tue). On Ortyga, **Archimede**, Via Gemmellaro 8 (tel 69 701), has wonderful seafood antipasti to start off a memorable meal of, perhaps, veal stew, and excellent desserts and wines (L30 000; closed Sun). Once *the* restaurant in Syracuse, the **Fratelli Bandiera**, Via G. Perno 6 (tel 65 021) has lost this accolade but it still provides a more varied selection of dishes than anywhere else in the city and is still worth a visit (L30 000). If pasta and seafood is taking its toll on your palate (and your purse) **La Pampas**, Via Gemmellaro 13, caters for carnivores. It's a charmingly rustic Argentinian-style restaurant where they cook the steak to your requirements (L20–30 000; closed Wed). Also on Ortygia there is **Minerva**, Piazza del Ducco 28, with pizza, mostly (L8000; closed Mon).

Inland from Syracuse: Palazzolo Acreide

West 44 km on the scenic SS124 (bus from Syracuse) is Palazzolo Acreide, modern successor of ancient Akrai, the first Syracusan colony, founded in 664 BC on a high hill.

Its ruins are the most extensive in the province after Syracuse itself: a 15-minute walk takes you there. The **Archaeology Zone** is open daily from 9 am to one hour before sunset. It includes a small (600-seat) but well preserved **Hellenistic theatre** with pleasant views; Roman silos and mills; the *bouleuterion* (council chamber); and the foundation of the *agora*. Behind the theatre are two quarries, or *latomiae*, the **Intagliata** and the **Intagliatella**, one containing Byzantine tombs, the other niches of the Hero cult, with a carved relief. Another *latomia*, more mysterious and 1 mile from the Archaeology Zone (note signposts), contains the **Templi Ferali** (temples of the dead), two great chambers with niches and inscriptions in honour of the deceased. Below, in an enclosure, are the *Santoni*—twelve rough-hewn statues representing various aspects of the goddess Cybele, a Phrygian deity. Her eastern origin may account for the very un-Greek repetition of the same figure in one place.

Palazzolo is a Baroque charmer with a complete lack of tourist facilities, but there is a museum, the **Casa Museo** on Via Machiavelli (open 10–1; closed Mon and Fri), with a fine ethnographic collection in a turn-of-the-century peasant home. Among the churches, note the asymmetrical *Chiesa dell' Annunziata*; the *Madonna with Child* by Laurano in the church of the **Convento dei Minori Osservanti**; and the exuberant Baroque interior of **San Paolo** in Piazza Umberto.

Another colony of Syracuse, **Casmene** (founded 644 BC), is located on top of Mt Casale, northwest of Palazzolo Acreide. The scenic river valleys around Casmene offer more than the excavations themselves, and the difficult access to the site makes it a destination for the adventuresome. **Buccheri**, the closest village to Mt Casale, is a modest summer resort, surrounded by forests and pretty views. Between Palazzolo and Syracuse lies another hill town, **Canicattini**, from where speleologists can visit the **Grotta del Monello**, or Monkey's Cave, with stalactites. The cemetery of Canicattini, set apart on a hill, is a true Baroque city of the dead.

Noto: Baroque's Ideal City

Alternatively, some 25 km south of Syracuse, you can visit a true, Baroque city desperately trying to stay alive. After passing a chain of beaches—**Lido Arenella, Ognina, Fontane Bianche, Lido di Avola**—where the deep blue of the sea is matched in intensity by the glistening green of the citrus groves, you arrive in **Noto** (pop. 22,500), set a few miles in from the coast. Not only in Sicily, but in the rest of Italy, Noto stands out as sharply as one of the magical towns described by Marco Polo in Italo Calvino's *Invisible Cities*; a new city, designed and built of golden sun-drenched tufa, in pure Sicilian Baroque, unabashedly theatrical, tacitly admitting in its set *piazze*, broad sweeping stairs, and the confectioner's façades of its churches and palaces that all life is indeed a stage. Sicilians call it a 'garden of stone'; then suddenly it was discovered that even a garden of stone could be in grave danger of total collapse.

Noto itself was born of destruction, when its parent, now called Noto Antico, fell prostrate in the great 1693 earthquake. The damage and loss of life were so great that the inhabitants had no desire to face the bleak ruins of their homes; instead they moved a few miles away and had the great priest-architect Rosario Gagliardi, Paolo Labisi, and Vincenzo Sinatra lay out a new street plan in accordance with the ideals of the early 18th century to set off their architecture, rational and symmetrical, with straight streets, stairs and sloping piazze to play perspective games with the eye. And when this Baroque paragon was finished, there was nothing more to do but sink discreetly into the national daydream and collect dust the way a housebound philatelist collects stamps from distant lands. The rude awakening occurred in September 1986, when a long-overdue structural survey discovered that Noto was so fragile that the slightest tremor of the earth would make it go down like a house of cards. Nuns were evacuated from convents, the Corso was closed to traffic, the museum hastily locked up. A conference was quickly called, and when the vote was yes to Noto, the tedious work of propping up the foundations of the city's monuments began—and is still underway.

TOURIST INFORMATION
Pro Loco, Piazza 16 Maggio (tel (0931) 836 744).

Walking in Noto
For the full effect, enter Noto through its monumental gate, the **Porta Reale** (1838) syphoning traffic down Noto's majestic main street, **Corso Vittorio Emanuele II**, which the planners placed along the flank of a hill, the better to build the wide ballroom stairs beloved of Sicilian Baroque. The Corso pierces three grandiose set-piece *piazze*. The first is adorned with the elliptical convent of **Santa Chiara** (attributed to Gagliardi), **San Francesco** (1745) at the top of the cascading steps, with the horizontal contrast of the monastery of **San Salvatore** (1703) running parallel to the stairway. The monastery houses the **Museo Archeologico**, housing an interesting collection of finds from Eloro and Noto Antica, but is at present closed for repairs and no one knows when it will re-open; it all depends on available funds.

The next square strung along the Corso, **Piazza Municipio**, is Noto's most important. Three flights of steps ascend to the monumental **Cathedral of San Nicola** (or **Corrado Confalonieri** as it is also known), named after the town's patron saint, with its twin bell towers, one of the last structures to be completed, in 1770; next to it stands the **Palazzo Vescovile**, and opposite, the beautiful, arcaded **Palazzo Ducezio** (the town hall), built in 1746 by Vincenzo Sinatra, the neo-classicist among Noto's architects. The effect is completed by another church, **San Salvatore**, and the **Palazzo Landolina di Sant'Alfano**. The Corso then enters a third square, **Piazza Sedici Maggio**, where a pretty little garden contains a fountain with a statue of Hercules salvaged from Noto Antica. Facing this is the **Teatro Vittorio Emanuele** (finished in 1842), and the beautiful convex façade of **San Domenico** (1727) by Gagliardi; adjacent is a former convent, now containing a library and municipal museum.

Off the Corso, you can seek out more works by Gagliardi: the concave church and collegio of the **Gesuiti** (1730s) and the **Church of the Carmine** (1743), a personal journey into the Rococo. Among the palaces, the **Palazzo Villadorata** (1737–60) on Via Nicolaci stands out, adorned with lovely wrought-iron balconies and curling Baroque grotesques. Up on the hill of Noto Alto, where the streets become increasingly austere, the principal monument is the church of **SS. Crocifisso** (early 1700s), a large basilica; inside is a statue of the *Madonna della Neve* (1471) by Francesco Laurana.

136

Around Noto

The meagre remains of **Noto Antica**, ancient Netum, lie some 20 km from Noto on Monte Alviano, off the road to Palazzolo. Founded according to tradition by the Sikel king Ducetius in the 5th century BC, Netum came under the rule of Syracuse, then of Rome. It was the only town to successfully resist the despoilations of the praetor Verres, and was also the last bastion of the Saracens before their surrender to the Normans in 1091. Never rebuilt after the earthquake, Noto Antica remains a wild, total ruin, which includes parts of a Norman castle, the gateway, churches and tombs (earliest of which are two Sikel necropoli excavated in the vicinity).

West of Noto Antica, **Castelluccio** was a prehistoric settlement, inhabited between the 18th and 14th centuries BC. The great archaeologist Paolo Orsi excavated the site and gave its name to the early Bronze Age culture of eastern and central Sicily. You can see the remains of the village and necropolis of Castelluccio, though all portable finds are now in the archaeology museum in Syracuse. More has survived of ancient **Eloro**, a few miles south of Noto. Founded by the Syracusans in the 7th century BC at the mouth of the River Tellaro, Eloro (ancient *Helorus*) has recently been excavated: at the entrance to the site stand the **Pizzota Column** (a Hellenistic funeral monument) and a **Sanctuary of Demeter and Kore**, both outside the well-preserved city **walls**. Within, a small theatre and the grandiose **stoa** of the 2nd century BC have been uncovered. Besides archaeological sites, a number of beaches can be easily reached from Noto: Noto Marina, Calabernardo, Marina di Avola, Lido di Avola. Further south and more isolated are Vendicari, Marzamemi and Pachino, which is heading for resort status after starting life as a simple fishing village, and likewise Portopalo di Capo Passero, a few kilometres south.

WHERE TO STAY AND EAT   (tel prefix 0931)
For an overnight sojourn Noto has one small pensione, the *Stella on Via F. Maiore 40 (tel 835 695; L35 000 with bath). At the trattoria **Il Giglio**, Piazza Municipio, you can expect some typical Sicilian dishes as well as the odd culinary surprise—the owner's wife is Spanish (L25 000). The trattoria **Carmine**, Via Ducezzio 9, is very much a family concern with wholesome fare for around L20 000. Down in Noto Marina the ***Eloro**, Loc. Eloro Pizzuta (tel 835 122), is large and has rooms for L80 000. Alternatively, the **Jonio, Viale Lido 1 (tel 812 040), is of more human proportions (L45 000). Avola has a couple of inexpensive pensioni—the *L'Ancora, Via Lungomare (tel 822 875; L34 000) and *Mignon, Via Maugeri 37 (tel 821 788) for about the same price. Of the few hotels in Portopalo di Capo Passero, the **Jonic , Viale V. Emmanuele 19 (tel 842 615), has rooms with bath for L42 000.

South of Noto

Continuing to the extreme southeast corner of Sicily, where the Ionian and Mediterranean Seas meet, are the lovely remote beaches of **Porto Palo** and **Marzamemi**. Just north of Pachino, at the farm **San Lorenzo lo Vecchio**, the skeleton of a Hellenistic temple transformed into a Byzantine church may be seen incorporated into the farm buildings. **Rosolini**, further west, has to be one of the ugliest, dustiest little nowheres in Italy, but even it has an interesting site. Beneath the **Castello del Principe** (1668) are catacombs and an early Christian basilica or crypt, with three irregular naves carved out of the rock.

Cava d'Ispica

Five km from Rosolino, **Ispica,** known as 'Spacca' in the Middle Ages, is the last resting place of the painter Sozzi (died 1765), buried in the church of **Santa Maria Maggiore** which is decorated with his frescoes. Like many of the surrounding towns, Ispica was destroyed in the earthquake of 1693 but, phoenix-like, re-emerged to become a busy agricultural centre. Between Ispica and Mòdica is the **Cava d'Ispica** (signposted and always open), a gentle 14-km-long gorge in rugged country, fascinating for its signs of continuous habitation from the Bronze Age right up to the 18th century. Throughout the length of the gorge are catacombs and cave dwellings carved in the rock face, silent testimonies of hardship and courage, dating mostly from between the 5th and 13th centuries. **Pozzallo,** south of Ispica, was the port for Ragusa and has a 14th-century tower and a fine wide sandy beach which is often empty, even in summer.

Mòdica

Mòdica was the old capital of the county of Mòdica (now the province of Ragusa). However, rather than being built on the surrounding hills, the town is situated in a deep valley: the town's defence depended not on fortifications but on the potential for guerrilla warfare once an invader arrived. In ancient times it was an important agricultural market centre, and its population grew steadily until at the beginning of the 18th century it was the fourth largest city in Sicily. The torrents that pass through Mòdica flooded the town in 1902, following which the rivers have been all but covered over. Mòdica may no longer be 'the Venice of Sicily' but it is still a lovely town where the houses on the hills peer discreetly over the shoulders of their neighbours, and many of the streets are stairways. It gave the world the now obscure 1959 Nobel prizewinner for literature, Salvatore Quasimodo.

Mòdica consists of two towns, the upper and the lower. In the lower town are the main shopping streets, the bus stop, etc., and the church of **Santa Maria di Betlem** where the highest point of the great flood is marked by a plaque. **Mòdica Alta,** the upper town is dominated by the 18th-century church of **San Giorgio,** reminiscent of San Giorgio in Ragusa, and perhaps also designed by Gagliardi. Dominated by its huge central spire, the church has a beautiful ornate façade, beckoning at the summit of a monstrous Baroque stair of 250 steps. The old conventual church on top of Mòdica Alta, **Santa Maria di Gesù,** now houses a prison, of all things. The **Cathedral San Pietro** and the 15th-century **church of the Carmine,** also in the upper town, offer other examples of the local style of architecture.

Ragusa

Ragusa (pop. 60,000) is one of the most picturesque and typical hill towns in Sicily, with its decaying, flamboyant Baroque buildings hugging the sides, its slow pace of life and lack of tourists. Set in a rugged, dry landscape of winding maze-like stone walls, carobs and olives, scented with the wild mint, rosemary, and lemon balm that lend a delicate taste to the local honey praised by Pliny, Ragusa's colours, grey and austere, become subtle and quietly beautiful as the eye adjusts; 'it needs patience and love to be understood and accepted', wrote Nobel laureate Quasimodo.

The most exciting thing to do in Ragusa is to take the hair-raising bus from the new part of town, Ragusa Superiore, to the ancient hilltop island of Ragusa Ibla, plunging down narrow winding streets, the busdriver cursing in the front and the conductor acting as navigator in the rear. Yet just past **Santa Maria delle Scale**, the marvellous panorama opens up of old Ibla, crowned by the dome of San Giorgio, sanctum of Ragusa's patron. For more thrills, come back on the last Sunday of April with a pageant presenting scenes and people from St George's life: his fight with the dragon, Emperor Diocletian, the sorcerer Atanasio, accompanied by allegorical figures of Hunger, War, and Faith.

History

The town of Ragusa, perched atop a hilly ridge, is divided into two parts, the lower of which—Ragusa Ibla—was the site of the original Sikel town of Hybla Heraea, one of their major settlements. Conquered by the Greeks and Romans in 258 BC, Hybla Heraea declined, only regaining some of its former importance when Count Roger created the County of Ragusa for his son in 1091, although in 1296 Manfred Chiaramonte incorporated it into the powerful County of Mòdica. This became the most powerful fiefdom in Sicily. Later kings rued its semi-independence under the counts of Chiaramonte, Cabrera and Henriquez–Cabrera, who only begrudgingly tipped their hats to Palermo and paid their tribute only when the king's army came to collect it. This state of affairs lasted into the 18th century, and was rather more benevolent to the local population than might at first be thought, with its unique set of laws uniting townsmen and farmers in a common cause, such as the reconstruction of towns after the earthquake. After the 1693 earthquake, work was begun on Upper Ragusa, which remained a separate town from Ibla—and its main rival—until they were united in 1926 when Ragusa became the provincial capital. Despite being a centre for asphalt production, since the war Ragusa has become a city of great charm.

GETTING AROUND

From Catania the fastest route to Ragusa is route 594; if you're driving from Syracuse, Gela, or Agrigento, take the hilly prickly pear route SS115.
By rail: to and from Syracuse and Licata daily (Stazione at Piazza del Popolo).
By bus: from Piazza del Popolo to Syracuse, Agrigento, Palermo, Gela and all other towns in the province. City buses no. 1 and 3 link Ragusa Superiore's Piazza del Popolo with Ragusa Ibla.

TOURIST INFORMATION

Via Natalelli 131, in the Palazzo Camera di Commercio (tel (0932) 21 421).

Ragusa Superiore

Ragusa Superiore is the address of most of the city's businesses, as well as the **Archaeology Museum** (open 9–2, holidays 9–1; closed Mon), located in the Palazzo Mediterraneo, on Via Natelelli. The museum contains a chronologically arranged collection of artefacts from the province, especially from the important Syracusan colony of Camarina: well-preserved painted vases of the 6th century BC imported from Attica, terracotta figurines, especially of the goddess Demeter in her flower-pot hat, the mosaic pavement of an Early Christian church, decorated with animals. From the museum, Via Roma leads to Piazza San Giovanni, site of the large Baroque **Cathedral of San Giovanni Battista** with its imposing campanile; inside, note the richly ornate stucco decorations in the interior of the cupola and an 18th-century terracotta *presepio*.

High on the isthmus dividing Ragusa Superiore from Ragusa Ibla stands the 15th-century **church of Santa Maria delle Scale** ('of the stairs'), one of the few buildings to survive the earthquake, though reworked in the 17th century. Of the original, the portal and pulpit beneath the campanile remain; a 16th-century bas relief inside is a work of the prolific Gagini. There are fine views from the church terrace and a choice of routes to Ibla, the 242 steps below the church or Corso Mazzini; fortunately the bus takes the latter.

Ragusa Ibla

In Ibla's narrow lanes and midget squares, the genteelly dilapidated palaces more often than not serve as planters for weeds and wild flowers; little Baroque monsters lurk just under the balconies and roofs. Crowning all is the high-domed, high-fronted master-piece of Rosario Gagliardi of Noto, the Basilica of **San Giorgio** (1738). One of the finest examples of Sicilian Baroque, its elegantly vertical convex façade is perfectly sited on a curving stair above the palm-lined Piazza del Duomo: although the interior is quite plain, the cathedral treasure, which includes Byzantine religious items dating back to the 7th century, may be seen on request. Down Corso XXV Aprile from San Giorgio, there's another fine church with a convex façade attributed to Gagliardi or an imitator, **San Giuseppe**.

The magnificent 15th-century portal of the original Gothic–Catalan **San Giorgio**, which collapsed in the earthquake, can be seen at the end of the Corso; in the lunette there's a weathered relief of St George and the dragon. Also on the Corso, **Palazzo Donnafugata** contains a number of works of art, including paintings attributed to Antonello da Messina and Ribera, and Sicilian ceramics. At the eastern end of the Corso and Ibla is the **Giardino Ibleo**, with views down the Valle dell'Irminio towards the sea.

Excursions from Ragusa

Short excursions from Mòdica or Ragusa are to the **Trabacche Cave** (11 km from Ragusa) with its large 4th-century catacombs, and to the south (take the train from Ragusa) the **Villa of Donnafugata** can be visited on request of the owners. If the name Donnafugata rings a bell, remember that Tomasi Giuseppe di Lampedusa borrowed it as the major setting for his novel, *The Leopard.* The closest beaches are Punta Secca, Randello, and the Ragusa and Mòdica Marinas.

Camarina

On the coast west of Ragusa Marina, Camarina was a Syracusan colony, founded in 598 BC. One of the Greeks' most important outposts, it was alternately destroyed and rebuilt by Gela, Syracuse and Carthage, and finally put out of its misery by the Romans in 258 BC. Little remains of Camarina, though the foundations of a 5th-century Temple of Athena can be made out, and the grid-pattern street plan and part of the wall. The necropolis, dating back to the 6th century, yielded many interesting objects, some of which are in Ragusa and others in the small museum on the acropolis (open 9–1; closed Mon).

Despite its name, **Chiaramonte Gulfi** is an inland village north of Ragusa, famous in Sicily for its food. Specialities include goats' cheese with peppers (*pecorino*), pork galantine, stuffed pork chops, roast lamb, salami and olive oil. The town sits on a hill and from the **public gardens** you can look down in the valley and see Comiso, Vittoria, Caltagirone, the beach at Gela and (on a clear day) Etna in the distance. For this view the town is known as the 'balcony of Sicily'. From Mòdica, a by-road leads to **Scicli**, small and Baroque, where the road forks for the beaches at Donnalucata, Cava d'Aliga and Sampieri.

WHERE TO STAY   (tel prefix 0932)
In town, the ***Montreal on Via San Giuseppe 10 (tel 21 133) is the most comfortable place to stay (rooms for L40–44 000, air conditioning available; always open). If it's full, try the *****Mediterraneo**, Via Roma 189 (tel 21 944; rooms L35 000, depending on the room). The only place cheaper is the ****Tivoli**, Via G. D'Annuzio 60 (tel 24 885; L20 000; rooms with bath extra). Near the sea west of Marina di Ragusa, the summer holiday centre of **Camarina** (tel 911 719), set in a pine grove, has swimming pools, tennis courts, and a riding area; there are three campsites near Camarina.

EATING OUT
Ragusa specialities are Caciocavallo cheese and *pecorino* (goats' cheese with pepper). Local wines include *Ambrato* and *Cervasuolo*. Ragusa does better with its restaurants than its hotels. **Fumia** at 23 Cappuchini is the best in town, with Italian fare for around L30 000. In Ibla, **U Satacinu** on Via Convento specializes in Sicilian dishes for slightly less. **Orfeo** in Upper Ragusa, at Via Sant'Anna 117 (tel 21 035), is a popular lunch spot, with meals around L15 000 and free TV entertainment. Least expensive is **Biffi** on Via Lupis, with typical trattoria fare. If you have a car, you may want to go to the **Osteria del Braciere**, a local favourite in the village of San Giacomo northeast of Ragusa, where the good food is plentiful and inexpensive (around L25 000). Five km along the road to Marina di Ragusa is **Villa Fortugno** (tel 28 656), a restaurant serving *salsicce alla siciliana* and *cavatelli al sugo di maiale*

Còmiso and Vittoria

West of Ragusa, after a stunning descent from the Iblean Hills, the road leads into the more fertile lands of Còmiso and Vittoria. Attractive, unheralded **Còmiso**, on the Ippari river (pop. 27,000), another town that had to be rebuilt after 1693, was ruled by the Naselli d'Aragona from the 15th–18th centuries; their 14th-century **Castello** has recently been restored. Near the town centre in the Piazza delle Erbe, the church of **San Francesco** (finished 1478) contains the **Cappella Naselli** and the sepulchre of Count Gaspare Naselli by Antonello Gagini, one of his finest tombs. Just off the piazza is an interesting 19th-century market—Còmiso is an agricultural centre. But Baroque is the dominant note in the town's palazzi and churches, especially the 17th-century **S. Maria delle Stelle** with its tall narrow dome, echoed by a similar dome crowning the vast **Basilica dell'Annunziata**. The Fonte Diana once supplied water for the Roman baths, now under the Municipio; in the library you can see a surviving mosaic. Còmiso's high vines produce excellent table grapes and *l'ambrato* wine.

Neighbouring **Vittoria** (pop. 47,000), city of peaches and spring produce, was named after its 1607 foundress, the daughter of a viceroy. Although the rest of the town isn't much to write home about, Vittoria has two elegant piazze, surrounded by Baroque and neo-classical buildings, especially the one containing the handsome church of **Madonna delle Grazie** and the adjacent neo-classical **Teatro Comunale**. which Berenson, in his *Trip to Sicily*, described as 'one of the best European theatres in this style'. **Scoglitti**, some 16 km away on the coast, with a pleasant wide beach, a few restaurants and one hotel, is the beginning of the 'Gela Riviera'.

The North Coast: Messina to Trapani

From the Arab–Norman–Spanish marriage that produced Palermo to the brilliant seas and sands of modern resorts like Cefalù, the northern coast from Messina to Trapani provides a bewildering variety of places to visit. Its popular beaches, some reached by secret little rocky paths, run a full 180 km and are framed, a few miles inland, by the Madonie mountains, whose gentle oak-covered slopes rise to a height of 2000 m. Rich in folklore and handicrafts and renowned for its wines, this part of the island is becoming a holiday favourite. It has enough diversity to suit all—from its shimmering seas and beaches, to its Norman monuments and bold Baroque villas.

Milazzo

In the centre of a narrow promontory, Milazzo is the main port for the Aeolian Islands, and one of the busiest in Sicily, with the island's largest single industry—a huge oil refinery. It's a pleasant town to stroll around and enjoy a *granita* in one of the numerous cafés while you're waiting for your island connection. Colonized by Greeks from Messina in 716 BC, Mylai, as it was then called, was the scene of Duilius' victory at sea over the Carthaginians in 260 BC and Garibaldi's victory over the Bourbons in 1860, which all but cemented the 'Risorgimento' in Sicily.

GETTING AROUND
The railway station in Milazzo is within easy walking distance of the port for the Aeolian Islands; the Giunta bus from Messina stops right in front of the hydrofoils. From Milazzo a good road leads to the tip of the cape, where there is a tourist restaurant (with unusable loos) and a fine view of the islands and the Sicilian coast.

The Castle
The castle on Mylai's acropolis is the main attraction in Milazzo, originally built by Frederick II in 1239, enlarged by Charles V, then restored in the 17th century. The Gothic door is very fine. Inside the castle walls, the domed **Duomo Vecchio** belongs to the 16th century but is being replaced by a new church. The old prison, **Palazzo dei Durati**, dates back to the 15th century.

The Nebrodi Mountains

Some of the towns in the Nebrodi Mountains merit a visit, including **Mistretta** (ancient *Amestratus*), dominated by its castle. The parish church of **Santa Lucia**, though reno-

142

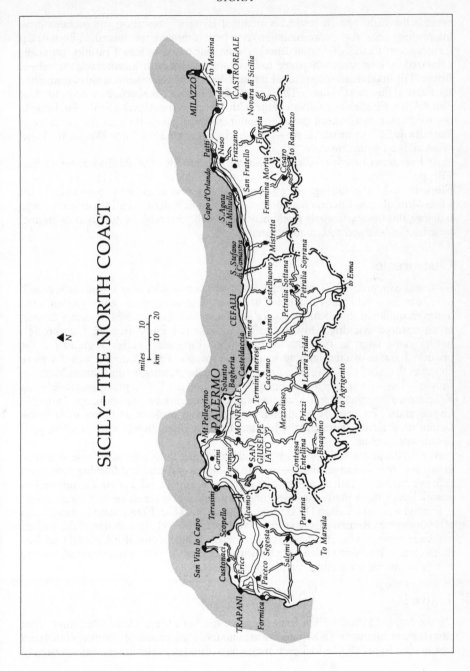

SICILY– THE NORTH COAST

N

miles 10
km   10   20

MILAZZO
to Messina
Tindari
CASTROREALE
Novara di Sicilia
Naso
Patti
Frazzano
Floresta
Capo d'Orlando
San Fratello
Femmina Morta
Cesaro
to Randazzo
S.Agata di Militello
S. Stefano di Camastra
Mistretta
CEFALÙ
Castelbuono
Petralia Soprana
Collesano
Petralia Sottana
to Enna
Imera
Mt Pellegrino
PALERMO
Bagheria
Soluntum
Casteldaccia
Termini Imerese
Caccamo
Lecara Friddi
Mezzojuso
Prizzi
MONREALE
SAN GIUSEPPE IATO
Carini
Partinico
Terrasini
Scopello
San Vito lo Capo
Custonaci
Contessa Entellina
Bisaquino
to Agrigento
Alcamo
Erice
Segesta
Partana
Custonaci
Paceco
Salemi
TRAPANI
Formica
To Marsala

vated in the 17th century, retains its medieval-fortress appearance, and contains some interesting works. A popular excursion from here is through the watershed Portella del Contrasto to Castel di Lucio. Another mountain town is **San Fratello**, originally colonized by Lombards who came to Sicily with Adelaide di Monferrato, the wife of Roger. The inhabitants still speak a Lombard dialect and retain various old customs, like the Feast of the Jews (Maundy Thursday/Good Friday). The simple Norman church of **Santi Alfio, Filadelfio e Cirino** of the 12th century is quite lovely. From San Fratello the road south to **Cesarco** (another mountain town) passes through the picturesque **Portella della Femmina Morta**—though why it is named 'the Little Door of the Dead Woman' is a Sicilian mystery.

At **Frazzanco** south of Capo d'Orlando, you can visit the Basilian abbey of **San Filippo di Fragala**, built in the 11th century. South of here (SS116 from Naso) is **Floresta**, at 1220 m the highest town on the island, remote and grey, dominated by Mt Etna. **Montalbano Elicona** has another example of Frederick II's 14th-century castle building, this one particularly monumental and well preserved. In its chapel its original frescoes can be discerned, though faintly.

Castroreale

Castroreale (pop. 8500), 10 km from Milazzo, was named after after a royal castle rebuilt in 1324 by the other Fred, Frederick II of Aragon, who spent a good deal of his time here; however, unlike his Swabian namesake's building, little has survived beyond a stumpy, much restored cylindrical **tower** and the oft-restored **Porta Raneri**. Castroreale's heyday came later, in the 16th century, when Emperor Charles V granted it the privileged status of city, igniting in the townspeople a fierce desire to build more churches than they could ever fill . Among the more interesting are the **Chiesa Matrice**, with its robust and crenellated campanile, restored in the 17th century but retaining its Renaissance interior, with a Madonna and St Catherine of Alexandria by Antonello Gagini, and a 17th-century inlaid choir among its many works of art. Other works by the Gagini are in **Sant' Agata** and the **Immacolata**, the latter church adorned with a good Renaissance ceiling.

Most of the people who spend any time in Castroreale these days have come to indulge in two favourite Italian pastimes—soaking in therapeutic mud and flushing their livers with mineral water, both in the coastal **Castroreale Terme** and **Terme Vigliatore**, just inland, both spas in shady garden settings and linked to Castroreale by a scenic road.

Further west on the coast (19 km from Milazzo), near **San Biagio** station, the remains of a 4th-century Roman villa have been excavated; they include a section of the ancient baths and some mosaics, the best of which shows a fishing scene. **Rodi**, inland from San Biagio, was a flourishing Sikel town known as *Longane*. As yet it is unexcavated, but you can make out the walls and a temple foundation.

Tindari

On the Capo Tindari, 65 km from Messina, the **Sanctuario della Madonna Nera** attracts many pilgrims on 8 September in honour of a miraculous Byzantine black-faced icon of the Virgin. This little church stands on a place long holy, the ancient acropolis of

Tyndaris. Founded by Dionysius of Syracuse in 396 BC, Tyndaris was born a garrison town to protect Sicily's north coast from the Carthaginians. Dionysius named the town after the *Tyndaridae* (another name for the Dioscuri, the twins Castor and Pollux), traditional battle gods worshipped by the colonists, who were mainly refugees from the Peloponnesian War. Although captured by Carthage in 264 BC during the First Punic War and used as an important naval base, Tindari was regained by Rome 10 years later. The Romans made the town one of Sicily's five colonies, and it prospered into the Christian era, when it became the seat of a diocese. All was demolished by the Arabs in 836, and when it was safe enough to re-establish a settlement on the coast, Roger I chose the present site of Patti.

The Archaeological Zone
The extensive excavations of Tindari (open daily 9–12 and 3–6) have revealed a large **Theatre** of the late 4th century BC, adapted and enlarged by the decadent Romans for gladiatorial contests and wild animal 'hunts', or *venationes*, requiring a corridor between the spectators and the dangerous activities in the ring. Like the theatre of Taormina, Tindari's belies past atrocities with a magnificent permanent stage set, including the Aeolian Islands and on a clear day, Mt Etna. In June it's used for performances of Classical drama. Some of the stone from the theatre was quarried in the late Roman and Byzantine eras to fortify the exceptional **walls and towers**, among the best and most impressive in all Sicily.

Along the *cardus* are the ruins of houses, some with mosaics; one, a mansion of the 1st century BC, has retained sections of the peristyle of the *atrium*, the *triclinium*, and the *impluvium*, where the residents saved precious rainwater. The *decumanus* leads towards the mighty arches of the partially restored **basilica** or *propylaea* (entrance) to the vast *agora*; originally a great vaulted gallery with nine arches, its massive stones were cannibalized in later years for the all-important walls—further fortifications, with the main gate and barbican, can be seen at the opposite side of town. On the *decumanus*, between the theatre and the basilica, is an **antiquarium** containing statues, including a massive head of Augustus, theatre masks, terracotta figurines, Roman glass, and an assortment of headless statues in togas. Although the Christians must share some of the blame for their decapitation, chances are they were first sculpted this way; just as the chairmen of the Communist Party tend to blackball their predecessors, provincial Romans would literally knock off the block of a dead governor or emperor and replace it with a politically correct head sent from Rome's busy bust factories.

Tindari to Cefalù

A number of small resorts dot the Tyrrhenian coast from Tindari to the west. The hilltop town of **Patti**, the main base for visiting the ruins of Tindari, has gone down in the annals for having been burned twice, by Frederick II of Aragon for its loyalty to the Angevins, and by Barbarossa in 1544, as part of a pirate's day's work. At the highest point of Patti stands the 18th-century **Cattedrale di San Bartolomeo**, of interest for the **sarcophagus of Adelasia**, the wife of Roger I, who died in 1118. There is a fine beach below at **Marina di Patti**.

Gioiosa Marea, Brolo, and Capo d'Orlando are popular Italian resorts with camp-sites near sandy beaches. **Brolo** is dominated by a distinctive medieval tower, and on **Capo d'Orlando's** sea-swept promontory is the 14th-century castle where Roger of Lauria, with the fleets of Catalonia and Anjou to back him up, defeated Frederick II; the church next to it dates from 1598. Capo d'Orlando has a unique beach at **San Gregorio**, the fine sand strewn with odd-shaped boulders. Oddly named **Naso** ('nose'), a small village about a mile inland, has a beautiful 15th-century church, the **Minori Osservanti** located just outside the town. Built partly in Gothic and Renaissance styles, it contains the tomb of Artale Cardona (died 1477) with allegories of the six virtues. The rosary chapel of Naso's parish church also has many works of art inside, belonging to the 14th and 15th centuries.

Sant'Agata Militello is one of the most important resorts on the north coast. From here you can visit pretty **San Marco d'Alunzio** (ancient *Aleuntine*), where Robert Guiscard built the first Norman castle in Sicily back in 1061, now in ruins. The roofless church of **San Marco** was built on the site of a temple of Hercules (you can see the ancient *cella*). One of the smaller resorts, **Castel di Tusa**, is near ancient *Halesa*, founded in the 5th century BC by Archonides of Herbita, a Sikel. The Romans granted Halesa special privileges in return for its loyalty in the First Punic War. Excavations of Halesa (open daily, 9 am to sunset), still in progress, have unearthed its grid street plan, part of the *agora*, walls and the remains of two temples. There are a few interesting churches in Castel di Tusa itself, notably the **Chiesa Matrice** with its medieval campanile and Gothic door, and the 14th-century church of **San Nicola**.

TOURIST INFORMATION

At Capo d'Orlando, Pro Loco, Via V. Veneto 54 (tel (0941) 902 471).

WHERE TO STAY AND EAT

Castroreale (tel prefix 090): Serving the baths in luxury, the ******Grand Hotel delle Terme**, Via Stabilimento has a garden and tennis court (tel 978 1078; L78 000). With its own beach is the ***Lido Marchesano**, in Via Marchesana (tel 978 1211; L26 000 with bath). There is also a **youth hostel** at Castroreale, on Via Federico II d'Aragona (open all year; L7000).

Patti Marina (tel prefix 0941): The recently rennovated *****Hotel La Playa**, Via Playa (tel 361 319), has a pool and most other up-to-date comforts and is on the beach (L65 000).

At Capo d'Orlando (tel prefix 0941) there's a good choice; on the beach and with its own pool *****La Tartaruga**, Lido S. Gregorio (tel 955 013; L55–70 000), which has an excellent restaurant serving *bottarga, pasta marinara*, superb fish and desserts (L25–30 000); *****Il Mulino**, Via A. Doria 46, also with a pool (tel 902 431), L55–70 000; the ****Bristol**, Via Umberto 37 (tel 901 390; L45 000 with bath) and the ***Piave**, Via Piave 125 is simple and cheap (tel 31 203; L35 000 with bath). Another excellent restaurant is **Il Gabbiano**, Via Trazzera Marina 146 (tel 961 065) where the menu is mostly fish, but they also have the standard meat dishes *bistecca, vitello arrosto* and pizza (L20–25 000, half that for a pizza meal).

146

Cefalù

Of all the seaside resorts that have popped up along the coast, Cefalù, the loveliest, is increasingly popular as an international holiday spot, with its Club Méditerranée and the occasional English paper in the kiosks. The dramatic site of the ancient Sikel town of Cephaloedium, Cefalù was settled in the 9th century BC, and later became a fortified outpost of Imera. The name comes from the craggy rock resembling a head (*cephalus*) that overlooks the town. Never large, Cefalù had been continuously inhabited before the arrival of the Normans, who used some of the stone from its ancient walls to build the Cathedral—one of the most magnificent in Sicily.

GETTING AROUND
Cefalù lies on the main bus and train routes from Palermo to Messina, from which there are frequent daily connections. In summer there is a hydrofoil service to the Aeolian islands of Lipari and Vulcano.

TOURIST INFORMATION
Via Amendola 2 (tel (0921) 21050).

The Cathedral
Founded by Roger II in 1131, in thanksgiving for his safe landing after a storm at sea, Cefalù's cathedral took 100 years to finish and was consecrated by a certain Monsignor Chat, whose arms of a cat rampant can still be seen. The façade designed in 1240 by Giovanni Panettera is very fine, but better are the Norman decorations on the east end and the three apses which are earlier. Inside, the long nave, with 16 Roman columns leading up to the altar and presbytery, the oldest part of the church, is decorated with the oldest Norman mosaics in Sicily (1148). By Byzantine artists, these seem quite oriental in comparison with the later ones in Palermo and Monreale; the depictions of Christ Pantocrator and the Virgin are excellent, and the former is considered one of the greatest portrayals of Christ in the world. The Madonna in a chapel by the choir is by Antonello Gagini.

Cefalù Cathedral, Palermo Province

147

On the rock above the cathedral (path above Piazza Garibaldi) the nimble visitor can explore the Arabian and feudal fortifications and the odd megalithic structure of trapezoidal blocks known as the **Temple of Diana** of prehistoric origin with modifications from the 5th century BC. Its purpose is a mystery, although with its splendid views some scholars believe it might have been a simple watchtower.

Museo Mandralisca
On Via Mandralisca is the private Museo Mandralisca (open 10.30–12.30 and 4.30–6.30 on weekdays; adm). Besides many local finds, the museum houses the *Portrait of an Unknown Man* by Antonello da Messina; if you've spent any time at all on the island, you may agree with the critics that it portrays the archetypal Sicilian, sensuous and cunning. Also of interest are the vases from the island of Lipari (one depicting a scene in an ancient fish market), a fine coin collection, Chinese boxes and other items collected by Enrico Piraino di Mandralisca. Towards the sea on Via Mandralisca are the medieval or **Arabic washrooms** at the foot of a curving stair, where the women of Cefalù did their wash in a picturesque arcade. The **Osterio Magno** a Norman palace at the corner of Via Amendola and Corso Ruggero, has beautiful arched windows with weeds growing out of them—as they do everywhere else in Sicily.

Although Cefalù is a growing resort (and one of the few places in Sicily where you'll come across British holidaymakers in any numbers) with beaches, a Club Méditerranée and various hotels and restaurants at Santa Lucia and Caldusa on either side of the Rock, it is still very much a fishing village. The arms of the town depict three fish holding a loaf on their noses. Fish is of course a speciality and the day's catch may be sampled in the many restaurants facing the sea on the Grand Promenade, or Lungomare.

WHERE TO STAY
(tel prefix 0921)

There are a number of hotels in town and spread out along the beaches to Santa Lucia in the west and Caldura in the east. One of the many with a beach, *****Baia del Capitano** at Mazzaforno (tel 20 005; L80 000 with bath), is in an olive grove. In Santa Lucia, the *****Santa Lucia** (tel 21 340) is a slightly less expensive alternative at L70 000. In Cefalù itself there's the *****Santa Dominga**, Via Gibilmanna 18 (tel 22 581; L68 000 considerably less in low season), which has the beach just outside its door, and if you're watching pennies the locanda ***Cangelosi**, Via Umberto I 26 (tel 21 591), has rooms without bath for L18 000.

EATING OUT
Cefalù, famous for its delicious seafood, offers a host of restaurants and trattorias to pick from. The keen competition keeps the standard high and you can expect a fine range of antipasti, main dishes and pizza. Particularly good are **Il Gabbiano** (tel 21 495) and, in a garden setting, **Da Nino** (tel 22 582), both on Lungomare G. Giardina, and **Al Gambero** (where you may come across emigrés from the Club Med.) at Via Vittorio Emmanuele 77; prices at all three are pretty regular, so expect to pay L25–35 000 for a full-blown fish meal, appreciably less if you opt for meat, of course, and around L10 000 for pizza.

South of Cefalù

The stretch of coast from here to the west was usually in ancient times the territory of the Carthaginians, but they left few souvenirs of their passing between the Madonie Mountains and the Tyrrhenian Sea. These mountains, especially at the eastern end of the province, are high enough (many over 1830 m) to have winter sports facilities. The villages of the province have some of the prettiest folk costumes in Sicily, which are on show at the summer festivals, particularly in the mountains in August.

South 9 km of Cefalù is the **Sanctuary of Gibilmanna** on a hill called 'Gibel el Iman' ('The Mount of Faith') by the Arabs, after they witnessed a miracle by the Madonna there, now the site of an annual pilgrimage (8 September).

From Cefalù SS286 heads south to **Castelbuono** in the Madonie Mountains. The castle here, built in 1289, was the seat of the powerful Ventimiglia princes of Geraci, the rivals of the Chiaramonte family. The main square, with a pretty fountain, has the 1350 **Matrice Vecchia** with frescoes and other artworks; **San Francesco** contains the Ventimiglia chapel and tombs.

Another castle of the Ventimiglia family stands in **Geraci Siculo** to the south, this one built in the 11th century; the local church of **Santa Maria della Porta** contains a *Madonna and Child* sculpted by Domenico Gagini. South of here the highway forks off, east to **Gangi** and west to Petralia. Gangi was the birthplace of the artist Zoppo Gancia, who painted a Michelangelo-inspired *Last Judgement* in the church of **San Nicola**; its lovely campanile was built in the 14th century.

The Two Petralias

There are two towns: **Petralia Sottana** (lower) and **Petralia Soprana** (upper). Hardly low at 1000 m, Sottana boasts many lovely churches in a variety of styles, in particular the **Chiesa Madre** with paintings by Zoppo Gancia and a fine belfry. In August the interesting festival of the Madonna dell' Alto takes place in the streets here, with a nocturnal procession on horseback and the Ballo della Cordella, an ancient dance. Some 150 m above Sottana, Petralia Soprana has become a major summer and winter resort. The sculptor of crucifixes, Fra Umile Pintorno, was born here in the 15th century and the Convento dei Minori Riformati contains an example of his art. Also notable is the 18th-century **Santa Maria di Loreto** with its two 14th-century campaniles adorned with colourful majolica tiles.

To the north, another picturesque old town, **Polizzi Generosa**—no, it does not mean 'Generous Policeman'—is more than generously endowed with churches. The best of these, the **Chiesa Madre**, houses a Flemish triptych, a Venetian organ and sculptures salvaged from other churches. Off the highway, the most ancient section of **Caltavuturo** (pop. 7000) perches beneath a Saracen castle, Kalat-Abi-Thur, captured by Roger I; called Terra Vecchia, it's as picturesque as it is jumbly, and nearly all the streets consist of stairs. The new village dates from the 16th and 17th centuries; in **Santa Maria di Gesù** hangs one of Fra'Umile's wooden crucifixes.

Imera

Imera, up on the coast near Buonfornello, was founded by Zancle (Messina) in 678 BC and was the home of the lyric poet Stesichorus, whose destiny was foretold as a child, when a nightingale alighted on his lips and sang. In 480 BC, the Greeks of Syracuse and Akragas defeated Hamilcar and an enormous force of Carthaginians in a decisive battle at Imera, winning great spoils and a measure of security; in honour of their victory, they erected a temple on the bank of the Fiume Grande. However, some 70 years later, Hamilcar's nephew Hannibal (not the one who worried Rome, but an ancestor) took revenge on the Greeks by demolishing Imera, slaying many of its inhabitants and sending the survivors as slaves to the Carthaginian town of Therma Himeraia (Tèrmini Imerese). Imera was never rebuilt. The large base (62 by 25 m), ruined *cella* and drums of the columns of the **Doric Temple of Victory**, perhaps dedicated to Zeus Eleftherios, stand outside the ancient walls, between the modern road and the railway. The elaborate lion-headed masks that once embellished the temple are now in the Palermo museum. In a sacred area in the city walls, excavations in 1963 uncovered remnants of temples of the 7th, 6th and 5th centuries BC, tombs, paved streets, and homes.

True warriors, it is said, have a sixth sense when it comes to old battlefields. While the Allies were fighting for Imera in 1943, the ghosts of the Carthaginians and Greeks rose up out of the ground and refought the Battle of Himera for the benefit of General Patton.

Tèrmini Imerese

East of Trabia and overlooking a gulf of the same name, Tèrmini Imerese (*Thermae Himerenses*) was a colony of neighbouring Himera. Unlike the mother city, however, Tèrmini thrived under the Romans, partly due to its mineral springs, a treatment for arthritis, which may still be drunk at the spa; according to the Italians, who get easily obsessed, the good water is the reason why Tèrmini produces its good pasta. The town is divided into two levels; in **Città Bassa** (the 'lower city') by the station are the ruins of the **Roman baths**; marbled pools, a large **Amphitheatre**, and a temple dedicated to Hercules.

In the attractive **Città Alta** ('upper city') Tèrmini's lumbering 17th-century **Cathedral** was designed to fit four early 16th-century statues on its façade and a cornice from a Roman house into the campanile. The church of **Santa Maria della Misericordia** houses a magnificent *triptych of the Madonna, St John and St Michael* (1453), attributed to Gaspare da Pesaro. One of the oldest churches, **San Giacomo**, consecrated by the great Pope Innocent III in 1208 and reconstructed after the Angevins wrecked it in the War of the Vespers, has an ancient watchtower for its campanile. The **Museo Civico** (open 8–12) contains both a collection of art—a Byzantine triptych and other medieval works, and paintings by Caravaggio's pupil, Mattia Preti—and archaeological finds from the area, including reliefs, sarcophagi, columns, mosaics, Greek, Roman, and Arab inscriptions, and the remains of the Aqueduct of Cornelius, used to fill Tèrmini's bath with its 'showers' made of lead. Oldest of all are the relics from the cave by the citadel where an Upper Palaeolithic family once lived, who lingered in Tèrmini long enough to learn how to scratch geometric designs on their pots.

Càccamo

The magnificent **Castello** at Càccamo, a mountain town 12 km south, was built in the 12th century and used as the seat of the local dukes into the 20th century. One of the largest castles in Italy, piled on the edge of the sheer escarpment, it is crowned with the typical swallowtail crenellations of the Ghibellines; some of its well-preserved rooms house a collection of arms and art. The **Cathedral** in the Piazza del Duomo was built by the Normans in 1090 but toyed with numerous times since then, and contains a number of Renaissance works—a quattrocento marble tabernacle and painted Crucifix, and a baptismal font by Domenico Gagini. Another church near here, the **Annunziata**, dates from the Middle Ages and was given a half-hearted 17th-century facelift; inside there's an *Annunciation* by the Flemish painter Borremans, an 18th-century wooden pulpit, and stuccoes by Serpotta. **San Domenico** (1486) has a Madonna by Antonello Gagini. Best of all, however, is the pavement in the nave of the 17th-century church of **San Benedetto**, done in fantasy majolica tiles by Nicolò Sarzana of Palermo, depicting marine and country scenes. Here, too, are stuccoes by Serpotta, and an overwhelming, gilt high altar. Further west along the coast are the two castles, **San Nicola d'Arena** (now a nightclub) and **Trabia** dating back to the Arabs.

Bagheria and the Villa Palagonia

. . . the coat-of-arms of the House of Pallagonia is a satyr holding up a mirror to a woman with a horse's head. Even after having seen the other absurdities, this seems to me the most peculiar of all.

—Goethe, *Italian Journey*

Despite his fascination, Goethe didn't take at all kindly to the mad and playful whimsies of the Prince of Palagonia, who like the rest of Palermitan nobility of the 17th and 18th century, built himself a summer villa in Bagheria, the next town west of Trabia, 15 km from Palermo, on the easternmost edge of the Conca d'Oro. A bit dusty here and there, intruded upon by ugly new buildings, and recently a focal point in the Mafia gangland wars, Bagheria is still the best place not only to get a sense of the pampered life of an old Sicilian aristocracy, but to see the extremes of the Baroque imagination in its most famous residence, the **Villa Palagonia**, off Piazza Garibaldi, built in 1715 by the great Palermitan architect Tommaso Maria Napoli for the Prince of Palagonia. By the time of Goethe, the attractive home had been inherited by his grandson, who proceeded to decorate it in what Goethe called a 'Palagonian paroxysm' of crudely leering, writhing, snarling, grinning monstrosities—62 of the most surreal creatures ever carved in stone ring the garden; the cornices are topsy-turvy, tormented with figures of dragons, gods, and monkeys; inside are frescoes of the Labours of Hercules in an elliptical vestibule, and a room lined with mirrors to further bedazzle the already weary eye . Now owned by the government, the villa has been restored (open daily 9–12.30 and 4–6, adm).

Another striking villa (though in a more normal sense) by Tommaso Maria Napoli is the lovely **Villa Valguarnera** of 1721, a lofty, rectangular palace with twin *exedrae*, a sweeping double stair leading up to the entrance at the *atrium*, their curves echoed in the semicircular colonnade of the courtyard in front of the villa. Other villas in Bagheria include the first, the 1658 **Villa Butera** on Corso Umberto I, a fine, more severe house despite later Baroque touches; its little crenellated tower adding a warlike touch. Today it is perhaps better known as **La Certosa**, or Charterhouse, for its waxwork figures of famous people, all dressed in Carthusian habits. On the road towards Palermo, the **Villa**

dei Principi di Cattolica, also from 17th century, has a gently concave façade and an elliptical stair, now housing the collected works of the local artist Renato Guttuso (open 9–1). One of the last places to paint Sicilian carts—or lamps, or vases, or ironwork—in the traditional style is Bagheria's Studio Ducato. In **Altavilla Milicia** just to the southeast there is the ruined church Chiesazza built by Robert Guiscard in 1077, at the site where he defeated the Saracens.

Solunto

A frequent train service takes you from Palermo some 16 km east to **Santa Flavia**, its station labelled Solunto after the ruins of ancient Soluntum which may be visited here (open daily from 9 am until 2 hours before sunset). Situated in a spectacular position on the heel of Monte Catalfano, Soluntum is the child of Solus, one of the three main Phoenician settlements mentioned by Thucydides, which has recently been located some 5 km to the southwest at Cozzo Cannita. Very little remains of the earlier town, destroyed by Dionysius of Syracuse in 398 BC in his campaign to rid Sicily of non-Greeks. Later Soluntum was built by Timoleon in a classic grid plan and was very Hellenized. During the First Punic War the Romans annexed it as a *civitas decumana*, and many of the ruins date from that period. At the entrance of the excavations a small **Antiquarium** contains a plan of Soluntum and some finds. Inside are the ruins of the *agora*, the theatre and Odeon, and Roman houses with mosaics (most famously, those of Leda and the swan) and traces of wall paintings. Most striking, however, is the view of the castle of Solanto, the Casteldaccia vineyards and Cefalù along the coast. Santa Flavia itself is a small fishing village turned resort.

PALERMO

A million people inhabit the hurly-burly of Palermo, the capital of Sicily and its largest city. With the odd-shaped Monte Pellegrino on one side, the plain of Conca d'Oro (Golden Shell) surrounding it and the Madonie Mountains in the distance, Palermo is splendidly situated, but what attracts most visitors are its magnificent Norman and Baroque monuments. Almost all of these are packed into a small section of the sprawling city. The division between new and old in Palermo is abrupt; around Piazza Ruggero Settimo and to the north of it are the chic shops, the modern apartment buildings and white-collar enterprises, whereas the south side has all the superb churches and palaces—and all the squalor. Here once-elegant residences rot in the exhaust fumes that have turned them black, and the narrow streets of the ghettoes are lined with every variety of rubbish imaginable, from horse heads to cheese rinds. Sporadic hole-in-the-wall trattorie, the children growing up in the streets, the shifty men who want to make a deal with you—it is all fascinating, colourful, and probably won't last much longer. The spirit of change and progress that has swept across this great island is most noticeable here in its capital, which like all capitals tends to reflect the best and the worst of the land. Crime (do watch your car, and conceal all valuables in it and keep your purse out of the reach of the infamous scooter-mounted *banditti*), drugs (the Mafia don't consign them all to the export trade) and poverty are still problems, but there is a growing public demand for something to be done about them. If it's been a while since you last visited Palermo, you may well be amazed at its bright new face. The only real setback in the growth of the economy is that everyone buys a car as soon as he can afford it, and there are times when this grand old city resembles a Baroque parking lot.

History

Palermo was colonized by the Carthaginians in the 5th century BC, in an effort to control the spread of Greek influence in Sicily. Its original name is unknown; the Greeks called it 'Panhormos' (many harbours) from the many safe anchorages that existed in ancient times, but these have since been filled in with silt from the two streams that once traversed the city near the present-day cathedral. Rome fought hard for Palermo in the First Punic War, finally capturing it in 254 BC. The father of Hannibal, Hamilcar Barca, tried for some years to recapture the city, basing himself on Monte Pellegrino, but did not succeed.

The Byzantines, who called it 'Balarma', took it from the Barbarians in 535, holding it until the Saracens defeated them in 831. Under the Arabs, Palermo became the splendid capital of an Emirate. The Arabs built a new quarter, separately walled, for their officials (*el-Halisah*, 'the elect', from whence comes the name 'Kalsa' still used today).

In 1072 Roger de Hauteville retook the city for Christendom, and under his son, King Roger, Palermo became the most splendid capital in all Europe with its beautiful Norman churches and pleasure palaces. The city continued as a famous cultural centre under Frederick 'Stupor Mundi' who was raised in Palermo's Palazzo dei Normanni. When Swabian rule gave way to Angevin, the rebellion of the Sicilian Vespers broke out in 1282 at a church in Palermo over a Frenchman's insulting advances to a bride at her wedding.

Under the distant tyranny of the Spanish and Bourbons, the city declined in splendour although it gained in population. By the 18th century it was the second largest city in Italy after Naples, and Ferdinand IV ruled from Palermo when the French occupied that city. Placed under British protection in the 19th century, Palermo rebelled on three occasions, the last of which in 1860 saw the entry of Garibaldi and the Thousand. During World War II, Palermo suffered badly from the American bombardment; even today, bombed ruins in some quarters of the city remind one of that evil time.

Two Palermiti in particular have made their mark on the world: Alessandro Scarlatti, the composer (1660–1725), and Alexandre, the self-styled Comte de Cagliostro (1743–95), a swindler who dabbled in the occult and was deeply embroiled in French politics at the time of Louis XVI, playing a major role in the Diamond Necklace Affair that brought about Marie Antoinette's fall. His reputation as the greatest charlatan of his day spread across the Continent from the islands of Rhodes and Malta to London. Finally in Rome he was sentenced for heresy and died serving a life sentence in prison.

GETTING TO AND AROUND PALERMO
By air: Palermo's airport is at Punta Raisi, 26 km west of the city; there's a regular bus to the airport and back from Piazza Ruggero Settimo, in front of the Politeama Theatre. The airport connects the city with Naples, Rome and Milan, and also with Italian

provincial centres such as Bergamo, Bologna and Venice. There is a shuttle service to Catania, and some overseas flights from London in the summer, as well as charter flights available all year round.

By sea: regular ferry services to Naples, Cagliari, Tunis (on Tirrenia; offices at Via Roma 385, tel 333 300 for bookings and information). There are also ferry and hydrofoil connections to Ustica Island (Siremar: Via F. Crispi 124, tel (091) 582 403), as well as occasional summer hydrofoils to the Aeolian Islands and Cefalù.

By rail: besides the central railway station on Piazza Giulio Cesare, at the foot of the Via Roma, there's another station in the new part of town, called Notorbartalo. (On arriving in the city, don't be alarmed when your train stops here first, then reverses out of Palermo; it has to circumnavigate the city to get to the Stazione Centrale.) There are connections to all points, most frequently those along the north coast route to Trapani and Messina, and the cross-island route to Enna and Catania.

By coach: most of the coaches for towns around Sicily and Palermo Province also stop in the Piazza Cesare near the station. Some exceptions are: to Agrigento, from the Botanical Gardens on Via Lincoln; to Trapani and Ragusa, from the Giardino Garibaldi; to Santa Flavia, Bagheria, Altavilla, and to the coastal area to the east, from the Piazza Florio (AST line). Several different companies run services around Palermo, which can be confusing.

Within the city, these municipal buses may help: buses 14 and 15 to Mondello Beach, 16 to the Sferracavallo campsite (catch them at the Piazza Cesare); 12 to Monte Pellegrino and 8/9 or 9 to Monreale (from the Piazza XIII Vittime near the port). Buy tickets at a tobacconist and validate them on entering the bus. Driving a car around Palermo is folly. Cab-drivers are predatory—as they tend to be elsewhere in Sicily—and don't be shy about reminding them to use the meter. If there isn't one, you've found a gypsy cab, which is all right as long as you negotiate the fare in advance. This is also true for the picturesque horsedrawn carriages that wait in the Piazza Cesare (though they're likely to be cheaper than the taxis). If you're walking in the old town, you won't get lost if you stick to the main streets, like the Via Roma, which were cut through the labyrinthine medieval city a century or two ago. If you stray too far from them you could end up in the Twilight Zone.

TOURIST INFORMATION (tel prefix 091)
Palermo's very able and active EPT has its main office at Piazza Castelnuovo 35 (an extension to the west of the Piazza Ruggiero Settimo; tel 586 122). It also operates these branches:
Stazione Centrale (tel 616 5914).
Punta Raisi airport (tel 691 405 or 691 698).
Piazza Cavalieri del S. Sepolcro (tel 616 698).
AAST, at Salita Belmonte 43 (tel 586 830).
Monreale, Piazza Duomo (tel 640 2448).

The Old City

The centre of the old city is known as the **Quattro Canti**, the 'four corners', where the main streets Via Vittorio Emanuele and Via Maqueda intersect. In 1611 the Viceroy

Vigliena built the four buildings at this crossroads and adorned their corners with fountains, allegories of the four seasons, the four kings of Sicily, and the patronesses of the four quarters which the Quattro Canti defines. For hundreds of years these four quarters—the **Kalsa** (southeast), **Amalfitani** (northeast), **Sincaldi** (northwest), and **Albergheria** (southwest)—had little to do with one another; indeed, they were so clannish that marriages between the quarters were very unusual.

The Norman Cathedral

Turning west from the Quattro Canti along the Via Vittorio Emanuele you pass a few blocks of small shops and then the **Cathedral** makes a sudden appearance on the right. Founded in 1185 by the Archbishop Gualtiero Offamiglio (the English 'Walter of the Mill'), this masterpiece of Sicilian–Norman architecture was only completed in the 19th century. In the meantime various alterations—most notably the dome, built in the 18th century by the Florentine Ferdinando Fuga—have spoiled the integrity of the building, but its beauty and fine proportions still hold true. The eastern end of the cathedral retains its fine 12th-century structure and embellishments. In the Gothic porch on the south side one of the columns bears an inscription from the Koran—it belonged to the mosque that once stood on the same site.

The spacious interior is stale fare after the lavish feast of the exterior (open daily 7–12 noon and 4–6.30 pm). At the back of the church is the **tomb of Frederick 'Stupor Mundi'** (died 1250); the Eastern style of symbols of the Evangelists and the lions supporting the sarcophagus pay homage to his syncretic character. Other sepulchres contain the remains of Peter II of Aragon (died 1342), Henry VI (died 1197), Roger II (died 1154) and his daughter Constance (died 1198), wife of Henry VI. Also, set in the wall there, are the tombs of Duke William of Aragon (died 1338), son of Frederick II of Aragon, and Constance of Aragon (died 1222), first wife of 'Stupor Mundi', whom he wed when he turned 14.

In a choir chapel are the relics of Palermo's favourite saint, St Rosalia, who lived and died on Mt Pellegrino (see below for her story). There are many fine statues by Antonello Gagini, as well as a Madonna by Francesco Laurana. The **treasury** contains some interesting items from the tomb of Constance of Aragon, including her crown—a cap with jewels stuck on it, reminiscent of nothing so much as a child's party hat with pieces of bright paper pasted on it. The **crypt** contains the sarcophagus of Gualtiero Offamiglio, among those of other archbishops of Palermo.

In the court of the abutting **Archbishop's Palace** (Via Matteo Bonello 2) is the **Museo Diocesano** (open Mon, Wed and Fri, 9–1; adm; tel 583 442), containing works of art salvaged from the churches bombed in the war, many quite lovely. The door of the Archbishop's Palace dates from the 15th century.

The Cappella Palatina

Via Vittorio Emanuele ends in shady **Giardino Bonanno** (the **Porta Nova** was built in 1535 for Charles V's victory in Tunisia), and the large, strange **Palazzo dei Normanni** (open 9–4, closed Thurs; Nov–Mar, open Mon, Fri and Sat 9–12.30). Originally a Saracen fort of the 9th century, Roger II and the Normans adapted it for their own uses, and alterations continued throughout the centuries, so that only the Torre di Santa Ninfa recalls the men of northern France. (From the observatory on its roof, Giuseppe

Church of San Giovanni Degli Eremiti, Palermo

Piazzi discovered the first known asteroid, Ceres, in 1801.) In the Palazzo is the royal chapel of Roger II, the **Cappella Palatina**, one of the jewels of Norman–Eastern art (open 9–1; donations; Sunday Mass 10.20). Like the more grandiose church of Monreale, the walls of the chapel glow with wonderful mosaics on a golden background, but here the scenes are more intimate and easier to study, and the rest of the chapel is spared the minor imperfections of Monreale. With its wooden ceiling—exquisitely carved by Roger's craftsmen—the mosaic floors and marble-covered walls, as a work of art the Cappella Palatina is flawless. The dais at the rear of the chapel supported the thrones of the Sicilian kings. The Palazzo also contains the **Royal Apartments** (second floor). After various sumptuous but unmemorable rooms you enter the Sala di Re Ruggero, where the Norman influence is most obvious, retaining a fine, though formal, mosaic of a hunting scene. Currently the Sicilian government meets here.

San Giovanni degli Eremiti
Off the main Corso Ruggero to the left of the Palazzo rise the four pink domes of San Giovanni degli Eremiti, a church straight out of the *Arabian Nights* (entrance on Via dei Benedettini; open 9–2, holidays 9–1). This Arab–Norman–Sicilian piece of confectionery, originally part of a mosque, was built by Roger II in 1142. The charming gardens and old cloisters nearby (part of an old Benedictine convent in the 18th century) complete this little oasis. The **Villa d'Orleans** in the gardens on the other side of Corso Ruggero is the palace where future French King Louis Philippe lived in exile in 1809, now the residence of the President of Sicily.

Kalsa Quarter

Turning eastwards down the Via Vittorio Emanuele one enters the Kalsa Quarter. A few blocks down from the Quattro Canti, by the Via Roma, is the church of **Sant' Antonio** destroyed in the 1823 earthquake, but restored to its original Chiaramonte style. A right turn down curving Via Paternostro takes you to the fine church of **San Francesco**

d'Assisi built in the 13th century, with a rose window. The interior is particularly lovely, despite bomb damage, and its **Cappella Mastrantonio**, carved in 1468 by Francesco Laurana and Pietro da Bonitate, must be Palermo's best example of Renaissance art. Eight statues by Palermo's genius of stucco Serpotta adorn the nave, and the two Madonnas are by Domenico Gagini. Next to it, on Via Immacolatella 5, the **Oratorio della Compagnia di San Lorenzo** is Serpotta's masterpiece, an extravaganza of Baroque decoration (open from 9 am until dusk on request).

Near the **Giardino Garibaldi**, further east on Via V. Emanuele, the 15th-century **Santa Maria della Catena** derives its name from the chain (*catena*) that once closed the Cala Harbour every evening. Built by Matteo Carnelivari, it is fronted by a simple but elegant Renaissance loggia. The entrance to the harbour is through the 16th-century gate, the monumental **Porta Felice** which has no arch in order to permit the passing of the great car of Santa Rosalia. Beneath the huge banyan trees shading the **Giardino Garibaldi** you can wander across to the Piazza Marina which as its name implies was once part of the sea until reclaimed by the Arabs in the 10th century as part of their Kalsa quarter. Here the Aragonese held their jousts, and the Inquisitors their *autos-da-fé*. In one corner note the pretty Renaissance **Santa Maria dei Miracoli** built in 1347.

In the southeast corner of the Giardino Garibaldi is the **Palazzo Chiaramonte**, built in 1307 by Sicily's most flamboyant noble family; like all Sicilian palazzi associated with the Chiaramonti, it was graceful and magical though made harsh by its later occupants—Sicily's viceroys, the Inquisition, Palermo's Law Courts—and now restored, it is owned by the University. Its courtyard has a lovely tri-lobed window adorned with zigzags; try to get in to see the ceiling of the Sala Maggiore.

The National Gallery of Sicily

From here, Via 4 Aprile gives on to Via Alloro, the finest street in the quarter, lined with palazzi in various stages of decrepitude. At no. 4 stands the grand **Palazzo Abatelli** 1488), a highly original creation of Matteo Carnelivari, its main portal a Renaissance take-off on Catalan Gothic which wouldn't look out of place in Flash Gordon; the tower has an elaborate headdress and elegant triple windows. Restored after the war, it houses the **National Gallery of Sicily** (open 9–2; also Tues and Thurs 4.30–7.30; Sun 9–1; closed Mon; adm), the richest collection of paintings and sculpture on the island. The masterpiece amid the fine collection of medieval and Renaissance painting is Antonello da Messina's *Annunciation*, which perhaps should be subtitled 'of the Right Hand', for along with the Virgin's expression, the gesture of her hand makes this one of the greatest yet simplest paintings in the world. The other highlight in the gallery is the large fresco entitled *The Triumph of Death* by a 15th-century (perhaps Catalan) artist who did not sign his work. This macabre scene of the Deadly Archer dealing it out to the wealthy, who tumble beneath the hoofs of Death's dying horse, originally hung in the Palazzo Sclafani—at that time a hospital. Other works include a beautiful ideal Renaissance marble *bust of Eleonora di Aragona* by Francesco Laurana, a fine 16th-century Flemish triptych of the Virgin with angel musicians, a sweet-faced *Coronation of the Virgin* by Sicilian quattrocento painter Riccardo Quartararo, and from the 1600s, the Caravaggesque *Angel liberating St Peter from prison* by Pietro Novelli. Next to the gallery, the church of **La Gancia** or Santa Maria degli Angeli was built in the 15th century, and contains works by Antonello Gagini, Serpotta and Vincenzo da Pavia.

Villa Giulia

South of here, across busy Via Lincoln, is the **Botanical Garden** (open mornings, closed Sun), and the geometrical neo-classical garden, the **Villa Giulia** with four pavilions adorning its centre. Not so very long ago the Villa Giulia was a wasteland of rubbish, dying shrubs, alcoholics and assorted human nuisances, its pompous pavilions crumbling into what would have been a perfect Italian *Cinema Verità* film set. Over the past couple of years, however, it's been spruced up, and you can take the children there without fear of bacterial or social contamination. Also interesting for children as well as adults are the exhibits at the **Marionette Museum** on Via Butera 1 (open 10–1, 5–7 pm, Sun 10–1).

Via Lincoln leads to the Central Station; halfway there, Via Garibaldi on the right leads to the **Piazza della Rivoluzione** where the 1848 rebellion began. The fountain here supposedly represents the spirit of Palermo. Just off the Via Garibaldi, the **Palazzo Aiutamicristo** ('Christ help me palace'), designed by Matteo Carnelivari, was the residence of Charles V after his campaign in Tunis. Its façade, in the usual happy Sicilian mélange, is Catalan–Gothic. Behind this, the large Norman church of **La Magione** in the piazza of the same name was originally built in the 12th century for the Cistercians, but in 1193 Henry VI donated it to the Teutonic Knights of Jerusalem. Like the rest of the rather scruffy Kalsa quarter, La Magione suffered frightfully in the wartime bombardments, but has been restored to its old stern Norman form.

La Martorana

Returning to the Quattro Canti, just off the southeast corner of Vias Maqueda and Vittorio Emanuele is the large **Piazza Pretoria**, locally known as the 'piazza di Vergonia ('of Shame') from its dreadful, grandiose, overpopulated fountain of nymphs, satyrs and other mythical whimsies, designed in the 16th century by two loony Florentines, Michelangelo Naccherino and Francesco Camilliani. This has to be the greatest abuse of decoration in Sicily; the nudes coy and cloying, though the animal heads popping out of the basin's arcade add a much-needed note of humour, sitting as it does before Palermo's city hall. Originally commissioned by a certain Don Pedro di Toledo for his Tuscan villa, it was sold to Palermo by his son, who had better taste. Besides the city hall, or **Municipio**, the piazza has two churches, **San Guiseppe dei Teatini** built in 1612 by Giacamo Besio with a lavish interior (entrance in Via V. Emanuele), and facing it, **Santa Caterina** (entrance in Piazza Bellini), built in 1566 and sumptuously Baroque, containing a statue of Santa Caterina by Antonello Gagini.

Adjacent to Piazza Pretoria lies the Piazza Bellini with the loveliest church of Santa Maria dell' Ammiraglio, familiarly known as **La Martorana**. Founded in 1173 by Roger II's 'Admiral of Admirals', George of Antioch, this Orthodox church was the site of the parliament of Sicilian barons following the Sicilian Vespers, where they elected to give the Sicilian Crown to Peter of Aragon (1282). In 1233 King Alfonso transferred the church to the convent founded by Eloisa Martorana (a part of the cloisters remains to the south). In the 19th century La Martorana was used as a post office, but in 1935 Mussolini returned it to the Greeks, who have made it an Orthodox cathedral.

La Martorana's beautiful, graceful campanile dates from the church's Norman foundation, surviving later adaptations. Inside are the earliest mosaics in Palermo, by Greek artists, golden and Byzantine, best lit in the morning. On the west walls are two

Norman mosaics, one of Christ crowning King Roger II and the other of the founding Admiral at the feet of his beloved Virgin. The 1717 frescoes by Borremans in the newer part of the church seem trivial beside the mosaics.

Immediately next to La Martorana, the small, distinctive **San Cataldo**, built in 1161, has been restored to its original Arab–Norman form, its three pink domes, stone latticework and palm trees adding up to an Arabian Night effect. The plain interior may be seen on request (ask in La Martorana). In the University, on the other side of Via Maqueda, there is a **Geological Museum** (open 9–1). Via Ponticello, beyond the University, leads to the Jesuit Church, the **Casa Professa** (1564–1636), restored after the war and containing two paintings by Pietro Novelli. The **Biblioteca Comunale**, on the west side of the church, houses early manuscripts and incunabula. The rest of Via Maqueda south to the Porta Sant' Antonio and the station is lined with 17th- and 18th-century palazzi. The best of these are the **Palazzo Santa Croce** and the **Prefetura** cornering each other at the intersection of Via Maqueda and Via Bosco, both built in the 18th century.

National Archaeology Museum

To the north Via Maqueda has been turned into one of Palermo's busiest shopping streets. From here, to the west, Via Sant' Agostino leads to the 14th-century church of **Sant' Agostino**, built by the Chiaramonte family, whose stoneworkers seemingly embroidered the elegant rose window and laid lava mosaics around the door.

To celebrate the unification of Italy with typical Sicilian excess, Palermo built not one, but two of the largest theatres in Europe. One looms up where Via Maqueda enters Piazza Giuseppe Verdi: the vast **Teatro Massimo** (1875–97) with the second largest stage in Europe after the Paris Opera; the two lovely Art Nouveau kiosks in the piazza condescend to a more human scale. From here, Via Giacalone gives directly on to the Piazza Folivella with the **National Archaeological Museum of Palermo** (open 9–1.30 Tue and Fri 3–5.30 pm, Sun and winter 9–1.30), housed in the former convent dell'Oratorio dell'Olivella. One of Italy's finest archaeological museums, the collections trace the civilizations of Sicily, from the Prehistoric to Classical eras; the **Sala di Selinunte** contains two remarkable Archaic *metopes* from Temple C (6th century BC), one of the Rape of Europa and the other, Perseus, protected by Pallas, slaying the Gorgon, the figures highly stylized, with enormous staring eyes; the *metopes* from the following century, from Temple E, show the amazing development towards realism. The **Sala d'Imera** is lined with the leering lion-head spouts from the Doric temple of Victory, each different. There are excellent Greek vases, which make an interesting comparison with those made by their contemporaries from Etruria, exhibited in the museum's **Etruscan room**; one jug, decorated with bas-reliefs of the Gorgon, is especially fine. Other highlights: the magnificent Hellenistic **bronze ram** from Syracuse's Castello Maniace; thousands of votive offerings from the Sanctuary of Demeter Malophoros in Selinunte; the 'Stone of Palermo'; a fine Roman mosaic of Orpheus enchanting the wild beast, discovered under Palermo's Piazza Vittoria; a beautiful bronze of *Hercules and the Stag*; and casts of the sensuous Paleolithic incisions from the Addaura Grotto on Monte Pellegrino (see p. 164).

Connected to the museum is the convent's church, the **Stimmate** (17th century) with a lavish 1700 interior by Serpotta. Another interior by the prolific Serpotta is nearby, on Via Monteleone, **Oratorio della Compagnia di Santa Caterina** (ring to enter).

Via Roma

Via Roma runs just east of the museum, passing the bulk of Palermo's central **Post office**, a Mussolini concoction that stretches the length of the block like a dull white elephant on this otherwise elegant 19th-century street. The brute power of the Corporate State demands its homage; an endless, oppressive flight of steps leads up to the enormous doors, the weight of which is enough to defeat all but the most determined postal customer. The Aztecs queued up for hours to ascend into similar temples for the privilege of having a priest tear out their living hearts.

A few blocks south of the Palazzo della Poste, still on Via Roma, rises the tall **Colonna dell' Immacolata** in the piazza before the large church of **San Domenico** built in 1670, although the façade dates from 1726. In its elaborate interior many of the island's favourite sons are buried, in 'Sicily's Pantheon' including Francesco Crispi, Pietro Novelli, and Giuseppe Pitrè. This is where Ruggero Settimo called together the rebel parliament of 1848. Behind the church, on Via Bambinai, is another of Palermo's fine oratories: the 17th-century **Oratorio della Compagnia del Rosario di San Domenico** with a beautiful altarpiece by Van Dyck depicting the four patronesses of Palermo, and some of Serpotta's finest and most graceful Rococo figures. (The chapel is open from 11–12 and 3–4; it may be necessary to ring for the custodian at Via Bambinai 10.)

A block south of San Domenico, a little stairway leads down to what seems at first to be a mysterious underground city: it is really one of Palermo's colourful street markets, covering a dozen old narrow streets, busy until late in the evening beneath festive lights, with steaming cauldrons of boiled potatoes, live eels, a veritable cornucopia of fresh fruits and vegetables, and popular delicacies in the many restaurants and stands. Also behind San Domenico, on Via Squarcialupo ('rip open the wolf street'), is the 16th-century church **Santa Cita** with various works of Antonello Gagini, despite heavy bomb damage. Far more interesting, however, is the adjacent Baroquissimo **Oratorio di Santa Cita** next door, one of Serpotta's masterpieces, decorated off and on between 1686 and 1718, its fantastical programme commemorating the great victory over the Turks at the Battle of Lepanto; on a backdrop of curlicued draperies are biblical scenes, surrounding a large, central picture of Lepanto, embellished with stucco swords and blunderbusses, *putti* playing with armoured torsos, helmets and a lion, creating an exuberant mix of the sacred and profane.

To Piazza Ruggero Settimo

At the end of Via Squarcialupo, by the Piazza XIII Vittime, is the fine Renaissance church of **San Giorgio dei Genovesi**, designed by Giorgio di Faccio for the sailors of Genoa. From this piazza (named after the thirteen leaders of the 1860 rebellion, executed by the Bourbons) Via Cavour leads to the centre of Palermo, the large **Piazza Ruggero Settimo**, busy bus terminus, stage for the evening *passeggiata*, and site of Palermo's other monster theatre, the **Politeama Garibaldi** designed in 1874 by Giuseppe Damiani Almejda, housing the **Gallery of Modern Art** (open 9–1; closed Mon). Most of the works here are regional efforts from the 19th century; some of the more interesting paintings are by Giuseppe Sciuti (1834–1911), from Zafferana Etnea, whose post-Romantic vast visions of ancient Sicily presage Cecil B. de Mille. Looking over the shoulder of Piazza Ruggero Settimo is a dour Fascist skyscraper in Piazzale Ungheria. Most of the new public buildings in Palermo were put up by Mussolini and company with unmitigated pretentiousness and shoddy workmanship, each building stamped with a striving symbolic relief and a bewildering inscription from the Duke of Delusion's slogan machine. In these respects, the Palazzo del Proveditorato stands out. The municipal fire station, however, is a real wowser.

On the Outskirts of Palermo

Palermo's outskirts (all within reach of the municipal bus service) have enough sites to occupy a couple of days' serious exploration. In the cemetery of Sant' Orsola, south of Palermo (Via del Vespro), is Santo Spirito, better known as the **Church of the Sicilian Vespers** built in 1173 by the founder of Palermo's Cathedral, Archbishop Offamiglio. At this severe Norman church, a pair of Sicilian newly-weds attended Vespers on 31 March 1282, Easter Tuesday. As they left, an idle Angevin soldier rudely insulted the bride—this, from a hated oppressor, was too much for Sicilian honour to bear and the nasty Frenchman was the first to die in the ensuing massacre.

A walk south on the broad Corso dei Mille (from the station) takes you to the **Ponte dell' Ammiraglio**, the bridge built in 1113 by 'the Admiral of Admirals', George of Antioch, over the River Oreto, although the river has since been diverted. On this fine piece of Norman engineering Garibaldi skirmished with the Bourbon defenders of Palermo in 1860. Further south on Corso dei Mille (no. 384) is the domed church of **San Giovanni dei Lebbrosi**, founded by Count Roger in 1072 and considered the best example of early Norman architecture in Sicily. Initially used as a leper hospital, it has been restored and may be visited by asking the guardian for the key. The Corso dei Mille continues to **Brancaccio**, where the half Norman, half German Frederick 'Stupor Mundi' spent his precocious childhood with his Swabian barons, learning Greek, Latin, and Arabic in the fabled but long vanished **Palazzo di Favara**, the 10th-century estate of the Emir Giafar; surrounded on three sides by an artificial lake, it was nicknamed 'Palazzo Mare Dolce', the Sweet Sea Palace.

Although the main palace is gone, hints of its Arabian–Norman beauty remain in **La Zisa** (from Porta Nuova take the Via Colonna Rotta to Piazza Ingastone and Via Zisa; bus 27). *Azis* means 'magnificent' in Arabic, and this Norman pleasure palace, built by William the Bad in 1160, must have once been dazzling. Tall and elegant, La Zisa's façade is adorned with shallow arches and crenellations. It's in the process of being restored; inside mosaics, fountains, bright stalactite ceilings and a central court are reminiscent of the Alhambra (inquire at the tourist information office about opening times).

Catacombs of the Cappuccini

From Piazza Ingastone, Via Cipressi leads west to the catacombs of the Convent of the Cappuccini (open 9–1 and 3–6; leave a donation), the most fascinatingly macabre site in Sicily. Capuchin friars elsewhere in Italy, most notably in Rome, appreciate the aesthetics of Death more than most, and have a knack for arranging curious tableaux of bones and skulls. Here, though, they simply hung their customers on the walls, though carefully arranged according to former occupation—monk, soldier, lawyer, virgin, spinster, and so on. The catacombs had a natural mummifying effect on their bodies, and today, like Palermitans of the 19th century, you can make a pleasant excursion through the corridors lined with the grinning remains of Sicilians of the last century, all dressed in their Sunday best. The last to be entombed, in 1920, was a little girl nicknamed 'The Sleeping Beauty'; she and the other small mummies in the catacombs are a sad reminder of how children used to drop like flies before the advent of modern medicine. As you leave, the plump, good natured, and lively friars will want to sell you wonderful colour postcards, useful for sending obligatory greetings home to relatives you don't like.

From here it is a short walk down Via Pindemonte to Corso Calatafimi, the main thoroughfare west of the gate, Porta Nuova. At no. 94 (a barracks), a soldier will guide you to **LFa Cuba**, another Arabian–Norman kiosk built by William II (the Good) in 1180, in what was then the great park of the Maredolce palace. In form it resembles La Zisa, massive and rectangular, embellished with shallow columns and arches; originally it was topped by a dome. Boccaccio used it as a setting for one of his tales (see 'Procida').

La Favorita and Museo Pitrè

On the opposite (north) end of Palermo is the pretty park of La Favorita just off Piazza Vittorio Veneto in the former aristocratic suburbs of Piana dei Colli. Within its landscaped grounds is a sight as unexpected as the Cappuccini catacombs—the **Palazzina Cinese**, a crazy, half neo-classical, half Chinese confection covered with tinkling bells, a Palermitan Xanadu. In 1798, when the French Revolution and the French themselves were storming Naples, the Bourbon King Ferdinand IV and his Queen Maria Carolina found refuge in Palermo, arriving aboard Lord Nelson's flagship *Vanguard*, with the British Ambassador Sir William Hamilton and Lady Hamilton for company. Upon arrival, the royal couple purchased what is now La Favorita Park and the old house on the grounds, known as the Villa of Bells. The bells gave Ferdinand the idea of having the villa redone in *chinoiserie*, the then fashion in England.

The result is charmingly inconsistent. The ground level forgets to be Chinese with a portico of orange-striped Gothic arches; flanking twin stairs in little fairy-tale stone turrets lead up to the pagoda *Piano Nobile*, the only part of the palace open for visits (on Saturday mornings, when it's used for civil weddings). Here you can visit the **Sala d'Udienza** with magnificent chandeliers and silken walls, and the **Dining Room**, where Nelson and the Hamiltons were frequent guests at the great oval table. To keep their conversations private, the table was equipped with a winch that lifted the food directly up from the basement, dispensing with the need for flunkeys. If someone wanted seconds of a dish, the king would inform the staff below with a complicated code of knocks. Unfortunately the rest of the Palazzina has been closed since 1982, when it was discovered to be structurally unsafe. The newly landscaped garden is open 9–sunset, closed Sun.

Underground passages connect the palace to the servants' quarters and kitchens, now housing the **Museo Etnografico Pitrè** (daily except Fri and Sat, 8.30–1). Founded in 1909, this is Sicily's best collection of ethnographic items, dedicated to the island's great student of folklore, Giuseppe Pitrè. The collection includes puppets, carts, costumes, torture instruments, carriages, religious items and utensils from everyday life decades ago, anarchically arranged à la Grandma's attic.

SICILY

WHERE TO STAY
(tel prefix 091)

Palermo has some renowned old establishments that truly deserve the appellation 'Grand Hotel'. In a garden overlooking the sea north of the port is the *****Villa Igiea famous for its 'Liberty' style (Art Nouveau) murals and décor by Ernest Basile and Ettore de Maria Bergler (Via Belmonte 43; tel 543 744; L280–350 000; tennis, swimming pool). In the centre of town, the ****Grande Albergo Delle Palme seems a perfectly preserved time-capsule of early 1900s elegance (Via Roma 396; tel 583 933; L155–200 000). For more modern comfort the ****Jolly Hotel del Foro Italico, Foro Italico 22 (tel 616 5090), has lower rates—L110 000, and the ****Politeama Palace, Piazza Ruggero Settimo 15, is about the same (L105 000). For the rest, like any of Italy's great cities, Palermo is crowded, and modest hotels usually take up one or more floors of a larger building—so you can guess little about an establishment from the street. Don't let this discourage you; most are quite decent. On Via Roma, the *Moderno has exceptionally nice rooms and an English-speaking owner (no. 276; tel 588 683; L55 000 with bath). Even many of the cheapest hotels—Palermo has dozens of them—are comfortable if not always quiet: the *Odeon (Via Amari 140; tel 332 778; L35 000) or the *Cavour Via Manzioni 11, near the Stazione Centrale (tel 616 2757; L25 000 without bath).

EATING OUT

The almond-paste sweets you see in every pastry-shop window in Sicily were first made at the Convent of La Martorana in Palermo, and are called *Frutti alla Martorana*. These 'fruits' come in a delightful variety of forms—tomatoes, cactus fruits, oranges, and even little dishes of marzipan spaghetti. Other specialities are *pasta con le sarde* (pasta with sardines), *involtini alla Siciliana* (rolled meat on a skewer), *caponata* (fried aubergine in sweet and sour sauce) and *pupi di zucchero* (special-occasion statues of people made out of sugar).

The best-known restaurant in Palermo, and possibly in all Sicily, is the **Charleston**, Piazza Ungheria 30 (tel 321 366), near the old skyscraper, with serious cuisine in Art Nouveau surroundings. In summer, like many of Palermo's finer establishments, the Charleston moves itself to Mondello Lido, in an old palace with a terrace on the Viale Regina Elena (tel 450 171; L45–60 000; closed Sun and 5–25 Sept). **Gourmand's**, which is decorated in an unusual ultra-modern style, on Via Libertà 37/E, is its closest competitor (tel 323 431; average price L35–50 000). There are plenty of more modest places with typical Sicilian food, but they are easier to find in the newer district around Via Libertà or in the suburbs than in the old town, such as the trattoria **Fusillo**, Via Carella 38, or **Fontanini**, 49 Via Sella, or **U Strascinu**, Viale Regione Sicilia 2286, all with Sicilian specialities in the L18–25 000 range. For a good, simple meal, that's easy on the purse, you can't beat the Trattoria **Trapani**, Via Gregorio (next to the Stazione Centrale). The famous, or rather infamous **Shanghai** restaurant sits on a balcony overlooking the Vucciria market (tel 589 702). Most of the entertainment is provided by the residents of the area hurling bags of rubbish off their balconies, the local Palermo yuppies trying to look at ease with this spectacle, and the owner quoting his own verses between trying to make you plump for the relatively expensive mixed seafood plate. If the filth of the square doesn't put you off your food, you can have quite a jolly evening for around L20 000. On your way to the Shanghai stop at the tiny bar on Via Roma near Piazza Domenica, adorned with enough plastic fruit to make Carmen Miranda drool. If you're suffering from an upset stomach try a glass of mineral water with a shot of lemon juice, like all the local businessmen seem to do. A local trattoria worth a visit is **Al Buco**, a few steps from the Politeama theatre, where the atmosphere and service are exceptional for such a reasonably priced spot (L20–25 000). Note also that Palermo contains some fine examples of that vanishing Sicilian amenity, the true *osteria*, with enormous, dusty wine barrels stacked up to the ceiling, meant for serious drinking; food is provided mostly to keep you sober enough to drink more. There are some on and around Via Americo Amari, near the port.

Around Palermo

West of Palermo, **Monte Pellegrino**, 606 m high, is the city's main landmark, known to the ancients as Heirkte. On the north side of the mountain, in the Grotta di Addaura rock incisions dating back to 7000 BC were discovered in three chambers, one depicting human figures, beautifully and sensuously drawn. Permission to visit these lovely Palaeolithic carvings must be obtained from the Soprintendente alle Antichità at the National Archaeological Museum in Palermo; it's much easier to see the casts in the museum itself.

You do not need permission, however, to visit the **Sanctuary of Santa Rosalia** (bus 12). Rosalia, a niece of King William II, renounced the world in 1159, and retreated to a hermitage on Monte Pellegrino, where she died. In 1624 when Palermo was suffering a disastrous plague, a holy man had a vision regarding Rosalia's bones; these were found, taken in a procession round the city, and the plague receded. So goes the legend, which is the reason for the great, festive pilgrimage on 15 July. In 1625, the small cave that held Rosalia's bones was converted into a chapel, where water of miraculous properties drips down the wall. From here you can walk to the cliff's edge to see the gigantic statue of the saint; another road from the sanctuary leads to the Semaforo near the summit of Monte Pellegrino. Below the sanctuary, the Scala Vecchia zigzags down to Le Falde, where the Fiera del Mediteraneo takes place and the long-abandoned Hotel Castello Utreggio presides over marvellous views of Palermo. Below Monte Pellegrino lies Sicily's most popular beach resort, **Mondello Lido** (bus 14). Goethe, during his Italian sojourn, described this area as the most beautiful promontory in the world (which is possibly as much a compliment to the strength of the local wines as it is to the region's natural beauty). It is, nevertheless, a pretty bay dotted with boats but teeming with people at the weekend, of course. There are plenty of snack bars, some of which are run by guys you wouldn't leave alone with your mother.

Monreale

Bus 8/9 from Piazza XIII Vittimi passes down Corso Calatafimi to Monreale and to its glorious **Cathedral** which should not be missed by any visitor to Palermo. It was built by William II in 1174, supposedly after a dream in which the Virgin revealed to him a great treasure, which he found and used to fund the cathedral, creating one of the greatest medieval monuments in the world (open daily, but closed 12.30–2.30).

Monreale Cathedral (Triple Apse)

From the outside, with only one of its towers completed, the cathedral seems stern, but go around the back to see the celebrated neo-Arabic decoration of the apse. The doors on the west by Bonanno da Pisa (1186) and on the north by Barisano da Trani (1179) are quite beautiful. Inside, however, the impact of golden walls of mosaics overwhelms you; it's as if you had just walked into an illuminated manuscript. The dominant figure in the central apse of Christ Benedicens presides over the stories of the Old and New Testaments, and over the angels, apostles, saints and martyrs—among them, surprisingly enough, Thomas à Becket, who suffered martyrdom by William II's own father-in-law, Henry II, only a few years before his depiction in the mosaics. A mosaic above the throne portrays William II offering his cathedral to the Virgin. He and his father William 'the Bad' are buried in a chapel by the choir; in another chapel lie the rest of the 'Bad' family, and a plaque marks the spot where the body of St Louis lay (before it was removed to Paris) after the defeat of Tunis. From here you can climb to the roof for a splendid view of the Conca d'Oro, or visit the rich treasury, or the 12th-century Benedictine **cloisters** (enter south of the cathedral; open 9–2.30, holidays 9–1). The columns all have elaborately-detailed individual designs in relief and mosaic. In one corner a pretty Arabic fountain adds a final touch. The 18th-century convent by the cloisters, now the **Istituto Statale d'Arte per il Mosaico** (open 8.30–12), contains an excellent painting of St Benedict by Pietro Novelli, who was born in Monreale in the 17th century.

In the **Municipio** (Piazza V. Emanuele) of Monreale you can visit a small art gallery. There are three good churches on Via Umberto Primo—the **Madonna delle Croce** affords a panoramic view. North of Monreale a road leads to the Castellaccio, once a monastery and now a refuge of the Sicilian Alpine Club.

Baida

Baida (Arabic for 'white'), a small village west of Monreale by Boccadifalco, may be reached by bus 23 from Palermo. In 1377 Benedictine monks founded a convent here, after Manfred Chiaramonte chased them from the Castellaccio above Monreale. The church, 15th-century Gothic, houses one of Antonello Gagini's best pieces, of John the Baptist. Beyond Baida, in the pine-forested Valle del Paradiso, is **San Martino delle Scale**, site of the vast **Abbey of San Martino**, also Benedictine and believed to have originally been founded by Pope Gregory the Great in the 6th century, rebuilt in the 14th. Today it is an orphanage and college; you can visit the convent with its grand stair and fountain, and the later church with many works of art. San Martino itself is a hill resort, popular with picnickers in the summer months.

West of Palermo to Terrasini

The suburban sprawl stretches out along the coast to the airport of Punta Raisi. **Isola delle Femmine** refers both to an offshore islet and to the fishing village facing it. This and Sferracavallo next to it have become small resorts with campsites, although the sea here is none too clean. In **Carini** further inland, there are caves with stalactites, and a 12th-century castle. **Terrasini** by Monte Pecoraro, a pleasant little fishing tourist resort, also has many caves, the most famous being the **Grotta delle Colombe** and the **Grotta Perciata**. The town's **Antiquarium** houses mainly marine finds from the rocky coast (Via Calalossa 4; open 9–1 and 3–6, Sun 9–12). A huge collection of painted Sicilian carts and related items recently acquired by the regional government of Sicily may be seen at the **Palazzo d'Aumale** which once belonged to the Duke d'Aumale, son of Louis Philippe of France; in the very near future the carts are to be installed in a new civic museum.

WHERE TO STAY AND EAT (tel prefix 091)
In Monreale, the best hotel is the ***Carrubella Park** (Via Umberto 1, tel 640 2187; L60–70 000), and in San Martino delle Scale the **Messina** is a modest place with modest prices (Via della Regiona 90, tel 418 153; L35 000 with bath). West of Palermo, along the beaches past Monte Pellegrino, the area is heavily built up and crowded. Most of the more expensive hotels have their own beaches, but a few more modest ones do too, like the **Piccolo Hotel Villa Esperia** (at Mondello Lido close to the city, Viale Margherita di Savoia 53; tel 450 004; L50–55 000), and the **Villa Azzurra**, Via Stesicoro 14 (tel 450 362; L48–55 000 with bath, L38 000 without). All the hotels have restaurants, and on the sea front in Mondello you'll find the **Charleston**; the restaurants serve mostly fish, which you'll see the restaurateurs buying straight from the stalls in front of the lido. Prices are, naturally, a little higher than the average in Palermo, but you can eat well for L35 000, less if you choose meat.

South of Palermo

South of Palermo, connected by a frequent bus service, lies one of the unique towns of Sicily, **Piana degli Albanesi**, a 15th-century Albanian colony (actually northern Greeks) where the people still speak Greek at home, attend Orthodox (Uniate) services, and wear their old costumes at weddings and feasts, especially at Epiphany and Easter. On the main road south to Agrigento, it's up into bandit country and some of the finest inland scenery that Sicily has to offer. The roads dip and rise with the contours of the grassy slopes through utterly serene pastures, so still that it's like a tableau; take a picnic and a bottle of heady Corvo wine, find a shady tree and listen for the tinkling of bells, as niggled goats are goaded to new grazing grounds. The town of **Misilmeri** (from the Arabic *Menzil el Emir*—the village of the Emir) saw Roger de Hauteville's victory over the Saracens in 1068, beginning the Norman rule of Sicily. Misilmeri produces the white wine *passito*, good strong stuff, but otherwise there's no need to linger here. **Marineo** totters on a hillside and has a cemetery which, fringed by cypresses, looks as though it's been in the closing sequence of many movies. At **Bagni di Cefalù**, the ruins of an old Arab town lie near the Castle of Diana. A small village further south on SS121, **Mezzoiuso**, produces an imaginative pantomime every Carnival Sunday (*Il Mastro di Campo*).

South of **Prizzi** (1013 m), sitting proudly in the breezy hills, are a lake of the same name and some unusual 'drunken' rocks to the west. Passing Bisacquino you can reach quaint **Contessa Entellina** where traditional sacred plays are performed during Holy Week. A long hike from Contessa (or drive from Bisacquino) takes you to the **Abbey of Santa Maria del Bosco** of the Olivetan Order, with a 17th-century church and 16th-century cloister.

The big town north of here, **Corleone**, will sound familiar to those who have seen *The Godfather*. Founded by the Saracens, it has a large population of Lombards brought there by Frederick II in the 13th century. Although a few modern housing blocks have sprung up on the outlying hills, the town is essentially Sicilian, with narrow cobbled lanes and its citizens eyeing intruders suspiciously. Look out for the rather comic statue of St Francis of Assisi; his frustrated expression and outstretched arms suggest he is bemoaning the loss of a big, prize fish, the one that got away. On the main Palermo–Sciacca highway, **San Giuseppe Iato** is near the site known as Monte Jato, recently excavated to reveal a Hellenistic settlement, with a theatre and stage, an arcaded *agora*, a temple dedicated to Aphrodite and a well-to-do residential quarter.

Alcamo

South of Terrasini, the A29 or SS187 follows the coast along the wide Golfo di Castellammare, passing by way of **Partinico**, long one of Sicily's most awful towns and long the headquarters of Danilo Dolci's efforts to improve the lot of the average Sicilian—if you're coming from Palermo you can take the shortcut along SS186. Another 20 km west will bring you to **Alcamo**, a town of pretty churches 6 km inland from its busy beach, Alcamo Marina. Frederick II founded Alcamo in 1233 and named it after the Saracen castle of *Alkamuk* above the town on Mount Bonifato (826 m). Ciullo d'Alcamo, one of the first poets to compose in Italian and a true troubadour, was born here in the 12th century. In the piazza named after him is the **Church of Sant'Oliva**, containing lovely works by the Gagini family. The Flemish painter Borremans painted the frescoes in the **Assunta**, with its 14th-century campanile. On the Corso Sei Aprile, there are three other fine churches: the **Madonna del Soccorso**, **San Tomaso**, with a beautiful 14th-century doorway, and **San Francesco**, containing sculpture by the Gagini. Paintings by Pietro Novelli may be seen in the abbeys, **Badia Grande** and **Badia Nuova**, north of town. **Santa Chiara** church contains stuccoes by Serpotta; while in the

167

Segesta, Trapani

ruins of the Saracen castle the church of the **Madonna dell'Alto** is worth visiting for the panoramic view.

Segesta

West of Alcamo are **Calatafimi** (with an obelisk commemorating Garibaldi's victory here in 1860) and **Segesta**, a 20-minute walk from the station Segesta Tempio. Segesta (the Greek *Egesta*) was one of the main Elymnian centres, along with Erice, but where Erice came under Carthaginian influence, Segesta became Hellenized, and was famous in Greek Sicily for its sulphurous springs.

History

The Elymnians may have settled Monte Barbaro and Segesta as early as the 12th century BC, but little is known about the city until the 6th century BC, when Segesta and Selinunte started squabbling over their borders, as productively as the Two Cats of Kilkenny each of which thought there was one cat too many. In the grand political arena of Greeks, Carthaginians and Romans, Segesta always sided with whoever was the strongest at any given moment. At one point, writes Thucydides, the Segestians were trying to curry favour with Athens to counteract arch-rival Selinunte's allegiance to Syracuse. To impress the envoys sent by Athens, they collected all the gold and silver drinking cups from their territory and sent them to each house the Athenians were entertained in, successfully tricking them into believing Segesta was an exorbitantly wealthy city; perhaps even the beautiful Doric temple was begun then to impress the Greeks. However, when the Athenians sent their Great Expedition to conquer Syracuse, Segesta reneged on its promise to pay for the venture, and the Athenians realized they had been fooled. It was only the first of their disappointments.

Afterwards, Segesta became an ally of Carthage, which destroyed Selinunte. Carthage protected Segesta from Dionysius of Syracuse, but couldn't do a thing when Agathocles of Syracuse captured the city in 307 BC, slaying 10,000 people and selling the rest as slaves. He repopulated it with Greeks and named it *Dikaeopolis*, but it drifted back to Carthage. However, when Rome took the upper hand in the First Punic War, the treacherous Segestans massacred the Punic garrison and pledged allegiance to Rome. In the 10th century the Saracens destroyed Segesta once and for all.

The Temple

But Segesta left behind one of Sicily's most celebrated sights, the great Temple of Segesta, high up on the itinerary of any Grand Traveller, although its lovely situation is now somewhat marred by the road-building mania of the Italians in the form of the A29. Although the temple was never finished (the 36 columns are unfluted, and the *cella* and roof were never built), this temple to an unknown deity is one of the most majestic monuments of the ancient world. An Athenian architect is believed to have designed it, and had the temple ever been completed, it would have been among the most beautiful. Views of the surrounding countryside are ravishing and you can get a pick-me-up at the nearby café.

On the other side of the unexcavated Hellenistic *Egesta*, the road leads up Monte Barbaro to the theatre, built in the 3rd century BC. Excellently preserved, it measures 631 m in diameter and has 20 rows of seats. Beneath the orchestra runs an underground passage from which actors could pop out from the 'underworld'. The theatre, which commands an extraordinary view over the Golfo di Castellammare, still hosts occasional summer performances of Greek drama. A rough path below it leads to the **Sanctuary of the Elymnians**, towards the hamlet of Magno. Although built in the 6th century BC, this walled enclosure precociously shows the Greek influence.

Salemi

South along the SS188A from Segesta (or take a bus from Trapani) is Salemi, site of the Sikan town of *Halicyae*, today dominated by a 13th-century castle. An earthquake in 1968 made the centre of town unsafe and it has been abandoned. Here in 1860 Garibaldi declared himself ruler of Sicily in the name of Vittorio Emanuele. Beneath it all you can see the ruins of a **Paleo–Christian basilica**, which dates, according to the local brochure, from the 5th century BC! The most curious thing about the basilica are its African-influenced mosaics.

If you wind 24 km east of Salemi, near **Poggioreale**, you can take a look at the excavations begun on Monte Castellazzo of a town believed to be the ancient *Entella*. What has been uncovered so far dates back to the 4th century BC.

Alcamo to Trapani, Along the Coast

On the Golfo di Castellammare, the largest town is **Castellammare del Golfo** on SS187, near the mouth of the River Freddo, a popular resort with hotels and a campsite. The Festival of Sicilian Songs takes place here each year on 2 August. Picturesque **Scopello**, with its little harbour dotted with sea rocks on the west side of the gulf, is an unspoiled fishing village, and there's a postcard view of it from the road.

The plunging shoreline along the western rim of the Golfo di Castellammare has defied even Italian road engineers. The Sicilian tourist board calls it 'Marble Riviera';

and the part inaccessible to motorists is now a protected bird and wildlife 'reserve' called **Zingaro**. To reach the towns of the peninsula, you must travel 24 km west to Crocevie, and veer north towards **Custonaci**, with its marble quarries; from there the road continues to the tip of the mountainous cape, **San Vito lo Capo** (frequent bus from Trapani), a growing resort with a fine beach, with Monte Monaco providing the backdrop. From 10 July to 10 September, the Pro Loco provides numerous distractions and a feast of the patron saint San Vito to keep sun-seekers amused, including a photography contest.

WHERE TO STAY AND EAT   (telephone prefix 0924)
In Castellammare del Golfo: there are many inexpensive hotels and locandas, mainly catering for Sicilian families on holiday. Best here is the ****Punta Nord Est**, Via Leonardo da Vinci 67 (tel 33 633; L40–45 000 with bath). The restaurant **Oasi Azzurra** (tel 31 575), on the waterfront, has good Sicilian staples such as pasta with eggplant, grilled meat and fish, and couscous (L20 000) and the pizzeria **Stella del Mare** has a wide variety of good oven pizzas at L10 000 for the full whack. There's no fussing in Scopello—everything is one-star only; the **Torre Bennistra** has rooms with bath for L38 000 (Via Natale di Roma 19, tel 596 003), with a restaurant serving pasta *con sarde e finochiello* (sardine and fennel), tagliatelle with shrimp, oven-cooked fish and local wine (L25 000). The locanda **La Tavernattea** is even cheaper (Via A. Diaz 2, tel 596 007; L30 000 with bath) and a few steps along is the restaurant–pensione **Tranchina**, with *pasta con fave* (beans), lentil dishes, fish soup and meat done over the open fire (L20 000).

In San Vito lo Capo (tel prefix 0923): The **Cala' Mpiso** pool, tennis, garden, beach, etc. (tel 972 287; open May–Oct; L45–55 000 with bath) and **La Ruota**, Via Cavour 88, with 5 rooms (tel 972 629; L30 000 with bath) and restaurant (L20 000). There are many inexpensive, simple places along this coast, and one of Italy's 4-star campsites, **El Bahira** on the beach at Macari, 7 km south of San Vito (tel 972 577). Fish is served nearly everywhere; look in the Via Savoia. Especially good is **Costa Gaia** at no. 125, with couscous, seafood, *involtini*, etc., and the trattoria **Mamma Teresa** in Via Cortese—it's good home cooking, with *risottoa alla marinara* and a selection of fried fish (L20 000).

Trapani

Trapani, a salty, Baroque-encrusted provincial capital, is built on the site of ancient Drepanon, on an odd hook of land beckoning to the Egadi Islands. Drepanon was the harbour of Eryx (Erice) and, like that city, populated by Elymnians, a rather mysterious people who claimed Greek descent but who were allies of the Phoenicians. Samuel Butler and Robert Graves have produced some clever arguments that the *Odyssey* ('the first Greek novel') was written in Drepanon by a woman, perhaps named Nausicaa, who disregarded the ancient myths to 'whitewash Penelope'—theories that Graves pursues in his novel *Homer's Daughter*.

In 260 BC Hamilcar Barca transferred people from Eryx to the port, making it a city in its own right. The Romans took it in 241 BC, Lutatio Catullus defeating the Carthaginians from his base on the islet of Colombaia.

Because of its position between Europe and Tunis, Trapani prospered from the 13th century; the crowned heads of Europe were always popping in and out. King Theobald of Navarre died here in 1270 from a Tunisian fever; Edward I of England landed here on his return from the Crusades and learned that he had inherited his kingdom; Peter of Aragon disembarked here in 1282 to accept the crown after the Sicilian Vespers, and Emperor Charles V used Trapani as a base in the Tunisian campaign. During World War II, bombing seriously damaged the city, especially the San Pietro quarter.

GETTING AROUND
By air: to Palermo, Rome and Pantelleria (airport at Birgi, 23 km away—bus from Corso Italia).
By sea: to Egadi Islands, Pantelleria (5 trips a week); Ustica, Cagliari, Naples (by hydrofoil) and Tunis (by Tirrenia).
By train: to Palermo (usually very slow), Segesta, Marsala and Agrigento (also slow) from Stazione Centrale in Piazza Umberto I.
By bus: from behind the station to Palermo, Sciacca and all towns in the province, including Erice.

TOURIST INFORMATION
APT, Via Vito Sorba 15 (tel (0923) 27273); information office in Piazza Saturno (tel (0923) 29 000) and at the airport.
Post Office: Piazza Vittorio Veneto.
Telephones: Via Scontrino.

Corso Vittorio Emanuele
The port of Trapani today still does a fair amount of business; the saltpans with their windmills and tuna fisheries also provide important income for the bustling little city. Although the post-war expansion inland is as ugly as any in Italy, the old town on the narrow peninsula has a well-kept charm, especially the main street, Corso Vittorio Emanuele, where traffic is prohibited. Here Trapani is only five blocks long—on one side lies the port with views of the Egadi Islands, and on the northern side, the powerful lighthouse and nearest beach, **Lido di San Giuliano**. The town has a number of artisan shops producing silverware, sculptures, bronze and coral work, and it seems as if there is a horsemeat butcher on every corner.

Facing the Corso Vittorio Emanuele on Via Torrearsa is the beautiful **Municipio** (1696), the focal point of the shopping area. On the Corso itself, the grandiose Jesuit **Chiesa del Collegio** (at present undergoing restoration after the 1968 earthquake) (1636) by Natale Masuccio has a fine Baroque façade and contains the wooden *Misteri*, the 18th-century processional figures representing Passion scenes carried about the city during the Holy Week celebrations. The sacristy houses an elaborate cupboard carved by a local sculptor, Pietro Orlando. An extension of the Corso leads to the **Torre di Ligny**, named after a Spanish prince.

Behind the Municipio, in the triangular Piazzetta Saturno (named after the fountain in the centre), is the church of **Sant'Agostina**, a 14th-century Templar church with a good rose window, but little else. South, on the Corso Italia in the San Pietro quarter, **Santa Maria del Gesù** contains a lovely *Madonna degli angeli* by distant Tuscan Andrea della

Robbia and a *baldacchino* by Antonello Gagini; the south door also dates from the Renaissance. On the other side of the Corso, off Via 30 Gennaio in the old Jewish ghetto is the towered **Palazzo della Guidecca**, embellished with the 16th-century Plateresque windows and grimacing faces. To the north, **San Domenico** (17th century) contains the sarcophagus of Manfred, son of Frederick III of Aragon.

At the end of Via Garibaldi on Piazza Vittorio Veneto is the **post office**, a 1930s confection with an elaborate art nouveau–art deco façade. The public gardens of the **Villa Margherita** nearby have a small zoo; operettas and plays are often performed here in summer. Just outside the park is a public trampoline, where you can bounce with the local children for a small fee.

Museo Regionale Pepoli

Bus no. 1 from Piazza Umberto I travels to the Museo Regionale Pepoli (open 9.30–4; Sun 9.30–1; closed Mon), founded by Agostino Pepoli in 1908 and located in an old convent in Via Conte Agostino Pepoli. It contains a wide variety of paintings, church art, glass and archaeological finds, a pompously amusing painting of Jupiter and Napoleon, and a figure of Christ on the cross carved from a single piece of coral by the Trapanese sculptor Giovanni Matera. The church attached to the museum, the **Santuario dell' Annunziata**, was founded in 1315 and badly restored in 1760, so that only the door and the rose window remain of the original structure. In the sanctuary stands a medieval Madonna of Pisan manufacture, the object of an annual pilgrimage and yes, there's also a Gagini Madonna to keep her company.

WHERE TO STAY (tel prefix 0923)

If you're just passing through on the train, you can't do better than the reliable ***Hotel Sole** at the station of Piazza Umberto I (tel 22 035; L32 000), or the ***Moderno**, Via Genovese 20 (tel 21247; L38 000 with bath). For something classier, just outside the town there is the ****Cavallino Bianco**, by the sea on the Lungomare Dante Alighieri (tel 2 1549; L55 000).

Seaside resort hotels include the *****Astoria Park Hotel**, at Cusumano on the Lungomare D. Alighieri (tel 62 400), with a pool, garden, beach, tennis courts and more for L90 000.

EATING OUT

Couscous with fish is the delicious speciality of Trapani (usually eaten as a first course), and you can get it in several forms at the trattoria **I Trabinis**, Largo Porto Galli 4, for L18–22 000. A treat awaits you at **P & G**, Via Spalti 1 (tel 47 701), where the chef prepares not only delicious fish couscous, but a wide variety of antipasti and a *pasta al pesto trapanese* (L35 000). **Dell'Arco**, Via N. Bixio 110 (near the sports ground, tel 27 796), is not as expensive but equally good, particularly the *pasta col nero delle sepie* (inkfish) and the fish served in a red sauce called *matarocco*, with a large selection of local wines (L25–30 000). Marsala wines and innovative cuisine are to be found at **Il Salotto**, Via N. Burgio 10 (closed Sun; L30–40 000). At the popular **Da Felice** on the waterfront at Via Amm. Staiti 45 (tel 47 822) you can sit outside and watch the day trippers pour off the island ferries as you tuck into some very good and reasonably priced food (L20 000 for a full meal). Least expensive, and often serving couscous, is **Safina** across from the station (tel 22 708; L15–18 000).

Erice

High above Trapani, connected by an hour-long bus ride (enjoyable for its lingering views of Trapani and the sea below, as well as the lovely wild flowers that blanket the hillsides) or a shorter cable railway ride, is Erice (known to the ancients as Eryx), on top of the 756 m mountain of the same name. Eryx was famous all over the ancient world for its temple of the fertility goddess Venus Erycina, mentioned as a landmark in the *Aeneid*. Indeed the mountain seems to rise straight out of the sea, a natural home to magic and myth. That eryx means 'heather' and that the symbol of the goddess was the bee attest to the extreme antiquity of this most sacred Elymnian cult. The Elymnians claimed descent not only from the Greeks but also from the Trojans, whose leader, Aeneas, was the son of Venus. Daedalus offered a golden honeycomb to the goddess when he visited Eryx; and in a later legend, Eryx, another son of Aphrodite, hosted Hercules when he came to Sicily.

Erice has always had an obvious reputation as being impregnable, but in 260 BC Hamilcar Barca seized and destroyed it, moving its population down to the port of Drepanon. The Romans captured it and Tiberius and Claudius rebuilt the temple, paying homage to the mountain. When the Arabs captured the town, they too felt the holiness of the place and named it Gebel Hamed (Mahomet's mountain). Count Roger named it Monte San Giuliano after a dream he had there of St Julian. In 1934 Mussolini re-dubbed it Erice.

Erice has been described as more like a hill town of Umbria than Sicily; in the right season (especially when the fog curls around the mountain) you do get a flavour of that misty, mystical hilly region in the centre of Italy.

GETTING AROUND
From Trapani, the most uplifting method of reaching Erice (20 km east) is by *funivia* (cable railway). The *funivia* station is a few km east of the city (take bus no. 2 from the station); cars make the trip up every hour. Buses run all the way to the top almost as often, making a circular route through Paparella. If you're driving, there's convenient parking just outside Erice's walls.

TOURIST INFORMATION
Viale Conte Pepole 56, by the Porta Trapani (tel (0923) 869 388).

A Stroll through Erice
The town today is more medieval than any in Sicily—perhaps even in all of Italy. Eerie silence reigns in the narrow, roughly cobbled streets (don't wear high heels!) that wind up and down the hills, making Erice seem much larger than it actually is. The houses have secretive stone façades, each hiding a delightful courtyard full of plants and cats, and sometimes a pretty girl. Whether or not the goddess of love has a hand in the matter, the women of Erice are reputed to be the most beautiful in Sicily. Nowadays, in addition to the day trippers, scholars from many lands descend on Erice for conferences on a wide range of topics, some as evocative as the town itself.

You enter the town through the **Porta Trapani**, of Norman construction, as are all the gates. By some of these, particularly on the north side of town, the ancient walls are well preserved, having been repaired by the Romans; their foundations date back to the

Elymnians. Off the Via Vittorio Emanuele is the **Cathedral**, founded by Frederick of Aragon in 1312 with a façade dating from 1426, which for once hasn't been touched since then. The dimly lit interior has an almost Arabic ceiling and contains a statue of the Madonna and Child by Francesco Laurana. Via Vittorio Emanuele leads into the central Piazza Umberto I, where in the Municipio you may visit the small **Museo Comunale** (open 10–12 and 2–4; Sun 10–1), with a lovely Annunciation by Antonello Gagini, a 4th-century BC head of Aphrodite, Punic and Greek bronze sculptures and a wax nativity scene, among other items; the Library in the next room contains various incunabula.

At the other corner of town, above the communal gardens, stand the medieval towers, the **Torretta Pepoli** and the **Castello Normanno**, the last with stupendous views in all directions; on a clear day it is said you can see to Cape Bon, Tunisia. Only the base remains of the **Temple of Venus Erycina** on the northeast side, thought to have been destroyed during the construction of the medieval castle. Unlike most Greek temples, which are oriented east–west, the base of this temple is aligned to the northeast and southwest. The Roman-built **Pozzo di Venere** (Well of Venus) can be seen here, as well as a mosaic floor. Fragments of the temple are incorporated in the castle walls.

WHERE TO STAY AND EAT   (tel prefix 0923)
There are few things more atmospheric than staying up at Erice and strolling through the town at night when the tourists have all gone: smartest here is the ******Ermione**, with a garden, on Via Pineta Comunale (tel 869 138; L85 000). Cosy and less expensive, the ****Edelweiss**, Cortile P. Vincenzo (tel 869 158), has centrally located rooms (L55 000 with bath). The **Re Aceste**, Via C. Ag. Pepoli, has spaghetti *alle vongole*, good couscous and other specialities for L20–30 000. Classier is the restaurant **Elimo**, Via V. Emanuele (tel 869 377), with a rarity in these parts, lasagna and *involtini di melanzane*, fish and steak (L35 000).

The South Coast and Interior

This part of Sicily holds very few natural attractions, and in places where the coast has been developed it's usually done very shoddily. Your impressions will depend largely on the time of year in which you come. In high summer the terrain is scorched and uninspiring, whereas in spring it is green and bedecked with wild flowers and fragrant almond blossoms. Inland there are some real treasures, the excavations of Selinunte and the Greek temples of Agrigento, and if your itinerary allows time for only one town in the interior of Sicily, it would be hard to choose between stalwartly medieval Enna lost up in the clouds or the handsome and chivalric Piazza Armerina, with the Villa Imperiale and its fabulous mosaics, only 3 km away.

Marsala

31 km from Trapani, Marsala is a pretty, shady town with a long wide palm-tree lined promenade, which helps preserve the atmosphere of calm pervading its streets and

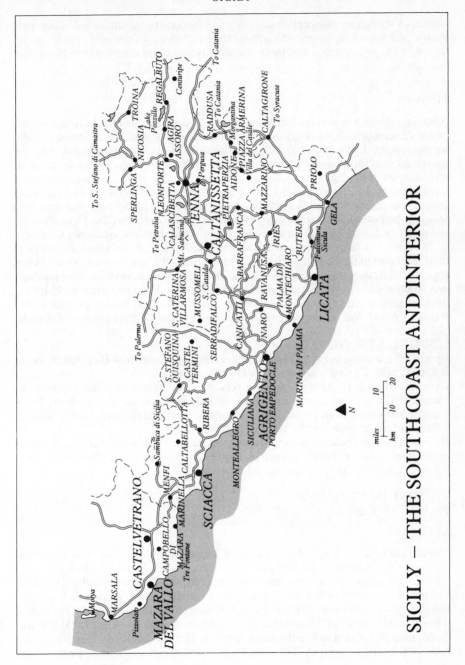

SICILY – THE SOUTH COAST AND INTERIOR

citizens. Although no stranger to visitors, Marsala has as yet been untouched by the cruel hand of mass tourism, but it's only a matter of time before the combined efforts of the tourist board and property developers launch Marsala on to the road of package tour stardom.

History

Nowadays synonymous with wine, Marsala is situated near ancient Lilybaeum, founded by the Phoenicians after Dionysius of Syracuse destroyed their base at Motya (see the section on the Egadi Islands). Although the original settlement occupied only the westernmost point of Sicily at Capo Boeo, the name Lilybaeum eventually came to include most of the land occupied by present-day Marsala. Powerfully fortified by the Carthaginians, Lilybaeum was the only place Pyrrhus failed to take in his whirlwind conquest of the island. The Romans besieged it unsuccessfully for nine years and only took it in the peace following their victory at Erice. Cicero described it as a splendid city, and in 204 BC Scipio Africanus and his fleet sailed from Lilybaeum to conquer Carthage.

The Saracens renamed the town Marsah-el-Allah ('the port of God') and made it their main port in Sicily. In the 18th and 19th centuries the English set up various wine import establishments, first the Woodhouse and then the Ingham–Whitaker firms, still very visible today. Garibaldi landed at Marsala in May 1860, and ever since then Marsala has been known as the *Città dei Mille*, the City of the Thousand. Its strategic position did it dirty in World War II, however, when the city was all but destroyed in bombing raids.

GETTING AROUND
By air: 15 km away, between Marsala and Trapani, the airport of Birgi has flights to Rome (75 min, 2 a day) and Pantelleria (30 min, 2 a day)
By train: Marsala is connected by train regularly with Trapani; the line continues to Mazara del Vallo and Castelvetrano, where it loops back up to the north. From Castelvetrano there is an erratic service along the coast to Selinunte, Menfi, Sciacca, Ribera and Montallegro on the way to Agrigento.
By bus: buses ply the same routes; Marsala, Mazara and Campobella di Mazara are all on the autostrada and quickly reached from either Trapani or Palermo. Services to other points originate in Marsala, Sciacca and Agrigento.

TOURIST INFORMATION
Pro Loco, Via Garibaldi 45 (tel 958 097).

The Town
Marsala has retained much of its Saracen air, if not any of its physical structures. One survivor of the bombing is the **cathedral** on the Piazza della Republica, dedicated to St Thomas of Canterbury. It's only fair—the supporting columns were on their way from Corinth to Canterbury when the ship carrying them took refuge in Marsala in a heavy storm. The columns were considered to be too heavy and were subsequently off-loaded. The cathedral contains the tomb of native son Antonio Lombardo (died 1595) who was Archbishop of Messina and Ambassador to Spain. The Spanish King Philip II gave him eight 16th-century tapestries illustrating the conquest of Jerusalem; these are on display

in the church and are quite remarkable. Of the Gagini works here, Antonello's St Thomas is the best. Via Garibaldi passes through the Porta Garibaldi. Various Spanish bastions mark the perimeter of the old city walls, and to the northeast, by the Scuola dei Cappucini, there is a large Punic–Roman necropolis.

Lilybaeum
Leaving Marsala through the western gate, head towards the flat, littered shore where the **excavations of Lilybaeum** can be seen at Capo Boeo (open daily 9–12 and 2 pm until dusk). The remains here are mainly Roman. Some vestiges of the city walls have been uncovered near Viale V. Veneto along with the baths and some well-preserved mosaics. At the Baglio Anselmi at the tip of Capo Boeo, a new, mammoth structure houses the marvellous Punic ship recovered by the archaeologist Honor Frost in the early 1970s. The ship, a liburnian, was found off Isola Lunga in the Stagnone group of islands, and may have been sunk in the Battle of the Egadi Islands, which, in 241 BC, ended the first Punic War. Measuring 35 m and manned by 68 rowers, it is a unique example of Classical warships, and amazingly well preserved (open 9–2, also Wed, Sat and Sun 3–5 pm, closed Mon). Here also stands a marble obelisk commemorating Scipio Africanus' departure, Garibaldi's arrival, and the Battle of Lepanto.

The best time to come to Marsala is Holy Thursday, when a sacred procession in costume a kilometre in length makes its way down the *contrade*; among the more typical 'masks' of figures from the Passion are the *verginelle addoloratine*, young girls in fabulous golden headdresses, each concocted from the family jewels, from which flow their sheer white veils.

Marsala Wine
Marsala, one of the most popular wines in England in the 18th and 19th centuries, was developed when a certain soap merchant in Liverpool named John Woodhouse noticed that Sicilian wine, when fortified with alcohol before the long trip to England, was much better than the plain wine. He moved to Marsala, reproduced the same effect in his winery, and shipped the first batch to England in 1773, where it soon became a roaring success. In 1806 Benjamin Ingham opened another winery; in 1833 Vicenzo Florio opened a third. For the next hundred years the three firms ruled the industry, until 1929 when Cinzano bought them up (though it continues to bottle the wine under their old labels).

The Florio Winery south of the town, on the Lungomare Mediterraneo, may be visited daily 10.30–1 and 3.30–6, with abundant tastings provided. The sweetest of the sweet wine brewed in those great wooden casks is *Marsala all'uovo*—with egg yolks. Others have various flavours added; *Marsala secco*—dry only by Marsala standards—may be your favourite as an aperitif. Besides Florio, there are a number of other wineries along the roads to Selinunte and the airport.

WHERE TO STAY AND EAT
(tel prefix 0923)
Marsala has several choices: ***President**, Via Bixio 1 (tel 999 333), with its own pool (L85–95 000). With the same standard of comfort and also with a pool are ***Cap 3000**, Via Trapani 161 (tel 989 055; L80 000), and ***Stella d'Italia** in the town centre (Via M. Rapisardi 7; tel 953003; L65 000 with bath, L52 000 without). The **Garden**, Via

Gambini 36 (tel 982 320), is small and cheap at L33–50 000, depending on whether you want a bath).

Zio Ciccio near the Florio winery on Lungomare Mediterraneo 211 (tel 981 962) has couscous and seafood specialities such as spaghetti with lobster sauce or shellfish for L30 000. On the sea **Marinella 'Gnaziu 'U Pazzu**, Contrada Stagnone 800 (tel 989 792), has similar dishes and is even better, but, naturally, pricier (L35 000). **Enzo e Nino**, a trattoria on Via Favorita 26, also has couscous and fish and—rare in an Italian restaurant—dessert specialities, for around L25 000 total.

Scaloppine al Marsala is a speciality at **Garibaldi** in Piazza Addolorata (L20 000) Every restaurant in Marsala, not surprisingly, serves the local wine, and the odd eyebrow may be raised if you ask for something dryer.

Mazara del Vallo

TOURIST INFORMATION
Piazza della Repubblica (tel (0923) 941 727).

South along the coast, past the resort of Lido Ponticello, is the important fishing town of Mazara del Vallo, at the mouth of the River Mazaro. Dusty and chaotic as it is, the town has a palm-lined waterfront, giving a hint of what's across the water in North Africa. Originally a colony of Selinunte, Mazara was destroyed at the same time as that city by the Carthaginians. In 827 the Saracens conquered Mazara, their first territory in Sicily, then Count Roger took it in 1075, and 20 years later the town saw the first Norman parliament. Over the door of the **Cathedral** stands a statue of Count Roger who founded the church, although nothing remains of the Norman structure. Inside are two Gagini works: a tomb by Domenico (1485) and a Transfiguration by Antonello. Antonello also sculpted the Santa Caterina in the church of that name. An old Palace of the Knights of Malta now containing a small **Roman museum** (open 10–1), is on the Via Carmine, near the harbour. For the Knights, Mazara was the nearest Christian city and port, as well as the home of the Spanish viceroys, to whom the Knights paid homage. West of the town is a long beach which is uncrowded, even in summer, and has not yet been transformed into a 'Lido', meaning there are no concrete walls with broken glass atop to deter non-paying guests and no umbrella forests, nor overpriced cafeterias.

Due east lies wine-making **Campobello di Mazara** where the parish church contains a 15th-century crucifix by Fra Umile da Petralia. From here take the Strada di Tre Fontane to the Greek quarries at the caves of **Rocche di Cusa** (from N115, turn off at Principe–Torre Cusa). It was from here that Selinunte took the stone to build its temples, and some of the column drums, still waiting to be taken in ox carts to Selina, can be seen amidst the trees. The Carthaginian invasion in 409 BC interrupted the work on Temple G, and the quarries have not been used since that day.

WHERE TO STAY AND EAT   (tel prefix 0923)
The hotel ****Mediterraneo**, Via Valeria 36, is reasonable at L52 000 with bath, L40 000 without (tel 932 688). The trattoria **Da Nicola**, Via Emanuele Sansone 21 (tel 94 270, closed Mon) is one of the best places to eat here, with couscous and a wide

selection of fish dishes, which are somewhat spicier than elsewhere (L35 000); and local specialities are served at **Del Pescatore**, Via Castelvetrano 191 (tel 947 580), including a crab pasta and swordfish (L20–30 000).

Castelvetrano

TOURIST INFORMATION
Corso V. Emmanuele 102 (tel (0924) 41015).

The largest town in the area, Castelvetrano is a wine- and furniture-making centre and the base for visiting Selinunte. In the Municipio in Piazza Garibaldi you can see the city's beautiful jewel—the *Ephebe of Selinunte*, an excellently preserved bronze statue of an athlete dating from 460 BC. The **Chiesa Madre** contains an altarpiece by Orazio Ferraro and works by Serpotta. Outside is the **fontana della Ninfa**, built in 1615. Those with time should not miss the Arabic-influenced Byzantine chapel **Santissima Trinità di Delia**, built in the 12th century and restored to its original state. To see the interior, ask the caretaker. The chapel is a couple of miles west of town (look for the yellow signs).

Selinunte

Buses leave Castelvetrano for the beach and village of Marinella Lido and for the magnificent and romantic ruins of Selinunte (you also go by train). Ancient Selinus, lying between the rivers Selinus and Cotone, was the most westerly of all Greek colonies, founded by Megara Hyblaea around 650 BC, an event that was considered so important that an official founding father, or *oikistes*, was brought in from Megara in Greece to lead the new colonists. Selinus' name derives from the Greek word for the wild celery (*selinon*), the symbol of the city, which still grows there on the fertile plain. This plain that attracted settlers so far westward was the cause of the city's prosperity, mainly in the 6th and 5th centuries BC, as well as its woes, for Segesta coveted the land and ceaselessly fought for it, by fair means and foul; for over two centuries its existence depended on the astuteness of its diplomats in dealing with the neighbouring Carthaginians to the west and Hellenized Elymians of Segesta just to the north. The latter were Selinus' worst enemies; in 409 BC they formed an alliance with Carthage, which sent 100,000 men against Selinus, capturing the city in only nine days, before its ally Syracuse could send aid. Although Hermocrates of Syracuse later attempted to found a new settlement on the plain, he was later killed and the site returned to Carthaginian hands. In 250 BC they removed the inhabitants to Marsala and destroyed Selinus for strategic reasons; earthquakes finished the job, leaving an impressive, highly evocative ruin.

As Selinunte was in non-Greek territory, it absorbed many foreign influences which, combined with Hellenic ideals, contributed to the high artistic traditions of the city. The metopes and vases at Palermo are examples of this, as well as the bronze athlete at Castelvetrano. The grid plan of the streets is one of the oldest in the world, dating back to a century before Hippodamus supposedly invented it. This is not all that surprising: Sicily was the 'New World' for the Greeks, and on virgin turf the grid is the easiest way to divide property—witness New York, Chicago, Detroit or a hundred other cities in America.

The Excavations
The excavations of Selinus (open daily, 9 until dusk) lie on rather desolate low hills facing the sea. The most interesting part of Selinus are the temples of its well-fortified acropolis, anciently divided by the harbour which the River Cotone has since filled up with silt. The temples are identified by letters, as their dedications are uncertain. Of the three temples on the eastern bank near the station, the most prominent is **Temple E** (480–460 BC) reconstructed in 1958, as can be seen by the different degrees of weathering that the individual columns have suffered. This gives the magnificent 5th-century BC structure a piecemeal, fragile look. Measuring 67 m by 25 m, the four *metopes* removed from here to the Palermo museum suggest a dedication to Hera. **Temple F** beside it belongs to the mid-6th century BC, and is unusual in that the spaces between its columns were filled in with 3-m walls, perhaps to prevent outsiders from watching the sacred rites inside. These unusual stone screens, original to Selinus, may have inspired the architect of the huge Temple of Olympieon Zeus at Agrigento when faced with the knotty problem of holding up such a large structure. As to size, the Agrigento architect was competing with the grandeur of **Temple G** on the other side of the road. Begun in the 5th or 6th century BC, this vast edifice measures 113 m by 54 m and was lined with columns 3.3 m in diameter, now broken and lying about like a giant's broken toys; like the Temple of Zeus, to which it is second in size, it was unfinished when the Carthaginian bully-boys came to town. Over the years of its construction, fashions changed, and the temple is partly Archaic, partly Classical. Only one column still stands, built of 100-ton drums.

THE WEST ACROPOLIS
The Acropolis stands on a small plateau on the other bank of the Cotone, where there are more temples, the remains of the walls (begun 6th century BC) and the site of the city itself, located just inland on another hill and connected to this westerly Acropolis by a path. Dominating the Acropolis is the 1927 reconstructed colonnade of **Temple C**, a large temple (63 m by 24 m) thought to have been dedicated to Hercules. The Archaic *metopes* in Palermo came from this temple, which was built in the 6th century BC. Some of the columns were monoliths instead of divided drums, and when these collapsed in an 8th-century earthquake, they flattened a Byzantine village on the hill.

Across the ancient street are the vestiges of **Temple O** and Temple A. Of Temple O only the platform (stylobate) remains, while pieces of the 36 columns of **Temple A**, as well as its stylobate, can be seen. Both of these temples date from 490–480 BC, the last and most refined temples built in Selinunte. Only the base remains of little **Temple B** constructed in the Hellenistic period. Temple D (56 m by 23 m), on the main street leading to the ancient city, was built in 535 BC. The nearby ramparts of the North Gate belong to 250 BC.

SANCTUARY OF DEMETER
To the west, on the other side of the ancient River Selinus (modern Modione), a path leads to the **Sanctuary of Demeter Malophoros** ('the apple-bearer'). The walled sanctuary, or *megaron*, was built around 575 BC, replacing an older one. Outside the sanctuary worshippers set up carved *stellae*, and more than 12,000 votive figures of Demeter have been recovered, attesting to the importance of the cult, which appears to

have had some connection with death as well as fertility; a vast necropolis is spread around the sanctuary, and for several miles along the coast tombs are visible in places.

Around Selinunte

Menfi to the east, once a picturesque feudal town, was destroyed by an earthquake in 1968. The new town has been constructed above the old, which remains in ruins. **Porto Palo**, 8 km south on the coast, has a fine beach. Inland, north of Menfi, **Santa Margherita di Belice**, the childhood home of Giuseppe di Lampedusa, has an elegant piazza worth visiting if you are passing through on the N188. A late Bronze Age settlement, **Monte Adranone**, has been found north of Sambuca di Sicilia. The inhabitants of the simple round huts here were Hellenized by Selinunte; the Romans destroyed the settlement in the 1st century. **Lake Arancio**, by Sambuca, reputedly offers excellent fishing.

WHERE TO STAY AND EAT   (tel prefix 0924)
Near Selinunte, at Marinella (Castelvetrano) you can stay on the beach at ****Giani**, Via Pigafetta 2 (tel (46222; L60 000 with bath), or at the ***Lido Azzurro** with an excellent seafood restaurant on the terrace (Via Marco Polo 98; tel 46057; L38 000 with bath). Both of these are at Marinella, officially part of Castelvetrano, and nearby at Belice di Mare is the **Paradise Beach Club** (tel 46 333), a large modern affair with all the trimmings for loners and families alike. It has a good buffet restaurant too. High season rates are around L140 000, but otherwise reckon on about L90 000. In Castelvetrano itself, if you're thinking of a quick overnight stop, the *****Selinus**, Via Bonsignore 22 (tel 41104; L60 000), has a good restaurant with typical Sicilian cooking, including the old faithful, pasta with eggplant and basil (L22 000), and the ***Ideal**, Via Partanna 26 (tel 901 454) lives up to its name pricewise—L28 000 (without bath). Try the good ravioli and meat dishes at **Efebo**, Via Campobello 6 (L25 000); in Marinella di Selinunte, after seeing the ruins, try one of the many pastas at the restaurant–pizzeria **La Scogliera**, Via Scalo di Bruca 25, among them *bucatini con sarde*, and lots of fish dishes for L20–30 000.

Sciacca

TOURIST INFORMATION
Corso Vittorio Emanuele 84 (tel (0925) 22 744).

To the east, Sciacca (pronounced Shakka) has been a thermal spa since ancient times, when it was known as *Thermae Selinuntinae*. During the 15th and 16th centuries one of Sicily's greatest feuds, the *Caso di Sciacca*, divided the town's population into factions loyal to the Luna and Perolla families. The feud left the town devastated and decreased its population by half. Sciacca today is the prettiest town in Agrigento Province, especially in the upper quarters, which recall places in North Africa, but it suffers from an overpopulation of cars. The thermal spa lies at the eastern end of town, and to the west are the beaches of Stazzone, Lido Salus and La Foggia.

The traditional way of entering this terraced town overlooking the sea is through the grandiose **Porta San Salvatore** built in the 16th century within the older fortifications. The lower town contains many fine churches—among them **Santa Margherita** (1342, rebuilt in 1595), a lovely Renaissance Catalan portal with sculptures by Francesco Laurana, and nearby, the peculiar church of the **Carmine** looking for all the world like a picture in a book with a torn page, so abruptly does its 18th-century restoration stop midway up. The **Norman Cathedral** of the early 12th century has since been modified with a curly Baroque façade, decorated on the outside with five statues by Antonino and Gian Americo Gagini, while the east side of the church is original and quite lovely. The interior is mainly Renaissance, with a statue of the Virgin by Laurana. Near here, in the central piazza, the **Palazzo Municipale** dates from 1615. On Via Incisa note the beautiful 15th-century palace of **Casa Arone** and the crenellated, diamond stubbly **Palazzo Steripinto**, also from the 1400s, on Via Gerardi. Near the Steripinto is the derelict 12th-century **Church of San Nicola**. Among the pretty houses in the upper town stands the solemn **Luna Castle**, built in 1380, and the church of **Santa Maria della Giummare**, a fine Norman church redone à la Catalan, with frescoes by Mariano Rossi (18th century).

Monte San Calogero

Six km north of Sciacca, Monte San Calogero is another thermal spa, where people since antiquity have come for the natural steam baths (the *stufe vaporose di San Calogero*). The seats and water channels were hollowed out in ancient times; legend has it that Daedalus made the baths, while other sources claim that St Paul sent San Calogero to Sicily to put an end to a plague raging there, and during his stay he found the caverns in the mountain that bears his name, as well as the natural saunas which are reputed to cure rheumatism and are still in use today. Beneath the steam baths, where the sulphurous vapours are more concentrated, lie two underground caverns, open since very ancient times, where archaeologists and speleologists have discovered huge Copper Age jars and the tiny arm bones of children sacrificed as an offering to the terrible gods inside. The sulphurous fountains near here are dedicated to the Madonna degli Ammalati.

Perhaps strangest of all the stories concerning San Calogero involves a small uncharted island offshore. In 1831, British seamen discovered and claimed it for Britain. Sicily, of course, disputed the claim, but before Britain could make a full reply, the island sank out of sight, disappearing as mysteriously as it had appeared.

Caltabellotta and Ribera

The Castello at nearby Caltabellotta saw the 1302 signing of the peace ending the War of the Vespers. Among the buildings of this medieval town is the Norman **Chiesa Madre** containing two works by the Gagini—the *Madonna della Catena* and a St Benedict.

Ribera was founded in 1627 by Prince Luigi Paterno who named the town after his wife Maria di Ribera. Here the famous Prime Minister Francesco Crispi was born in 1818. Ribera is also famous for its strawberries, which make Sicilian mouths water at their mention.

Eraclea Minoa

Monteallegro, an 18th-century town built below the old hill town, is the base for visiting Eraclea Minoa (*Heracleia Minoa*) near the mouth of the River Platani. Although no public

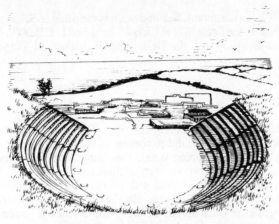

Eraclea Minoa, Agrigento

transport goes to the excavations, the beach and campsite near the ruins attract enough traffic to make hitchhiking a viable way to get there in the summer. The old place name, *Minoa*, suggests the legend of King Minos, who came to Sicily in search of Daedalus and was killed by the daughters of King Cocalos in his bath. Indeed, when Akragas captured the city, Theron supposedly discovered the tomb of Minos, considered by the inhabitants to be the founding father.

The town as it exists was founded in the 6th century by Selinunte; the name commemorating Hercules was added later, perhaps in the 4th century when the city belonged to Akragas. During the Carthaginian Wars, Eraclea Minoa was depopulated, as the River Platani (the ancient Halykos) formed the boundary between Greek and Punic territory. Timoleon repopulated the city with a mixed Greek–Carthaginian population; it changed hands a few times and suffered so much in the 1st-century Slave Wars that it was abandoned for good. The **excavations** (open 9 until dusk, shown by custodian) date mainly from the 4th century BC and include the powerful walls built in four stages, though landslides have destroyed the southern part of the walls. The interesting theatre, built of soft marl and now covered over to protect it from further weathering, was designed after the main theatre in Athens. An Antiquarium on the site contains a few items from the digs and a plan of the ancient city, which is still being excavated.

Further east towards Agrigento, **Siculiana** has a large castle dating from 1356 and a beach at Marina Siculiana.

WHERE TO STAY AND EAT (tel prefix 0925)
In Sciacca, one of the big resort hotels is the ***Torre Macauda** on the N115, (tel 26800; L90 000; garden, tennis courts, beach and pool). Smack next to the spa is the ***Grand Albergo delle Terme**, Piazza delle Terme (tel 23 133; L80 000), conveniently located for those patrons suffering from indigestion pains that alka-seltzer just can't handle. The **Piccolo Mondo** in Siculiana, Contrada San Rocco, has a garden and tennis court (tel (0922) 815531; rooms only L50 000, with the dubious chance of

watching Italian TV in your room). Seafood again is the pride of Sciacca, and you won't find any better than at **La Ferla**, Via al Lido 26 (tel 23 621; L25 000), but there's a lot more choice than that—try also the **Bella Napoli**, Viale della Vittoria (tel 25 448; L20 000).

Agrigento

Agrigento is a slick town, or so it seems at first sight. The young people on the tree-lined Viale della Vittoria, with the splendid panorama of the temples below, wear the latest fashions, and in the main shopping street, Via Atenea, the shops compete for your attention with shiny glittering displays. Outside these centres, however, Agrigento is just another dusty, shabby provincial capital with its modern extensions of dull concrete apartment blocks. The surroundings are all: the sloping hills covered with almond orchards, dazzling the eye when they blossom in February, and the magnificent Valley of the Temples, one of the major Greek sites in the world that keeps visitors coming all the year.

History

Colonists from Gela and Rhodes founded Agrigento, then known as *Akragas*, in 581 BC, on a landshelf between the rivers Akragas (San Biagio) and Hypsas (Sant' Anna), easily defensible and very fertile. The early colonists must have been very confident about Akragas' future, for unlike most ancient cities, it is thought the new colony was laid out with a large plan to grow into, and its extensive walls were built at one time in the 6th century.

Akragas soon became one of the major cities in Sicily, owing to an early tyrant, Phalaris, who reigned until 549 BC. Credit is given to him for the city walls and grand building programme and for annexing Licata from the Sikans. Pindar, who lived as a guest in Akragas under the later tyrant Theron, wrote that Phalaris roasted his enemies alive in a large brazen bull, a recurring theme in Rhodian mythology but not very likely to have happened in reality.

Under Theron (who ascended to power in 488 BC) Akragas expanded its territories up to Himera (Imera) on the north coast of Sicily, provoking the mass attack of Carthage on that city. Theron and his ally, Gelon of Gela, won a sweeping victory here, and the captives and disbanded soldiers of this campaign were set to work erecting the temples and other public works. The city became fabulously wealthy—'the people built temples as if they would live forever, but lived as if they would die the next day', marvelled an ancient writer. The pre-Socratic philosopher Empedocles was born here; he theorized that all matter was made of Earth, Water, Fire and Air (he was the first to discover air as a substance) and that Love and Strife moved them. Believing hot air would make him rise like a god, Empedocles jumped into the fiery crater of Mt Etna. Akragas was also famous for its horses, which won the great Games of the Ancient Greeks and were depicted on contemporary coins that have been found.

Time was running out for Akragas, however. When the city's great enemy, Syracuse, defeated the Athenians, the Carthaginians saw their chance to extract revenge for Imera.

They besieged Akragas for eight months before capturing it. Many of the citizens took refuge in the Temple of Athena and set fire to it and themselves as the Carthaginians looted the city. Later the Carthaginians allowed some inhabitants to return; it became independent, was rebuilt by Timoleon in 340 BC and eventually enjoyed a bit of its old prosperity under the Romans, when it became a centre of the coin market. By the 3rd century, however, *Agrigentum*, as the Romans called it, began a slow decline. The medieval town was built up around the ancient acropolis (Rupe Atenea) and was known as *Girgenti*. Mussolini, in his name campaign, changed it back to Agrigento in 1927.

Modern Sicily's most famous son, the playwright Luigi Pirandello (1867–1936), was born in Agrigento. In July and August performances of his plays are given in the Settimana Pirandellana.

GETTING AROUND

Agrigento is connected by rail directly with Trapani, Caltanisetta and Ragusa; connections to the rest of Sicily are patchy—one or two trains a day, with a change to make. The station is on Piazza Marconi, in the exact centre of the city. Buses for the temples and Porto Empedocle (for Lampedusa) leave from here as well; for connections outside the town of Agrigento, buses leave from Piazza Fratelli Roselli, though there are some that stop around the Piazza Vitt. Emanuele.

Regular city buses make the circuit of the Valley of the Temples, starting from Piazza Aldo Moro.

TOURIST INFORMATION

The city's AAST information booth is just around the corner from the station on the Piazza Aldo Moro (tel (0922) 20454). The EPT office is at Via della Vittoria 255 (tel (0922) 26926).

Up Via Atenea to Old Agrigento

Sloping Piazza Roma just north of the station (Piazza Marconi) is the centre of the city and one of the few green spots in Agrigento. At the bottom of the square, the Via F. Crispi leads down to the Archaeological Museum (open 9–2, Sun 9–1, closed Mon; adm) and the temples; on the opposite side, the Via Atenea takes you to the old town. On this street, the 17th-century church known as the Purgatorio, with fine sculptures by the Palermitan Serpotta, stands over the entrance to a complex underground system of cisterns of the 5th century BC (stone removed from here was used to build the temples). The Municipio, also on Via Atenea, is in a pretty 11th-century convent on the same square as the Teatro Pirandello and the Museo Civico (open 9–12 and 3–5; closed Sun), the latter containing a variety of paintings from many centuries. Up the stairs and alleyways from here you reach the old whitewashed Greek quarter of town, which indeed looks more Greek than Italian; signs will direct you to the old Orthodox cathedral, **Santa Maria dei Greci** (open 9.30–12 and 4–7; leave a tip). This little church with a lovely portal was constructed in the 13th century and incorporated a temple, perhaps of Athena. Six bases of Doric columns remain inside, as well as some frescoes and ceiling painting.

Via del Duomo

Further up you will find the Via del Duomo and the large 14th-century **Cathedral** at the very top of Agrigento. This and the Diocesan Museum next to it were damaged in a landslide in 1966 and the museum's collection has since been moved to the Archaeology Museum. Founded by San Gerlando, Roger I's bishop, the church was dedicated to him in 1365 and contains his relics in a silver casket. Partly painted, partly coffered, the ceiling offers the main interest in the interior, along with the grand arch in the nave. The phenomenon known as *porta voce* allows someone in the apse, beneath the cornice, to hear whispering in the main doorway, and so the priest could discreetly listen to comments on his sermon as the parishioners departed. Also on Via del Duomo is the Biblioteca Lucchesiana founded in 1765 by the Bishop of Agrigento as a public library, now containing 40,000 volumes.

The finest church in Agrigento, however, lies towards the east side of the old town, at the top of dead-end Via Fodera, not far from the round *fascisti* Post Office. Known as the **Badia Grande**, the Cistercian convent and church of Santo Spirito was founded by Marchisia Chiaramonte in 1290. The windows of the convent belong to that lovely style in Sicily known by the Chiaramonte name. The church preserves a beautiful doorway (on the west) and a white interior with stuccoes by Serpotta and a Madonna by the school of Domenico Gagini.

At the Rupe Atenea (Via San Vito on the east side of town), the old acropolis of Akragas, were temples of Zeus and Athena and the oldest part of the Greek colony. Some ruins of ancient structures remain, as well as the hypogeum.

The Valley of the Temples

The Archaeological Zone below Agrigento (Via F. Crispi) is always open, with the exception of the Temple of Zeus and the Temple of the Dioscuri (open 9 to dusk) and the Hellenistic quarter by the church of San Nicola (open 10–12 and 2–4 in summer; 9–2.30 in winter; closed Mon). Every night the temples are illuminated from 9.30–10.30.

ARCHAEOLOGY MUSEUM

Spread across 3 km in the valley, the temples take a good part of the day to explore, and you may consider stopping first at the National Archaeology Museum near the 15th-century cloisters of San Nicola—the first stop of the bus to the temples (open 9–3; Sun and festivals 9–12; closed Mon). This fabulous collection of vases, statues, coins, etc. found on the site makes a fine introduction to the splendour of ancient Akragas and its unique temples. Particularly good are the Greek vases and the heads and one body of the giant telemons of the Temple of Zeus. Beside these a display of models offers various conceptions of what this monstrous temple—the Radio City Music Hall of its day—used to look like. Among the sculptures, there is a Praxitelian torso and the Phaedra sarcophagus of the 2nd century AD, moved here from the damaged cathedral. A small Greek theatre was discovered next to the museum during its construction, and near the so-called Oratory of Phalaris, actually a shrine dedicated to an unknown woman of the 2nd century BC, converted to a chapel in the Middle Ages.

Across the Passeggiata Archeologica (the main road to the temples) lies the **Hellenistic–Roman Quarter** where along the grid streets some of the houses have good mosaics with protective coverings, and reconstructed columns of their peristyle courts. From here you can continue south on the Passeggiata to the main temples on either side of the

Posto di Ristoro (a café–bar) or backtrack a bit to the north turning east (right) for the Strada Panoramica and the Via Demetra; this, along with some ancient wheel ruts, leads up to San Biagio at the edge of the Rupe Atenea shelf.

SAN BIAGIO AND GATE I
The Normans built the San Biagio chapel over an important **Temple of Demeter and Persephone** begun shortly after the Greek victory at Himera in 480 BC. Of the temple, part of the foundation can be seen by the chapel and two round altars remain to the north; in one of them, a hole called the *bothros* received the wine, piglets, male members made of dough, etc. offered to the chthonic (underworld) gods, to whom the cult of Demeter and Persephone was naturally closely attached. Even more interesting in this respect is the **Rock Sanctuary of Demeter** below San Biagio (steps in the rock). Pre-dating the temple of Demeter and the Greek colony of Akragas itself by 200 years, the sanctuary is of Sikan origin, although the walls they built demonstrate how Greek influences infiltrated Sicily very early on. The sacred area consists of three natural caves, once filled with votive statues of Demeter and Persephone of various periods, the oldest dating back to the early 8th century BC, when water deities apparently were worshipped (channels and drains for the water can still be seen in the caves). Timoleon added the Nymphaeum to the sanctuary. A short walk south of here, by the wall of the cemetery, is the first of eight city gates, **Gate I**, and the V-shaped Bastion located at a particularly vulnerable point in the defences.

GATE II AND THE TEMPLE OF JUNO LACINIA
The Strada Panoramica heads south from here, taking you past **Gate II** (known as the Gela Gate) from where the ancient road to the mother city-state can still be seen. At this important gate, more votive offerings to Demeter and Persephone have been uncovered. The **Temple of Juno Lacinia**, the easternmost of the great temples, comes clearly into sight as you descend to the south. Its name derives from an 18th-century confusion with another temple, and its original dedication is unknown. Built around 460 BC, the temple still shows signs of when the Carthaginians set fire to it; the Romans later restored it, only to have their good work undone by an earthquake. Only 25 of the original 34 columns remain, windblasted on the southeast by the sirocco. The temple is currently undergoing restoration and cannot be entered.

GATE III AND THE TEMPLE OF CONCORD
Between this temple and the Temple of Concord, **Gate III** has suffered the borings of Byzantine tombs. These continue throughout the natural rock wall up to the **Temple of Concord**, which along with the Theseion in Athens is one of the best-preserved Greek temples in the world, owing to its conversion into a church by the 6th-century bishop of Agrigento, San Gregorio delle Rape ('of the turnips'). Dismantled in the 18th century, the church left this Doric structure of the mid-5th century BC almost intact, with its 34 columns, stylobate, *cella* etc. Originally coated with ground marble stucco and painted in bright colours that have long since worn away, the rough, dull-golden limestone beneath surprises people who expect all temples to look like the Parthenon or their local bank branch.

TEMPLE OF HERCULES
Still heading west you cross an unusual deeply-cut street known as the Street of Tombs

which passes through an early Christian cemetery. The Roman catacombs north of here were adapted by the Christians in the 3rd century, and continue all the way to the garden of the Villa Aurea, the old Antiquarium (whose collections have been transferred to the main Archaeological Museum). The columns near here, rising above the Passeggiata Archeologica, belong to the oldest temple in the valley, the **Temple of Hercules**. Built around 500 BC, on an artificial platform, it measures 67 m by 25 m—longer than most. The Carthaginians burned it and the Romans repaired it, although the predatory Praetor Verres did his best to make off with a famous statue of Hercules that once graced the temple. For once the outrage of the citizens deterred him. In 1923 eight of the temple's columns were re-erected by Sir Alexander Hardcastle.

GATE IV AND THE TEMPLE OF AESCULAPIUS

The Passeggiata leads south to the **Tomb of Theron** which you can see from the Temple of Hercules. Like almost everything else it is erroneously named, for this two-storey monumental tomb belongs to the 1st century BC. It is located just outside the city walls, where the city's main gate, Porta Aurea (**Gate IV**), once stood, through which a road ran to the port. A large Roman cemetery, partially destroyed by landslides, spreads out over the hill from the gate. South of the Tomb of Theron, on the other side of the SS115, lies the **Temple of Aesculapius**, built in the 5th century and different from the other temples in that it has solid walls instead of columns. Aesculapius was the god of healing, and this temple, along with all others dedicated to him, is built beside a spring with curative properties. The treatment offered by the priests, however, was more psychological than medicinal and consisted of dream interpretations, restful surround-ings, and taking of the waters. The success of this simple cure is attested to by the great popularity of the cult throughout the Greek world.

TEMPLE OF OLYMPIAN ZEUS

The next temple within the walls, across the Passeggiata and next to the Posto di Ristoro, is the Temple of Olympian Zeus, the largest Greek temple in the world and one of the most remarkable. Although totally ruined by an earthquake and its stone quarried to build Porto Empedocle, what remains is still very impressive, measuring 113 m by 54 m (larger than a football field). The columns, thought to have been 16 m tall, were made of small stones plastered over to look like whole marble pillars—the flutings in these, as Goethe noted, are wide enough to hold a man with his shoulders scarcely touching the sides; it would take twenty men standing side by side to embrace the pillar's great girth. Walls and buttresses filled the spaces between the mock columns and on top of these stood the enormous telemons, or stone giants, supporting the architrave. A copy of one of these Atlas-like figures lies within the temple, to give you an idea of the vast scale the Carthaginian slaves were forced to work on: columns, telemons and architrave com-bined, the whole thing stood over 30 m high. Begun in 480, after the victory at Himera, the temple was still unfinished in 405 BC when the Carthaginians invaded the city.

GATE V AND THE SANCTUARY OF THE CHTHONIC DEITIES

West of here, the newly excavated **Gate V** once had a tall projecting tower, designed as many of these gates were to hamper the shield arms of opponents trying to enter. Here also are four temples dating from the foundation of Akragas, known collectively as the

Sanctuary of the Chthonic Deities. The first two temples, begun in the 6th century BC, were never completed and the third, commonly known as the **Temple of Castor and Pollux** or of the Dioscuri, was finished at the end of the 5th century. In 1836 four columns and a piece of architrave were pieced together for picturesque effect but without any attempt at historical accuracy: it's a mishmash of items from the numerous ruins of altars and sanctuaries that litter the area, some of which date back to the Sikans (like the Sanctuary of Demeter), and one altar is prehistoric. The fourth temple, with its platform and fallen columns, is from the Hellenistic period. Below this sacred area the River Hypsas runs through some extraordinary countryside.

GATES VI–IX
A path from the sanctuary (look for signpost) leads to the **Temple of Vulcano** beyond the railway. Difficult to reach, it is only recommended for enthusiasts. Two columns remain standing of this temple, thought never to have been completed, and certainly not dedicated to the smithy god. **Gates VI–IX** are also in this area if you are intent on making the complete circuit of the ancient walls.

Porto Empedocle

Just below Agrigento on the road to Porto Empedocle, in a hamlet called **Caos** (!) the **birthplace of Pirandello** has been turned into a museum (open 12.30–2.30), which is well worth a visit if you are a fan of *Six Characters in Search of an Author*, Pirandello's ashes are buried in a rock underneath a pine tree nearby. Connected by frequent buses is Porto Empedocle, Agrigento's port, named after the famous philosopher. On the harbour stands an 18th-century tower partly made from the stone of the Temple of Zeus, as was the mole. Porto Empedocle is one of Italy's main mineral ports and the port for the islands of Lampedusa and Linosa. Unless you have to go there, avoid this town: there isn't a good word to be said for it. The nearest beach to Agrigento is at San Leone (bus every half-hour from the station).

WHERE TO STAY   (tel prefix 0922)
The only hotel actually located in the Valley of the Temples is the elegant and serene ****Villa Athena, built around an old villa and garden near the Temple of Concord (tel 56 288; L130 000). Further up the slope and looking down on part of the valley is the ***Colleverde, Via Athena (tel 29 555; L80 000). In the town, the **Bella Napoli is good and less expensive than the others (Piazza Lena 6; tel 20435; L45 000) and you don't have to hike or bus into town every evening from the temples. There's a campground at San Leone.

EATING OUT
Cuscusu (a sweet made of almonds and pistachios by the monks at the monastery of Spirito Santo); *coniglio in agrodolce* (sweet and sour rabbit). The **Aurora**, just off the Via Atnea, is one of the better cheap trattorias you'll find, and there aren't many (L18 000). **Prinzinelli** is a popular, animated pizzeria on the Viale della Vittoria. Opposite the tourist office on Aldo Moro the restaurant **Kalos** serves excellent food (it should, the name is Greek for good, but the cuisine is strictly Italian; L25–35 000). For atmosphere,

a view of the temples, and their own *scaloppine Pirandello, fave* specialities and sole fished from the waters around Porto Empedocle, the **Taverna Mosè** is at San Biagio, Contrada Mosè (tel 26 778; L30 000 with fish).

In the Interior: Sant' Angelo Muxaro

In the centre of the province, near the small village of Sant' Angelo Muxaro in the Platani Valley, *tholos* (domed tombs) have been excavated which seem to link the site to Camicos, the ancient capital of the legendary King Cocalos who lived around 2000 BC. Long famous in Greece before Sicily was even colonized, King Cocalos supposedly built Camicos for Daedalus, said to have made many wonderful things here. None of these things remains, although some of the ceramics and gold found in the tomb bear a remarkable resemblance to items in the eastern Mediterranean, suggesting a link between Greece and Sicily a few centuries before the first colonies. The rock-carved tombs in the walls around the modern town also show eastern influences, the lower ones dating back to the 10th century BC. The largest of these is known as the Tomba del Principe or 'tomb of the Prince' (inquire in Sant' Angelo for directions). It is well worth the effort to see this; it is the finest such tomb in Sicily.

In **Aragona** south of here, you can find a guide to visit the Macalube—funny little volcanoes only a few feet high, bubbling with mud. Nearby **Raffadali** has a Roman sarcophagus in the church, in an ancient necropolis on Busone Hill. Two villages in the north of the province, **Bivona** and **Santo Stefano Quisana**, have notable churches. **Cammarata** to the east is an increasingly popular mountain resort, although it has only one hotel. **Racalmuto** (from the Arabic *Rahal-maut*) was the birthplace of Pietro d'Asaro (1597–1647), whose works may be seen in some of the churches. Nondescript **Canicatti** to the east is an important wine centre, though nowadays the whole area is coated with plastic during the winter, as if all the farmers had been inspired by Chrysto.

Licata

The next town to the east along the coast, **Palma di Montechiaro** with its fine mother church, was founded in 1637 by an ancestor of Giuseppe di Lampedusa, who inherited it. There is a beach at the Marina di Palma below.

44 km from Agrigento and located at the mouth of the River Salso (known as the Himera in ancient times) **Licata** developed on the site of ancient Phintias, a colony of Agrigento named after its founder, who transferred the inhabitants of Gela here when that city was destroyed. Excavations have recently begun, the finds of which are in Agrigento's museum and in the **Museo Civico** in Piazza Linares (but soon to be moved to Via Dante). Besides the ancient reliefs, this building, designed in 1935 by Ernest Basile, contains a small art gallery and a statue of the Madonna by Domenico Gagini (1470). The **Palazzo Canarelli** on the Corso is embellished with monstrous heads, while the Cathedral at the end of the street has a highly decorated chapel. Of the squares, Piazza Sant' Angelo is the finest, surrounded by Baroque buildings. A wide sandy beach at Mollarella Bay attracts its share of sun- and fun-seekers in the summer. Along the coast from here to Agrigento totter a ruined string of medieval defences.

North of Licata on the bank of the River Salso are the ruins of a **proto-historical settlement on Monte Saraceno** later Hellenized by Gela and Agrigento. Little of the town has been excavated; you can see the acropolis on top, vestiges of a temple and the town plan on the hillside. To visit the site, go to Ravanusa and ask for precise directions.

Gela

Gela is a prosperous little city, with its large oil refinery; its long sandy beach (with a splendid view of the refinery) also attracts many tourists, mostly Italian, in the summer. However, between the Carthaginians, the Mamertines and the shifting sand dunes of the coast, little remains to tell of Gela's ancient glory. The town itself is not much to look at although the people are friendlier than most Sicilians.

History
Gela, on the coast to the east, was once the most powerful city in Sicily, founded by colonists from Crete and Rhodes in 680 BC. Under the Rhodians the city prospered, producing mainly wine, oil and grain. By the 6th century BC the southern coast of Sicily belonged to Gela, and the Geloans founded Akragas in 582 BC (modern Agrigento). The city specialized in terracotta votive figurines, some of them prefabricated.

In 498 BC the grasping tyrant Hippocrates seized control of Gela, and he and his mercenaries proceeded to conquer half of Sicily, including Leontinoi and Naxos. Jealous of their harbour, Hippocrates defeated the Syracusans but later returned their city to them in exchange for the colony of Camarina. At this point Gela was the strongest city on the island. However, Hippocrates attempted to force the native Sikels into Greek ways; he started the one and only national uprising among the Sikels (led by Ducetius) and died in a Sikel battle. He was succeeded by his cavalry commander, Gelon. With his father-in-law, the tyrant of Akragas, Gelon defeated the Carthaginians at Himera in 480 BC. Subsequent political turmoil in Syracuse provided Gelon with a chance to muscle in, and he took control, moving half of Gela's population to Syracuse because of its fine harbour. A few years later, though, the Geloans were allowed to go home, and the city prospered once more, on terracotta and literature—Aeschylus wrote his *Oresteia* trilogy here, and died in Gela in 456 (when an eagle dropped a turtle on his head!). Another poet, the comic Apollodoros, was born and raised in Gela.

In 405 BC the Carthaginians destroyed Gela; when the inhabitants returned, their fine city was no more. Timoleon, the good tyrant of Syracuse, had Gela laid out anew in 338 and sent colonists to repopulate it. However, by the ascendancy of Agathocles, Gela had allied itself with Carthage, and Agathocles conquered the city, putting 7000 Geloans to death. The town was again destroyed by the Mamertines in 282, after which Phintias of Akragas removed the Geloans to what is now Licata. The site was repopulated in 1233 and known as 'Terranova' until 1928, when the city was renamed Gela.

During World War II Gela was the site of the American landings on 11 July 1943, and was the first town in Europe to be liberated.

GETTING AROUND
Bus and train connections from Caltanissetta, Syracuse and Agrigento.

TOURIST INFORMATION
Via Navarra Bresmes (tel (0933) 913 788).

Archaeology Museum

The best treasures of ancient Gela are housed in the new Archaeology Museum at the eastern end of the long main street, Corso Vittorio Emanuele (open 9–2, Sun 9–1, closed Mon). The museum contains some excellent examples of Gela's terracottas, coins and vases, and two magnificent horse heads. Next to the museum is the Mulino Vento Acropolis, mainly with Hellenistic houses from Timoleon's re-colonization. One Doric column in a garden setting is all that remains of a temple of Athena.

Capo Soprano

At the other end of the town (Corso Vittorio Emanuele to Via A. Manzoni and Via Indipendenza) are the Capo Soprano fortifications (open daily 9 to dusk). These 5th-century BC Greek walls are the best-preserved in the world, having been covered by 21 m sand dunes until they were excavated in 1954–8 (in some places the walls are still 8 m high). The fortifications have been covered in part by a plastic shield to protect them from the sea winds, especially the upper parts of the walls which are made of brick rather than stone. Very near Capo Soprano, next to the hospital on Via Europa, are the sheltered **Greek public baths** (always open). Dating from Timoleon's time, they are the only ones found in Sicily and the only hot baths to have seats.

Gela Riviera

The sandy beaches of the 'Gela Riviera' stretch all along the bay, and you have the choice of bathing with the crowd or on your own. West along the coast is **Falconara Sicula** with its isolated 15th-century castle housing a fine ceramic collection. On either side of it are huge sandy beaches.

WHERE TO STAY AND EAT   (tel prefix 0933)
Fortunately there's a little more choice than the *****Motel Agip** (N115, tel 911 579; L85 000) for business visitors to the oil refinery. The *****Hotel Delle Mimose**, right by Capo Soprano on Viale Independenza (tel 935 271) is well priced at L45 000 with bath, or cheaper still the grandly named but humbly furnished ****Excelsior**, Via E. Mattei 25 (tel 914 113; L33 000 with bath, L26 000 without). At **Da Giovannini**, also known as 'The World Famous' (Via Cairola), Giovanni is an old sea salt who's been to many a port, and his jovial chatter adds as much to your enjoyment as his sauce does to the fish; his inexpensive restaurant is a sort of landmark in nondescript Gela and should not be missed (L15–20 000).

Inland from Gela: Butera

On a low hill by the junction of N190 north to Caltanissetta stand the lonesome, romantic ruins of **Castelluccio**, a castle built by Emperor Frederick II. North of here, by

192

Lake Disueri, is a Pantalica-like oven-tomb necropolis of the late Bronze Age. A by-road north of Gela will take you the 19 km to **Butera**, the prettiest town in the undistinguished province of Caltanissetta, built on a hill which is dominated by an 11th-century castle. In the **Chiesa Madre** you can see a Renaissance triptych and a painting of the Madonna by Filippo Paladino. In the Middle Ages the princes of Butera, the Barresi, held sway over most of the region. They founded **Mazzarino**, 17 km north along N190, where their palace still exists. Another Barresi palace may be seen at **Pietraperzia**, 14 km north. Southeast of here is a site known as **Sofiana** or Castellazza where some 1st-century thermal baths have been discovered; they remained in use until the 4th century. A small basilica and necropolis have also been excavated, their contents now housed at Gela.

Caltanissetta

From Norman times Caltanissetta's economy depended on the sulphur and potassium mines, now closed down, which made it a modern and prosperous town, but unfortunately not very interesting for tourists. The old part of the town, however, has a few memories of its medieval and Baroque heritage. Thought to be located on the site of ancient Nissa, whence its name 'Kalat' (Arabic for castle) Nissa is derived, Caltanissetta was captured by Count Roger in 1086 and presented to his son. In the 15th century it fell into the hands of the Moncada family. The city suffered various bombardments in World War II.

GETTING AROUND
Frequent trains and buses from Palermo, Catania, Agrigento and Enna.

TOURIST INFORMATION
Corso V. Emanuele 109 (tel (0934) 21731).

WHAT TO SEE
The most striking of Caltanissetta's monuments is the **Castello di Pietrarossa** whose ruins from the 1567 earthquake are perched high on a crag. During the war between the Chiaramonte and Ventimiglia families, Frederick II found shelter here, and the castle became a favourite residence for his son, Frederick III. The 16th-century **Cathedral**, in the central Piazza del Duomo, was unfortunately hit in the war, the bombs damaging the masterpiece ceiling of the Flemish artist Borremans, painted in 1720. A prettier church is **Santa Maria degli Angeli** built in the 14th century, with fine reliefs on the main door. The Civic Museum, on Via Napoleone Colajanni (open 9–1; Sat 9–12; closed Sun and holidays), contains finds from the province, mainly from Sabucina; the early Bronze Age figures are the oldest found in Sicily. For geology buffs, the **mineralogical museum**, with exhibits from the area and all over Sicily, is at the western end of Viale della Regione.
    Just east of the town, by the new museum, is the **Badia di Santo Spirito**, its basilica founded by King Roger and Queen Adelasia, and consecrated in 1153, which contains some good 15th-century frescoes.

WHERE TO STAY AND EAT   (tel prefix 0934)
Presumably the two hotels in the town cater for people whose car has broken down. It's

hard to imagine any other reason for spending a night here. The ***Diprima, Via Kennedy 16 (tel 26 088), charges L62 000 for a room with bath, and you can try the local *Libecchio* wine in its restaurant. In the same price bracket is the ***Europa, Via B. Gaetani 5 (tel 21051).

Of the restaurants, which are not many, **Cortese**, Corso Sicilia 166 (tel 31 686), is the best with traditional Sicilian food for around L25 000.

Around Caltanissetta

Caltanissetta Province is the least visited in Sicily. However, some of the hill towns are quite charming and certainly untainted by tourism, and there are a few minor archaeological sites scattered throughout the area. One of these is **Mount Sabucina**, 9 km northeast of Caltanissetta, by the Salso river. Inhabited originally by Sikels in the first millennium BC, the site was later Hellenized and fortified. Excavations have uncovered the 6th-century BC town, huts and tombs from the Bronze Age and a small Sikel temple outside the town wall. To visit the digs, ask at the Museo Civico, Caltanissetta.

Near San Cataldo (5 km west) **Vassallaggi** is another archaeological site, spread over five hills. This was a Greek settlement in the 5th century BC, under the wing of Agrigento; you can still see the sanctuary, the fortifications, part of the town, and a rich necropolis of fine painted vases and urns, now in the museums of Gela and Agrigento. High on a crag (Rocca di Mussomeli) at Mussomeli, northwest of San Cataldo, stands the castle of the same name, built by Manfred III of the Chiaramonte family around 1370. (The nearest railway station to Mussomeli is at Acquaviva, north of Agrigento.)

Enna

At 948 m above sea level, Enna is the highest provincial capital in Italy. Favoured by both Frederick II of Hohenstaufen and Frederick II of Aragon for its unique position, Enna has not only marvellous panoramas in all directions, but some fine medieval and Aragonese towers and churches.

History

Ancient Sikan 'Henna', in one of the most strategic positions in Sicily—high in the Monti Erei, almost in the dead centre of the island—was also the centre of the cult of Demeter and her daughter Persephone, whom Pluto abducted into the underworld. According to Diodorus Siculus, the Sikans made a peace treaty with those other early Sicilians, the Sikels, after a brief conflict. This, if true, would make it one of the earliest peace treaties in the world (8th–7th century BC).

Enna was gradually Hellenized by Greek colonists who lived in peace with the natives (the Via dei Greci still runs through the ancient Greek quarter) and Gelon built a temple of Demeter here in 480 BC. The Romans called Enna 'Castrum Hennae' and their government of the town could hardly be termed happy. In 214 BC the Consul Pinarius had the leading citizens massacred, fearing they would side with Carthage, and later, in 135 BC, a slave from Enna named Euno led the First Slave War, giving the Romans no end of trouble until they recaptured the city two years later. In 859 the Saracens took Enna from the Byzantines, who had made it their headquarters, by climbing through the sewer—so impregnable was Enna's position. Under the Saracens, the town's name was corrupted to 'Kasr Janna'. Count Roger manipulated his way into Enna in 1087 and called it 'Castrogiovanni', but in 1927 Mussolini returned its Classical name and made it a provincial capital.

GETTING AROUND
Enna's station lies along the Palermo–Catania railway line. When you arrive you may look at the surrounding fields and orchards in disbelief—no trace of a city can be seen. It's up above the clouds, and a bus timed to meet the train will soon arrive to take you up (this bus also connects Enna with Calascibetta). Rail connections along the main line are easy; travelling to or from Agrigento and the south will probably mean an exasperating stop at a junction called Caltanisetta–Xirbi, the black hole of Sicilian railways. Enna's new bus station, with connections for Piazza Armerina, villages in the province and the rest of Sicily, is in the newer part of the city, in the Viale Diaz.

TOURIST INFORMATION
In Enna the EPT is hard to miss, the three giant letters pointing the way to Piazza Garibaldi (tel (0935) 21184), and the city AAST is nearby on the Piazza Colagianni (tel 26119; very good maps of the entire island are available here).

Via Roma
Via Roma, the main street of Enna, takes a sharp turn in the heart of town at Piazza Matteotti, and is strung with lovely piazze, like pearls on a necklace. In the first of these to the east, Piazza Vittorio Emanuele, is the **Church of San Francesco** which has a fine 15th-century tower. In the adjacent **Crispi**, with its extraordinary belvedere, is a copy of Bernini's *Rape of Persephone*. Continuing east along the Via Roma, the Piazza Umberto stands out like a sore thumb with its *fascisti* public buildings. The next square, Piazza Coppola, is named from the Arabic cupola on the elegant tower of San Giovanni. Just around the corner the city has opened its new Archaeological Museum in an old palace (open 9–1, 4.30–6.30, closed Mon). None of the finds is of special interest, but if you read Italian it will provide a good background to the region's ancient history.

The Cathedral
Still heading east on the Via Roma you come without warning upon the cathedral. Founded in 1307 by Eleonora, wife of Frederick II of Aragon, it caught fire in 1446 and was restored the following century, which may account for its idiosyncratic façade and the few remaining Gothic elements on the south side, including the walled-in Holy Portal. Inside, the iron gate of the baptistry once guarded the Saracen harem. The two stout columns near the entrance, carved with puzzling allegorical monsters, are the work of one of the Gagini—a peculiar work to have come out of that normally tradition-bound clan of Sicilian masters. Another Gagini work, the font, rests on a pedestal of ancient origin, perhaps from the Temple of Demeter. Filippo Paladino painted the scenes in the choir and the nave ceiling in the 16th century, and Giovanni Gallina—a local artist— sculpted the marble pulpit. Three works by Borremans are among those which adorn the walls.

195

Across the street from the cathedral, spread about the rooms of a house, is the **Museo Alessi** (open 9–1, closed Mon). It contains a good collection of coins and a few antiquities from Enna Province, along with some neglected paintings, but the extremely rich cathedral treasury, formerly housed here, has been removed and is in the custody of the priest.

Emperor Frederick's Castle

The eastern end of Via Roma opens out on the Castello di Lombardia (open 9–1 and 5–7 pm), constructed by the Swabians under Frederick II, and used as a residence by Frederick III of Aragon who proclaimed himself 'King of Trinacria' here and summoned the Sicilian parliament in 1324. 'Lombardia', an unusual name in Sicily, is thought to derive from the Lombard troops that Frederick quartered here to keep them out of trouble. Six towers remain of the original twenty, the tallest of which—the Torre Pisano—can be climbed for its commanding view of the surrounding countryside. Below, in the courtyard, where excavations are in progress, is an underground chapel with odd incisions on the wall resembling upside-down tridents, dating from ancient times and of unknown origin. Legend has it that King Sikanus and the goddess Demeter are buried together under the castle.

On the promontory east of the castle is the Rocca di Cerere (or di Demeter) where a temple once stood—perhaps the one built by Gelon. Only a few traces of it remain today.

Taking the Via Roma south of the Piazza Matteotti, you can visit the lower town, passing the church of San Tommaso with a distinguished altar, and the Carmine. Both have 15th-century campaniles (the good people of Enna like their church bells and ring them often). Further down, on a knoll in the public garden, is the Swabian Torre di Federico II (entrance on Viale IV Novembre, open daily until dusk). Scholars believe that 'Stupor Mundi' built this 'tower of the winds' to mark the crossroads of ancient Sicily's three main thoroughfares, symbolized in the three legs of the Trinacria symbol. Considered to be in the absolute centre of the island, the tower (as well as the rest of Enna) acquired the name Umbilicus Sicilae ('Sicily's navel') and served to divide the island into three districts: the Val Demone, the Val di Noto, and the Val di Mazara—a partition borrowed by the Arabs during their domination. The tower itself is octagonal with three floors. It is rumoured that at the bottom there is an underground passage to the Castello di Lombardia. A spiral stairway leads you up inside the 3-m-thick walls to the top unfinished floor. From here, on the clearest of days, the three corners of Sicily are visible.

THE TEMPLUM CAELESTI

Frederick's tower was not the first on this site, and it is an open question whether the subtle emperor was aware of the true significance of this spot. Thirty years ago a Sicilian historian, Umberto Massocco, propounded a theory that this was the centre of a giant geomantic construction, created perhaps by the Sikans, that covered the whole of Sicily. Like the leys in Britain (which Massocco appears not to have known about), there seems to be a network of alignments of holy places and landmarks, meeting at right angles and running the length of the island. Massocco, with the aid of aerial photography and the writings of Diodorus Siculus, discovered that many of the oldest sites on the island— Mount Erice, Segesta, Selinunte, Ortygia Island and Eraclea Minoa among them—fall along these alignments. He calls the work the *Templum Caelesti*, an attempt to make the whole of Sicily into one great geometrical temple. In Enna, he notes that the two central alignments that cross at Frederick's tower pass through the churches of San Marco (Piazza VI Dicembre) and San Bartolomeo (Piazza San Bartolomeo) and that these three sites form a neat Pythagorean triangle of sides proportionately 3, 4, and 5.

WHERE TO STAY   (tel prefix 0935)
The ***Hotel Belvedere**, facing the pretty Piazza F. Crispi on one side and half of Sicily on the other, truly lives up to its name. Its friendly staff and gracefully mouldering art deco furnishings will win a place in your heart; make sure you get a room with a balcony (tel 21020; L52 000, open all year). A cheaper, unlisted place in town is the cosy little **Albergo Enna** on Via S. Agata (L25 000).

EATING OUT
An old favourite (Mussolini dined here) is the **Centrale** at 6 Via VI Dicembre, off Via Roma (tel 21 025), where they have some unusual vegetable pasta dishes (L25–35 000). Just around the corner from the Torre di Federico, off Via Liberta, is a small family trattoria, where the portions of pasta are plentiful and inexpensive; the Enna football team eats there regularly, win or lose (L18–25 000). Least expensive of all (and with good scaloppine) is the **Grotta Azzurra**, a hole in the wall off the Piazza Matteotti (L15–20 000).

Around Enna

Enna Province, the only province in Sicily without a coast, compensates for this lack with its six large natural and man-made lakes and beautiful mountain scenery. Its inland position has also made it less vulnerable to outside influences and change, and almost all the towns retain a medieval aspect, especially Calascibetta and Nicosia. The Norman–Aragonese town of **Piazza Armerina** is the second city of the province, famous for the mosaics at the Roman villa and thus on the itinerary of many package tours; in mid-August it hosts one of the major festivals in Sicily, the Norman Joust.

Calascibetta and Persephone's Lake

The attractive hill town across the valley from Enna is **Calascibetta** (go by bus or train from Enna), its Arabic origins apparent in its old reddish buildings as well as in its name. It is a quiet, brooding place. The nearby Necropolis of Realmesi, its 'oven tombs' hollowed out of the rock, dates back to the 9th century BC. On the edge of Leonforte northeast of Calascibetta, the lavish great fountain (La Gran Fonte), constructed in 1651, has 24 spouts along its unusual length. Leonforte was founded by Prince Nicolò Branciforte in the 17th century. His family's funeral chapel is in the Capuchin Church on Piazza Margherita; also in the chapel is *The Election of St Matthew* by Pietro Novelli.

South of Enna, the town of **Pergusa** borders on the famous lake of the same name. But don't expect any Classical epiphanies here, where Pluto abducted the goddess of spring, Persephone, from her flowery fields. The lake is now encircled by a motor speedway, and motorboats and waterskiers skim the surface of the lake instead of demons patrolling its sullen depths.

Assoro and Nicosia

Assoro, 19 km east of Enna on the N121, is worth a visit for its 14th-century **Church of San Leone**. On the exterior note the late Gothic portal; inside are a fine wooden ceiling and floral reliefs decorating the pillars. Another 19 km north on N117 will take you up in the mountains, to beautiful **Nicosia** as fine a medieval backwater as one could hope to find. As a free city, Nicosia prospered under the Arabs and then the Normans who settled the town with Lombard and Piedmontese colonists; the local argot is said to contain their northern influence. Upon a crag above the town stand the ruins of the **Norman castle**. In **Santa Maria Maggiore** (Via Francesco Salomone) is an early 15th-century marble polyptych of the Virgin's life, by Antonello Gagini, as well as the throne used by Emperor Charles V when he visited Nicosia in 1535. The **Cattedrale di San Nicola** has a lovely 14th-century doorway and a campanile in a mixture of styles. The ceiling dates back to the early 13th century. Among the works of art inside are paintings by Velázquez, Pietro Novelli and Salvatore Rosa, sculptures by the Gagini, and a crucifix carved by Fra Umile da Petralia. Just west of Nicosia rise the picturesque ruins of the **Castle of Sperlinga**, the only safe refuge the French found in the War of the Vespers.

Troina and Agira

The 32-km by-road from Nicosia east to Troina takes in some impressive scenery as it climbs to its goal. **Troina** qualifies as one of the highest towns in Sicily, 1030 m above sea level. Captured by Roger I in 1062 from the Arabs, it retains many Norman souvenirs, including **San Basilio** founded by Roger himself in 1082, making it the first Norman diocese in Sicily. The **Chiesa Madre**'s tower is also Norman, and its treasury contains a famous 13th-century silver pastoral staff. Inhabited since the Sikel period, Troina still has a few parts of its Greek walls.

Agira, the ancient Sikel *Agyrion*, is another picture-postcard hill town, 30 km south of Troina. In 339 BC Timoleon of Syracuse captured and Hellenized *Agyrion*, the birth-place of the great Diodoros Siculus, the 1st-century historian who was the first to attempt a history of the world. In later days San Filippo Sirriaco (or of Agira) performed many miracles here—actually thought to be the deeds of ancient Agyrion's patron god Hercules in Christian clothing. The church of **San Salvatore** contains a good treasury.

Regalbuto and Centuripe

Regalbuto, 14 km east of Agira is only a few kilometres from the large artificial **Lake Pozzillo**, a favourite of anglers. In 1261 the inhabitants of Centuripe decimated Regalbuto, which had been populated largely by the hated Swabians. The present town was rebuilt by Manfred. To the east the old enemy **Centuripe** is magnificently situated in front of Mt Etna and the sea; Garibaldi nicknamed it the 'balcone della Sicilia'. Known in ancient times as 'Kentoripa', Centuripe was the site of an important Sikel town. The 1st-century physician Celsus was born here. Despite this antiquity, the present town dates back only to 1545, as both Frederick II and Charles of Anjou razed Centuripe for its defiance of their authority. During World War II the Nazis made the town a key base, and its fall to the 38th Irish Brigade forced the Germans to abandon Sicily. Centuripe has a small but extremely interesting Museo Civico (open 9–1; closed Mon) housing the distinctive locally-produced polychromatic pottery and ceramics renowned in Hellenistic times. On the outskirts of town a road leads to the so-called **Mausoleo Romano**, a 2nd-century ruin, perhaps of a tower.

Piazza Armerina

South of Enna (27 km, frequent bus) is Piazza Armerina, known in Sicily simply as 'Piazza'. Its excellent hill site was inhabited in antiquity, but only became more than passingly important in the Middle Ages. In 1161 King William 'the Bad' destroyed the old town in retaliation for a massacre of Saracens by its citizens, but three years later the Normans rebuilt what they had demolished and the new town prospered. In 1240 Frederick II elevated Piazza to one of the eleven imperial towns in the parliament of Foggia. Throughout the medieval and Spanish periods the town retained its importance, and it was often the centre of factional rivalries and feudal plots against the overlords of the day.

TOURIST INFORMATION
Piazza Garibaldi (tel (0935) 81201).

WHAT TO SEE
The rectangular Piazza Garibaldi is the heart of the old town, with the Municipio, the Church Fundrò (1613), and various palazzi. Turn west up Via Vittorio Emanuele for the Baroque Church of Sant' Anna and the 14th-century **Aragonese Castle** where King Martin I of Aragon once resided. At the summit of the city, in the Piazza del Duomo, is the **Cathedral**, built in 1627 with funds donated by Baron Marco Trigona, whose portly statue and palazzo also adorn the square. The Catalan campanile is a hundred years older than the cathedral, while the façade is some hundred years later. Inside is the Byzantine icon of the Madonna given to Count Roger by Pope Nicolas II, and a medieval crucifix painting on wood by an unknown artist. The treasury contains a statue of Roger among the more typical church vestments and reliquaries.

Of the many other churches in this elegant town, the best are the 13th-century **San Giovanni dei Rodi** (the chapel of the Knights of St John before they moved to Malta), also called the Commendo; the Collegium of St Ignatius and, north of the town, the **Church of Sant' Andrea** built in 1096 by the Normans and containing some intriguing early Sicilian frescoes.

Villa Casale
To reach the excavations of the Roman villa of Casale (open daily from 9 until sunset), 7 km southwest of Piazza, you must either walk or take a taxi from the Piazza Gen. Cascino, as there is no bus. Unless there are many in your party, the taxi isn't much of a bargain, but the walk is very pleasant if it is not too hot. But whatever the means, the journey

rewards the visitor with the magnificent, uniquely well-preserved mosaics. This is the best Roman site in Sicily and one of the most interesting in all Italy.

Scholars generally hold that the villa was built as a summer retreat near the end of the 3rd century AD for a member of the Imperial family, perhaps even for the Emperor Maximilian, Diocletian's co-emperor, who ruled from 286 to 305. Later, the Arabs made some use of it, as did the Normans, until William the Bad ordered its destruction for its pagan artwork. A landslide covered it and only since 1950 have serious excavations revealed the treasures that were buried.

There are some 40 mosaic floors in all, now covered with a clear protective roof supposedly following the ancient design. After passing the aqueduct that supplied the villa, one comes to the monumental entrance and the baths where the mosaics represent various stages of the elaborate Roman bath ritual and some mythical sea creatures. The remains of the plumbing are visible in the *tepidarium* (warming room), where the floor was built on brick pillars, allowing heat to rise into the room through vents (the hypocaust). The central latrines are also nearby. The vestibule contains damaged mosaics of guests being welcomed into the house, and leads into the large rectangular court (the peristyle), with mosaic animal heads along the side floors and a fountain in the centre. Following the walkway to the left, the Hall of the Circus (*palaestra*) is named after its mosaics depicting a chariot race at the Circus Maximus in Rome, the four contestants bearing the colours of the four teams of Rome—red, green, blue and white.

Passing a series of bedchambers with intricate geometric designs you reach the Room of the Small Hunt with realistic scenes of a local hunting expedition and the hunters' subsequent picnic. Whimsical mosaics of the Fishing Cupids, a very popular theme of the age, follow this, as well as the main hall, the 61-m-long Hall of the Great Hunt whose mosaic masterpiece depicts the hunt and capture of wild animals for use in Roman games. Remarkable for their lively and realistic details, the various scenes seem to move before your very eyes. At either end are allegorical figures of Africa and the Middle East. An adjacent room contains the bland but very famous Bikini Girls desporting on some Roman lido, and the next room has a mosaic floor that shows Orpheus enchanting the savage beasts.

The walkway leads out to the Elliptical Courtyard where the mosaics portray industrious *putti* harvesting grapes, pressing wine and fishing. Entering the villa once more, the walkway ascends into the Banquet Hall (*triclinium*) with powerful mosaics of the Labours of Hercules. The five giants, struck by Hercules' arrows and writhing in pain, are particularly impressive, reminiscent of Michelangelo. Another remarkable room follows, showing the Cyclops and Odysseus; the wily Greeks are offering Polythemus wine, hoping to intoxicate him and thus make their escape. Next is the so-called Chamber of the Erotic Scene followed by the private apartments that compose the rest of the villa, including two charming nursery mosaics, one showing the Children's Hunt with youngsters chasing rabbits and ducks, the other showing the Small Circus with children racing carts pulled by birds in imitation of their elders. There is also a room with mosaics of Greek instruments and musical notation, and another representing the myth of Arion the musician.

Other important excavations northeast of Piazza Armerina are of **Morgantina**, a few miles from the old Lombard village of **Aidone**, excavated by Princeton. This Sikel–Greco town of the 6th century BC rebelled against the Romans in the 3rd century and was given to their Spanish mercenaries. Located at the Serra d'Orlando, the **excavations** (signposted; open 9 until dusk, Sun and holidays 9–2) include the large *agora* and trapezoidal stairway, a theatre, a gymnasium and Hellenistic houses, many with mosaics. Finds from Morgantina are housed in the Capuchin convent in Aidone.

WHERE TO STAY AND EAT   (tel prefix 0935)
The *****Park Hotel Paradiso**, Loc. Ramaldo, is adequate (tel 680 841, L50 000 with bath. **Da Toto** on Via Mazzini 29 (tel 81 153) serves excellent pasta from the oven and some very good local wines (L25 000). The attractive, if remote, **Al Ritrovo**, on the Strada Statale 117b (tel 80 648), makes a pleasant spot to have lunch after you have visited the impressive mosaics. Particularly worth trying are the tagliatelle with a special thick sauce (*ragu*) and the kid cooked over the open fire (around L25 000).

Caltagirone

Caltagirone, 32 km south of Piazza Armerina, has the sobriquet 'Queen of the Hills'. It spreads out in a charming array over three hills, some 630 m above sea level. Originally inhabited in 2000 BC by the Sikels, the Syracusans Hellenized it. The name 'Caltagirone' dates from the Arabic occupation (*kalat*, or castle, and *gerum*, orcaves). The Genoese briefly conquered the town in 1030, the earthquake of 1693 destroyed it, and the bombs in 1943 caused much damage and some 700 deaths.

Caltagirone's other nickname is the 'Faenza of Sicily' from its ceramics, a tradition in the town since the 10th century. Its golden age came, as in many ceramic towns, from the 16th–18th centuries, when demand was high for its typical blue, green and yellow painted ware. By the early 20th century, the art was at the verge of dying out, when local priest and folklore student Luigi Sturzo gathered the surviving craftsmen and founded Caltigirone's school of ceramics. In the **Museo della Ceramica** (Via Roma; open 9–2, Sun 9–1, closed Mon) are examples of the town's craft, from prehistoric potsherds to the 19th century. Here also are the **Villa**, the public garden, the **Teatrino** (1792) and the **Chiesa del Gesù** (16th century) with a painting by Caravaggio. Near the centre of town is the **Piazza Umberto Primo**, a survival of the earthquake, dominated by the **Corte Capitaniale**, decorated by members of the Gagini family (Antonello is thought to have lived part of his life in Caltagirone).

What impresses visitors most in Caltagirone is the grand **Scala di Santa Maria del Monte** running through the centre of the oldest part of town, each of the runners of its 142 steps adorned with colourful ceramic designs, reproducing the colours and motifs of local designs from the 10th century on. On 23 July it is brilliantly illuminated for the *festa* of San Giacomo.

WHERE TO STAY AND EAT   (tel prefix 0934)
The only place to speak of here is the *****Grand Hotel Villa San Mauro**, Via Portosalvo 18 (tel 26 500; L75 000) with its own pool, and a couple of run-o'-the-mill trattorias.

Part V

ISLANDS OFF THE COAST OF SICILY

Il faraglione, Lipari, Aeolian Islands

Even in the early 1970s, the numerous small islands off the Sicilian coast were a secret for most Italians, and those who did visit were the rare birds who could do without typical Italian necessities like stainless steel bars, smart shops, motorscooters and most importantly, lots of other Italians to keep them company. Since then a few islands, especially the Aeolians, have had to bear the stigma of fashion; prices have risen, and the natural friendliness of the islanders has been somewhat blunted by dealing with the demands of anonymous throngs in reflecting sunglasses. Little of this, however, detracts from the islands' unique natural beauty and the translucent sea that embraces them; only chances are you'll enjoy them rather more if you don't have to share their charms with a thousand suitors: try to avoid August and early September in particular.

The Aeolian Islands

One of the loveliest constellations of the night sky is the Seven Sisters, or Pleiades, and one of the loveliest constellations of islands anywhere are the Aeolian, also known as the Lipari Islands, the seven sisters of Lipari, Vulcano, Salina, Panarea, Filicudi, Alicudi and Stromboli. Along with numerous smaller islets, they form one of the most unusual little archipelagos in the world. All are volcanic—Vulcano and Stromboli actively so. They are also the islands of the wind, and the sea surrounding them is the most violent in the

Tyrrhenian if not the entire Mediterranean. The islands' beauty is almost other-worldly. Volcanic eruptions and wind erosion have left their coasts sharp and menacing, in strange formations and colours, and within a mile of the soft, rolling green hills there are inhuman regions of unmitigated white (the pumice slopes of Lipari) or black (the *Sciara del Fuoco* of Stromboli's volcano). On calm days each island has its own little cloud over its highest peak, like a genie or the ghost of some ancient volcanic emission.

Homer first mentioned the Aeolian Islands in the *Odyssey*; Odysseus landed here after passing through the Strait of Messina. Aeolus, the king of the islands and god of the wind, welcomed him and gave him a gift to speed his voyage home to Ithaca—a bag of wind. Overcome with curiosity, the Greek sailors opened the bag as soon as they left port, and the wind rushed out, pushing them right back to the island. Seeing his great gift so squandered, the king berated them and sent them on their way.

History

According to legend, the first people to settle the islands were from Asia Minor, who fled westwards at around the same time as the Elymnians of Segesta, at the time of the Trojan War. Diodorus Siculus, the ancient historian from Sicily, recounts the following tale: Liparo, son of King Auson of southern Italy, left home to found a colony on the islands, which he named after himself. One of his companions was Eolo, or Aeolus, who married a girl on one of the islands (Lipari or Stromboli) and stayed there as king when Liparo returned to Ausonia. It was he who entertained Odysseus and whose sons colonized parts of Calabria and Sicily.

Prehistory

A castle on Lipari has proved to be an archaeological goldmine, with each successive culture neatly layered one on top of the other, and so we know much more about the early inhabitants of the Aeolian Islands than did Diodorus. Lipari was first inhabited in 3000 BC by a people from the Near East, who also settled the east coast of Sicily: their first pottery bears the same Stentinello decorations of simple incisions or impressions.

Then, it appears, the islanders discovered obsidian, and began to mine and export it on a large scale. Obsidian, hard volcanic glass, was highly prized in the Neolithic Age as being superior to flint for making tools. Obsidian from Lipari found a wide market; examples have been discovered in France, Spain and Malta. The contact with different peoples introduced different styles of ceramic decorations—the Capri style, the Serra d'Alto style, and a rather charming style thought to have been developed locally, the Diana style, named after the fertile Diana plain around the castle, the first part of the island to be cultivated.

Around 2350 BC, this flourishing obsidian-exporting civilization suddenly vanished, for reasons unknown, and was succeeded by what is known as the Aeolian Medieval Period, towards the end of the Neolithic and beginning of the Copper Age. The pottery found on Lipari, at Punta Conte, is primitive compared to the Diana style.

However, what importance the islands lost through the decline of the obsidian trade, they eventually made up as ports on the east–west trading route between the Aegean and the Tyrrhenian Seas. This, too, shows up in their ceramic ware, similar to styles found in the eastern and northern Aegean. Settlements were found on the islands of Salina,

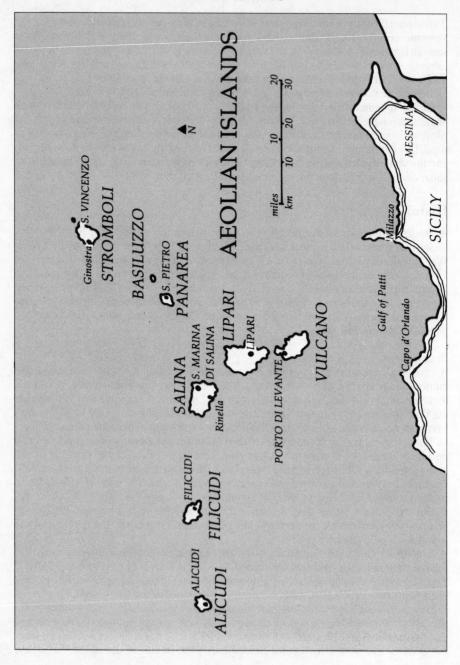

ALICUDI

ALICUDI

FILICUDI

FILICUDI

SALINA

S. MARINA
DI SALINA

Rinella

LIPARI

LIPARI

PORTO DI LEVANTE

VULCANO

Ginostra

S. VINCENZO

STROMBOLI

BASILUZZO

S. PIETRO

PANAREA

AEOLIAN ISLANDS

N

miles
km

10   10
10   20
20   30

Milazzo

Gulf of Patti

Capo d'Orlando

MESSINA

SICILY

Filicudi and Panarea, and later at Ginostra on Stromboli. They became thriving commercial centres, producing their own ceramic styles (Piano Quartara, Capo Graziano and Milazzese cultures). Particularly interesting is the Milazzese style of Panarea; the motives adorning the vases are distinctly of Cretan origin.

Sometime in the 13th century BC Bronze Age peoples from Ausonia and Sicily invaded the islands, burned the settlements and killed or enslaved the inhabitants. They were resettled by the Ausonians, themselves an Appennian tribe, initiating the cultures known as Ausonia I and II, producing the typical bull's-head vessels of the day. During this period lived Diodorus' Liparos and Aeolus, but their civilization, like the one they destroyed, didn't last long. In 850 BC it suddenly declined, leaving a wretched population barely surviving at subsistence levels.

The Greeks

In 580 BC a group of Greek colonists from Cnidos and Rhodes attemped to colonize the west coast of Sicily, but were pushed out by the Segestans and Carthaginians. Discouraged and with their leader Pentathlus dead, the would-be colonists made for home, stopping at Lipari on the way. The 500 Liparesi then living on the island received the Greeks well and entreated them to stay—which they did, attracted by the rich volcanic soil of Lipari.

One of the first things the new colonists did was refortify the castle against the constant menace of the Phoenician and Etruscan pirates. It wasn't long before the islanders established their own fleet to fight the pirates on the high seas, and the Liparesi, intimate with the local coasts and conditions, were more than a match for the marauders. Pausanias, the 2nd-century tour-guide writer, relates how Apollo's oracle at Delphi told the Liparesi that if they wanted victory they should fight the pirates with the bare minimum of ships. As usual, this seemingly ill advice saved the day. When the Etruscan pirate captain saw only five Liparian ships defending the island against his squadron, he confidently sent only five of his ships against them. They were all captured. Again the captain sent five ships, with the same result, then another five, and another five—all captured by the Liparesi. In disbelief and awe, the Etruscan captain withdrew the remaining ships of his fleet and escaped from these 'sea devils' while he still could. In thanksgiving, the islanders built a treasury at Delphi and raised a statue of Apollo for every ship they had captured. But the Liparesi were not only thwarters of pirates; they themselves indulged in the occasional spot of piracy to augment their income.

In 427 BC, Lipari—as an ally of Syracuse—was attacked by the Athenians, who wanted to establish a base there during their Great Expedition against Syracuse. They failed utterly, losing some 30 ships and more than 3000 men to the Aeolian defenders. In 396 BC, a ship bearing golden ex-votos to Apollo at Delphi for the Roman victory at Vei was ambushed and taken in the Strait of Messina by the Liparesi pirates. When the commander at Lipari found out from the Romans what they had been carrying and to whom, he convinced the sailors that the sacred nature of the cargo demanded that they not only return the ship to Rome, but escort it to Delphi themselves. In gratitude the Roman senate made the pirate commander Timasiteos an *ospitum publicum*—an honorary citizen of Rome.

Perhaps the most worthy accomplishment of these brave islanders was their communal system of self-government. All land, ships, houses and other goods were owned by the people and redistributed amid great festivities every 20 years. The inhabitants divided themselves into 'people of the earth', who farmed Lipari and the other Aeolian Islands and parts of the mainland as well; and 'people of the sea'—fishermen, pirates and defenders of Lipari. Whatever loot was captured was shared by all, and annual tributes were sent to Delphi.

The Liparesi remained faithful allies of Syracuse for many years in their battles against Carthage. The islanders were thus caught totally unawares when the cruel tyrant of Syracuse, Agathocles, landed in the guise of a friend, then proceeded to sack the rich temples of Aeolus and Hephestos (the smithy god, associated with volcanoes), filling eleven ships with their gold. In rage at this sacrilege the god of the wind blew the sea into a terrible storm, and all eleven ships sank with their cargoes of stolen gold. Only Agathocles' ship escaped destruction, the tyrant to die a more lingering death from plague.

In the Punic Wars Lipari sided with Carthage, as did most of Sicily. Some of the most important naval engagements of the First Punic War were fought in Aeolian waters, but Lipari's luck finally ran out. In 251 BC the Romans sent 60 ships to take and destroy the island, leaving few survivors. Later there is mention of Romans coming to bathe in the volcanic hot springs.

Henceforth the history of the Aeolian Islands more or less follows that of Sicily. In 1340, however, the island passed into the hands of the King of Naples, Robert I, although the formation of the Kingdom of the Two Sicilies brought Lipari and Sicily together once more. In 1544 the pirate Barbarossa left the islands depopulated and in smoking ruins. Because of their strategic position the Emperor Charles V had them recolonized a few years later. In the 19th century the island-hopping Archduke Luis Salvator de Hapsbourg 'discovered' the Aeolians and wrote a book about them, published in 1896.

In the early 20th century a prison was established in Lipari's castle, much to the anger of the islanders, who stormed and destroyed it in 1926. However, a few years later, when the Fascists began to send political undesirables to the island, they were made welcome, and not only shared the islanders' toil but founded a lending library in the little town.

The Aeolian Islands Today
Until only 20 years ago, accounts of the Aeolian Islands told of extreme destitution, of the inhabitants' struggle for survival on their windswept rocks, scratching out a living in the pumice mines, or fishing or tending the vines. Many have migrated to the mainland and to Australia since then, so that while life is much the same, there is more to go around for the islanders who have remained.

Tourism continues to grow on the islands and forms an ever larger chunk of the local economy. Of all the islands off Sicily's coasts, these are the most popular, and with good reason. Few travelling experiences are as magical as sailing out of Milazzo to the islands, watching them rise up on the horizon, one by one, green mountains floating mysteriously in an indigo sea. The Aeolian Islands have an intimacy which larger archipelagos lack, but enough variety, beauty, eccentricity and history to occupy an entire holiday.

GETTING AROUND
The main port for the Aeolian Islands is Milazzo, and if you're flying into Catania, a Giunta bus in the summer can pick you up at the airport at 2 pm and get you to Milazzo in

time to take a steamer out to the islands. Giunta buses also provide a year-round service connecting Messina and Milazzo nearly every hour, taking you directly to the port (a far easier manoeuvre than taking the train, which requires a walk that seems particularly long if you have baggage). Giunta buses depart from the piazza in front of the Stazione Centrale in Messina; for information contact their office at Via Terranova 8 (tel (090) 773 782).

By sea: steamers to the islands are few, and unreliable after October; they depart only from Milazzo. In the summer, however, there are connections from Messina, Naples and Reggio Calabria, mostly by hydrofoil. Siremar runs all the ferry services from Milazzo and Naples as follows:

From Naples to Stromboli, Panarea, Salina, Lipari, Vulcano, and Milazzo; 5 a week; 15 hours.
From Milazzo to Lipari, Panarea, Stromboli; 3 a week; 6 hours.
From Milazzo to Lipari, Filicudi and Alicudi; 5 a week; $6^{1}/_{2}$ hours.
From Milazzo to Lipari and Vulcano; 2 a day; 2 hours.
From Milazzo to Vulcano, Lipari and Salina; daily all year round; $3^{1}/_{2}$ hours.

Although the ferries do take cars, their main purpose is transporting goods to the islands. Only Lipari and Salina are large enough to justify the trouble and expense of bringing a car, but they also have efficient bus services, as does Vulcano on its one stretch of road. Panarea, Stromboli, Filicudi and Alicudi all have virtually no roads to speak of. The main advantage of the ferries is their lower prices and leisurely pace, which allows you to drink in your fill of delicious island scenery. The Naples ferries leave at night, so you save a night in a hotel.

Most people, however, want to get to the islands as quickly as possible; they choose the hydrofoils (*aliscafi*) from Messina or Milazzo and go thumpety-thump to their destination at top speed. Don't confuse the two hydrofoil lines (SNAV and SIREMAR) and their sometimes confusing schedules; always make sure that you buy the right ticket and get on the right boat. The SIREMAR hydrofoil schedules are as follows:.

From Milazzo to Vulcano and Lipari; 3 a day (4 in summer); 1 hour.
From Lipari to Salina; 2 a day; 40 minutes.
From Lipari to Salina, Panarea and Stromboli; daily; 1 hour 20 minutes.
From Lipari to Salina, Filicudi and Alicudi; daily; $1^{1}/_{2}$ hours.
SNAV Aliscafi runs the following daily hydrofoil services in the summer:
From Messina to Lipari, Salina and Stromboli; 5 hours 20 minutes.
From Reggio Calabria to Messina, Lipari and Vulcano; 2 hours.
From Naples to Stromboli, Panarea and Lipari; $5^{1}/_{2}$ hours.

The hydrofoil from Reggio Calabria coincides with ATI flights to the airport there. There are other summer hydrofoil services out of Milazzo (COVEMAR), and a ship out of Patti Marina (also daily from July to September).
Note: Exchange your money before you go. Lipari has the only bank on the islands; Stromboli, Panarea and Vulcano have only summer branches, opening 2 June. Underwater enthusiasts, however, will find a bottle service on all islands except Alicudi.

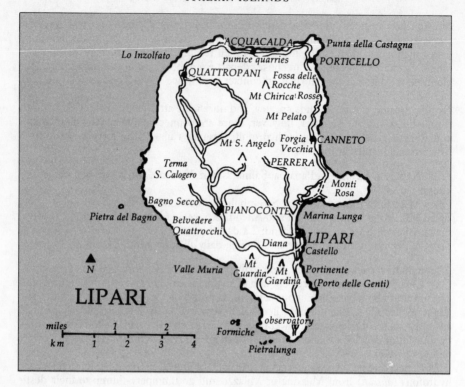

LIPARI

The largest of the Aeolian Islands (33 square km), Lipari was formed by a number of volcanic eruptions. The last eruption was around the 18th century BC, when Monte Pelato spewed out the lava that solidified into the Rocche Rosse and obsidian streams, as well as the snowy pumice slopes on the northeast of the island which occupy about a quarter of its entire surface area. The volcano today is dormant.

That may be the only sleepy thing about it; these days Lipari is decidedly 'in' amongst the Italians. The town's streets, and yachts moored in the harbour, are draped with people sporting the latest Valentino fashions and dripping in colourful, expensive jewellery. The main street serves as a catwalk for this colourful crowd, and part of the fun is to sit in one of the cafés and be part of the spectacle. If this isn't your scene there's a crummy 'wine bar' (ties not required) 100 metres up from the port where you can sit with the local fishermen, who scoff good-naturedly at the whole affair as they down the local *Malvasia* wine.

GETTING AROUND
The URSO company's buses leave Marina Lunga four times a day for Canneto, Porticello and Acquacalda; and for Quattrocchi, Pianoconte and Quattropani (also four

times a day); and buses run twice a day to Pirrara on the slopes of Monte Sant' Angelo, and twice a day to Lami, by Pianoconte.

TOURIST INFORMATION
Corso Vittorio Emanuele 253 (tel (090) 981 1190). Information office (summer only): Via Marina Corta (tel 911 108).

Lipari Town

The main town on the island, Lipari, serves as the seat of the *comune* of the Aeolian Islands—except for Salina, which is autonomous. The intimate **Marina Corta**, the town's hydrofoil port, lies between the castle walls on the north side and the natural rocky mole and church of the **Souls in Purgatory** on the south. This prim reminder of the wages of sin does not seem to deter any of the Proud, Lustful, and Greedy from swilling Campari and flirting over an icecream in the many bars and cafés line the waterfront.

The charming main street, the Corso Vittorio Emanuele with most of the shops and the tourist office, divides the town rather neatly into new and old. The old part is dominated by the castle with a grand pebble stairway penetrating the walls, built in the 16th century by the Spanish after Barbarossa's rampage and incorporating the massive blocks of a Greek tower of the 4th century BC.

The Castello and Museum

The Castello, Lipari's ancient acropolis, has been inhabited since at least 3000 BC. In places you can see the pits dug by archaeologists into the strata of various millennia. Such excellent time capsules are very rare, and the pottery finds of the Castello have been used to date prehistoric discoveries elsewhere in the Mediterranean. The two buildings of the **Archaeology Museum** near the digs contain one of the best Neolithic collections in the world (open daily, 9–1 and 3.30–6; 9–1 Sun from May to Oct, and 9–1 from Nov to April, adm). Chronologically arranged, the exhibits begin with Stentinello potsherds and continue to the Roman era, taking you past carefully reconstructed necropoli of the Middle Bronze Age and the Ausonia II cultures; beautiful, many-coloured vases and carved stone masks made during the Greek era, attesting to the island's importance in the artsy avant-garde of western Greece; and a fascinating and amusing collection of small figurines representing characters from Greek drama, displayed in models of the sets of the various comedies and tragedies.

Cathedral of San Bartolomeo

Between the museum buildings is the Cathedral of San Bartolomeo, patron saint of the Aeolian Islands, after whom many of the islanders are named. San Bartolomeo's body in a marble coffin floated ashore at Porto delle Genti on Lipari in 264, and as depicted on the doors of the Cathedral, he once saved the town from fire. The Cathedral was originally built by King Roger of Sicily in the 11th century, but reconstructed in 1654, and given a pseudo-Baroque facelift in 1861. Inside are 18th-century frescoes and a silver statue of San Bartolomeo (who, having suffered martyrdom by being skinned alive, traditionally carries his skin under his arm), as well as a fine late 15th-century *Madonna del Rosario* by Girolamo Alibrandi. The Baroque church of the **Addolorata** nearby is built on an older, Byzantine plan.

Along the cobbled street of the castle are various excavations, with placards explaining

209

what you see. Although nothing remains of the once-famous temples of Aeolus and Hephestos there is still a Neolithic shrine. The **Archaeological Park** (open 9–1 and 4–6) contains a collection of Greco-Roman tombs found on the Diana plain. Above the little theatre the walls offer splendid views of the Marina Corta and the town. On the other side of the castle are the campsites, the youth hostel (open March to Oct) and the gate and road leading down towards the Marina Lunga.

Marina Lunga, where the ferries dock, is also the major beach on the island. It curves around the small bay formed by the Monti Rosa promontory, where a small pleasure port has been created, the **Pignataro**, crowded in the summer with yachts and other boats from many shores.

In the garden of the Esposito house on Via Garibaldi you can see the 1st-century BC sculpture of a woman found near there. Behind the town, towards Porto delle Genti in the south, are the e..cavations of a vast necropolis whose some 1300 tombs produced many of the finds in the Archaeology Museum.

Around Lipari

A road completely encircles the island, but to see it all by bus you have to double back twice. Two routes leave Marina Lunga for **Canneto** to the north, the prettier one being further inland. Canneto, the second largest centre on the island, depends mainly on fishing. To the north rise the white slopes of **Monte Pelato** (472 m) and behind Canneto a road leads up to the old obsidian fields of **Forgia Vecchia** and the tiny hamlet of **Pirrera** beneath Monte Sant' Angelo.

Monte Pelato's slopes are snow-white with pumice. Pumice, formed by obsidian filled with volcanic gas while being cooled, is the lightest rock in the world; it even floats. It has diverse uses, in the soap, toothpaste and glass industries; remember when you next see Chicago's Sears Tower that part of it once had its home here. The pumice of Monte Pelato, mined in long galleries, is shipped off from the long docks beneath the mountain. At **Porticello** the beach is made of pumice and obsidian, the veins of which are red and black. These obsidian streams can be seen most spectacularly at the **Rocche Rosse** where huge blocks of it remain in the old quarries. To visit the site, take the path from Porticello or Acquacalda to Monte Pelato; the Rocche Rosse are on the way. Other pumice quarries are behind Acquacalda on the slopes of Lipari's highest mountain, **Monte Chirica** (596 m).

Pianoconte

Quattropani with its simple church, the Chiesa Vecchia, overlooks the distant island of Salina. The stretch of water between the two islands is an inviting area for the yachts which tack regularly through the channel, furiously so when the winds are up. Scattered white houses, gardens, vineyards and trees give this whole area a contented rural appearance. The road south winds past the Lipari hospital toward **Pianoconte**, where Bronze Age lava weapons have been discovered, and then the road branches off to the **Terme San Calogero**, the only exploited thermal establishment on the island (open July to Sept). According to legend, St Paul sent San Calogero to Lipari, where he found the spring—just as he did in Sicily, in the province of Agrigento at San Calogero. Famous for their curative powers in the Roman era, a few remains can still be seen of the ancient baths, near the modern establishment built in 1867. To take the baths you need a certificate from a doctor at Pianoconte (and also a reservation). The waters are recommended for gout, rheumatism and skin disorders.

From Pianoconte a path winds up to the crater of the extinct volcano, **Monte Sant' Angelo** (594 m). Although the path is steep, the climb rewards your effort with lovely views of the entire island and the unusual stratification inside the crater. Next to Pianoconte you may also visit the fumaroles, or little volcanic steam kettles, at **Bagno Secco**. On the south side of Pianoconte is the **Belvedere Quattrocchi** with a magnificent, much photographed panorama of Vulcano and the four craggy towers sculpted by nature, the **Faraglione**, shooting up from the sea between the two islands. Another path descends from here to the Valle Muria and a lonely beach.

Monte Guardia

The large promontory to the south largely consists of **Monte Giardina** and **Monte Guardia**, volcanic cupolas formed in a relatively recent eruption of Monte Sant' Angelo. South of Monte Guardia (a 45-min walk from Lipari town) is the **Geophysical Observatory** run by the National Research Centre and funded by UNESCO. The scientists here make volcanic and seismic observations of the Aeolian Islands and the Tyrrhenian Sea, pinpoint the epicentre of Mediterranean earthquakes, and correlate volcanic and seismic phenomena, their data being sent to geological institutions throughout the world. Peripheral stations are located on Vulcano, Alicudi, Panarea, San Fuscaldo in Calabria and at Novara di Sicilia, whose joint data determine where regional earthquakes shake the Richter Scale. For the average visitor, however, the main interest at the observatory is the wonderful view of Vulcano, pouting publicly for all to see.

Portinente, or Porto delle Gente, a short walk south of Lipari, has several hotels. The church of **San Nicola** near here has an ancient architrave. If at all possible, take a sea excursion around Lipari (there's no shortage of boat trips available), or at least to this southernmost part of the island where the dashingly coloured cliffs loom over the intense blue of the sea and monumental rocks like **Le Formiche** and **Pietralunga** lend a fantastical air to the seascape; just under the surface of the water they support a happy colony of oysters.

WHERE TO STAY   (tel prefix 090)

The *****Carasco**, Porto delle Genti (tel 981 1605) takes pride of place for best hotel on the island. It sits on its own private stretch of rocks and overlooks the broad expanse of blue, blue sea, with views across to the town from its swimming pool terrace decked with bougainvillea—a perfect setting. Hermione, the owner's English wife, is a resident of twenty years' standing and doubles as unofficial British Consulate and mother confessor. The hotel has excellent buffet lunches for L15 000 (without wine), and its half board rates are L130 000 in the high season. In town near the port is the small and charming pensione ****Poseidon**, Via Ausonia (tel 981 2876; L35–55 000 with bath). Also in town and for the same price is the ****Oriente**, Via Marconi 35 (tel 981 1493). Less costly on average is the ****Odissea** in Canneto, Via N. Sauro (tel 981 2337; L40–50 000 with bath). For real peace and quiet, stay in Quattropani at the little ***Nenzyna**, Via Castellana 10 (tel 982 2265; L40 000); there's a good little restaurant and garden as well, but you'll have to rely on taxi, or bus and foot, for getting to and fro. There's also a youth hostel (L7000).

Other accommodation may be found in private houses and locandas, but remember that in summer the island has a saturation point, so a phone call in advance is always a good idea.

EATING OUT
There are some very good restaurants on Lipari, which gets enough tourists to stimulate competition. Nearly all close by the end of October, however. Like all the Aeolian Islands, Lipari's cuisine centres around fish. The base for many fish dishes is *ghiotto* sauce, a lively blend of olive oil, locally produced capers, tomatoes, garlic and basil; black rice, given its colour by the *sepia* or inkfish, octopus and swordfish abound. To savour these, and many other exciting dishes, up in the Piazza Municipio the restaurant **Filippino** is the island's, and the archipelago's, jewel, with a choice of *risotti*, a delicious pasta *alla Filippino* with a wealth of goodies in it, and some very refined haute-cuisine main courses. Count on L40–50 000 for a memorable meal;in summer you'll have to book a table in advance (tel 981 1002). Also good for Aeolian specialities is **E' Pulera** in Via Diana (tel 981 1158), in a pleasant garden setting with *coniglio all'Aeoliana* (rabbit in a caper and olive oil sauce) a feature of the menu, and a very good icecream dessert called **Gigi** (L30–40 000). A little cheaper, but with good local dishes are **Il Pirata**, on the waterfront at Marina Corta (L25 000), and **La Nassa**, just out of town near the hospital and with a garden (L30–35 000). In a back street off the Corso Vittorio Emmanuele is **A Sfiziusa**, a trattoria whose tables totter on the sidewalk, and which attracts a young crowd. The food is good, if not particularly original, and inexpensive at L18 000 for a full meal. In Acquacalda, **Da Lauro** is a good bet (tel 982 1026; L25 000) and between Acquacalda and Lipari, with a balcony and (albeit somewhat obscured) view of Salina, is **A Menza Quartara** with a good *pasta alla melanzane* and *arosto misto di pesca* (L20–25 000). In Pianoconte **A Cannata** serves local cuisine and pizza (L25 000).

VULCANO

Vulcano, anciently *Iera* (the sacred island) or *Thermessa*, has at present much volcanic activity but no active volcanoes. This certainly wasn't true in the past: Aristotle, Diodorus Siculus, Strabo and Thucydides all record various eruptions, one so destructive as to cover the town of Lipari in ashes in the 4th century BC. Vulcanello, on the extreme north of the island, rose out of the sea only in 183 BC. The main crater, the Fossa (375 m), has been quite active for centuries, last erupting in 1890 when it obliterated the alum-extracting industry of a Scotsman named Stevens, who once owned the entire island.

Composed of five different volcanic structures, Vulcano is a bizarre island of strange colours and bitter odours. Legends breed here as naturally as wild flowers. The ancients believed that Hephestos, the god of fire and blacksmiths, had his headquarters on the island, and in the Middle Ages the island was thought to be the entrance to Hell. San Bartolomeo was accredited with separating Lipari from Vulcano to protect his island from eruptions.

TOURIST INFORMATION
In summer only, at Porto di Levante (tel (090) 985 2028).

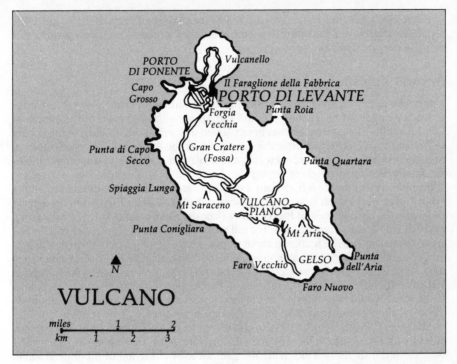

Vulcano

Hold Your Nose

The emergence of Vulcanello off the north coast, connected by a narrow isthmus, conveniently formed the island's two harbours: **Porto di Ponente** (for pleasure boats), lined with warm black sand, and **Porto di Levante** where hydrofoils and ferries dock (at the moment only the vehicles of islanders are permitted, so don't try to bring your car; the same holds true for the other islands except Lipari and Salina). Your nose is immediately insulted by sulphurous fumes rising from the steaming fumaroles on the isthmus. To the immediate north of the Porto di Levante lies the great rock known as the **Faraglione della Fabbrica** where alum was once extracted. (Alum, a whitish astringent mineral, is used in tanning, dyeing, medicine and fireproof materials.) The colours here are otherworldly—ochres, yellows, reds and oranges—and they paint the earth around the two hot springs of **Acqua del Bagno** and **Acqua Bollente** very near the port. In these shallow pools of stinking mud the pale rubber-capped heads of bathers bob up and down surreally as they wallow in its therapeutic virtues. If you join them, follow your soak with a wash in the sea (in this case, whoever jumps in, first or last, is a rotten egg). But even on the beach you can't escape the murmurs of the volcano; underwater fumaroles cause the sea to bubble, creating Mother Nature's own jacuzzi, though sulphur deposits on the sea bed give the coast a scabrous appearance. In another part of the port miniature but disconcerting geysers sometimes shoot warm mud into the air.

213

There are hotels and restaurants at each of the ports, and most of the island's 400 people live nearby, in a disarming Legoland of little rustic houses and flower gardens that defy the busy mudpies by the sea.

Around Vulcano

The only bus on Vulcano takes the one road up to **Vulcano Piano**, a very scenic drive across the middle of the island up to the earthquake-shattered ruins of the church of **Sant' Angelo**. The entire route has been planted with pink flowers. Most of the houses at Vulcano Piano were built after the earthquake in the 1950s and are mainly used as summer residences. There are a few bars and small restaurants, and many opportunities for quiet walks in the woods or among the sheep grazing on the hillsides.

From Porto di Levante it is an hour's walk (in sturdy shoes!) up to the summit of the **Gran Cratere di Vulcano**, otherwise known as **Vulcano della Fossa**. On the way up you'll pass the obsidian vein at **Pietre Cotte** ('cooked rocks') and clouds of smoke rising from the side of the mountain, near the red rocks. Further up, a large number of 'bread crust' volcanic bombs lie scattered about from the last eruption; above them at 500 m is the eerie hollow of the great crater, more than 460 m in diameter. The floor is completely solid, but it is hardly recommended to descend into it; the acrid gases from the fumaroles makes it difficult to breathe, even on the crater's rim. Bereft of vegetation, the whole area of the crater would look at home on the moon; from the highest point of the mountain you get a moon's-eye view of the entire Aeolian archipelago.

Also from Porto di Levante you can visit the crater of **Vulcanello** across the isthmus of lava with its toy-like volcanoes and stinking fumaroles. Passing the summer villas clinging to the slopes of Vulcanello, the path ascends to the top of the little volcano, notable for its brilliant colouring. Inside the crater visitors can enter a brightly hued cave where alum used to be mined.

The only way to see the rest of the island is by boat, unless you are something of an alpinist. Made of old and more recent lava, the coasts of the island are rugged and often spectacular; sailing between Lipari and Vulcano in the narrow **Bocche di Vulcano**— less than a mile wide and adorned with monoliths such as the 72-m **Pietralunga**—is a unique experience. On the south side of the island, beneath the tallest mountain, **Monte Aria** (495 m), are two lighthouses, **Faro Vecchio** and **Faro Nuovo**, and the tiny village of **Gelso**. One of the truly forgotten places on the Aeolian Islands, Gelso is visited by only one boat a day. Although there are no hotels or rooms to be found at Gelso, there are two restaurants. On the west side of Vulcano there is a fine beach at **Spiaggia Lunga** near the pretty Punta di Capo Secco and the boulder called **Pietro Quaglietto**.

WHERE TO STAY   (tel prefix 090)
The island's oldest hotel, ***Les Sables Noirs** at Porto Ponente, has, as its name suggests, a beach of black sand, as well as a garden (tel 985 2014; L85 000; open April–Oct). For the totally up-to-date, the ***Archipelago** at Vulcanello is built beside the sea, with a garden and pool for those who'd rather not swim off the rocks (tel 985 2002; L90 000). In Porto Levante there is the very simple but clean *Casa Sipione** (tel 985 2034; L35–45 000, some rooms with bath), and there's a campsite on the Via Provinciale (open June–Sept).

EATING OUT
The island's best restaurant, **Lanterna Blu** is a family concern providing a taste of wholesome home cooking. The choice is never great (but is it at home?)—rabbit is a regular appearance and whatever that day's fishing catch may be (tel 985 2287; L18–25 000). In Porto Levante **Il Palmento** has appetizing *antipasti* and also offers pizza (tel 985 2109; L20 000, less for pizza). In Piano **Scaffidi** is for more robust palates—rabbit, various salami and strong cheese dishes (L20–25 000), and of the two places in Gelso, head for **Maniaci**, where the menu is mainly fish, and it's up to you to decide if the management really are maniacs (L25 000).

SALINA

The twin volcanoes that gave Salina its ancient name, *Didyme*, are long extinct—Monte Fossa delle Felci (962 m), the tallest peak of the Aeolian archipelago, and Monte dei Porri (914 m). From a distance the island looks like a child's drawing—simple, painted green (unlike the other Aeolian islands, Salina is endowed with natural springs) with two rounded mountains and a smooth coastline. It is the second largest of the islands, but unlike the others Salina (pop. 2290) does not belong to the commune of Lipari; instead it supports three autonomous communes of its own: Santa Marina di Salina, Leni and Malfa.

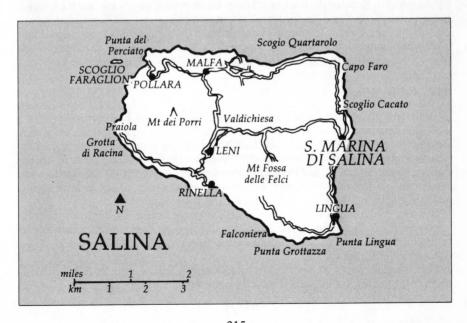

Tourism has made few inroads here, and most of the people earn their living from the very fertile land, producing tons of capers for export and the best sweet white *Malvasia* of the archipelago. Despite its name, Salina no longer has any saltpans, although these used to be an important industry at Lingua.

GETTING AROUND
Ships and hydrofoils to the island call at Santa Marina di Salina, and occasionally at Malfa and Rinella as well. All villages are connected by reasonably good roads, and Salina's bus schedules coincide with the arrival of the ferries.

TOURIST INFORMATION
Santa Marina di Salina (tel 984 3003).

Santa Marina di Salina

The main port is a straggling little village at the foot of the Fossa. Like every other town on Salina, it has little to 'see', but offers much in the way of peace, quiet and friendliness (many of the inhabitants are returned Australian migrants and speak a variety of English). By the lighthouse to the north a Bronze Age settlement once flourished; among the finds here was a necklace of Egyptian beads, a popular style in Mycenean days (similar necklaces have been discovered in England).

On the southern side of Santa Marina, the road leads to **Lingua** some 3 km away. The small lake near here was once used as a saltpan, on one side of which stretches a pebble beach where the sea is renowned for its clearness. In the 18th century the ruins of a typical Imperial Roman villa were noted here, but they have since sunk into the ground. Behind Lingua and Santa Marina, on the slopes of the Fossa, several Roman tombs have been excavated. A path from Santa Marina leads to the summit of the mountain (about two hours' climbing), from where on a clear day you can see not only all of the Aeolian Islands, but also Reggio Calabria and Mount Etna.

Around Salina

The coastal road north of Santa Marina passes many curious offshore formations of lava and basalt, and lonely beaches of pebbles and rock. Much of the land is neatly cultivated, although for lack of labour large tracts have become overgrown. The first village on the route is **Malfa** in the north, located on a wide plain overlooking the sea. West of here lies **Pollara** by the natural arch of **Punta del Perciato**, the only place on Salina where you can see the white pumice attesting to the volcanic origins of the island; the last eruption took place here in 10,000 BC, from the crater near the village.

Between Malfa and Leni, in the saddle known as Valdichiesa between the twin volcanoes, is the **Sanctuary of the Madonna del Terzito** built in 1630. The religious centre on the island, it attracts pilgrims on the main feast days of Mary, especially the Assumption (15 August).

Leni, another small community, is notable mainly for its location in Valdichiesa, overlooking the tiny fishing port of **Rinella** at the end of a steep winding road. The bus there stops by the overgrown public garden and a wide shady piazza with a café and fine

216

views of the sea. The small beach down below has a series of grottoes behind it. Fishermen will often take you on brief excursions along the coast—westwards to the interesting **Grotto di Racina** or eastwards to the **Grotto di Basalto** at Punta Grottazza, which easily wins the prize as the loveliest on the island (it can also be reached from Lingua).

WHERE TO STAY   (tel prefix 090)
The nicest hotel on Salina is in Rinella: ****L'Ariana** (tel 984 2075) with a beach and good restaurant (L50–60 000 with bath). In Santa Marina there are two 1-star hotels, **Punta Barone**, Lungomare Giuffre (tel 984 3172), and **Mamma Santina**, Via Sanita 26 (tel 984 3054) with rooms for L35 000. ***La Marinara** at Lingua (tel 984 3022) has an attractive garden and some rooms with bath (L35 000). In Malfa the ****Punta Scario** (tel 984 4139) has a pleasant little restaurant and pleasant rooms (L38–50 000 with bath).

EATING OUT
The restaurants are inexpensive and simple on Salina. **Da Santa** in Santa Maria is one that stands out (L20 000). In Lingua the trattoria **Il Gambero** serves, naturally, fish and prices are higher; in Rinella the best choice is **Da Peppino**, with the normal range of Aeolian dishes based on the capers–olives–eggplant theme, fish and straightforward grilled meats (L18–30 000).

FILICUDI

Small, lacking such basic amenities as water and electricity and a safe port, Filicudi is not for everyone—most of those who check into its sparse, Spartan lodgings are willing to sacrafice earthbound delights for the more rarefied pleasure of a tranquil, crystal sea. Yet despite the difficulties it presents, Filicudi has been inhabited off and on throughout history. The Greeks left an inscription near Pecorini, and later peoples left the numerous terraces cut like grand stairways in the mountains; although many of these have since been abandoned, from a distance they give the island a striped look. Many of Filicudi's 450 inhabitants make a living from the sea. Although the coral they once gathered is virtually gone, men still harvest the sponges, as well as fish.

The ancient name of Filicudi, *Phoinikodes*, referred either to its abundant ferns or (according to Strabo) to its palms. Capo Graziano, the first settlement on the island, is thought to date back to the 18th century BC. Eventually abandoned and then extensively resettled all the way up to the slopes of Montagnola, Capo Graziano became an important trading centre. Potsherds from Mycenae and the Cyclades attest to links between Filicudi and the Aegean in 1500 BC. In 800 BC the village was invaded and destroyed.

Capo Graziano

Filicudi Porto, where the ships and hydrofoils call, is one of the three main communities on the island. A long beach curves towards the promontory of Capo Graziano. To see the excavations there, apply in the port for the custodian, who will open the gate for you.

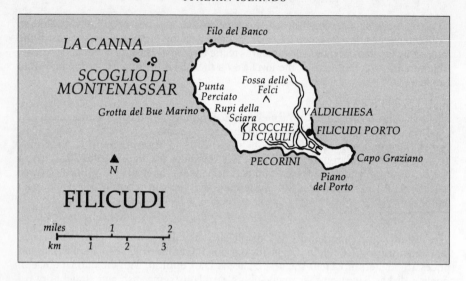

LA CANNA

SCOGLIO DI
MONTENASSAR

Grotta del Bue Marino •

Filo del Banco

Punta
Perciato

Fossa delle
Felci
∧

Rupi della
Sciara

ROCCHE
DI CIAULI

PECORINI

VALDICHIESA

FILICUDI PORTO

Capo Graziano

Piano
del Porto

▲
N

FILICUDI

miles   1   2
km   1   2   3

Capo Graziano, on a natural rock terrace some 90 m above sea level, was actually the successor to an earlier village on the plains, which was entirely indefensible. Some 20 oval-shaped huts have been uncovered on the cape, and the ceramics found here, with simple undulating scratched designs, gave their name to the Capo Graziano culture in the southern Tyrrhenian Sea (1800–1400 BC). All the ceramics are now in the Archaeology Museum in Lipari, but in one of the huts you can still see the smooth rocks and what appears to be a prehistoric altar. The necropolis of Capo Graziano extended up the steep sides of Montagnola, where people were buried in communal graves in the rock, much like those found in Sicily.

Around Filicudi, by Land and Sea

From the Porto you can also climb to the tallest of the island's three peaks, **Fossa delle Felci** (727 m), passing through **Rocche di Ciauli** (with post office and public telephone) and **Valdichiesa**, the main village of Filicudi, with the large church of **Santo Stefano** (constructed 1650) perching on the rim of an ancient crater. From here the path continues up to the summit of **Monte Fossa** and its charming views of the island. The only proper road on the island, built in the mid-1970s so that cars could replace the mules previously used, connects the Porto with the other seaside village of **Pecorini** where the ancient Greek inscription may be seen on the rocks.

From here, or the Porto, you can hire a boatman to take you around the island, the highlight of a stay on peaceful Filicudi. The west coast of the island is particularly lovely, with the famous volcanic obelisk called **La Canna** (91 m) towering out of the sea, popular with nesting seagulls. Next to it is another rock, the black **Scoglio di Monte-nassari**. Also along the west coast, a pointed natural archway forms the entrance to the marvellous **Grotta del Bue Marino** ('of the sea bull', after the hooded Mediterranean monk seals that once lived there). You can enter this large cavern in a small boat or swim around its ample perimeter; the intense silence and ever-changing light patterns are almost unreal. Other grottoes include the deep **Maccatore** and **Perciato**. The steep precipice **Rupi della Sciara** and the **Fortuna coast** offer further delightful visions of volcanic landscaping.

WHERE TO STAY   (tel prefix 090)
Underwater enthusiasts flock to Filicudi in the summer, and if you want to join them, book far in advance. Other than rooms in private houses, the only choice is the modern *****Phenicusa**, Via Porto (tel 984 4185; L55–70 000 with bath, open May–Sept), with a restaurant and beach. There are also a few rooms at the **Pensione La Canna**, Rocche Ciauli (tel 984 4187; L24–30 000).

EATING OUT
There is more choice here. **A' Tana** on the waterfront has fish-based antipasta and pasta dishes. You can get meat but it seems a trifle urbane to do so with the sea so close to the terrace. They often have lobster, and if you are tempted, reckon on L50–60 000, otherwise L25 000. On Via Porta there's **Lopes** and **Paino** both serving local hearty fare for L18–25 000; at Canale there's **Ristorante Ferlazzo** with seafood for L25 000.

ALICUDI

The furthest west of the Aeolian Islands, and one of the most remote islands in the entire Mediterranean, Alicudi is a round green bump on the sea, some 5 square km in size, a

miniature version of Filicudi. Its ancient name, *Ericusa*, derived from the heather that still covers this fertile little island, which is formed by the cone of an ancient volcano. In 1904 some tombs of the 9th century BC were discovered at Fucile, made out of lava, but it is not known if Alicudi was ever settled in ancient times; lacking any natural defences it may have been only used as a burial ground.

The gently sloping eastern part of the island is corrugated with green terraces and has the only village on Alicudi, the **Porto** (pop. 130). Lacking electricity, it couldn't be more peaceful. The one public telephone serves the bar as well as the hotel, and among the humble pink-and-white houses scattering the terraces there is only one prominent building, the **Church of San Bartolomeo** splendidly situated at the top of a small stairway.

High above the Porto is the steep **Serra della Farcona** where women used to hide from the pirates in a spot called the **Timpone delle Femmine**. Higher still is the depression of the very old crater, called the **Filo dell' Arpa** (669 m). The western side of Alicudi is too steep for houses or farming, but there are small scattered beaches and natural grottoes made by the wind, such as the **Grottazzo**. The few outsiders who visit Alicudi come mainly for the perfectly limpid water and the excellent fishing, especially for the Mediterranean lobster, the *aragosta*, lurking below and discreetly, if not always successfully, trying to avoid ending up on the evening menu.

WHERE TO STAY AND EAT   (tel prefix 090)
There's one hotel a few metres from the beach, the ***Ericusa**, Via Regina Elena (tel 981 2370; 12 rooms with showers, L35 000). Otherwise, you'll have to seek accommodation in private homes. The trattoria at the hotel **Ericusa** (it's a good idea to stay there and take full board for L60 000) has tasty food but no one knows from one day to the next what is going to be on the menu; it all depends on the day's catch (L20 000). **De Salvatore**, nearby, is equally good and prices are the same.

PANAREA

Panarea, the smallest of the Aeolian Islands (3.4 square km), is nevertheless one of the most charming, and is slowly but surely developing its tourist potential. Film buffs will know it from *L'Avventura*, which was shot here. Surrounded by numerous small islets and rocks like the Byzantine-named Basiluzzo, it is the queen of its own little archipelago. Known in ancient times as *Euonymos* ('of good omen'), it was the site of an early settlement at Piano Quartara (contemporaneous with the Capo Graziano culture on Filicudi), as well as a more famous settlement at Capo Milazzese (1400–1250 BC), a culture that produced the zigzag ceramic designs displaying symbols closely associated with the Minoan civilization on Crete.

The inhabited area of the island is spread across three neighbouring shores—Ditella, San Pietro and Drauto connected mainly by mule tracks. By the little quay at San Pietro there is a locally utilized hot spring, said to have medicinal powers. Among the picturesque rocks off the coast of Panarea is **Bottaro** where underwater fumaroles make the sea seem to boil.

Punta Milazzese

From San Pietro it's an hour's walk south, or a leisurely sail to the landing at **Cala Junco**, a lovely natural rock pool hemmed in by dark cliffs of outlandish volcanic prisms. Beyond Cala Junco crooks the thin knobby finger of **Punta Milazzese**, a basalt-walled promontory where in 1948 23 stone oval huts were excavated. Between 100 and 200 people lived here and maintained religious cults at Calcara and Punta Cardosi. Some of the pottery found at Milazzese bears a Minoan-like script which the early inhabitants may have been able to read. In approximately 1250 BC, however, the settlement was gutted by fire and ruined by Bronze Age tough-guys, who used their new metal-working technology mainly to destroy—behaviour unfortunatley repeated often throughout history.

North of the village of Ditella, **Calcara Beach** is reached by following a hairpin path down the rocky cliffs that comprise much of Panarea's coast. At Calcara fumaroles have left the stone a variety of colours; in places steam still rises from the ground and patches of sea and land are quite hot. In Neolithic times the fumaroles were worshipped as infernal gods, and deep pits were dug on the beach to receive their votive offerings.

From Drauto another path leads towards the **Contrada Castello**; from here you must make your own way up the terraces to the highest point of Panarea, the **Timpone del Corvo** (418 m), with splendid vistas of Stromboli and its active volcano. Just below Punta Corvo archaeologists have found traces of the ancient cult at Punta Cardosi.

Basiluzzo

Anyone coming to Panarea will not want to miss a visit to the unique cluster of rocks and islets off its west shore; hire a boat in the port. One islet, the **Dattilo** (Greek for finger yet pyramidal in shape), was until recently used by the islanders as grazing ground for their sheep, which they would ferry back and forth in boats. Now it's home to seagulls. The mountainous west coast of the island has many unusual formations of hardened lava, like the **Pizzo Falcone** above San Pietro. An unusual submerged shelf created by a seismic disturbance long ago extends from here, and on it, poking over the sea, are shoals and peculiar natural knick-knacks, the largest of which is the fascinating islet **Basiluzzo**, a more recent creation of the underwater volcano thought to have formed Panarea itself. Much of Basiluzzo consists of stratified lava in delicate shades formed into giant columns and pipes. By the landing point the ancient Roman dock wavers under the water; traces of Roman habitation dot the entire islet. It's uncertain whether the Romans were attracted by the weird beauty of the place, or merely used the islet as a cruel prison for political deportees; traces of mosaics found on Basiluzzo suggest the former. The rosemary and capers that grow on the little plain of the islet are harvested by the people of Panarea. The other rocks and islets in the area are also remarkable, in particular the many-coloured **Lisca Bianca** and **Lisca Nera**.

The sea itself is rich with life and, if you're lucky (and observant), you'll be treated to the sight of flying fish and dolphins leaping boastfully, while their more modest cousins, the tuna and swordfish, offer more subtle delights beneath the surface.

WHERE TO STAY   (tel prefix 090)
At San Pietro there's a small selection of hotels—**La Piazza** (tel 983 003; L60 000), with a garden but no restaurant. For the same price and facilities the tourist village

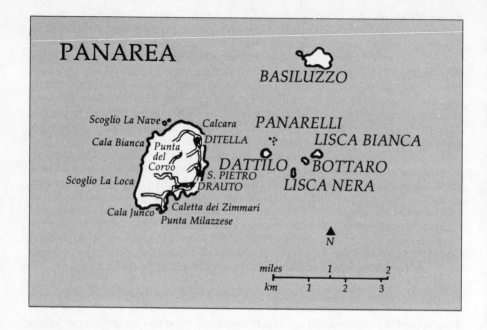

PANAREA

BASILUZZO

Scoglio La Nave • Calcara PANARELLI

Cala Bianca Punta DITELLA LISCA BIANCA
del
Corvo DATTILO BOTTARO
S. PIETRO
Scoglio La Loca DRAUTO LISCA NERA

Cala Junco Caletta dei Zimmari
Punta Milazzese

N

miles 1 2
km 1 2 3

Cincotta is nearby (tel 983 014), and the locanda ***Roda** (tel 983 006; L25–35 000). At Costa Galletta there's the modern ****Raya**, (tel 983 013), each room fitted with a private bath and terrace overlooking the sea; there's a garden, restaurant, and a small private port with boats to hire for island excursions (L40–55 000). There are also a number of locandas, like **Stella Maris** with one of Panarea's restaurants (tel 981 2558; rooms for L25 000).

EATING OUT

Like the other islands in this group, fish features prominently on all the restaurant menus, and prices tend to be a little higher—especially on items such as wine, which has to be 'imported' from Sicily. Because it's a stopping-off point for day trippers, in San Pietro there are a number of places on, or overlooking, the small harbour, all offering standard island pasta fare, but where fish seems to have a higher price tag. Among the better establishments are **La Sirena** (L25–35 000) and the restaurant in the hotel **Cincotta**. Like the accommodation, food tends to be simple on Panarea; a couple of the best establishments are **Trattoria La Sirena** on Via Drautti, and **G. Tesoriero** on Via San Pietro. Both will charge around L18–25 000 for a full meal.

STROMBOLI

In the 1950s the island of Stromboli became a household word with Rossellini's really awful Cinéma vérité film of the same name starring Ingrid Bergman, and it is still the most famous of the Aeolian Islands for its active volcano—although as islands go, Stromboli is a newborn, only 40,000 years old, and has yet to settle down. Its belching cone is the first thing you see when you begin your island odyssey from Naples, 211 km away.

Little has changed since the 2nd century AD, when Pausanias succinctly observed: 'On Strongyle "the round island" you may see fire coming up from the earth'. This may sound a bit dangerous for the 400 inhabitants of Stromboli, but it's not—all volcanic activity takes place on the Sciara del Fuoco ('the fiery trail'), confined by the nature of the mountain itself. From the two parishes on the northern part of the island, all you can see are puffs of smoke, and at night only the apogees of the fireworks.

Stromboli, the island furthest north and east of the Aeolian archipelago, had a special importance before the advent of steamships as the main port between Naples and Sicily. It seems a little hard to believe today, as the black beaches of San Vincenzo and San Bartolo have no protection from the raging winds, but the sailing ships used to anchor here, and the islanders made it a hereditary profession to ferry men and supplies between the ships and the shore. The new concrete mole at Scari has unfortunately eliminated the need for these brawny sailors and their romantic rowing-boats.

GETTING AROUND

Boats and hydrofoils arrive daily in Scari from Milazzo, Naples and the neighbouring islands; at least once a week one of the Milazzo steamers calls at the island's second port of Ginostra. Otherwise, regular transport on the island is shoe leather, as no roads as such exist.

The Volcano of Stromboli, Aeolian Islands

TOURIST INFORMATION
At Ficogrande, in the summer only.

The Stromboli Metropolitan Area
Visitors disembarking at **Scari**, the main port, are met by little three-wheeled vehicles which take your luggage up the hill to your hotel, for only they can manoeuvre the narrow streets of the villages; the one main road that skirts the shore from Scari to its seaside suburb of Ficogrande is scarcely used. **San Vincenzo**, the 'centre', is named after the large parish church of San Vincenzo Ferreri, which overlooks the village and the bizarre islet of Strombolicchio. Here the houses, mostly whitewashed, are of a delightful simplicity and proportion known as the Aeolian style. There are particularly fine examples at **San Bartolo**, the other parish, with an equally fine church. Most of the tourist amenities on the island are to be found here or below on the beautiful black sand beach of **Ficogrande** ('big fig'). These settlements have a melancholy air, however, thanks to the numerous abandoned houses and farms. No one seems to want to stay on this rarest of islands, and the delicious white wine of Stromboli, subtly flavoured from the volcanic soil—the finest in the Aeolian Islands—grows increasingly scarce for lack of labour.

Up the Volcano

Malcolm Lowry's unhappy characters sloshed their way to trouble *Under the Volcano*, but Stromboli offers you the chance to get on top of the situation. From the west end of San Bartolo it is about half-an-hour's walk to the **Osservatorio di Punta Labronzo** (follow the signs painted on the lanes). The Osservatorio, at the northernmost point of the island, offers a fine view of the volcano if you aren't up to climbing to the summit; come at night with binoculars to see the volcanic sparks.

To visit the crater of the volcano itself, allow 3 or 4 hours for the ascent and perhaps another 2 hours for the descent. You would do well to take a powerful torch, along with sturdy shoes, a flask of water, a bite to eat, and warm clothing—ideally a windcheater—not only because it's much cooler on top than at sea level, but the summit of Stromboli is the very citadel of the wind god, and he's lusty enough to blow cinders into every crevice in your body. The more adventurous bring a sleeping bag and sleep on the warm ground to take in the spectacular view of the day dawning over the archipelago. Ideally the climb should be made at full moon, beginning around 5 pm, allowing time to see the sun set over the islands. Of course, many people do go up during the day, but in summer it's too hot, and during the hours of daylight all you'll see is smoke. If you are wary of making the trip alone, trained guides may be hired on the island.

The ascent begins from the Observatory, where the well-made path has lately become somewhat overgrown. Beaten and narrow, it passes through thick undergrowth and prickly bushes, which become gradually thinner until they peter out all together. Here the track becomes a bit difficult to discern, paths cut through cinders wandering every which way over the rocks, but it doesn't matter which one you take as they all eventually meet. Little red and white stripes have been painted on the boulders to guide you, and you may have to do a little Alpine climbing to reach the peak, or the **Serra Vancura** observation point, at 927 m, the highest point of Stromboli and covered with sand which has a nasty tendency to blow into your eyes. However, from the peak you have an excellent view of the crater 213 m below; the amount of volcanic activity, the wind and your own stamina will determine how much closer you get.

It is an extraordinary sight. Stromboli has given its name to the constant, explosive nature of a certain type of volcano: every ten minutes on the nose red sparks flare up in an enormous fountain of fire, accompanied by appropriate deep rumblings inside the volcano. On busy nights the volcano spews chunks of molten volcanic debris and smouldering magma down the infernal Sciara del Fuoco; and when the fog gathers around the crater, as often happens, the effect is even more eerie. On good nights (little wind and no bitter volcanic gases), it is easy to stay up until dawn, always a magnificent sight from a mountain top, and particularly breathtaking on top of the world's most active volcano.

In summer there are evening boat excursions to the base of the startling, uncanny **Sciara del Fuoco.** The contrast between the verdant hills of the rest of the island and the hellish black slag of the Sciara couldn't be greater, and while the volcano isn't as immediate or awe-inspiring as when you make the big climb, the red sparks spraying over the side of the Sciara provide a truly memorable sight.

Ginostra and Strombolicchio

Other possible boat excursions on Stromboli are to Ginostra and Strombolicchio. **Ginostra** (pop. 30) lies very near the Sciara del Fuoco, on the far western side of Stromboli. This perfectly charming, remote village—much diminished through wide-spread emigration to Australia and America—has literally the smallest port in the world; no more than two tiny fishing boats can fit in it at a time. Lava rocks in the sea form a natural protective wall against the frequent violent storms. The fishermen and their families who have remained in Ginostra are amongst the hardiest of all Italians, served by a commuting priest who occasionally performs mass in the tiny church among the fine white houses, many built on ledges carved out of the lava. A mule path once connected Ginostra with San Vincenzo, but it has become impassable. The only contact that Ginostra has with the outside world is by boat, either from other parishes on the island, or the steamers from Milazzo. If the sea is rough, Ginostra is unapproachable.

One last excursion by sea is to **Strombolicchio** a couple of km off the north coast of Stromboli. From the distance this mass of volcanic rock looks like a Gothic cathedral; it is surrounded by strange currents, and its spires turn out to be petrified monsters. Between 1920 and 1927, some 200 concrete steps were hewn in Strombolicchio's side, leading up to the lighthouse, a vital installation in these frequently rough seas. Up to forty years ago, at *festa* time, the people from Stromboli would hop over in their boats to dance on the high terrace of the lighthouse—and magical it must have been beneath a full moon. The views from the summit of the islet sometimes extend to the peak of Mount Etna, although perhaps most interesting of all are the many queer shapes and the sheer sides of the rock carved by the wind.

WHERE TO STAY   (tel prefix 090)
For resort facilities and a pool, ***La Sciara**, Via Cincotta (tel 986 004) has rooms for L140 000, open April to Sept. ***La Sirenetta**, Via Ficogrande (tel 986 025) has a pool and garden and beach (L70–90 000, with bath). There are a number of inexpensive locandas, the best of which is the **Villa Petrusa**, Via Soldato Panettieri (tel 986 045) which has some rooms with a bath, and a restaurant. **Mario Lo Schiavo** (tel 981 1760) in Ginostra has five double rooms to let in the village, the sole accommodation.

EATING OUT
Il Gabbiano is a long-standing favourite at Via Vito Nunziante 10, with fish and meat dishes for L25 000. Less expensive choices are **Roma** on Via Roma and nearby **Saccavino**, The three trattorias in Ginostra—**Internazionale, Lo Schiavo** and **Merlino**—serve mainly day trippers in the summer.

USTICA

The 8 square km that make up the black island of Ustica lie a lonely 67 km north of Palermo, looking for all the world like a giant turtle swimming away from Sicily; it is just far enough away to escape the pollution of the larger island. For this reason Ustica, its transparent sea and bright submerged gardens of aquatic flora and fauna are well known among scuba divers, who take classes in the local diving school and gather here every July for the 'International Festival of Underwater Activities' to discuss new scientific discoveries and compete in numerous underwater sports.

But Ustica has many charms for landlubbers, too. Its volcanic structure has created some marvellous scenery, easily accessible on foot or by donkey. Wild flowers cover the island except in the hottest months, and a well-maintained little wood offers possibilities of shady picnics and afternoon snoozes. It is a fertile island and most of the land is taken up with agriculture of some sort—capers, figs, lentils and vines; its *Albanella* wine is

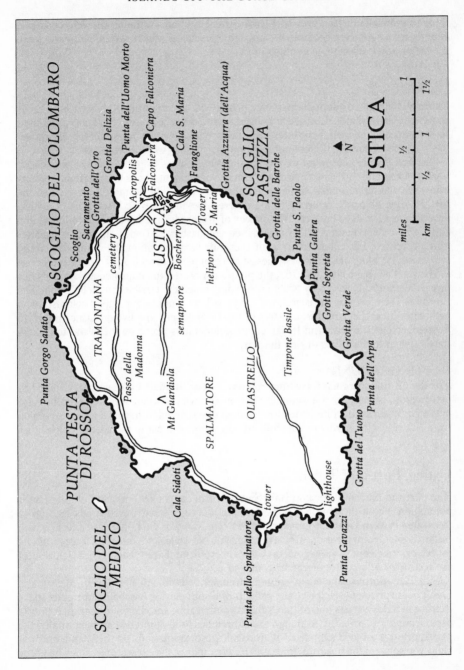

shipped to mainland Italy and, to a lesser extent, abroad. Although the wild coastline, dotted with magnificent grottoes, has no sandy beaches, there are several rocky coves and the major hotels all have swimming pools.

History

Ustica was inhabited about 2000 BC by a people with close cultural links with both Sicily and the Aeolian Islands. Located at Falconiera and near the present Saracen castle, their settlements have yielded many interesting finds, but have yet to be completely excavated. In the nearby Grotta dell'Uomo items from early tombs were discovered.

The first historical account we have of the island comes from the Greeks, who called Ustica *Osteodes* ('bony island'), from the remains of 6000 mutinous Carthaginian soldiers who were abandoned here to die of hunger and thirst. The Romans, who named the island *Ustum* ('burnt'), referring to the charred-looking volcanic black rock of Ustica, probably used it as a base. As the power of Rome declined, pirates took over, and although the Benedictines briefly maintained a monastery on Ustica, the pirates successfully prevented any colonization until the 18th century, when the Bourbons under Ferdinand IV, King of the Two Sicilies, sent a group of settlers from Trapani and Lipari to Ustica. Two years later, in 1762, the pirates massacred the unprotected colonists in a three-day rampage, with only two men escaping to tell the terrible tale in Palermo. The Bourbons then fortified the island, and ten years later sent a new group of colonists, who had better luck; they are the ancestors of the 1000 people who live on Ustica today. In September 1943, British and Italian commanders met secretly on the island to discuss Italy's switch to the Allies during the war.

GETTING AROUND

The daily 2-hour Siremar ferry from Palermo (not on Sundays in the winter) is joined by two hydrofoils daily in the summer, one in the winter when weather permits, also operated by Siremar. The boats are conveniently scheduled to make a day excursion from Palermo. (It's hardly worthwhile bringing your own car to the island, unless it's a jeep.)

Ustica, Port and Town

The port and town of Ustica on **Baia Santa Maria** contains 90 per cent of the island's population. From the landing, steps and one of Ustica's few paved roads lead up to tree-filled **Piazza Umberto**, the centre of town. Many of the houses are adorned with bright contemporary frescoes of every imaginable style and theme, a legacy of the mural-painting contest sponsored on Ustica in even-numbered years; several lanes sport the festive air of an outdoor colour comic strip.

San Bartolomeo, the main church, occupies a dominant position in the square. Don't be surprised to see the young gallants of Ustica playing baseball in the open space in front of it; Ustica has one of Italy's finest youth teams, and the boys wear their purple caps bearing a U proudly. Although the church has little of interest architecturally, the parish priest is an avid supporter of archaeological explorations on the island, and will show you some of the beautiful finds and photographs of the excavations which he keeps in the back. The **Museum** contains items from the offshore wrecks found by undersea explorers, but it is closed except for July, during the subaqua festival. Above the church, on the site of an 11th-century Benedictine monastery, is the **Palazzo del Commune** of 1763, Ustica's grandest building.

More steps and another path lead up from the town to the ruins of a Saracen castle on **Falconiera**, the highest point of the island, from which you can see Sicily. Here a number of ancient sites have been excavated. The modern inhabitants constructed the nearby Calvario and further down on the Guardia di Mezzo, a ridge that divides Ustica in two, there is an abandoned lighthouse.

Around Ustica: by Boat

The principal port of Ustica, **Baia Santa Maria**, has been in use since ancient times, when the Phoenicians constructed a long mole of volcanic rock where the concrete mole stands today. In the season it is easy to hire a boat or a boatman to take you around the splendid little island. Some of the most impressive parts of Ustica's coastline lie just to the south of the port, with the steep ochre cliffs of stratified lava and the **Grotta Azzurra**, which, like its namesake in Capri, derives its chief beauty from the reflections of light on the blue sea. While the entrance to the cavern is quite narrow, inside it is an ample 91 m long. The walls of the grotto are caked with petrified shells, and in the centre a steep greyish rock with stalactites drips water reputed to cure skin diseases.

The next sea cave, **Grotta Pastizza** just to the south, is almost as lovely as the Grotta Azzurra. Near it, just under the water, are a large bank of petrified shells and the half-submerged entrance to another fair-sized grotto, **Naiada**. Further south still is the majestic **Baia San Paolo**, one of the prettiest bays on Ustica, with a giant lava arch and yet another grotto, known as the **Barche** ('of the boats'), where fishermen beach their boats during storms, and where 18th-century 'ladies of scarce virtue' who accompanied the Bourbon soldiers to the island used to frolic in the evenings. Off the Punta San Paolo a Roman ship went down, and scuba divers still find amphorae here.

The entrance to the **Grotta Segreta** ('secret cave'), next to Punta Segreta, will keep its secrets since its mouth has been blocked by a chunk of lava, but the exquisite turquoise colour of the water inside the nearby **Grotta Verde** is impressively visible. Next are the rich fishing grounds of **Cala Sciabica** and **Punta dell' Arpa**, and a long stretch of rugged coast towards the Punta Gavazzi with one of the island's two lighthouses. Beneath the lighthouse is the **Piscina Naturale**, a natural sea pool that attracts swimmers and sunbathers. Another local feature is the **Torre Spalmatore**, an 18th-century defensive tower at the southern end of the Spalmatore coast, with numerous inlets and pebbly beaches. The **Baia Sidoti** is the most striking cove, with the **Scoglio del Medico** ('the doctor's rock'), a little way out to sea, a popular nesting place for seagulls. The bay is surrounded by orange cliffs of tufa, and has a reputation for its remarkable quantity of fish. The steep cliffs north of Sidoti bear the hilly tract known as the **Passo della Madonna**, one of the highlights of a walking tour of Ustica (see below). Here the rocks are coloured a deep red at the **Testa di Rosso**, a mighty precipice; at the bottom is a small pebbly beach.

Following this you pass a series of fantastic volcanic rocks—the **Colombaro** or Faraglione made of black and green crystals, the **Sacramento** rock with its unusual stratification, and two grottoes with curious mineral formations in their walls. The lighthouse on **Punta dell'Uomo Morto** (Dead Man's Point) stands on a cliff, where a deep cave contained vestiges of ancient tombs.

Around Ustica: on Land

If you prefer to explore the island, rather than merely admire it from a boat, you can easily see it all on foot (or hire a donkey) within 3 or 4 hours, circling around the Guardia di Mezzo. You can see many of the same things mentioned above along the coast from new and sometimes better angles, as well as the **Torre Santa Maria**, a watchtower (built 1766) with pleasant views over the sea. Signs remain of prehistoric villages at Punta Spalmatore (along with the modern tourist village) and in the Tramontana region. The **Passo della Madonna**, with its sheer precipices, forms the most dramatic part of the journey—that is if you don't encounter the red bees of Spalmatore. These pesky little blossom-suckers like to buzz around your head and legs when you cross their turf, but they rarely sting.

WHERE TO STAY   (tel prefix 091)
On the beach on the Contrada S. Paolo is *****Diana**, a comfortable hotel with a good restaurant (tel 844 9109; L60–70 000), and the ****Ariston**, Via della Vittoria 3, is small and reasonably priced (tel 844 0942; L45–55 000 with bath).
Also: ***Locanda Castelli**, Via S. Francesco 16 (tel 844 9007; L16 000, no rooms with bath) and the ***Clelia**, Via Magazzino 7 (tel 844 9039; L40 000 with bath) are the least expensive, and the ****Stella Marina**, in Via C. Colombo is where the subaqua team, the Diving World Group, are based in summer (tel 844 9014; L55 000 with bath). Resorts have appeared at a few of the most choice spots along the coast: at Spalmatore, the *****Punta Spalmatore** (tel 844 9323) is a large and well-equipped tourist village with cottage accommodation for 350 and a good selection of sport facilities. Rates are L80 000. Book through a travel agent of the Club Punta Spalmatore, Piazza Tricolore 1, Milan, tel (02) 799 205.

EATING OUT
Ustica's specialities are its wine and the day's catch, and quail in April/May and Sept/Oct. **Centrofiori**, in Via Tramontana, is one of Ustica's most traditional trattorias where Sicilian specialities abound—seafood is, naturally, de rigueur (L25–35 000). **Da Mario**, Piazza Umberto, and **La Rustica**, Via Petriera, are two fish restaurants where a pasta course and fish, with wine and salad, will work out at L30 000. **Le Campanelle** in an old house just outside town, has excellent fish and pasta dishes, including *spaghetti all'aragosta* (lobster) in the L20 000 range. The Clelia Hotel, Via Magazzino 7 (tel 844 9039), also has a good and inexpensive restaurant, where *lenticchie all'usticese* (Ustican lentils) is a speciality (L20 000).

The Egadi Islands

The three Egadi (sometimes spelt Aegadi in English) Islands—Favignana, Levanzo and Marèttimo—are just off the west coast of Trapani in western Sicily. Between them and the coast lie the Formiche ('ant') islets, one of which has an abandoned tuna cannery. As islands go, all are relative newcomers. Marèttimo, the island furthest from Sicily, was separated from that land mass 600,000 years ago during the Quaternary period, while Favignana and Levanzo, inhabited by Paleolithic Man in 10,000 BC, were parted from Sicily *c.*5000 BC, due not only to earthquakes but also to the glacial periods and the rising level of the sea.

Each of the Egadi Islands has a unique beauty and personality of its own. Favignana, the largest and by far the most populated, is the island of tufa and tuna, and nowadays of tourism too; Levanzo, the smallest island, is quaint and rocky; mountainous Marèttimo has fascinating rock formations and grottoes and a charming fishing village scarcely touched by the passing of time. In his book *The Authoress of the Odyssey* Samuel Butler claimed that Marèttimo was the Ithaca of Odysseus (see Trapani).

Because of the currents, the sea around the Egadi Islands is extremely rich with fish, especially tuna. Between April and July, the period of the famous *Mattanza* or slaughter, scores of tuna pass through the channel dividing Favignana from the Formiche islets. Among the Neolithic paintings in the Grotta del Genovese on the island of Levanzo are several of tuna fish, perhaps a mainstay in the diet even then. A sacred ritual developed around the *Mattanza* which still exists today, although modern techniques of catching the tuna have made inroads on the tradition. The oil company Agip is searching for minerals beneath the waters between Favignana and Marsala; if they strike lucky, who knows but the tuna might abandon this busy and dangerous route.

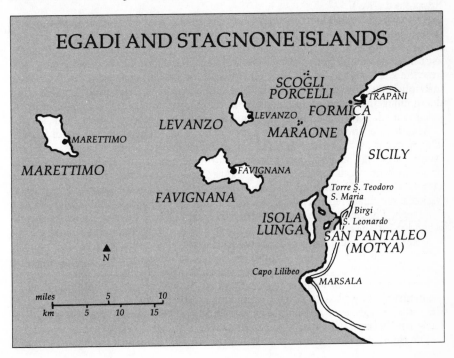

EGADI AND STAGNONE ISLANDS

History

What earliest traces remain of the various people who lived on the islands for the last 12 millennia are concentrated in the caves of Favignana and Levanzo, many of which were inhabited up to the 17th and 18th centuries AD. Most beautiful and moving, however, are the very first signs left in the Grotta del Genovese some 12,000 years ago, where the people of the Old Stone Age carved pictures of bulls, dancing figures, an ass and a marvellous deer, with incredibly natural and fluid lines. The much later inhabitants of the cave in Neolithic times further adorned the walls with simple black and red paintings, crude beside the art of their Palaeolithic ancestors.

Early on, the Egadi Islands found themselves sitting on an important Phoenician trade route and were settled by these Semitic people, although their main centre was Motya, just to the south (see the Stagnone Islands). During the First Punic War, the islands saw many of the sea battles between Rome and Carthage, including the final one in 241 BC. After 20 years of war, both Rome and Carthage decided to end it once and for all, sending their fleets to Lilybaeum (Marsala), the last Punic stronghold on Sicily. The two armadas met just northeast of Favignana, the Romans with 200 new warships, the Carthaginians with 400 ships crammed full of soldiers coming to the rescue of besieged Lilybaeum. Before they could land, however, the Romans demolished them, sinking 120 and capturing some 10,000 prisoners. So many Phoenicians died and were washed ashore on a small inlet of Favignana that their blood supposedly gave it the name of Cala Rossa ('red cove').

Although the inhabitants of the islands eventually adopted Roman ways—as witnessed by several buildings, mosaics and the development of the tufa quarries of Favignana—their hearts perhaps were still Phoenician, for several inscriptions from the 1st century BC found in the grottoes are in Punic characters. These same grottoes also bear the later symbols of the early Christians (4th and 5th centuries). An interesting inscription found in the Grotta della Stele on Favignana is linguistically important for determining the evolution of languages in the Mediterranean, as well as offering an insight into the life of the island's troglodytes: translated it means 'House, tomb, stable'.

After the decline of Rome little is known about what happened to the Egadi Islands. The Saracens used them as a base for their conquest of Sicily, and afterwards, under the Normans, Favignana and Marèttimo were fortified. Under the Aragonese the islands became a port of call for Genoese merchant vessels; some of the sailors from Levanto near Genoa gave Levanzo its modern name. When the Spanish established a base at Marsala, the Egadi Islands saw many of their comings and goings and encounters with the Turks. The Spanish were the first to develop on a large scale the great banks of coral around the islands, although most of the profits of this went to the Trapanese.

Spain's never-ending wars caused ever-increasing debts, and to help pay them off she sold the Egadi Islands to the Marquis Pallavicino of Genoa in 1637. The Pallavicino family did much to develop the islands economically, and the islanders were finally able to leave their caves to found a town around the Castello San Giacomo (the modern penitentiary), as well as to develop their farms, excavate the tufa of Favignana, plant vineyards on Levanzo, and cut down the forests of Marèttimo. The cave houses of Favignana became stalls for sheep and donkeys.

The Bourbons, always looking for somewhere to send their cons and political prisoners, turned Favignana into a penal colony. However, the islanders welcomed the extra income they made selling supplies to the prison and even became known throughout Italy for their kindness and tact as prison guards, so that even today a large proportion of prison guards in Italy are Favignanese.

Since the Egadi Islands lie so close to Marsala, they were liberated from the Bourbons early by Garibaldi, and soon achieved a new prosperity, fishing, farming and digging the tufa to build homes not only on the island but also in Trapani and Tunis. After World War II, however, their economy nosedived, and many emigrated to other parts of Italy and the New World. Only the advent of tourism in the late 1960s and 1970s has begun to turn the tide and keep the young people at home.

GETTING AROUND
Siremar operates all the ferries to the islands, and all depart from the port of Trapani. Three days a week (Tues, Fri, and Sun) the ferry makes the grand tour of all three islands, leaving early in the morning for the 3-hour cruise, returning immediately. On the other days (Mon, Wed, Thurs, and Sat) there is no service to Marèttimo, but 2 daily runs (3 in the summer) to Levanzo and Favignana only.

You needn't inconvenience yourself, though, unless you have a car, for there are always hydrofoils—the 'school buses' for the Egadi children. Even in winter there are 6 a day to Favignana, 4 continuing to Levanzo, and 2 reach Marèttimo, with a few extra in the high season. It's always easy to hop from one island to another—providing you can decipher the complicated schedules.

FAVIGNANA

A charmer of many names—the Phoenician *Katria*, the Greek *Aegusa* and the medieval *Faugnana* (from 'Favonio', the name of a wind), Favignana today is the capital of the Egadi Islands, and is the biggest and most populated. Tourist brochures tend to emphasize the island's butterfly shape, although the 'wings' hardly match—the eastern wing is a level plain, pitted with tufa excavations, while the western wing is mountainous. Beyond the Montagna Grossa, the Boschetto ('little wood') consists mainly of abandoned farmland but has several very fine examples of Siculo–Arab architecture.

GETTING AROUND
Favignana has no regular public transport. Although you can see a great deal on foot, people with only a short time to spend on the island will probably wish they had a car or bicycle since most of the roads here have been asphalted; bikes may be hired in the town. Hotel minibuses collect guests as they arrive on the hydrofoils or ships. The Arte Sport Sub (Via Roma) will care for the needs of underwater sportsmen, and boats may be hired at Leonardo, the fishermen's port (north of the commercial dock).

TOURIST INFORMATION
Piazza Madrice 7 (tel (0923) 921647).
Post office: Piazza Madrice.
Telephones: Piazza Europa 4.

The Port
On an island where fishing is such an important industry, it hardly comes as a surprise

that the main town is also the port. Known simply as **Favignana**, its dock has two impressive structures on either side of it: the large abandoned tuna canneries by a rocky beach, and the house of their founder, the **Palazzo Florio**. This palace, built in 1876 and surrounded by an unkempt garden with only two palm trees and a pine for company, is impressively melancholy. Built for Ignazio Florio and his family to use during the tuna season, it serves today as Favignana's Town Hall.

Ignazio Florio, son of a successful tuna entrepreneur in Palermo, bought the Egadi Islands from the last of the Pallavicino family in 1874, and applied his father's new techniques to the industry on Favignana. He built two processing plants (one on Favignana, the other on the islet of Formica) which are outstanding examples of 19th-century industrial architecture, the Alhambras of tuna fish canneries with their arches and ogival doors. His son Vincenzo, through high living and personal tragedy, managed to ruin the business, and a Genoese company took over in 1937, then the S.p.A. da Florio. Today, however, the canneries are just empty galleries; the tuna caught in the *Mattanza* is either served fresh in Sicily or taken to Japan and canned there.

Giving onto the port, the Piazza Europa has a statue of the portly Ignazio Florio, benefactor of Favignana. Behind him stands the **Old Municipio** in typical 19th-century Italian provincial style with a clock on top. A busy street of shops leads from here to the main Piazza Madrice, named after the **Chiesa Madrice** at the end of the long square. Built in 1704, the Marquis Pallavicino insisted that it should be out of range of the Forte San Giacomo directly in front, which is why the church was constructed in its unprepossessing location.

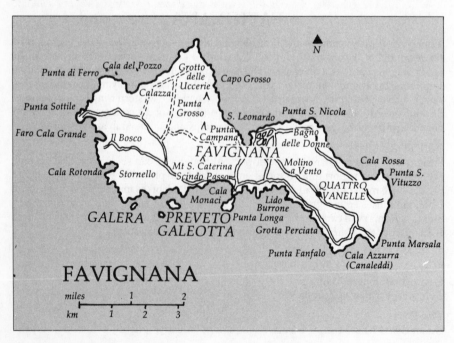

Forte San Giacomo, today a maximum-security prison, served an important role in Favignana's defence from the time of its foundation in 1120 by King Roger. Rebuilt in 1498 under orders of Ferdinand II the Catholic, it was converted into a prison in 1837 by the Bourbons, who had many uprisings to deal with that year. Unfortunately, the Forte cannot be visited. But near here is the studio of local artist Zu Sarina, whose smiling, childlike tufa heads add a charming note to many homes.

To the right of the church lies the old part of town, the **Rione Sant'Anna** with its narrow streets and typical houses made of native tufa. Just behind this are several examples of abandoned tufa quarries, unremoved bricks carved in the walls and a luxuriant garden invariably at the bottom, protected from the wind. There are tufa dovecots and tufa well covers and tufa roadside shrines. Some of the newer buildings on the outskirts of town have been unhappily whitewashed, as modern architecture in the Mediterranean seems to dictate.

Eastern Favignana

Heading east from the town along the coast, it is a short walk to the **Punta San Nicola.** Ancient and more recent tufa excavations are very much in evidence, and many of the caves have been inhabited for thousands of years. At San Nicola the island's cemetery has been used since ancient times; indeed, the whole area is full of signs of the generations who lived and died here from the Palaeolithic era onwards. Everything looks unorganized and uncared for, since the State hasn't the funds to excavate and explore the area properly. Nearby you can visit the **Grotta del Pazzo** ('Madman's cave') with late Punic inscriptions and early Christian symbols, and the **Grotta degli Archi** with several tombs of a Palaeo-Christian necropolis dating from the 4th and 5th centuries. To the right of the Cala San Nicola lies the entrance to the so-called **Bagno delle Donne** ('the women's bath') of Roman date, where water was pumped in from the sea. Traces of mosaics found here were put in the Antiquarium, but this too has closed for lack of funds.

A cross on the road to Cala San Nicola marks the crossroads to **Cala Rossa** at the eastern end of Favignana. Among the abandoned fields are two enormous abandoned tufa quarries. An overgrown path from the electric plant nearby leads to a prehistoric tomb cut in the rock, and further up there is a ledge with an excellent view of Favignana's coast. At Cala Rossa ancient tufa quarries in the rock have left wonderfully unnatural towers of clean-cut angles and long underground galleries, like a ruined, imaginary city. If you can get to Cala Rossa before dawn, the chances are very good of seeing a meteorological phenomenon called the *Fata Morgana* that causes mirages over Punta San Vituzzo similar to the one in Messina. According to the islanders, the mirage once saved the island from Turkish pirates, when it formed the illusion of a great fleet approaching on the horizon. At other times they say it looks like a vast army marching over the sea, or an invasion of Japanese movie monsters.

Those determined to walk around the eastern wing of Favignana can take the path from Cala Rossa south to Punta Marsala and the distant lighthouse facing the port of the same name. The dirt road west of here passes the **Cala Canaleddi,** also known as Cala Azzurra from the intense blue of the sea next to the almost snowy whiteness of the rocks around it. At the far end of the bay stands the modern white hotel complex of Villagio Punta Fanfalo.

The road continues up the wild coast to the picturesque **Grotta Perciata** ('pierced cave'), on the other side of which a tiny harbour can hold a total of three small fishing boats. Then comes Punta and **Lido Burrone**, a 15-minute walk from the port. This long stretch of sand facing a shallow sea is the best beach on Favignana, and although there are several villas nearby it could hardly be said to be spoiled. To the west the rocky coast towards the promontory of Punta Longa constitutes the 'head' of the Favignana butterfly. A seldom-used road covers the short distance from here to the town.

The West Wing of the Butterfly

From Favignana town a mule path zigzags up the mountain to **Forte Santa Caterina** but, sad to say, this is a military zone and it cannot be visited without special permission. Originally built by the Saracens, Roger II of Sicily renovated it in the 12th century and used it as a watchtower. Further additions were made in 1498 and 1655, and during the reign of the Bourbons it held some of the most notable figures of the Risorgimento, the Italian national renaissance leading up to the unification of Italy.

The **Montagna Grossa** (highest peak: Monte Santa Caterina, 308 m) makes a fairly effective barrier to the west side of the island; the one paved road skirts the extreme southern edge of the mountains at the Passo di Scindo. Numerous islets and rocks adorn the coast here, offering safe havens for the much pursued fish of Favignana. The largest islet, **Preveto**, once supported a colony of wild rabbits, but eager hunters have since eliminated them all.

This part of the island, euphemistically called **Il Bosco** ('the wood'), is nothing more than several hectares of abandoned farmland. Near the Case Casino the paved road forks, one branch leading to the south side of **Cala Grande** and the Villagio Approdo di Ulisse, the hotel for underwater enthusiasts, for this part of the island is richest in fishy prey. Near the village you can see an ancient well with a pendulum mechanism, still used by the few farmers who live in the area.

The northern fork of the paved road leads to **Punta Sottile** on the northern point of Cala Grande, where there is a lighthouse. An unpaved track to the right, halfway to the lighthouse, leads past the coast at Calazza to **Faraglione**, a strange rocky landscape more typical of Utah than the Mediterranean. The Faraglione itself, a steep-edged peninsula, offers a fine view of Levanzo a short distance away. Just below the Faraglione lies the entrance to a wonderful cave, the **Grotta delle Uccerie** (take an electric torch) with beautiful coloured stalactites which join the roof to the floor of the cave like columns. There are actually two chambers, the second less desecrated by souvenir-hunting shepherds.

ACTIVITIES

In May and June it is possible to witness the *Mattanza* (the tuna massacre), a wild and bloody spectacle. The tuna return from the Atlantic through the Straits of Gibraltar to breed in the warmer waters of the Mediterranean, the currents pushing them towards their destiny off the island of Favignana. Here, beside the upside-down cross of St Peter suspended over the water, they swim into the tuna corral (the *tonnara*) where they are trapped. Under the command of the *Rais*, the Mattanza chief, the fishermen chant their traditional songs about the saints while slowly raising the great net. The fish struggle and squirm in their frenzy as the net is hoisted higher and higher in the water. Then, one by one, the fishermen impale and drag their silvery victims into the boats, and when the last 140–180-kg fish is lugged aboard, then the fishermen gather their great net and take the catch home. Usually the fishermen make enough money from the two or three months of the *Mattanza* to tide them over until the next year.

WHERE TO STAY   (tel prefix 0923)
Favignana is the only Egadi island equipped to handle a large number of visitors, with hotels and campsites. Two resort hotels with pretensions are the *****L'Approdo di Ulisse** 'Ulysses' landing' at Cala Grande, (tel 921 287; L70 000), and the *****Punta Fanfalo**, Punta Fanfalo, (tel 921 777; L80 000). Both have pools and a stretch of seashore. The pensione ***Egadi**, Via Cristoforo Colombo 17 (tel 921 232), is simple and cheap—L38 000 with bath, L30 000 without. There are no pretensions at all at the **Tourist Village 4 Rose**—named by the owner, a retired migrant from Trenton, New Jersey, after his favourite bourbon. He also runs a campsite, restaurant, and disco, with the aid of his several cats and one monkey (tel 921 223, L24 000 for a bungalow).

EATING OUT
An inexpensive restaurant on Favignana, where you can try several different seafood and pasta concoctions, is **Angelo e Peppe**, Piazza Madrice 63 (L18–25 000). **La Tavernetta**, a few doors away at no. 59, is a little dearer but the seafood is a little better. Couscous, the speciality of Trapani province, is also the speciality at Trattoria **Da Matteo**, Via V. Emmanuele 19, for L20 000, and the best of North African and Italian cuisine comes together in the pensione–restaurant **Egadi**, Via C. Colombo 17 (tel 921 232), where couscous is a speciality. From May onwards tuna is a regular feature; excellent local *pecorino* cheese and a healthy selection of wines (L28–35 000).

LEVANZO

At 5.7 square km, Levanzo is the midget of the Egadi Islands. In ancient times it was known as *Phorbanzia* or *Bucinna*; the Saracens called it 'dry' (*Gazirat al ya bisah*), and in the Renaissance it became Levanto. Unlike Favignana and Marèttimo, Levanzo has no fresh water, which keeps its population down to a minimum (about 200), concentrated around the **Cala Dogana**. The entire coastline is rocky and inaccessible except for a few inlets. Inland, a charming valley used mainly as pastureland is surrounded by hills, the highest being the **Pizzo del Monaco** (277 m). Although there is but one small hotel on the island, Levanzo has a major attraction in its prehistoric artwork at the Grotta del Genovese.

The town and port of **Levanzo**, its houses gazing over the sea towards Favignana, exemplifies Schumacher's theory that 'small is beautiful'. Even the dogs have nothing better to do all day but sleep in the middle of the street, letting cats and even tourists walk by unmolested. Fishing and dairy cattle provide a decent, simple living for the islanders, although some of them commute to work in Trapani. They are an extraordinarily friendly folk, and seem to spend a good deal of their free time collectively spoiling the three or four little children who live on Levanzo.

Port of Levanzo, The Egadi Islands

Grotta del Genovese

A 20-minute walk along the dirt road west of the port takes you to the **Faraglione**, an odd-shaped rock off the rugged coast. This same track leads up the coast and through the hills to the Grotta del Genovese, although the route through the centre of the island is shorter and more scenic. To see the Grotta you must contact its custodian, Giuseppe Castiglione, who lives directly above the hydrofoil dock (Via Calvario 11; tel 921 704). The ideal way to get there is by mule; you may get a ride in a jeep or else you can walk—a pleasant enough proposition if it's not too hot. Ideally you can go out in the morning with Signore Castiglione.

The main road branches off to the left after about an hour's walk, descending towards Punta del Genovese (named after the 16th-century Genoese who used Levanzo as a port for their sailing ships). About 30 m above the sea opens the dark entrance of the Grotta del Genovese discovered in 1949 by an artist, Francesca Minellono, who was on holiday on Levanzo. The incisions on the walls were made by Palaeolithic Man while Levanzo was still part of Sicily, 6000 years ago, and are as fragile as they are magnificent. The beautiful deer beside the entrance is under a protective glass because the slightest touch causes the stone to crumble. The stylized paintings of men and women, tuna fish and unfinished animals by Neolithic artists, 5000 years later, are not as skilful; their magic was apparently of a different variety. In all there are 29 animals and 4 human figures by the earliest artists, and several confused rows of painted figures by the later ones, all in the second, closed-off chamber of the cave to which Signore Castiglione has the key.

The public telephone is at Vita Azzaro's. For bottle service contact Nitto Mineo, Via Calvario 39. Besides the port, there are isolated rocky 'beaches' at **Cala Fredda, Cala Minnola, Cala Tramontana** and **Cala Calcara** (easier to reach by boat).

WHERE TO STAY AND EAT   (tel prefix 0923)

Levanzo's only hotel, as such is the ***Paradiso** on Via Calvario, with eight rooms and a restaurant (tel 921 580; L35 000, or L65 000 with full board); the accommodation is rustic and simple; other than that rooms are available in private houses. Of the simple

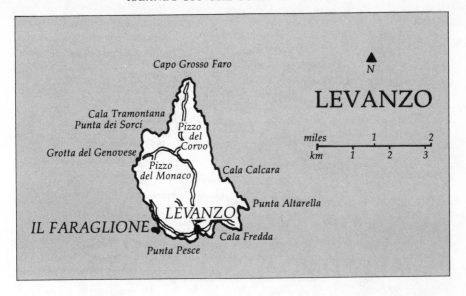

trattorias **Zio Mario** has a tiny veranda which seats ten. Zio (uncle) Mario himself is proud of his pasta sauce and fish dishes and says so (L20 000).

MARETTIMO

Marèttimo, the first island to break away from Sicily, is also the furthest—and not only in distance. The men of Marèttimo, invariably fishermen, have little to do with Favignana or Sicily; proud, soft-spoken and independent, they stick to their magnificent rocky island, their simple houses, their families and their brightly painted boats. The glamour and money of the tourist industry hold no attraction for them, and even though the big names of tourism have plans for the construction of x number of hotels with x number of beds, the islanders haven't made any moves towards that goal. Visitors are kindly received into their own homes, and several Italians from the mainland have built summer villas on Marèttimo. That is the extent of tourism on Marèttimo.

The sheer dramatic beauty of its coastline and numerous grottoes puts Marèttimo into the same class as Capri, yet you can only know it by sea. The mountainous hinterland of the island is almost inaccessible. One bumpy track follows the southern coast to the lighthouse, another winds up to the **Semaforo** on Punta Lisandro. The highest point, **Monte Falcone** (681 m), is by far the highest peak in the Egadi Islands. These mountains, apart from the *macchia*, are barren rocks, although pine trees have been planted with some success. The ancient names of the island, *Iera* (sacred) in Greek, and *Malitimah* in Arabic (whence comes Marèttimo), are of uncertain derivation.

Punta due Frati
Grotto dell'Tuone
Punta Mugnone
Scalo Maestro
Castello di Punta Troia
Capo Bianco
Cala Manione
Cala Bianca
BARRANCO
Grotta Perciata
Grotta Cammello
Mt Falcone
GIRODIFALCO
Punta Pegna
Roman houses
Scala Vecchio
Grotta Presepio
MARETTIMO
Grotta della Bombarda
SPALMATORE
Scalo Nuovo
Punta Libeccio
lighthouse semaphore
N
Punta Lisandro
Punta Cretazzo
Cala Marino
Punta Galera
Punta Martino

MARETTIMO

miles   1   2
km   1   2   3

The **village of Marèttimo** on the eastern side, is the only inhabited place on the island, its growth limited by the dominating mountain directly behind it. There are two piers protruding on either side of town: the **Scala Nuovo**, recently constructed for the delicate hydrofoils, and the **Scala Vecchia**, the fishermen's port, with the fine red, white and blue fishing boats—some purchased with money raised in Anchorage, Alaska, expressly for the purpose of buying boats for Marèttimo. The main street has the few shops needed to supply the 80 residents, as well as Marèttimo's one church which is built over an old warehouse, and takes care of their religious needs. The silent side streets, many quite narrow, have several pretty corners, although decoration is certainly minimal. There are beaches on either side of the town's promontory, the only ones on Marèttimo.

All excursions from the town on foot are a bit on the arduous side, and shouldn't be attempted in the noonday sun of August. The path leading up to the abandoned Semaforo also leads to a spring, and to the **Case Romane**, about a 45-minute climb from the port. The Case is a late Roman defensive work and quite well preserved. Next to it lies a tiny **anonymous church** built in the 12th century and showing very obvious Arabic influences, with barrel vaulting and central rounded drum, a design unique in Italy. Thought to have been built by the Byzantine monks allowed to pursue their religion in Sicily by the two Rogers, this lovely little piece of ecclesiastical architecture has become dilapidated over the past few decades and needs some major restoration work.

The one road south of the village leads to the lighthouse on the western coast. Pine trees have been planted along the sides of the road, making the walk shady and pleasant, although the way is often tortuous. The scenery is splendid, especially on the western coast, where the sight of the steep vertical cliffs plunging into the sea is awesome. Just beyond the lighthouse, a path leads down to **Cala Nera**, where you can swim off the rocks.

A path north of the town (or take a boat) leads to the **Castello di Punta Troia** built on a precipice over the sea, and connected to Marèttimo by an isthmus. There is a spring of fresh water by the isthmus to refresh the weary traveller before making the winding climb up the 116 m to the castle. The original tower on this site was built by the Saracens in the 9th century; Roger II enlarged it, and the Spanish completed the existing building in the 17th century. They also constructed cisterns here, and a small church (the only one on Marèttimo until 1844), and a prison so inhuman and cruel that when Ferdinand II, the Bourbon King of the Two Sicilies, visited it in 1844 he ordered it closed—he who founded so many other prisons all over the Italian islands. Marvellous views of Marèttimo and the sea can be had from the castle terrace.

WHERE TO STAY AND EAT
You can find limited accommodation in private houses, but that's all. There are simple, but good fish restaurants on Marèttimo, but they're open only in the summer. Lobster, in a variety of ways, is the prize dish at the trattorias **Aragosta Rossa** (tel (0923) 923 023) and **Brigantino** (tel (0923) 923 027); L25 000 for the big crustacean; much less for less exalted fare.

The Stagnone Islands

Just off the coast north of Marsala in western Sicily are the three Stagnone Islands: Isola Lunga, Isola San Pantaleo and Isola Santa Maria. Isola Lunga (or Grande) runs along the coast, protecting the two smaller islands from the high seas. This neat arrangement wasn't always the case. In the 4th century BC Isola Lunga was connected to Sicily at Capo San Teodoro; by the 3rd century BC the Carthaginians had dug two canals (*fretum*) through Isola Lunga, dividing it in two and separating it from the mainland, although not at Punta di Tramontana but across the present saltpans. Today Punta di Tramontana and San Teodoro are separated by a strait less than 400 m wide. Even more remarkable is the road 1 m under the sea, built by the Phoenicians, connecting San Pantaleo (ancient *Motya*) to the mainland necropolis at Birgi, near where the airport is today. Of all the islands in this book, San Pantaleo is the only one you can walk to if you don't mind getting your trousers wet. All three islands belong to the commune of Marsala and are uninhabited except for the caretaker and his family on San Pantaleo.

ISOLA LUNGA

Isola Lunga, strangely beautiful with its saltflats (exploited since the 15th century), lagoons and numerous windmills, has been declared a Regional Park. The few men who still work the saltpans live on the mainland. What the park authorities are really interested in, however, is fish farming on or near the island. Archaeologists, for their part, have a treasure trove off the coast of Isola Lunga; here Honor Frost and her team discovered the Punic ship dating from the wars with Rome that is now in Marsala Museum. To visit Isola Lunga, see the tourist office in Trapani or Marsala for information on obtaining permission from the park authorities. **Isola Santa Maria** is off limits, being owned by a private family who spend their summers in a villa here.

SAN PANTALEO AND MOTYA

To visit San Pantaleo and the extremely interesting ruins of the Phoenician city of Motya, 8 km north of Marsala call the caretaker on (0923) 959 598 to make an appointment (visiting hours are 8.30–1 except Mon) and he'll pick you up in his boat from the quay near San Leonardo. There's a sign on the quay in front of the island.

History

The Phoenicians founded Motya in the 8th century BC, and it soon became one of their most important trading posts in Sicily, mainly doing business with the mother city Carthage. Some of the ceramics excavated from this earliest period have distinct Cypriot and Palestinian influences, examples of the extensive cultures the Phoenicians came in contact with through trade.

Motya soon became a force to be reckoned with in western Sicily, and the rapid colonization of the eastern part of the large island by the Greeks gave them much concern. For the Phoenicians, control of the trade route was of vital importance, and the Greeks were muscling in on their business. To protect themselves, other colonies were founded on Sardinia at Nora, Sulcis and Tharros. When a company of Greeks attempted to colonize Lilybaeum (Marsala), Motya and Segesta, the Punic ally in the northwest of Sicily joined forces to kick them out. The few Greeks who survived the battle ended up on Lipari in the Aeolian Islands.

To keep the Greeks on their own side of Sicily, Carthage and Motya mounted a successful campaign between 560 and 550 BC. Motya was heavily fortified, and the city became so large that the necropolis had to be transferred to the mainland at Birgi—hence the famous submerged road, which oxcarts carrying goods could use as well as funeral processions.

In 510 BC, Motya and Segesta again united to drive out a hopeful Greek colony on the west coast. This was the beginning of the long-drawn-out war between Greeks and Carthaginians for the rule of Sicily, a war that never really ended until the Romans defeated Hannibal in the Second Punic War. The Greeks and Romans regarded the Phoenicians not only as a powerful enemy but also as heathens who believed in the ritual sacrifice of infants—not people they wanted living next door to them. When the united Greek forces defeated the great Carthaginian army in the Battle of Himera (480 BC), the Greeks took the usual prisoners and demanded ransoms and fines, and also ordered the Carthaginians–Phoenicians to stop sacrificing babies. Motya survived the war and continued trading with the Greek cities—one of the reasons, perhaps, why the Greeks didn't rout the Phoenicians once and for all from Sicily when they had the chance. They probably wished they had when in 409 Motya assisted Segesta and Carthage in destroying Selinunte and, three years later, Akragas, one of the most splendid Greek cities that ever existed. Only the outbreak of plague in the Punic army prevented the destruction of mighty Syracuse and the rest of Hellenized Sicily.

Catapults, and Other Marvels

At that time the tyrant Dionysius was holding the reins in Syracuse. Dionysius was one of history's great politicians; he faked a peace treaty with Carthage, then began to amass his forces. He summoned engineers from all corners to invent new weapons, and sent out propaganda to unite the independent Greek cities against the Barbarian threat. After nine years all was ready and in 397 BC the Greeks set sail with a powerful fleet to destroy Motya, the heart of Phoenician power in Sicily.

The ensuing battle was one of the most curious in ancient history. The Motyans boxed themselves in on their tiny island, walled up their gates and cut their marvellous road to Birgi, then sent to Carthage for help. At this time Isola Lunga was a huge peninsula surrounding Motya, and the only outlet to the sea was to the south, near Marsala. It was so narrow that only one ship could pass through at a time.

Dionysius landed 80,000 soldiers, who camped at Birgi. They destroyed the Carthaginian–Elymnian strongholds of Segesta, Eryx and Soluntum and repaired the underwater road to Motya to transport their secret weapons. Carthage meanwhile sent a fleet to attack Syracuse, to lure Dionysius from Motya. But Syracuse was well defended, and Dionysius couldn't be distracted from his prey. Himilco, the Carthaginian general, then decided to make a sneak attack on the Greek ships, beached at Punta Palermo.

At dawn the Carthaginians struck. Dionysius quickly brought his army from Birgi to Punta Palermo, along with his secret weapons—the catapult, huge spiked flaming projectiles and other war machines never seen or used before. These caused such destruction and panic among the Punic fleet that Himilco could do nothing but withdraw, but he withdrew in such a way that the Greek fleet was left trapped in Motya's unusual harbour: only one ship could leave at a time, and it would be a sitting duck for the Carthaginians.

Quickly assessing the situation, Dionysius had a brilliant idea. While leaving part of his army to hold off the Punic fleet with their horrible weapons, he ordered the others to chop down hundreds of trees and lay the trunks along the 2400-km peninsula of Isola Lunga to the open sea. As Himilco and the Carthaginians watched in disbelief, the Greeks then pushed their entire fleet across land and in turn began to surround them. At that Himilco had had enough. He ordered a quick retreat and sailed for Africa to escape the Greeks' monstrous weapons and ships that 'sailed' across the land. Without even giving battle, he left Motya to its fate.

Dionysius destroyed the city and its inhabitants with a vengeance. The Greek residents of the city who took refuge in Motya's Greek temple were either spared to become slaves, or, according to another account, crucified. The island city was never rebuilt; when Himilco returned to the scene of battle he chose Lilybaeum (Marsala) for his new base.

The Excavations

At the beginning of the 20th century, one of the great English wine merchants of

Marsala, Joseph (Pip) Whitaker, took an interest in the island of Motya, by now known as San Pantaleo. Strange rocks had been found under the roots of the vineyards planted there, and Whitaker, fascinated by the excavations of Troy and Crete, bought the island in order to do some archaeological research of his own. He spent so much time digging on the island that he built a villa, and planted the trees that beautify the island today.

The fascinating ruins of ancient Motya occupy most of the island, many of them still unexplored. Near the port are the **city walls** that proved so useless without the power of the Punic fleet to support them, and a **cemetery** dating from the 8th–6th centuries BC, before the necropolis was established at Birgi. There is also a temple dedicated to the goddess Tanit who protected the Phoenicians in return for the lives of their first-born, and you can still see the **Cothon**, the artificial harbour surrounded by walls. Near here begins the submerged highway to Birgi. In the residential area of Motya are the ruins of numerous **houses**, some with mosaics, especially the **Casa dei mosaici** with a particularly fine black and white pebble carpet of lions fighting with a bull.

The foundations of a 6th-century **Greek-style temple** illustrate the Phoenicians' knack for imitating techniques from the countries they traded with; while the **Tophet**, where the babies were sacrificed, betrays their true barbaric sentiments. More than 1000 small burial urns (some still containing the tiny bones of the victims) and grave-marking steles carved with the various fashionable symbols of cruel Tanit have been uncovered and may be seen in the **Whitaker Museum** on the site. Other interesting items in the museum include a beautiful enamelled vase in the Egyptian style of the time, and a carved group of lions attacking a bull, found at Motya's north port and believed to be of Mycenean origin.

PANTELLERIA

The island of Pantelleria lies 112 km southwest of Sicily and 80 km west of Cape Bon, Tunisia. Its 83 square km merit a dot on most maps, but its distant location attracts few foreigners apart from archaeologists who study its peculiar *sesi* and anthropologists who come to look at one of the last truly agricultural communities in Europe. Students of architecture come to examine the *dammuso* style of homes built by the natives, and ecology students come to observe their admirable management of natural resources.

In short, Pantelleria is one of the most unusual islands in the Mediterranean. Despite determined efforts to develop it as a holiday paradise, with the same bright white hotels you see everywhere else along the coasts of the Mare Nostrum, there is an equally determined group of people who want Pantelleria to retain its ethnological identity, encouraging visitors to stay in the traditional *dammuso* houses, to understand the way of life that once existed throughout Europe. It isn't easy, however, to compete with the easy money that tourists will pay to lie in the sun. At the moment, 60 per cent of Pantelleria's income still comes from agriculture (zibibbo grapes and capers), while 40 per cent derives from tourism. Perhaps both sides can claim victory from these figures.

History

The elusiveness that characterizes Pantelleria begins with its history. The product of innumerable volcanic eruptions, the island may once have been landlocked between

Sicily and North Africa before the continents drifted apart. Volcanic eruptions occurred well into the period of human habitation. One clue, a fragment of handworked stone found under the basalt of a late eruption in the Quaternary period, suggests some kind of aboriginal people.

A little more is known of the people who settled Pantelleria in the 18th century BC. These Neolithic immigrants were probably a tribe of Pelagians, a name which confusingly includes many different people in different places, in this instance from Tunisia. At Mursia, on the Cimillia shore of Pantelleria, they built a village and the strange stone *sesi* unique to the island. Although they bear a resemblance to the Sardinian *nuraghes* and the Neolithic monuments on the Iberian peninsula, Paolo Orsi, the great Sicilian archaeologist, believes they were built by a different people; the *sesi*, more primitive in construction and technique, may have been the ancestor of more refined structures found elsewhere.

Sesi are circular domed structures made of natural volcanic rock, somewhat resembling the modern *dammuso* house of the island. Within the thick walls are various entrances into tomb-like cells, still in the wall itself, while the actual interior of the *sesi* with a floor of beaten earth and pebbles, has no entrance at all. Their purpose is a mystery, but defence has been almost ruled out, for the Neolithic village itself is protected by such strong walls that it has been dubbed **Alta Mura** ('high wall'). An upsurge in volcanic activity is thought to have caused the village's abandonment. A poor place, it must have only been a base for those sailing on to bigger and better things.

In the 7th century BC, the Phoenicians founded a colony on Pantelleria and named it

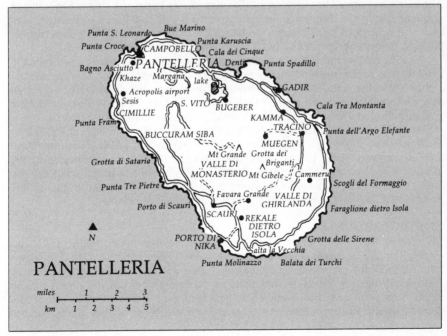

Hiranin ('isle of birds') or *Cossyra* ('the smaller'), referring to the larger size of Malta not far away. The wealth of *Cossyra* was earned by trade, and the island's settlements were invariably clustered around small harbours providing refuge in bad weather. The main town stood at the site of the modern 'capital', with an acropolis on the northeast side of San Marco hill.

Because of its location, Pantelleria became a bone of contention in the Punic Wars. Rome took it during the First Punic War in 255 BC, but lost it a year later. In the Second Punic War Rome regained and kept it, an event celebrated by the minting of coins and a holiday in Rome. The Romans administered the island from Lilybaeum (Marsala) and used it as a place of exile for over-demanding soldiers during times of peace.

The Romans were succeeded by the Vandals, the Byzantines and most importantly the Arabs, who perhaps more than anyone shaped modern Pantelleria. They called it *Ghusiras* at first, and then *Bent el rion* ('daughter of the wind'). Many place-names on the island—such as Zighidi, Khagiar and Bugeber—recall the Arabs' domination, like the names of towns in modern Malta. Unlike all the previous inhabitants of Pantelleria, the Arabs were farmers, and they were the first to cultivate the rich red soil of the island. They introduced vineyards, cotton, vegetables, citrus and palm trees, as well as barley, with which they made a long-lasting hard bread, common until recently. They also built irrigation systems and *dammuso* houses all over the island to be near their fields.

When the Normans conquered Sicily they took Pantelleria as well, and it has been ruled from Sicily ever since. Politically its history is the same, but the constant flow of events made little difference to the good islanders, who lived mainly around the port. The island was owned by various noble families who had done the king of Sicily a good turn; one family, the Requesens, proudly attached the title of 'Prince of Pantelleria' to their leading male. Their presence was noticeable only at tax time. Their ownership of the land, however, prevented all but 12 per cent of it from being cultivated.

The 19th century brought winds of change. In 1845, feudal rights were abolished in Sicily and the land was redistributed among the people, so that by the turn of the century 50 per cent of the island was under cultivation. Because both male and female children were now equally entitled to inherit their parents' land, the farms of Pantelleria were gradually divided into smallholdings—and the people now have fewer children.

During World War II the Fascists made Pantelleria their main base in the central Mediterranean, fortifying it and building an airport. When North Africa fell to the Allies, the base became crucial to both sides; the Allies had to take it before beginning the invasion of Sicily, to protect their rear. On 8 May 1943, the bombs began to fall, day and night. Pantelleria held out until 11 June; then, flattened and blockaded, the 11,000 soldiers stationed on the island surrendered and were taken prisoner.

GETTING AROUND

The Siremar ferry from Trapani makes the $4^{1}/_{2}$-hour trip daily in the summer, and 6 days a week (Sunday excepted) from September to June. In addition, there are daily flights from Palermo and Trapani all year round, with some additional services in the summer. The Alitalia office by the AGIP station in Pantelleria has a bus which connects with all flights to and from the island—get there an hour before your plane leaves. In summer the agency Santoro (Via Borgo Italia) runs chartered day excursions by air to Tunis. Santoro and Nautica Cossyra (Via Punta Croce) have boats to hire for excursions around the island, as well as for skindivers.

TOURIST INFORMATION
Palazzo Ufficio on Via San Nicola (tel (0923) 941 838). If you're interested in the cultural aspects of Pantelleria, contact the **Gruppo Etnologico Pantesco**, Corso Umberto 66 (tel (0923) 911029), which among other things can arrange for you to spend a night in a *dammuso*. In July you can talk to the professors at the Centre for Advanced Studies in Environmental Design at Cala Tramontana.

Pantelleria Town

Pantelleria has one souvenir of the war that won't go away: the brutal concrete reconstruction of its main town, after the pleasant original was bombed beyond repair (see photos in lobby of Hotel Agadir). At best it's ugly and functional, at worst it's as spooky as any post-war town in Italy. If you come to Pantelleria by ship, it's a wretched introduction to an otherwise exceptionally charming island. The one old building still standing, the black reconstructed Spanish castle, isn't even very interesting. Next to it stands a hideous church; from here buses depart for Scauri and Tracino 5 times a day.

Around Pantelleria

The ideal way of seeing the rest of Pantelleria is to take one of the two buses to some point in the countryside, and then walk. You have to take your time in order to absorb what is special about the island, the subtle beauty of the domed *dammuso* houses surrounded by drystone walls and the neat vineyards that form beautiful designs all over the landscape. On one side stands the Monte Grande, a spent volcano (836 m) and a major landmark in this part of the Mediterranean; on the other is the crystal blue of the clean sea, with a wealth of lobsters, sponges and coral, which is exported to the coral-working industries of Torre del Greco in the Bay of Naples. In places you can see the old Arab irrigation system and the cisterns, some of which were originally catacombs—on Pantelleria nothing is wasted.

Along the road behind the town towards the airport, a branch to the right leads to *Cossyra*'s **acropolis** directly above the ancient town. Although only a few walls and foundations remain, there are some nice views. Another old road before the airport leads to the church of the **Madonna della Margana** dedicated to the patroness of the island, which contains a picture of the Virgin and Child (15th or 16th century) salvaged from a shipwreck. When the oxen pulling the cart with the image refused to budge when they arrived at Margana, it was interpreted as God's will, and a church was built on the spot. In the winter months the image is kept in the Chiesa Matrice in town.

Siba and the Grotta dei Briganti
Past the airport, the road across the centre of Pantelleria passes the pretty and ancient town of **Siba**, site of the oldest *dammusos* on the island, with barrel roofs; the weight of the dome rests on the two longer walls of the houses. A rough track from here, suitable only for jeeps or mules, leads to the summit of Monte Grande with a panorama of the

entire island. The nearby **Grotta dei Briganti** is associated with legends of brigands and other undesirables who made it their secret headquarters. Below Monte Grande lie two of the finest valleys on Pantelleria: the **Valle di Monasterio** named after a derelict Benedictine abbey, and the **Valle di Ghirlanda** to the east, with the most fertile soil on the island, where the grapes are reputed to grow as large as plums.

The North Coast
(bus terminus at Tracino)

At **Campobello** just east of Pantelleria town, the shore is level enough to permit bathing—but don't expect any wide stretches of sand; the coast, for the most part, is a picturesque tumble of volcanic rock. The round lake near Campobello known as the **Specchio di Venere** ('Venus' mirror') is actually an old crater, 535 m in diameter. Supplied by the sea, a volcanic phenomenon called the *Mofette* makes the shores of the lake white, warm and highly alkaline. In summer, the fastest horses on Pantelleria take part in the festive races around the lake. A paved road along the shore leads up to the ancient town of **Bugeber** with the best view over the constantly changing colours of the lake.

The main road (and the bus) continues further east to the wild, lovely **Cala dei Cinque Denti** ('inlet of five teeth'), where the craggy blocks of lava under the cliffs do indeed look like a set of monster teeth. Just past the lighthouse to the east is **Gadir** with its little bay, the prettiest fishing village on Pantelleria. The mildly radioactive black sand and hot spring on the shore make for a remarkable rustic spa; when you swim off Gadir you can feel the heat in the sea. Still further east is **Kamma**, a large sprawling village just above the **Punta dell' Arco Elefante** ('the elephant's head rock') beside the sea. The innovative *dammusos* built by the people of Kamma have been studied by the students of the Environmental Design Centre near **Tracino** (the bus terminus), but even people who know nothing about 'environmental design' can appreciate the skill and imagination of the native builders. Above Kamma a path leads up to **Muegen** an abandoned village of very old *dammusos* on the slope of Monte Grande. Enthusiastic hikers can follow the trail down to the **Ghirlanda valley** (road also from Kamma) where among the richest vineyards are Neolithic tombs and grottoes. Off the coast are some rocks with an unusual name: Cheese Reef (**Scogli del Formaggio**).

The extreme southeast coast of Pantelleria is known as **Dietro Isola** ('back of the island'), only accessible by private transport, for there are no villages in this harsh dry area. One of the coves, the **Balata dei Turchi**, was supposedly the place where Turkish pirates landed and were thwarted by the islanders. Nearby, to the west, a 180-m precipice towering over the sea has been curiously dubbed the **Salta la Vecchia** ('old lady's leap').

The Southwest Coast

Only a few miles from Pantelleria town there are a number of hotels at **Mursia** near the ruins of the Neolithic village of the Pelagians, and the *sesi* themselves, mysterious and exotic and massive. At **Khazen**, a natural sauna called **Bagno Asciutto** was carved here in ancient times and may still be used; at **Punta Fram** to the south you can see the obsidian mines of the Pelagians.

The **Grotta di Sataria** further down the coast contains a notable hot spring, known for curing rheumatism and skin diseases. The water flows into a Roman basin. Here the lava forms canals of volcanic glass known as 'liparite' after the same material on the island of Lipari. Another cave, the **Grotta dello Storto** may be entered by boat; it is the nesting place for numerous birds.

Scauri, the bus terminus, has been the second port on the island since Phoenician times, although the town itself stands on a shelf some 90 m above the sea. The pretty white church forms the focus of the typically pretty cluster of white *dammusos*. Paths lead down to the **Valle di Monastero** with Phoenician tombs, and to the fumaroles and hot springs at **Favara Grande** on the other side of the Torrente Nika, which runs from Monte Grande only in winter and when Pantelleria gets a bit of rain. By the beached fishing boats at Scauri another hot spring is collected in two basins, where it is possible to bathe.

Yet another hot spring rises in the **Grotta di Nika** near the tiny village of the same name. Best reached by boat, Nika acts as a good base for a tour of the splendid sea grottoes on this part of the coast; also nearby are the awesome cliffs of Dietro Isola. Above Porta di Nika you can walk up to the scarcely-visited village of **Rekale**, another of those places on Pantelleria that does not seem to be a part of the 20th century.

WHERE TO STAY   (tel prefix 0923)
Among several hotels in Pantelleria town, the ****Agadir**, Via Catani (tel 911 100; L55 000), and the ****Miryam**, Corso Umberto 1 (tel 911 374; L55 000), are comfortable. Several holiday hotels have opened, all quite near town, all in the area of Punta Fram–Mursia to the south, except the secluded ****Turistico Residenziale** at Bue Marino north of the town, which has a garden and park (tel 911 054; L53 000). In the Punta Fram area the *****Sporting Club**, on the beach, has lots to offer if you're tired of lying around in the sun (tel 918 075; L75 000) and *****Punta Tre Pietre** in Scauri has rooms for L55 000, with bath (tel 916 026).

To stay in a *dammuso* house, contact one of several firms offering short holiday lets, among them **Dammuso** on the Contrado San Vito (tel 911 827).

EATING OUT
Sun-drenched Pantelleria is famous for its high octane wines: *Moscato*, a sweet, amber, fragrant desert wine, and a raisin wine called *Tanit* made from zibibbo grapes; other quite drinkable table wines come from Scauri, both reds and whites. Other favourites are soft *tumma* cheese, made from cow's milk; fish and vegetable couscous; *pesto pantesco*, a sauce made from tomatoes, garlic, pepper and basil; and *ravioli amari* made with ricotta and mint and wild rabbit. Look, too, for the island's variation of south Sicilian couscous—*cuscus ai pesce* which you may try at the ristorante **Miramare** in the town on the Via Catania 4, along with another house speciality, spaghetti with shrimps in white wine (L20–25 000) or at the trattoria **Castiglione** on Via Napoli, with a good selection of Pantelleria's famous wines (both about L22 000). In Mursia, the restaurant of the Mursia hotel has rare treats like pasta with *pesto pantesco* or with a lobster sauce, followed by fish, and an icecream dessert seeped in Tanit (L30–40 000).

The Pelagie Islands

The remote, arid and sparsely populated Pelagie archipelago (from the Greek *Pelagia* or

A fishing harbour, Pelagie Islands

'sea islands') consists of three islands: Lampedusa, Linosa and the uninhabited Lampione. Flat, pistol-shaped and wind-whipped, Lampedusa is the largest of the group and the southernmost point of the Italian Republic, just a mile closer to Monastir in Tunisia than to Porto Empedocle in Argrigento Province. Even Malta is further north. Geologically Lampedusa belongs to North Africa, while Linosa, a volcanic island, is the last tiny cone to the south of the great volcanic chain stretching from Etna to Vesuvius and the Pontine Islands. Only recently have the Pelagie Islands attracted many visitors, who come almost exclusively for 'the cleanest sea in Italy' and for the miles and miles which lie between these islands and the industrial regions of the rest of Europe.

History

Although finds prove that Lampedusa and Linosa were inhabited in ancient times, and the former perhaps used as a Roman base in the Punic Wars, the islands have merited scarce mention in the annals of history, and for the most part were uninhabited and undefended. In 813 they were captured by Saracens who established small colonies on them. A few centuries later, in 1430, King Alfonso V of Aragon ceded the islands to the barons of Caro di Montechiaro. In 1553 the pirate governor of Tunis, Dragut, paid a visit to Lampedusa and carried off 1000 people—the whole population—as slaves, and a few years later the Montechiari built a fortress to defend Lampedusa from further such outrages.

In 1630, Carlos II of Spain gave the title 'Prince of Lampedusa' to Giulio Tomasi di Lampedusa, ancestor of the famous modern novelist Giuseppe Tomasi who wrote *The Leopard*. In 1800, the princes allowed some Maltese colonists, the Gatt family, to farm Lampedusa. Ten years later the Gatts subdivided the island with an Englishman named Alexander Fernandez, who brought 300 colonists of his own.

The modern visitor will find it hard to believe that in those days Lampedusa had trees, fertile soil, deer and wild boars—so totally has all this been destroyed by unwise deforestation and farming (all the topsoil blew away). But Lampedusa appears to have prospered in these early years.

In 1839 the princes of Lampedusa changed their minds about the island, and told the Gatt family and Fernandez they had revoked their rights. The Bourbons were helping neither to maintain nor to defend Lampedusa, so the Tomasi family tried to sell the island to England, who already had nearby Malta. This the Bourbon King Ferdinand II refused to permit, and instead purchased the islands himself for 12,000 ducats.

The first Bourbon colonists arrived on Lampedusa and Linosa in 1848. Thirty years later, the Italian Republic established penal colonies on the islands, much to the colonists' resentment. At the end of the 19th century a vast bank of sponges was discovered off the coasts of Lampedusa and Lampione, but the Italian government failed to establish either a sponge industry or telegraph wires to Lampedusa, so the hundreds of sponge fishermen from all over the Mediterranean made Sfax, Tunisia, their port instead.

During World War II the people of Lampedusa were evacuated and the island was turned into a fortress during the North African campaign. On 12 June 1943, the Allied fleet surrounded and bombarded it non-stop until the troops surrendered the next day. The peace treaty of 1947 stipulated that all fortifications on the island be destroyed; a minor point as it was already shot to hell. As undefended as it is, in 1986 Lampedusa was attacked again by Col. Gaddafi, who in response to the American bombing of Libya sent a torpedo addressed to Lampedusa's small American coastguard station (set up to emit ships' navigation signals in the Mediterranean). The Colonel missed, but shook the Italians up so much that they sent the Americans packing, fearing similar reprisals.

LAMPEDUSA

Lampedusa is an extreme example of neglect and misuse of natural resources, its 20 square km an ecological disaster area. Only a few of the oldest inhabitants can recall the days when the neat drystone walls enclosed rich farmland instead of piles of rock. One of the biggest jokes on the island is the 'national park'—two scrubby trees forever dwarfed by the wind and lack of rainfall. However, the lush greenery and flowers around the Sanctuary of the Madonna di Porto Salvo and a few vineyards recently planted demonstrate that the children of Lampedusa needn't grow up on such a lunar landscape. A lot of hard work could improve the islanders' surroundings, but at present their attitude seems to be 'the Italians cut down all the trees—what can we do? The Italians only think of Lampedusa when they need her'.

Over 4000 people live on Lampedusa; 70 per cent earn a living from the very rich fishing grounds surrounding the island, catching more fish than the small ice-packing plant can freeze. Fish is certainly one of the staple items of the islanders' diet, since the island lacks proper refrigeration for large imports of meat. The tourist industry employs another 15 per cent of the work force—the lack of greenery apparently does not deter visitors in search of perfectly clean beaches and sea, and fresh fish.

GETTING AROUND
There are two ways to do it; on the daily flight from Palermo's Punta Raisi airport to Lampedusa, and by the Siremar ferry from Porto Empedocle, the unattractive port town

251

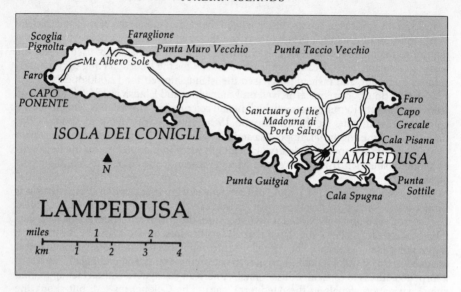

of Agrigento. The ferry service runs daily in the summer (less frequently in the winter), a 9-hour overnight trip that calls at both Linosa and Lampedusa.

Post office: by the main square.

Telephones: Cartoleria Brignone, Via Vittorio Emanuele 15.

For information, guides, bottle refills, etc. see Salvatore Lo Verde at the Centro di Pesca e Assistenza Subacquea on Via Roma, or go to Boutique Lo Verde Sport on Via Mazzini.

Lampedusa Town

The town of Lampedusa is only one minute's walk from the airport and the wharf where the Siremar ferry calls. Whether you arrive by ferry or plane, you are bound to meet Lampedusa's one-man welcoming committee, Oreste, who will, among other things, take your baggage to your hotel in his van for a slight fee. Oreste is a good person to know if you plan to do some skin-diving during your holiday—he is the self-acclaimed 'Oreste la Peste, Il Terrore del Pesce' (Oreste the Plague, the Terror of Fish). He'll even give you a bumper sticker and read you his poetry.

After Oreste, the town seems colourless and dusty. The width of the empty main street would better suit a grand boulevard in Rome; out of season, it wants only tumbleweeds to complete the air of total desolation. The houses on the side streets are plain and unadorned, each with a padlocked little cistern resembling an oven, rarely used; most of the island's nasty-tasting water comes from a desalination plant.

It is a 15-minute walk from here to the fine sandy beach at **Guitgia** on the other side of the fishermen's port. Most of the hotels are here as well. On the way there you'll pass one of the landmarks of the island, the old prison, converted into a car repair shop (the rocks of Lampedusa destroy the average car in less than three years).

Around Lampedusa

The rest of Lampedusa is shared by a few Italians, some wild rabbits, two species of poisonous snake and rocks and boulders that jump out and trip the unwary. North of the town lies an abandoned, brand-new hospital built by the government, and the even more abandoned construction work of a *dammuso*-style tourist village begun by Giuseppe Sindona, the Sicilian who caused the Franklin National Bank of New York to go under when millions of dollars were unaccountably lost. After being on the run for a long time, Sindona was captured in Italy in 1981, slipped a poisoned espresso in prison before he could implicate any accomplices, and the work on Lampedusa's tourist village has been at a standstill ever since.

Towards the centre of the island, the **Sanctuary of the Madonna di Porto Salvo** is the garden spot of Lampedusa, with real flowers and bushes. The legend behind the much venerated statue of the Madonna claims that it was sculpted in Cyprus in the 8th century, and was being transferred from Jerusalem during the Crusades when the ship carrying it foundered off the coast of Lampedusa. The grotto where the statue was taken had long been a place of hiding from the Saracens and slave traders and was then transformed into a small chapel. In 1619, a sailor from Imperia was taken slave by the Barbary pirates and forced to cut wood on Lampedusa. He escaped to the grotto, and there he carved a canoe of sorts in which he managed to flee Lampedusa, using a painted banner of the Madonna, Child and Santa Caterina as a sail. In gratitude for his miraculous escape, he turned the grotto into a sanctuary. A more mundane account claims that when the Bourbon colonists arrived, the statue was found broken on the floor of the church and had to be restored, and that the September festival actually celebrates the anniversary of the day the first colonists arrived.

The road continues to the far western end of Lampedusa, where the old coastguard station and a lighthouse may be found. Halfway there, a track branches off to the left, leading down to a lovely sandy beach facing the **Isola dei Conigli** ('rabbit island'), easiest to reach by sea; at certain times of the year the island is off-limits, to protect the colony of tortoises who come here to deposit their eggs.

Around Lampedusa by Sea

Circumnavigating Lampedusa by boat is rather more picturesque than the trip by land. Among the excursion's highlights are the steep cliffs of **Albero Sole**, at 137 m the highest point on the island, with its *faraglione* just a few feet out in the crystal-clear sea. Just to the west are the stratified cliffs of **Punta Parise**, full of grottoes and boasting a curious rock formation resembling a Madonna with Child. The north coast of Lampedusa has jagged bare precipices dotted with fish-filled grottoes, and an exploratory oil-drilling platform that has yet to turn Lampedusa's waters into a new North Sea.

WHERE TO STAY   (tel prefix 0922)
Lampedusa has a surprising number of modest establishments for its enthusiasts.

***Baia Turchese** (tel 970 455), just outside the town on a beach, has 42 tidy rooms, all with showers and balconies (L80–95 000). The pleasant, family-run **Lido Azzurro** has a good restaurant (tel 970 225; L50 000). For the same price is **Le Pelagie** (tel 970 211). A number of basic pensione dot the shores, like the *Belvedere (tel 970 188; L26 000, with bath) and *Oasi (tel 970630; L25 000 with bath). There are two-room cottages available at Cala Creta, each equipped with a small kitchen, bath, towels, and sheets and able to accommodate from 2–4 people each. To book, contact Moteltour SEMI, Via San Donato Milanese, Milan (tel (02) 512 820).

EATING OUT
Seafood is everywhere: in *Pagghiata di pesci* (a sort of paella with rice and several different kinds of fish), spaghetti with sardines, grilled tuna fish. Try them at **Da Tomassino** or the restaurant **Del Porto** where you'll pay in the region of L25–30 000.

LINOSA

About 50 km north of Lampedusa lies its little sister Linosa (almost 5 square km). The two islands have little in common, though, mainly owing to Linosa's volcanic origins. Linosa consists of three extinct craters: Monte Vulcano, the tallest (186 m), Monte Rosso and Monte Nero, also known as Monte di Ponente. These volcanoes have not only enriched the soil but have also prevented the wind from blowing it away, as happened on Lampedusa. The disadvantages to this becomes obvious in summer, when the lack of

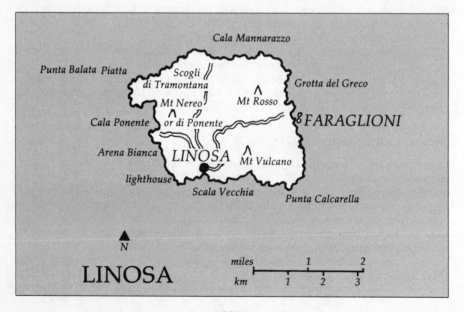

wind and the black soil and rock combine to make roast Linosians—it is one of the hottest places in Italy. Unlike Lampedusa, where the sea bed slopes gradually, the waters surrounding Linosa drop down quickly to great depths, as the island is only the peak of a much greater submerged volcano.

Ancient cisterns and other scanty traces reveal that Linosa was inhabited by a few people in the Roman era, then by the Arabs, and again in the 16th century, when it is believed Linosa was a port of refuge for pirates and slave ships. In 1845 the first real settlers arrived, the Bourbon colonists, mostly hailing from Agrigento. They cultivated the good earth and fished and built their brightly coloured little village (pop. 400) between two craters and the sea. In the 1940s the government built a prison on the island, which has since been closed. Rome still has a bad habit of dumping its *personae non grata* on this charming little island, despite the protests of the islanders.

As Italian islands go, Linosa today is as far out of the way as you can get. Here is civilization in miniature: 2 miles of road, a tiny church, a few cars, 40 telephones, one tobacconist and a few descendants of the rats that were once such a menace on Linosa. There are several 'beaches' of lava, the cliffs of **Scogli di Tramontana** and the three craters to explore, adorned in spring with several species of wild flowers. At **Scala Vecchia**, where the fishing boats are moored, there is an impromptu campsite.

Linosa is the idyllic isle of peace and quiet, and visitors looking for more should probably avoid it. Agriculture still occupies most of the people; their lives are extremely simple and natural. Unless the new barbarism of our society breeds another generation of pirates, life on Linosa will remain the same long after we've begun to sift through the rubble of our car factories and nuclear power plants.

WHERE TO STAY   (tel prefix 0922)
A resort hotel has recently opened up on Linosa, the *****Algusa** (tel 972 052; L80 000) and a locanda, **Saltalamacchia** (tel 972 095; L28 000, open all year round) with ten rooms. Otherwise there's the campsite and rooms to rent in houses in summer.

LAMPIONE

The uninhabited islet of Lampione lies to the west of Lampedusa and Linosa. Like Lampedusa it is geologically part of North Africa, and has almost no vegetation at all. At one time the ruins of a possible hermitage could be seen there, but no longer. The islet (about 1.3 km in area) is very popular with scuba divers, for the fish are exceptionally large in these protective, unfrequented waters, which are alive with all sorts of types of shark. It can be reached in two hours in a small boat from Lampedusa.

Part VI

SARDINIA

Cala Gonone in Nuorno, Sardinia

Where, oh where in Italy can you find clean seas and uncrowded beaches, surrounding Wild West landscapes dotted with hundreds of Bronze Age castles and watchtowers? Where might you encounter wolves, flamingoes or herds of wild horses, mountaineer sheep rustlers and fishermen who live in reed huts? Where else but Sardinia; in its splendid isolation, as the Mediterranean island furthest from the mainland, history and geography have conspired to create a world apart, altogether the least Italian corner of all Italy.

The uncrowded beaches, inevitably, are beginning to attract some notice. Especially among the Italians, Sardinia has become an increasingly popular holiday destination in recent years. The Sards, a people who hold on to their distinctive language and customs as tenaciously as anyone, look on all this with good-humoured disdain—just the latest and least worrisome in a long series of invasions that began with Phoenicians and Romans. They would be glad to argue with you about it (politics is their passion and their greatest talent). After that they'll bend your ear about nuraghes or NATO bases or seafood or Antonio Gramsci. And after that, if you're not careful, they might drag you off to one of their village festivals, where they will subject you to droning Sard choruses and show you a very good time. Somehow, this exotic island full of u's and x's and sheep cheese and dolmens, this least Italian corner, is also the part of the nation with the greatest knack for making the visitor feel at home.

History

The fact that Sardinia is the island in the Mediterranean furthest from the mainland prevented its settlement at an early date. The first inhabitants seem to have arrived about

256

3000 BC, perhaps by way of Corsica. About 2000 BC a second migration of peoples occurred, culturally in transition from what we would call 'Neolithic' to 'Megalithic'. Their origins are mysterious to an extreme; they may have come from Iberia, or from Africa—Africa is more likely.

We have the name 'Shardanas', one of the troublesome sea peoples that combined with Libyan tribes to invade and almost conquer the mighty Egyptian empire in the 15th century BC, and we have the legend of a Libyan Hercules (the use of that name by classical authors reflects religious practices similar to those of the Greeks), whose sons Sardus and Kyrnos settled Sardinia and Corsica respectively. The story is probably the echo of a migration of a people from Libya called Shardana or perhaps Iolai.

About 1500 BC, a division of some sort occurred in their society, and some of them moved north to found the Torréenne culture in Corsica. Whoever the Shardana were, they brought with them a new religion and built dolmens, menhirs and large, often decorated, rock-cut tombs called *domus de janas*. This Sard word is usually translated as 'witch's house', but *janas* in fact, means something closer to 'fairy'. The associations that Neolithic monuments acquire in the popular imagination are often interesting; in Corsica, similar tombs are called 'devil's forges'. Most of these remains are found in the northern part of the island, and archaeologists distinguish two distinct but closely related cultures: the Ozieri or San Michele culture in the northwest, and the Arzachena in the northeast.

The Nuraghes

About the time of their expansion into Corsica, this society began to change, though whether it was subject to some foreign influence or did it on its own is an open question. The most obvious sign of its evolution is the construction of the first *nuraghe*. A *nuraghe*, a word of ancient and unknown origin, is a tower-like structure of mortared large stones which stands one to three storeys in height. They clearly served a defensive purpose and may also have been the homes of chiefs. The Corsican *torres* are derivative of these, and the *talayots* of Minorca and Mallorca are very similar.

By this time, the Sards were developing into a large, powerful and culturally advanced nation, one of the greatest in the Mediterranean world. Expanding from the north, they occupied the entire island and made their presence felt far from home, as we see from their part in the alliance against Egypt. They created expressive works of art, bronze statuettes of kings and warriors and ritual ships. Their nuraghi evolved into true castles, as at Torralba or Barumini, with huge central towers surrounded by a wall containing four or five more. Picture reconstructions of these can be seen in the museum at Sassari—they are certainly imposing, even in the ruined forms that remain today. Archaeologists have counted the incredible number of 30,000 nuraghi Of these, only 7000 remain, the rest picked clean for building stone over the centuries.

The largest nuraghi often have the remains of large villages of round stone huts adjacent to them, reflecting the increasing wealth and complexity of the culture. Metal-working appears to have been their chief trade. The great number of nuraghi and the absence of foreign enemies until the arrival of the Phoenicians suggest an island of tiny, but contentious and competitive city-states, an atmosphere that is always a hothouse for cultural advancement.

Modern Sards cannot look at these works of their ancestors with detachment, as mere cultural relics. They reflect, after all, the greatest period of their people's history and are both a source of pride and a symbol. Their ubiquity ensures the visitor an opportunity to explore at least one of them. The towers have walls sloping inwards, giving them the appearance of the lower half of a cone. There is a low entrance with a lintel over it and perhaps windows in the upper storeys. The classic nuraghi—and the vast majority of them are simple defensive outposts or strongholds—have a single central chamber with storage areas dug out of the corners of the floor. Often, the structure has a double wall with a staircase spiralling around the central chamber to the roof or second floor, where some of the earlier nuraghi have recesses in the wall that perhaps served as beds for the warriors. In the later nuraghic complexes, which must have looked for all the world like medieval European castles, only the conical shape of the towers being different, there were originally corbelled roofs with platforms above them for the defenders to shoot down at their enemies. Almost always, a nuraghe was within sight of several others. In a few places where many still remain standing, we can have some sense of how impressive a picture they must have made, pulling together the entire landscape in a single piece of architecture.

A great incentive to nuraghe-building was provided in the 9th century BC by the arrival of the first Phoenician traders, who set up trading posts in the relatively unpopulated south at Nora, Tharros, Cagliari and elsewhere. The Phoenicians, tolerably peaceful trading partners, were soon succeeded by their more aggressive western cousins, the Carthaginians. In the 6th century BC, Sardinia became involved in Mediterranean power politics, as Carthage sought to add the island to its growing empire. They occupied the western coasts and warred continuously with the Sards, gradually pushing them back into the interior. Olbia was founded as a foothold on the east coast and Karalis (Cagliari) and Nora grew into important towns. To secure the south, Carthage settled large numbers of their Iberian and Balearic allies there. The Sards defended their island with tenacity; some of the large nuraghi that they built at the time, such as the one at Barumini, were important fortresses marking the borders of the Carthaginian conquest.

The Carthaginians brought new methods and ideas to the island. They introduced their militaristic and oppressive state, slaves to grow grain for their army, and their thoroughly unpleasant religion. One of the major features of their archaeological remains is the *tophet*; a particularly interesting example can be seen at Sant' Antioco (ancient Sulcis). At these combination temple-barbecues, the nobles would sacrifice their first-born children to the glory of Tanit and Baal. Being culturally closer to the natives than other people, they were the first to call the island by its true name, Sardinia. The Greeks, who had touched the coasts but never settled there, called it *Ichnoussa*, meaning 'footstep', either because of its shape (according to Pausanias) or because it was used as a stepping-stone for Greek traders on their way to Corsica and Provence.

The Roman Era

During the First Punic War, the Roman general Sulpicius invaded the island and won a victory at Sulcis. It was only after the conclusion of hostilities, however, that Rome was able to gain control, aided by a rebellion of Carthage's mercenaries in 238 BC. The Sards made the Romans feel as unwelcome as they had the Carthaginians, putting up a fierce resistance that wasn't even quelled by the tremendous Roman victory of 177 BC in which contemporary historians claimed that 12,000 Sards were killed. The remnants of the free Sards fled to the eastern mountains, a land the Romans called *Barbaria* from the barbarous valour of the people (the women, they said, were especially fierce and untamable).

The great age of nuraghe-building, and the civilization of their builders, was drawing to its close. The last nuraghi to be built were complex maze-like structures—by then the Sards assumed that the dogged Romans would get in eventually and designed their last fortresses to enable them to split up and ambush their enemies inside. It was a futile gesture, but the difficult terrain of the east was to defend them as well as the nuraghi had. Despite all Rome's efforts, Barbaria was never fully brought under control.

Apart from constructing their usual public works, the Romans treated Sardinia as a simple agricultural reserve and largely neglected it. The island became one of the major sources of the Republic's grain, but received as few favours from Rome as it does today. By a stroke of luck most of the island sided with Caesar in the civil wars, and he and his successors rewarded it. Karalis (Cagliari), by then emerging as the leading city, received the status of a Roman municipality.

Under the emperors Sardinia did well. Karalis, Nora, Olbia, Tharros and the other towns became prosperous and up-to-date cities. Latin became the dominant language; the modern Sard language is closer to Latin than even Italian. The island received more than its share of exiles; Tiberius sent 4000 Jews there and later emperors used it to be rid of Christian soldiers spreading dissension in the legions. As a result of this, the early Church was particularly strong there—and Sardinia today is particularly rich in early Christian churches. The island produced two 5th-century Popes, Hilarius and Symmachus, and was a refuge from persecution for several others. The Christians had a rougher time among the more independent mountaineers. By AD 600, Pope Gregory was complaining that the Barbarians still worshipped 'stones and wood' (in fact, the ancient Sard religion was a cult of springs).

Middle Ages

Records on Sardinia are scarce after AD 500, but the Dark Ages brought the Sards as much trouble as any of the other Mediterranean islands. The Vandals under Thrasamund came in 535 and, after a short stay, were expelled by Justinian's resurgent Byzantines. Ostrogoths and various bands of Saracens came and went. Through it all, the Sards of the interior were relatively safe but most of the coastal cities shrivelled and disappeared. As late as the 11th century, Muslims from Africa were attempting to settle the coasts. By this time, Sardinia had once again achieved, by default, a *de facto* independence.

Under the Byzantines, the administrator of the island was called the *judex* or judge. This position gradually evolved into four *giudicati* democratically elected and responsible to a popular assembly, each serving one of the four *giudicati* into which the island had been informally divided: Torres, Olbia (Gallura), Cagliari and Arborea. The emerging powers of medieval Europe, however, refused to leave them in peace. Early in the 11th century, the Papacy invited Pisa and Genoa to help it grab the island. The Pisans helped expel the last Saracens and insinuated themselves in the south of Sardinia while the Genoese sought a foothold in the north. The two city republics fought over the island for almost 300 years, with the Hohenstaufen emperors keeping their hand in by proclaiming the Giudicato of Arborea as King of Sardinia. During most of this period the Pisans had the greatest influence on the inhabitants—not political but artistic. The Sardinians called architects and artists from Pisa to build and embellish their churches. As in Corsica, these Pisan churches comprise most of the important architecture of the island. Some are severe, almost naive country chapels, some are large and ornate, but all have the seemingly effortless grace that marks all Pisan religious buildings.

The Pisans were soundly defeated by Genoa at Meloria in 1284, effectively putting an end to their dreams of dominating the region. By now, the Genoese had become bitter enemies of the Popes, who turned to the Kings of Aragon to advance their interests. The attempts of King Jaime II to conquer Sardinia were met with strong opposition, particularly in the north. The Aragonese responded with strict repression, going so far as to expel the entire population of Alghero, replacing them with Catalan settlers. In the south, they took a year to prise the Pisans from their last stronghold, Cagliari.

The Giudicati
The greatest problem of all for the Aragonese came from the Arborean Kings of Sardinia. No longer imperial pawns, they gathered Sardinian opposition around them to become the island's leaders against the invaders. By the 1360s they had established themselves squarely across the path of conquest, beating off repeated Aragonese attacks on their capital of Oristano and even managing to capture a few towns themselves. King Mariano IV is one of the Sardinian heroes; upon his death, however, and that of his son seven years later in 1383, prospects for the Sardinian cause looked dim.

Here the hopes of the Sards were placed in the hands of the first and only *Giud-ichessa*—Eleonora of Arborea, daughter of Mariano. This Eleonora became Sardinia's national heroine, its Joan of Arc; from the first she proved herself a political and military leader equal to her father. The Aragonese were kept at bay in spite of treachery from within; even Eleonora's husband deserted to the scheming Spaniards. Perhaps her greatest contribution to Sardinia was her codification of the law, the *Carta de Logu*, which remained in effect for 466 years.

After her death in 1403, however, the Sardinian resistance crumbled. Oristano fell to the Aragonese in 1409, and Sassari, an independent city-state and the last hope for Sard liberty, in 1417. As if the Aragonese weren't bad enough, after the marriage of Ferdinand and Isabella in 1479, Sardinia passed under the rule of a united Spain. To be a Spanish possession in those times was perhaps the worst fate that could befall any people. The Spaniards were greedy and cruel; they introduced feudalism to an island where it had been largely unknown all through the Middle Ages. Free thought was stamped out by the terror of the Inquisition, and city and countryside alike suffered and grew poor from Spanish avarice and mismanagement. A crushing burden of taxes was imposed to pay for Spanish imperialism abroad. Armed opposition on the part of the Sards was not completely quelled until the end of the 15th century, and even after that it continued in the mountains as 'banditry'. Like all previous rulers, the Spaniards were for the most part confined to the coasts; their hold over the mountainous east was always tenuous at best.

The Kingdom of Sardinia
The Spanish were not deposed until the 18th century. During the War of the Spanish Succession the Austrian Hapsburgs temporarily occupied the island, and in the Treaty

of London that followed the war (1718) Sardinia was given to the Dukes of Savoy on condition that they dropped their claim to Sicily. Sardinia's first Savoian kings ruled from the mainland—their Kingdom of Sardinia included much of northwest Italy—but after the Spanish they were a welcome change. One of them, King Carlo Emanuele, was a reformer who sought to rehabilitate the island's economy. His efforts to repopulate Sardinia (the number of inhabitants had dropped steadily under the Spanish) can be seen on the island of San Pietro, where Genoese colonists—actually refugees from their original colony on a Tunisian island—were introduced, naming their town Carloforte after the king.

The tumult of the revolutionary era came to Sardinia in 1793 with a French attack from Corsica, which was unsuccessful. One of the leaders of the revolutionary troops was the young Napoleon Bonaparte. Shortly after this Sardinia had its own revolution against the king and the nobles, led by Giommaria Angioy. The revolutionaries controlled much of the island by 1796 and captured Sassari, but after a defeat near Oristano, Angioy was compelled to flee the island. During the Napoleonic Wars, the Savoian kings for the first and only time held their court in Sardinia, at Cagliari, as the Piedmont was occupied by France. After 1815, two more able kings of Sardinia, though now back in Turin, proved themselves reformers with an interest in the island's welfare. Carlo Felice continued economic development—he built the main road from Cagliari to Sassari that still bears his name—and Carlo Alberto finally abolished feudalism in 1847.

The Kingdom of Sardinia (of which Sardinia, of course, formed only a small and rather unimportant part) was becoming an important force in European affairs; it even played a role in the Crimean War against Russia. It was to play the major role in the unification of Italy. Garibaldi began his campaigns on the peninsula and in Sicily from Sardinia, encouraged by King Vittorio Emanuele and his clever minister, Cavour. Through force and diplomacy, the Kingdom grew until, in 1861, Vittorio Emanuele became the first king of a united Italy.

This did not mean any particular benefits for the island itself. In spite of the efforts of Carlo Felice and Carlo Alberto, Sardinia was a poor and isolated place and continued as such into the 20th century. Many Sards were forced to emigrate, though not as many as those who abandoned Corsica, Sicily or other Mediterranean islands. Just the same, Sardinia proved its attachment to the new Italy by fighting enthusiastically for it in World War I. The famous Sassari Brigade was among the most effective and most decorated in the Italian army.

Mussolini probably did more for Sardinia than any of his royal predecessors. Roads, dams and irrigation systems were built, land was reclaimed from swamps and the cities of Arborea (originally Mussolinia), Fertilia and Carbonia were founded. Many Sards still think kindly of the dictator, not so much for his politics as for what he did for them. In the old town of Cagliari and elsewhere you can still see Mussolini slogans and pronouncements which were painted on the sides of buildings in the 1920s.

Since World War II
Sardinia did not suffer battles and campaigns in the last war, but parts of it were heavily bombed, Cagliari worst of all. After the war the new Italian Republic made a creditable effort to improve the island's economy. Most importantly, the Sards were granted autonomy with their own assembly and executive to decide internal affairs, just as the

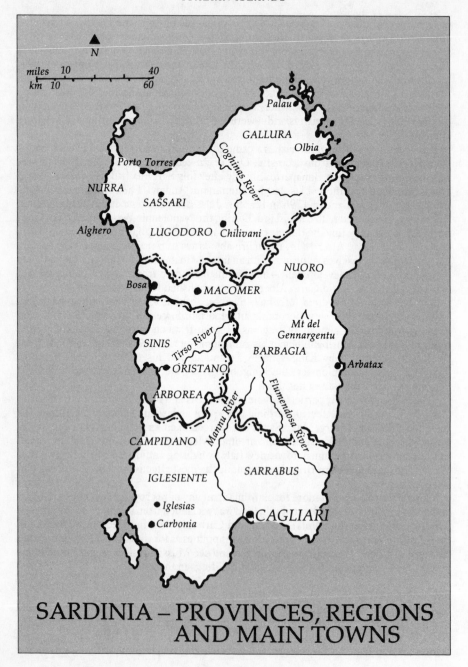

miles 10   40
km 10   60

N

Palau

GALLURA

Olbia

Porto Torres

Coghinas River

NURRA

SASSARI

LUGODORO   Chilivani

Alghero

NUORO

Bosa   MACOMER

∧
Mt del
Gennargentu

SINIS   *Tirso River*

BARBAGIA

ORISTANO   Arbatax

ARBOREA

Flumendosa River

Mannu River

CAMPIDANO

SARRABUS

IGLESIENTE

Iglesias

Carbonia   CAGLIARI

SARDINIA – PROVINCES, REGIONS AND MAIN TOWNS

Sicilians were. The developed activities of the *Cassa per il Mezzogiorno* include Sardinia, and a further impetus came with the *Rinascita* plan of 1962. Unfortunately, most of the public and private efforts have been unhelpful; all too often, 'development' efforts mean big factories in Cagliari or Porto Torres that foul the air but employ few workers. Lack of opportunities still force many younger Sards to emigrate to the mainland or beyond.

As in Corsica, one of the most encouraging events was the elimination of malaria by the US Army, with money from the Rockefeller Foundation, directly after the war, making the settlement of many fertile coastal areas possible and allowing a burgeoning tourist industry to develop on the island's many beaches.

For many Sards, autonomy and industrialization are not enough; they would like an even greater control over their homeland. A recurring complaint is the fact that there are no less than 24 NATO bases in Sardinia, unpleasant to live near and probably ensuring that the island would be quickly reduced to its component molecules in the event of war in Europe. Many Sards also see the process of modernization and industrialization turning their land into a colony of big business and the central government. They take a new look at their old way of life and compare it to what they can expect from the present. It is not surprising, then, to see the graffiti appearing on the walls of cities and villages over the last decade—proclaiming older, truer values, a less mechanized and regimented existence and Sard independence and self-sufficiency. These ideas are very much in the air in Sardinia and the visitor curious enough to ask will find them proposed by people in remote Sardinian villages with more sophistication and down-to-earth pragmatism than the intellectuals of Europe's big cities can ever manage. Politics, as we have said, seems to be one of the Sards' greatest talents. The famous socialist philosopher Antonio Gramsci came from a village near Oristano, and many of Italy's leading politicians today are Sards.

Geography

Sardinia is the second island in the Mediterranean in size, only a little smaller than Sicily. Its topography could best be described, perhaps, as confusing—it has certainly done a good job of bewildering various invaders over the centuries. Mountains, valleys, plains and plateaux are scattered across the map without any pretence of order or reason on the part of the Creator. Mountains come in patches instead of ranges, the greatest of them the Gennargentu, in the east–central part of the island.

This is a landscape where the native has a great advantage; the Gennargentu, particularly, has been equally effective in protecting the Sards from Romans and Spaniards and protecting sheep thieves from the *carabinieri*. Nowhere are the mountains as high as in the central range of neighbouring Corsica, but like Corsica most of the island is volcanic in origin. Not a few of Sardinia's peaks are long-extinct volcanoes; another feature of the volcanic heritage are the *giaras*, large, steep basalt plateaux, several marking the border of Nuoro and Cagliari provinces.

Sardinia's coasts are a different matter altogether. There is a tremendous variety of coastal landscape: high cliffs, mountains diving straight into the sea, numerous marshes and lagoons (*stagnos* in Italian) that made it possible for Sardinia to supply almost all of Italy's salt, and everywhere there are caves. From the great marine grottoes full of tourists to the million little potholes around Nuoro, Sardinia has more caves than anywhere.

In the last hundred years, man has brought great changes to the Sardinian scene. The 19th century saw the virtual deforestation of the island; the big forests of holm oaks, cork oaks and pines you see now are only a small fraction of what was here before. More recently, dams have been built all along the four great rivers, the Tirso, the Flumendosa, the Coghinas and the Mannu, creating over a score of artificial lakes.

A great variety of fauna exists on the island, including some comparatively rare species. There is the usual Mediterranean array of rabbits, weasels and game birds such as the partridge, woodcock and duck, and tuna, shellfish and lobsters off the shores, and eels and trout in the rivers and streams. Wild boar are numerous. Among the more exotic inhabitants of the island are the cranes of Sinis, small deer, eagles, wild sheep called *muflone* in the mountains, the Queen's hawk (which gets its name from Eleonora of Arborea, who reserved to herself the right to hunt them), and the Mediterranean seals of the caves near Dorgali. Not to be left out are the unique miniature wild horses that inhabit the Giara of Gesturi, and the world's only albino donkeys, on the island of Asinara.

People and Customs

There is a cliché about Sardinia that one visits not for the sights but for the atmosphere. This isn't entirely true; Sardinia will prove more than sufficiently entertaining for the visitor interested in nature, in history and archaeology, in art, or in just sitting on a beach. However, what makes the island special and compelling is something more than these; it is the Sardinian way of life in its uncompromised integrity. This is truly 'the unconquered island' as the title of a recent book described it. Not the various hosts of invaders, not even the conformist pressures of modern society have succeeded in changing it much.

The Sards maintain their costumes and festivals not to impress tourists but to remind themselves of who they are. A nation as old as their nuraghi, they have seen Phoenicians, Romans, Spaniards and the others come and go without really altering the stock—this is especially true in the mountains of the east. Today, they think of themselves as Sards first and Italians second. Part of this feeling is expressed in the jealous maintenance of their language, which betrays its non-Romance origins in strange words like *nuraghe* and the use of the *u* and *x* (which is pronounced, incidentally, as *sh*).

Much of the vocabulary and grammar, however, is straight from Latin. The word for 'house', for example, is *domus*, not *casa*. It is enough of a living language to have many dialects; Lugodoro, Nuoro and the Campidano have the most important. Besides this, accidents of history have placed other tongues on the island. San Pietro still speaks a version of 16th-century Genoese dialect, and Catalan is still common in Alghero. Surprisingly, this makes life easy for the visitor with only an imperfect knowledge of Italian. Almost all Sards speak Italian, and they do it with clarity and without colloquialisms.

Many of the ancient customs survive in country districts. The Sards had their own calendar, with the new year starting on 1 September, and special names for each of the months. Old traditions persist in marking life's milestones—birth, marriage and death.

Magic is used to guess the sex of an unborn child, and christenings and weddings are elaborate occasions. There is a courtship ritual called the *precunta* where the successful suitor and a friend visit the bride's father pretending to look for a 'lost lamb'; together they search the house until they find her—and the couple is betrothed on the spot. At the wedding they are showered with grain, salt and sweets, and at the wedding banquet they eat from the same plate, which is then broken at their feet and the pieces are counted to see how many children they will have.

Poetry, music and dance are an important part of the old traditions. The shepherds in particular are masters of extemporaneous versifying (in Sardo, of course) and often compete before a jury of their peers at weddings and festivals. Sard music is ancient and fascinating. The styles of Gallura, Lugodoro and Campidano show some Italian influence, but the music of the mountain people isn't diluted by anything foreign—indeed, it is probably unlike anything you have ever heard. The classic form, in Nuoro Province, is a *coro* (chorus) of four male voices, one singing the verses and the other three responding in a weird droning chorus. There are traditional instruments, such as the *launedda*, a difficult contraption of three pipes, which the nuraghic-era bronzes in the Cagliari museum prove to be a survival of the remotest past. Of course, you are more likely to see such modern additions as the accordion or concertina accompanying the folk dances. For an introduction to Sard music, vendors in Cagliari's Piazza Matteotti sell an infinite variety of tapes of *coro* music and other specialities from all over the island.

One of the most important features of Sardinian folk life is costume. In the villages the older women still favour traditional dress, but the real costumes, the beautiful and expensive outfits handed down from father to son and mother to daughter, are brought out only for the festivals. Every town and village has its own style; the best, predictably, are from the mountain villages of the Barbagia. For both men and women, black and red are the predominant colours. The men's costumes, with their loose white trousers and high boots, look more like eastern European than other Italian styles. At the new museum outside Nuoro you can see examples from all over the island, but you are sure to see them being worn if you are fortunate enough to attend any of the Sardinian festivals.

There's one subject we shouldn't neglect to mention, not because it is important, but because it is the average newspaper-reader's first impression of Sardinia—banditry. Stealing sheep is an old custom in the Barbagia and Nuorese regions, done more often than not out of need. The institutionalized banditry and vendetta that grew out of this way of life, never as common as in Corsica or Sicily, have largely dissipated, though the Gennargentu and Sopramonte still shelter outlaws today. In the seventies, they made the world's headlines by kidnapping wealthy tourists or their children. Those of us not falling within this category have little to fear (much less than, say, in Palermo or New York) and should take it in good humour when the Sards explain that, after all, the bandits at least conduct themselves as gentlemen.

Festivals

Here is where the visitor will really get to know Sardinia. In truth, they're hard to miss; most villages have at least one *festa* each year, and in the spring and summer there can be as many as a dozen at the same time across the island. They range from simple festivals honouring a patron saint to the great events in the big towns that attract people from every province. Among the most interesting are those celebrated in the sanctuary villages in the countryside. These villages, a huddle of small structures encircling a church, often with the back walls joined together to turn a blank face to the outside as if they were walled towns, are empty all year. For the festival, families from the nearby villages move in for a week of singing, dancing and carrying on. The best-known of these festivals are at San Cosimo, near Mamoiada (27 September), San Salvatore, Sinis, and San Francesco, near Lula (4 October). Some of the biggest festivals are listed below.

Sant' Efisio at Cagliari (1 May), with costumes and performers from all over Sardinia. The highlight of the festival is a pilgrimage to the saint's shrine at Nora, with the saint's image on an elaborate float and decorated oxcarts called *traccas*.

Cavalcata Sarda, the 'Sardinian Cavalcade' (Ascension Day) at Sassari. This is only 30 years old, but it has become one of the most popular festivals, a showcase for the costumes, songs and poetry of all Sardinia's villages.

Festa del Redentore (29 August) at Nuoro, with a pilgrimage to Monte Ortobene, processions through the streets of the city, and folklore exhibitions and performances.

Sa Sartiglia (at carnival time) at Oristano. The main event of this folk festival is a kind of medieval joust, introduced by the Spaniards but given a curious Sardinian flavour. Among the displays of equestrian prowess is this very strange piece of dream-imagery: a rider called Su Compoidori, wearing a costume with red ribbons tied on his arms and legs, a feminine mask and a top hat, gallops at full speed towards a silver star suspended from a ribbon, and tries to impale it with a short spear. They've been doing it since the days of the Giudicato of Arborea.

Carnival (in Mamoiada, Ottana, Bosa, Tempio). Carnival in the mountain villages of Mamoiada and Ottana, more than anywhere else, betrays its pre-Christian religious origins. A common practice in many cultures was the driving out of a 'scapegoat' at the beginning of the agricultural year to take the community's bad luck with it, and this is just what happens in Mamoiada. The *Mamuthones*, a group of men dressed in animal skins with wooden masks and thirty pounds of bells, are chased out of town by the *Socadores*, onlookers sometimes getting lassoed in the process. The similar festival at Ottana is called the *Boes*.

The word 'Mamuthones' is of an ancient and unknown origin, as is the festival itself. It may be a clue that, according to Frazer's *Golden Bough*, the ancient Romans had a similar ritual, driving out of the city each March a man dressed in skins called the 'old Mamurino' or old Mars. Mars, before he became a god of war, was an agricultural deity, a 'god of the year'.

Li Candelieri (14 August), at Sassari, is something altogether different: not of religious origin at all, but a ritual of a medieval free city unique on the islands. The main event is the procession of the *gremios*, the medieval guilds, each group carrying a giant 'candle-stick' decorated with emblems of the guild and its patron saint, and includes an act of symbolic submission of the city officials to the leader (*obriere*) of the Farmers' Guild, the *gremio* on whom the life of the city depends, and the 'judgement' of the mayor and council by the people during the *Faradda*, the 'descent' of the candlesticks.

In all of these Sardinian celebrations, visitors are more than welcome. Particularly in the village festivals, you are likely to leave overfed and inebriated. The local tourist office or Pro Loco can probably get someone to introduce you around. The mountains around Nuoro are the best place for festivals—there are more than a hundred of them each year.

Traditional Costume for the Ascension Day Procession, Sassari

The EPT in Nuoro keeps a complete list, and chances are they can direct you to one any time during the spring and summer (also, see Festivals, pp. 15–21).

Food and Wine

The Sardinian table is a rich one, with many dishes derived from the Italian and many entirely Sardinian. Antipasti include many things similar to Corsican charcuterie: the sausages (*salsiccie*) and ham, either from pigs or from wild boar. There are also such delicacies as *bottarga* (roe of the mullet) and minced boiled octopus.

Most restaurant menus on Sardinia will feature some variety of Sardinian pasta, such as the truly peculiar *malloreddus*, little dumplings, or *sa fregula*—something like couscous. There is also *culingionis*, a Sardinian type of ravioli, and many kinds of *minestra* (vegetable soups with or without pasta).

Fish is of course popular and widely available around the coasts; the Sards make several different varieties of fish soup. Mutton and kid are also popular. You're less likely to encounter the more exotic traditional dishes, in which thrushes and blackbirds and the entrails of various animals figure prominently, such as *accarraxiau* or *sa frixioredda*.

Sardinia is famous for its wonderful artichokes, and a few kinds of strong cheese; one, called *casu beccio* is eaten with the cheese mites still in it (an acquired taste, to be sure). Bread is as much an art form as a staple, and some special kinds are baked for special occasions: in the shape of towers, or castles for weddings, or something that looks almost like lace, and also the *carta da musica* (music paper), made for festivals. It is very thin and keeps for a long time; the shepherds carry it on their long trips into the mountains. Sards, particularly those around Cagliari, are very fond of sweets, and an almost infinite variety is produced.

Wine is cheap and very good (much better than in Corsica). The island is best known for dessert wines of a formidable alcoholic content, such as the *Vernaccia* of Oristano and Sulcis. Every province has its wine-making regions, and some of the best wine, such as *Anghelu Ruiu* (red) and *Torbato* (white), comes from Alghero. Other varieties include *Muscatel*, *Aleatico* and the strong *Cannonau*.

Handicrafts

Unlike many places, any souvenirs you buy in Sardinia are almost certain to have been made there. The most popular with the tourists are baskets, decorated with geometric designs that have probably changed little since the nuraghi were built. Sardinian carpets are beautiful, and often exported overseas, where they fetch high prices. Isili, Uras and Mogoro are centres of carpet-weaving. Other crafts include leather goods, carved wooden objects such as the bridal chests of the Barbagia, and moulds for cheese and bread. There is a new 'artisan' movement, a reaction against cheap tourist trinkets (though you'll still find plenty of those) in favour of genuinely traditional quality goods. There are over 50 craft centres around the island.

Agriturismo

One of the most interesting possibilities for getting to know Sardinia and the Sards is this organization, operated by a cooperative of stock breeders in Oristano province. They can arrange for you to stay quite inexpensively in the home of one of their members in a number of villages around Oristano. For details, write to the Cooperative Allevatrici Sarde, Casella Postale 107, Oristano 09170 (tel (0783) 418006).

GETTING TO SARDINIA

By Air

Frequent domestic flights from all major Italian cities (as well as scheduled and charter flights from London in the summer) to Sardinia's three airports: Cagliari–Elmas, Alghero and Sassari–Fertilia, and Olbia. The only internal flights are between Alghero and Cagliari on Air Sardinia (4 daily, a trip of about 30 minutes), and between Cagliari and Olbia on Alisarda Airlines (1 daily, a trip of 35 minutes).

By Sea

There are many daily connections between Sardinia and the mainland, and they increase by half in the summer. Nearly all are overnight services. If you plan to go in July or August advance bookings are essential.

Tirrenia offers the following connections:

Genoa to Porto Torres: daily, depart 8 pm, arrive 7.30 am.
Genoa to Olbia: daily depart 6 pm, arrive 7 am.
Genoa to Cagliari: 3 a week, depart 5 pm, arrive 1.30 pm.
Civitavecchia to Cagliari: 3 a week, depart 7 pm, arrive 8.45 am.
Civitavecchia to Olbia: 2 daily, depart 11 pm & 11 am, arrive 6 am & 6 pm
Genoa to Arbatax: 2 a week, depart 6.30 pm, arrive 12.30 pm.
Tunis–Trapani to Cagliari: 1 a week, depart Tunis 11.30 am, depart Trapani 10 pm, arrive 8 am.
Livorno (Leghorn) to Porto Torres: 3 a week, depart 7 pm, arrive 8.30 am.
Naples to Cagliari: 2 a week, depart 5.30 pm, arrive 9.30 am.
Livorno to Cagliari: 2 a week, depart 5 pm, arrive 10 am.
Palermo to Cagliari: 1 a week, depart 7 pm, arrive 8 am.

Nuova TranTirreno Express:
From Livorno to Olbia daily from mid-July to September, and several times a week at other times between 6 April and 2 November.
Italian Railways has several daily crossings from Civitavecchia to Golfo Aranci.
Grandi Traghetti has a service once or twice a week between Genoa and Porto Torres.
NAVARMA links Sardinia and Corsica (Bonifacio), as do Tirrenia and others.
There are also frequent ferry services by Tirrenia and others to the offshore islets of Carloforte (from Portovesme or Calasetta, reached from Cagliari by frequent FMS buses) and La Maddalena (from Palau).

GETTING AROUND IN SARDINIA
Like Sicily, and unlike its French neighbour Corsica, getting around is relatively easy. Rail and bus systems are cheap, surprisingly efficient and extensive. Unfortunately most of Sardinia's attractions, natural wonders, nuraghes and Pisan churches are out in the country, and if you intend to see more than a few of them you'll need a car.

By Rail
The service of the Ferrovie dello Stato on Sardinia consists of a Cagliari–Oristano–Macomer–Sassari–Porto Torres line, with a branch off at Chilivari for Olbia and Golfo Aranci. There are usually several trains a day at weekdays. The trip running the length of the island takes about 5 hours.

In addition, there are several subsidiary lines: one from Bosa to Nuoro, intersecting the main line at Macomer, and one to Carbonia–Iglesias–Decimomannu–Cagliari. Two old narrow-gauge lines are still in service: a scenic trip through the Barbagia from Cagliari to Mandas–Sevi–Lanusei–Arbatax, and the Alghero–Sassari–Tempio Pausania–Palau route operated by the Strade Ferrate Sarde (SFS).

By Bus
As in Sicily, and for that matter almost everywhere else in Italy, riding the bus is almost a pleasure. The lines are subsidized by the state, so the fares are very cheap, and the coaches themselves new and clean.

From each of the four provincial capitals, regular services run to all the towns and villages in the province. In Cagliari and Oristano, the company is SATAS, in Nuoro and Sassari it is ARST. Both companies' buses are painted blue. Services between the provincial capitals are provided by the PANI line, with buses painted red.

It is possible to reach nearly every village from its provincial capital, but it's tricky. Buses are of course arranged for the convenience of the villagers, and schedules can be a problem; if you're making a day trip out to a village, check in advance if there's a bus coming back when you need it. Tourist information offices in Sardinia are very helpful (they often know more than the bus line employees) and villagers will usually know all the local routes.

Have faith: with a little foresight, you'll find even the most unlikely connections will materialize—including long, scenic trips on the back roads from one province to another.

The best map of Sardinia is that published by the ACI (Italian Automobile Club) and available throughout the island. It's indispensable for exploring Sardinia's out-of-the-way places, and it shows all the major natural attractions, country churches and nuraghi.

The Old City, Cagliari

Cagliari and the South

CAGLIARI

The Sardinian capital is a very busy place. A city over 2500 years old, Cagliari has usually been the centre of Sardinian life and culture. Since the war, it has been expanding in all directions, though parts of the centre have become somewhat neglected—a pity, as the old town is quite an attractive place. Often choked with heavy traffic, the busy city has, however, a charm that is immediately evident, with its smart boutiques, places of entertainment, noisy cafés and popular eating spots. The city can meet all the visitor's holiday needs with its sporting, bathing and recreational facilities, and is an excellent starting point for the lovely coastlines which stretch east and west.

As for the industrial and residential sprawl surrounding the two great swampy lagoons, Stagno di Molentarguis and Stagno di Cagliari, the less said the better, except that they provide feeding ground for the abundant bird life—flocks of cranes in competition with

270

the city's fishermen for the day's catch. The latter lagoon has saltpans that meet much of Italy's need for that product.

History

Cagliari (pronounced KAI-lyar-ee) made its first appearance as *Karalis*, a military and trading post of the Phoenicians. Under them, and later under the Carthaginians and Romans, the city prospered as a trade outlet for the island's grain and timber. Sant'Efisio, one of the numerous Sardinian martyrs in the reign of Diocletian, met his end here.

Cagliari's fine harbour, one of the best in the Mediterranean, kept the city from disappearing entirely during the Dark Ages. The steep hill overlooking the port made an admirable defensive position; when the Pisans seized the town in the 11th century as a base for expanding their influence in Sardinia, they built the walls of the Citadel that exist today. In spite of Pisa's string of military defeats at the hands of the Genoese, it managed to hold Cagliari until the Aragonese conquest in 1397. The Aragonese and later the Spanish and Savoian kings made Cagliari the island capital, ruling through a viceroy. In the 17th century the Spanish founded Cagliari's University.

The city reached its greatest period of prosperity, perhaps, only in this century. During the last war it suffered heavier bombing than any other Italian city; one-third of its buildings were destroyed, and the town was decorated for its bravery under fire. Since 1945, Cagliari's reconstruction has been dramatic. Most of Sardinia's new industries are located here, and one in six Sards call Cagliari home. The city has an impressive collection of tall buildings around its harbour; without the old Citadel to give it away it would look more like an American city than an Italian one.

GETTING AROUND

Cagliari is conveniently centralized for most of your needs. Hotels, restaurants, and cafés can be found mostly around the arcaded Via Roma. Piazza Matteotti is the transportation hub, with both the rail (FS) and bus (ARST) stations. For the FCS rail line to Arbatax, the station is in Piazza Repubblica; some buses to the villages leave from the FMS station on the Viale Colombo. Both of these are in the eastern part of the city.

TOURIST INFORMATION

Regional Tourist Board, Viale Trento 69 (tel (070) 650 971).
Sardinian Tourist Information Office (ESIT), Via Mameli 95 (tel (070) 668 522).
Provincial Tourist Board (EPT), Piazza Deffenu 9 (tel (070) 654 811 and 663 207).
City Tourist Office (AAST) Via Mameli 97 (tel (070) 664 195), and Piazza Matteotti 9 (tel (070) 651 604).

The Port

Cagliari's front door is its port, where the ferries to the Continent can dock almost in the centre of town. Along the port runs the wide Via Roma, the arcaded main thoroughfare with its many cafés. Where Via Roma meets the Largo Carlo Felice is the Piazza Matteotti with the rail and bus stations, the tourist information booth, and the 19th-century neo-Gothic Town Hall. Giacomo Matteotti, by the way, after whom streets and

271

squares are named everywhere in Italy, was a Socialist deputy of the 1920s who led the opposition to Mussolini until his murder by blackshirt thugs. A block north is the shady Piazza del Carmine with the port office and the offices of the provincial government.

Behind the Via Roma is a district of old, narrow streets on a grid plan that has changed little since Roman times. Here, especially in and around Via Sardegna, are many of Cagliari's restaurants and hotels. The northern boundary of the district, the Via Mannu, a lovely street with many old Spanish buildings, connects the Piazza Yenne, where there is a statue of King Carlo Felice, with the Piazza Constituzione. A network of narrow alleyways and stairs lead up to the Citadello, the old Pisan fortress, and one fancy marble stairway ascends from the Piazza Constituzione to the San Remy Bastion; at the top is the Terrazza Umberto I with a view over all Cagliari. Cagliari's unusually decadent teen-agers, a social phenomenon of this fast-changing city, have made it their meeting-place.

In the Citadello
Around the Terrazza is the old University with its fine 18th-century buildings on the Via Universita, where a 19th-century Cagliarese professor of physics, Antonio Pacinotti, invented the dynamo. The buildings are in a sad state of semi-abandonment (and there are few sights as sad as an abandoned library) while the University is gradually being moved to new quarters in the north of town. The move, like most of Cagliari's public improvements, has already been in progress several decades. Next to the University is the Torre dell' Elefante, one of the remains of the Pisan fortifications. It still has its portcullis, and takes its name from the marble elephant over the gate. This tower and its twin, the Torre San Pancrazio on the northern end of the Citadello, have the aspect of being stage props; the tight-fisted Pisans built only three sides, leaving open the side facing inwards.

On the Piazza Palazzo, besides the Archbishop's Palace and the Governor's Palace, is the Cathedral. There is little left of the original 13th-century structure, and only the interior remains from the 17th-century rebuilding. The present awkward façade was added in 1933—a clumsy copy of the Cathedral of Pisa. Inside, however, are two beautiful pulpits carved by the Pisan Maestro Guglielmo in the 12th century (he also did the four big stone lions). Other works of art and religious artefacts can be seen in the Cathedral's treasury, the Museo Capitolare. The crypt is also worth a visit for its ornate vaulted ceiling.

From the Piazza Palazzo, the Via Martiri leads to the Piazza Indipendenza and the Archaeological Museum. This collection was given by Carlo Felice, and has become, along with the museum at Sassari, the major exhibition of Sardinia's distant past. There are Neolithic finds, the 'little Venus of Macomer', and a fertility goddess from Decimo Lutzo that bears no small resemblance to the Maltese 'fat ladies', but the stars of the collection are definitely the nuraghic bronzes. At once elegant and homely, these little bronze figurines have a lot to say about the people who built the nuraghi. There are archers and warriors, scenes of combat, men playing the *launedda* just as Sard shepherds do today, animals, and the goddess with her child. The most artistic, perhaps, are the ritual boats, with bull or deer heads, and sometimes dogs or other symbols of the underworld. The Carthaginians are also represented, with artefacts from Tharros, Nora and Karalis, including some grotesque masks and idols of the god Bes. Bes, always a kind of smiling Buddha, looks out of place in the gruesome Phoenician pantheon. Roman and

Greek art, gems, and grave steles, a collection of coins, and a Pinacoteca containing Sard and Italian paintings complete the list.

Around the City
From the Torre San Pancrazio, the Viale San Vincenzo leads down from the Citadel to the Municipal Art Gallery (open daily 9–1, 4–6 pm) which includes some of the most important works of Sard sculptors and painters of this century. Nearby are the ruins of the Roman amphitheatre, constructed in the 3rd century and one of the most striking reminders of imperial Rome to be found in Sardinia. In its day it seated 20,000. During the Middle Ages much of the masonry work crumbled, but you can still see the underground passages, the corridors for the wild animals and an impressive series of grandstands. The Botanical Gardens, a short distance away, were founded in 1865 and house over 500 species of tropical plants. Friendly and helpful professors are willing to conduct special visits if previously arranged (details at the tourist office, open Mon–Fri, 8–1). On Via Tigellio are the remains of a Roman house believed to be that of the poet Tigellius, and dating from the 2nd to the 4th century. To the west, between the quarters of Stampace and Sant' Avendrace, rises the Tuvumannu hill, with the Punic–Roman necropolis where some of the objects in the museum were found. The necropolis contains the tomb of Attilia Pompilia, also known as the Grotta della Vipera from the snakes decorating it, on Viale Sant' Avendrace.

On the east side of Cagliari, just off the Via Dante, the Basilica di San Saturnino stands in a small piazza. This is the oldest church on the island, dating from the 5th century, named after a Sardinian martyr under Diocletian. Part of the structure was actually added in the 11th century and the whole was severely damaged in the bombing, as were most of Cagliari's churches. The church has been lovingly restored—it looks as if they're still working on it, but what you see are excavations for the ancient cemetery that was discovered during the process of restoration. On the slope of Montixeddu hill is the Santuario di Bonaria, a large 19th-century basilica and adjacent 17th-century church with a statue of the Madonna that attracts many pilgrims.

As you drive into town from the east you'll be impressed by the wide boulevards speeding you into the centre of Cagliari. The enormously long and lively beach flanking the left-hand side adds a touch of Miami to your first impressions. This lido, the **Poetto**, is frequented mostly by Cagliarese, and along its shore of fine soft sand you'll find plenty of spots to relax, swim and eat.

WHERE TO STAY   (tel prefix 070)
Certainly the queen of hotels in Cagliari is the ******Regina Margherita**, Viale Margherita 44 (tel 670 342; L170 000). Otherwise there's nothing particularly special in either the high or low categories. *****Al Solemar**, Via Diaz 146 (tel 306 211), has rooms with bath for L85 000. The *****Italia**, Via Sardegna 31 (tel 656 832; L75 000), and the ****Quattro Mori**, Via Angioz 27, just off the Largo Carlo Felice (tel 668 535; L45 000, with shower, L30 000 without), are both good bargains and centrally located. Cagliari has an infinity of very inexpensive hotels. Most are small and often full, and you may need to look around a bit—on side streets off the Via Roma or the Corso Vittorio Emanuele. The ***Firenze**, Corso Vittorio Emanuele 50 (tel 653 678; L20 000), may be the nicest, but the ***Caocci**, Via Garibaldi 42 (tel 651 907), is the cheapest at L12 000; it's clean, but don't expect luxury.

EATING OUT

In and around the Via Sardegna, just behind the Via Roma, are any number of very good restaurants, mostly inexpensive; Cagliari is altogether a wonderful town for dining. On the inexpensive side, try the **Due Archi**, Via Napoli 38, for grilled trout (L15 000 for dinner), or the **Su Furriadorgiu**, Via Angioy, for ethnic surroundings and cuisine. In the old quarter of the marina, **L'Antica Hostaria**, Via Cavour 60 (tel 665 870) is deservedly well patronized because of its faithfulness to fine old Cagliaritana recipes. The owner spent years in Brazil, where he claims to have discovered the most wonderful things in life. His enthusiasm and warmth spills over into his restaurant. Try the fish soup, *antipasta di mare*, and the *risotto di mare*; it's reasonably priced at L35 000 (closed Sun and Aug). In the centre of Cagliari **Il Gatto**, Viale Trieste 15 (tel 663 596; closed Sun), has built up a good reputation for its local cooking, especially good are the grilled fish and king crabs (L30 000). In Cagliari eating meat or fish *alla brace* (grilled on the open fire) is almost a cult, and when you have experienced this at the **Italia**, Via Sardegna 30 (tel 657 987), you'll understand why. Home-produced wine to complement the meal, L25 000 (closed Sun). Moving well up the scale **Dal Corsaro**, Viale Regina Margherita 28 (tel 664 318), in an old nobleman's palace, is, in many people's opinion, the finest restaurant in Sardinia, not solely for its traditional Sard food, but also for its innovative dishes and extensive selection of wines from Sardinia, mainland Italy and abroad (L50 000; closed Sun).

Around Cagliari Province

GETTING AROUND

The services of the FS can take you to San Gavino Monreale (en route to Oristano) or else to Iglesias and Carbonia on the western spur, but to get anywhere else in the province without a car you'll have to rely on the buses. Another possibility is the antique FCS narrow-gauge railway that passes through Dolianova, Senorbi and Suelli on its way to Mandas, where it branches off for either Arbatax or Sorgono in Nuoro Province. Service is erratic but the scenery is some of the best in southern Sardinia.

TOURIST INFORMATION

Besides the information booth in Cagliari's Piazza Matteotti, where the staff are well versed in what's going on throughout the province, these towns can offer assistance: Muravera (for the southeast coast), Piazza Europa 5 (tel (070) 993 760); Villasumius, in the Piazza Incani (tel (070) 791 393).

East of Cagliari

Not too far beyond the city begins an empty but ruggedly beautiful region called the Sarrabus, dominated by the peaks of the Setti Fratelli ('seven brothers'). The road hugs the coast, leading towards the recently developed resorts on the southeast corner of the island: Solanas, Capo Boi (a romantic setting with its old watchtower) and Villasimius near the small peninsula called Capo Carbonara. 2 km of wide road link the village, which is attractively set among almond trees, with the broad sandy beach of **Simius**, almost hidden between the point of the **Asini** and the bay of **Porto Giunco** to the south.

The transparent turquoise water and the flour-like sand have made it an increasingly popular resort.

Despite the number of new hotels and villas that have grown up around this corner of the island, at Capo Carbonara, Capo Boi, and other spots as far north as Muravera, the lovely coast is still pure primeval Mediterranean, with quiet coves and broad beaches everywhere, ideal if you're touring the area by car. The road through the mountains is just as scenic, passing through the lonely gorge of Sa Picocca with its grotesquely-eroded rock forms. North of the junction of these two roads are the market towns of Villaputzu and Muravera at the end of the rich Flumendosa valley where almonds and figs grow. The red flowers of the oleander add a wild splash of colour to the otherwise rather gloomy landscape. The beaches near Muravera are a popular vacation spot, and almost any road you take will lead to a fine, sandy beach, the most outstanding being Torre Salinas, Cristolu Axedu, Feraxi, Capo Ferrato, Piscina Rej, Costa Rej, Cala Sinzias and Cala Pira. Should you time your trip well, and not go in August, you'll have miles of empty beach to yourself. The coast to the north features two ruined castles, Castello Gibas and Castello Quirra, and the 12th-century Pisan Church of San Niccolo

North of Cagliari

To the northwest the Carlo Felice (SS131), the island's main highway, traverses the

Campidano, the broad plain stretching towards Oristano. Here, **Sanluri** saw the battle in 1709 that marked the end of Sardinian independence, when the forces of Arborea were finally defeated. Sanluri's castle (14th century) was a stronghold of the Giudicati of Arborea. There is a small historical museum inside, containing relics from World War I and the colonial wars. Another castle of the same era, the Castello di Monreale, can be seen near Sardara, a centre of the carpet-weaving craft with a large cooperative enterprise.

Directly north of the city, secondary highways and the old narrow-gauge FCS railway lead to Arbatax and the mountains of the Gennargentu, passing through a region of rolling hills and grey, quiet, resolutely Sardinian villages. In the little town of **Dolianova** the medieval church of San Pantaleo is built on the site of an early Christian structure; in the crypt are the original baptismal fonts cut from the rock, and the hanging arches along the side walls of the church are an interesting feature. Some of the decorations are Moorish in style.

Farther to the north, the small plain of the Trexenta, a recently reclaimed agricultural area, lies between the mountains and the artificial Lake Mulargia, created by the damming of the Flumendosa. **Senorbi** has two interesting churches, the parish church with its carved wooden altars and the 13th-century Santa Mulargia in the hills overlooking the town. **Suelli** has another restored Romanesque church, which served as a cathedral in the Middle Ages when the town was an episcopal see. South of the town lies the Nuraghe Piscu. **San Gavino Monreale** is a lead-smelting town, in the centre of the Campidano. The scenery, both here and in the surrounding hills, is very reminiscent of parts of the American West: Utah, Arizona or Texas. It isn't surprising that Italian directors often chose to film their 'spaghetti westerns' here.

The northernmost part of the province, the Marmilla with its dozens of small villages, is dominated by a huge basalt plateau called the **Giara di Gesturi**. This natural wonder, covered with dense vegetation and some nuraghi and home to a band of small, wild horses, has no roads; it's a steep climb if you wish to visit it. **Barumini** boasts the most important nuraghic complex of the south, **Su Nuraxi**, also one of the most visited. The central fortress is one of those resembling a medieval castle, and provided a bulwark in the defence against the Carthaginians. Remains of a nuraghic village surround the towers. Su Nuraxi was unknown until 1899, when a mudslide uncovered it. Most likely the nuraghe builders used wood for their domestic buildings. For that reason, and also because complexes like this are so rare, it is believed that these ruins are no mere village, but a palace or capital, or perhaps a trading centre for the Sards and their erstwhile Greek, Punic and Roman enemies. The collection of smaller towers and odd-shaped chambers, built of the same huge stones as the castle and connected by narrow, winding alleys, evokes the nuraghic civilization more clearly, perhaps, than any other site on the island. Especially interesting are the two well-carved circular fountains. In the castle itself there's a small central courtyard and a maze-like network of stairways and passages hardly large enough to walk in—more like an anthill than a castle, and obviously meant for defence. Altogether, the complex resembles quite clearly one of the larger *talayot* complexes of Minorca

From the top of the castle, the view takes in an incredible sight, the ruined 12th-century **Castle of Las Plassas** at the summit of a bare, steep, perfectly conical hill, visible for many miles in any direction. There are a number of these hills in Sardinia;

with ruins of a castle on top they are like something seen in a dream, and it is impossible to convince oneself these are natural formations and not the work of men.

One other village in this region, **Villamar**, is well known for its murals, literally dozens of them, covering its houses and walls, depicting aspects of Sard life, old and new, as well as contemporary political issues. Just beyond the village of **Mandas** is **Serri**, set on a plateau 650 m above sea level; one of the most striking reminders of the 'cult of the waters', practised by the nuraghe, can be found at the well and temple of **Santa Vittoria**.

West of Cagliari

Beyond the Stagno di Cagliari, the coastal road plunges southwards towards Capo Spartivento, the southern tip of the island. On the way, it passes through the villages of Sarroch, with a large nuraghe nearby, and Pula. It also passes what seems to be the biggest oil refinery this side of Dubai, blighting the coast for almost a mile. On the coast near Pula are the ruins, recently excavated, of the great Punic–Roman city of **Nora** (open 8–1 and 3 pm to sunset). Here better than anywhere else in Sardinia one can get an idea of what Roman provincial cities were like. On Nora's narrow streets—often with the sewers underneath—can be seen the theatre, a temple to Tanit, and the mosaic floors in the homes of the wealthy. Part of the city, including the port, founded by the Phoenicians to provide protection from the *Mistral* and west winds, is today under the sea. Near the ruins a Pisan watchtower stands guard.

Also in the vicinity of Pula are the 11th-century church of Sant' Efisio, goal of pilgrims during the saint's festival in Cagliari in May, and the beach resort of **Santa Margherita** near a small pine wood. This is probably the most popular resort on the southwest coast of the Gulf of Cagliari, and has hotels, tourist villages and bungalows to rent; it comes as a welcome surprise after the hideous coastline preceding it. More excavations, these of the ancient city of Bithia, are farther down the coast near Capo Spartivento, as well as another watchtower, the Torre di Chia (16th century), and another resort **Porto Pino** on Capo Teulada. Near San Giovanni Suergiu with the turn-off for Sant' Antioco (see below) is a 13th-century church in the hamlet of Tratalias dedicated to Santa Maria. It was once a cathedral.

Another road west from Cagliari (route 130) passes through industrial sprawl north of the Stagno di Cagliari, past Elmas Airport and the road and railway junction of Decimomannu. Nearby are two towns, **Uta** and **Villaspeciosa**, both with interesting 12th-century churches built by French monks. With Siliqua we leave the Campidano and enter the mountainous mining country of the southwest. Near the town is the old feudal castle of **Acquafredda**. Further west are two big mining towns, one very old and one very new: Iglesias and Carbonia, respectively the fourth and third largest cities on the island.

Iglesias and Carbonia

Iglesias dates from the early Middle Ages; some of its original fortifications can still be seen, and the Aragonese Castello Salvatore (begun by the Pisans) still looms above. Mariano IV besieged and captured this fortress in 1365. Two medieval churches are of interest: the 13th-century Cathedral in Piazza Municipio, and the Nostra Signora di

Valverde on Via Valverde. The centre of town is the Piazza Quintino Sella, named after the famous vintner, whose respected label Sella & Mosca is bottled in Alghero. Via Matteotti, leading from the piazza, is the main shopping street. The Technical Institute has a small mineralogical museum.

Iglesias has always been a mining town, though a more pleasant one would be hard to find. Today the mines are becoming uneconomical to operate—at least according to the government monopoly that runs them. The community is being forced to reconsider its future, and this is reflected in the murals that are appearing around the town. Some are celebrations of the old Sard ways, and some have political messages, but none is without artistic value (there's a good one on an elementary school a block from the railway station). Lead and zinc *aficionados* can visit the mines at Monteponi on a hillside 3 km to the southeast.

Carbonia, just west of Iglesias, is a new town, founded by Mussolini in 1938. When he invaded Ethiopia in 1936 the League of Nations imposed economic sanctions, and Italy had to mine its own coal. The town centre reeks of Mussolinian pomposity, with wide dusty streets and squares. Like Iglesias, though, it is pleasant enough for a mining town, not at all the horrible place most writers accuse it of being.

Islands off the Coast

SANT' ANTIOCO

This isn't really an island now, though it once was. The Carthaginians began, and the Romans completed, a causeway over the shallow straits that still survives. Some arches of the Roman work are still visible. On the middle of the causeway are two standing stones, or *faraglioni*, that were an object of worship by the nuraghic people. The legend has grown since that they are a monk and a nun turned to stone by God when they attempted to flee the island together.

The aboriginal Sards had a sizeable colony on Sant' Antioco; of the original dozens of nuraghi not many are left. The island was one of the first footholds of the Phoenicians. For them, and for Carthage, Sulcis (now Sant' Antioco) was the largest city in Sardinia. This city has been continuously occupied for 2600 years; ancient remains are found everywhere. This is not readily apparent to the visitor, who sees first the new town by the sea, with its tree-lined main street that sleeps all day but comes noisily alive for the evening *passeggiata*.

TOURIST INFORMATION
Piazza de Gasperi; Calasetta, at Piazza Municipio 10 (tel. (0781) 82 031).

Catacombs, and a Tophet
The old town is up on a height, surrounding the 11th-century Church of Sant' Antioco. Island, town and church are named after this saint, who took refuge here from Africa.

Behind the simple Baroque façade the old church seems almost like a cavern, lit with candles. Besides the relics of the saint, and some interesting early medieval reliefs, this church boasts two catacombs underneath, entered from the transept; also underneath are parts of a Punic hypogeum, which the Christians expanded in the 4th century to create the catacombs. Above the old town is the Castello rebuilt in the 16th century by the Aragonese.

Just outside the old town are the Punic–Roman necropolis and one of the most interesting small museums on the island. Some of the tombs have been converted into living quarters, inhabited to this day. The collection is presently housed in a farmhouse, but a new structure is being built next to the necropolis, a 5-minute walk away. Among the Punic artefacts are a number of gems decorated with mythical scenes, many toys of the children who perished on the *tophet*, grave steles and pottery. There is a tablet inscribed in Hebrew, testifying to the large number of Jewish settlers brought by the Romans, and some columns from the acropolis (where the Castello is now). The necropolis and *tophet* are predictably grim. The *tophet* is one of the best preserved anywhere; you can see the stone slab where the sacrifices were performed, and the urns in which the ashes of Baal's little victims were deposited.

The remainder of the island is devoted to agriculture; some very good strong wine is made here. Off the southern tip are three islets—the 'Bull', the 'Cow' and the 'Calf'. Tourism is of major importance and there are a number of beaches all around the coast, but the only other town is Calasetta, founded in the 12th century, the point of departure for San Pietro.

SAN PIETRO

This island was originally settled by the Carthaginians, though in the Dark Ages its population drifted away (or were carried away). San Pietro takes its name from a spurious legend that St Peter was shipwrecked here and taught the inhabitants how to catch tuna. King Carlo Emanuele, in his efforts to repopulate Sardinia, brought the Tabarchini, Ligurians from the town of Pegli who had started a colony on Tabarca Island near Tunisia, to San Pietro in 1737. More emigrants from Pegli arrived in the decades that followed. One of the last great pirate raids, in 1798, saw most of them abducted to Tunisia again, but piracy had become fairly civilized and the Sardinian government was able to buy them back five years later.

As a result of this colonization, San Pietro is a very atypical corner of Sardinia. The inhabitants still speak their Genoese dialect, and most of them are fair-haired. The most obvious difference is in the town of **Carloforte**, named after the king. Carloforte is a tidy and very pretty town of pastel-coloured houses, looking not surprisingly like any similar town on the Ligurian coast. It lies between a hill, with remains of an old fortress, and the extensive saltpans to the south. Life in Carloforte centres on the Via Roma, the shady esplanade with most of the restaurants. The town, indeed all of San Pietro, is fast becoming popular with the tourists. Apart from being a well-known seaside resort the island has fascinating sea caves and geological formations, and the typical maquis vegetation of the Mediterranean.

One of the island's major attractions is the *Mattanza*, the ritual bludgeoning of tuna that is the island's chief source of income. A circle of boats, led by the *rais* or chief (the word is Arabic and means admiral), surrounds a group of tuna and draws closer together, finally pulling up the nets and catching the tuna all at once. It's done the same way off Trapani and the Egadi Islands, and the spectacle takes place here by the islet of Piana just off San Pietro's northern tip, between April and July.

From Carloforte, a winding road crosses the centre of the island, past Guardia dei Mori, the highest point, where the Saracens are said to have had a fortress, through pine woods to Cala Fico. There are beaches along the western coast, near Carloforte, and on the western coast, where another road connects the town with La Caletta. Two grottoes on the coast, at Mezzaluna and Punta delle Oche, can only be reached by sea; excursions are arranged from the harbour at Carloforte.

At the southern tip of the island is the San Vittorio tower. Exactly on the 39th parallel, it houses an important astronomical observatory. Offshore here are twin *faraglioni*, called the 'columns'.

From Iglesias to Oristano

Iglesias' mines ship their products from the growing industrial town of **Porto Vesme**, the home of yet more oil refineries. This is also the embarkation point for San Pietro and Sant' Antioco. Almost adjacent to Porto Vesme is **Portoscuso**, an older port with an Aragonese tower and a beach. Just to the northeast, the nuraghic village of **Serrucci** retains some buildings that are entirely intact. Perhaps because of the vicinity of the mines, the coast north of here has not been developed. The scenery is spectacular even by Sardinian standards, featuring the tall *scoglio* called Pan di Zucchero (sugar loaf) in the bay, with purple and green mountains and cliffs for a backdrop. There are fine beaches at Fontanamare and Porto Flavia.

East of Iglesias is another mining town, **Domusnovas**, to the north of which is the famous **Grotta di San Giovanni**—really a natural tunnel in the rock. It's the only cave in Sardinia you can drive your car through. Once you go through, though, turn right back around—the road fizzles out into a track which winds its way past disused mines, and nobody knows where it ends. Taking the road north from Iglesias towards Guspini will take you to one of the most unusual and little known archaeological sites in Sardinia, the **Tempio di Antas** (signposted on route 176, 14 km north of the city). This nuraghic temple was taken over by the Phoenicians; later, under Roman rule, the mixed population constructed their own version of a Classical temple with odd Ionic-style columns. Many of these, along with a sculpted frieze above, still stand.

North of Iglesias, there are holiday villas on the coast, the 'Costa Verde', while a few miles inland are the old mining centres of Arbus, Guspini and the surreally-named Gonnosfanadiga, all on the slopes of Monte Linas. **Guspini** has a fine 15th-century Aragonese church, and nearby, ruins of the ancient city of Neapolis. For one of the loveliest diversions you can make in Sardinia, take the back road from Arbus to Marina di Arbus, then south through the centre of the Costa Verde to **Piscinas Beach**—lonely acres of formidable dunes of ultra-fine sand (some of them reaching 30 m in height), driftwood and gulls. The travel brochures' claim to miles of empty beaches is, for once, a reality in this region.

It may not be so for long, but this is still one of the most beautiful and unspoiled places on the Sardinian coast.

WHERE TO STAY   (tel prefix 070)

Consult the provincial hotel listing for which villages in the interior are likely to provide accommodation. Most of them will be quite simple, like the *Hotel Italia, in San Gavino Monreale (tel 933 9053; L28 000, no rooms with bath). You may be lucky, though, and find another piquant institution like the **Santa Lucia in Barumini (tel 936 8064; L20–22 000) which is exactly like staying at your grandmother's.

Beach hotels here are mostly expensive, self-contained complexes built in the last decade. Santa Margherita, near Pula, has the fanciest, with swimming pools and private beaches, such as the ***Flamingo (tel 920 8361; L100 000).

Capo Boi and Capo Carbonara, near Villasimius, have similar complexes which are popular with groups. You can take your golf clubs along and stay at the ***Is Molas Golf Hotel (4 miles outside Pula (tel 920 9457; L115 000).

Less expensive holidays can be spent on the coasts near Muravera in the east or Portoscuso in the west, or on the islands of Sant' Antioco and San Pietro. In Calasetta (Sant' Antioco) there is the **Stella del Sud (tel (0781) 88 488; L60 000) and less expensive hotels in the area such as the *Bellavista, Loc. Sottotorre (tel (0781) 88 211; L40 000 with bath).

EATING OUT

On the islands, you can wash down fish dinners and unusual specialities with *Vernaccia* wine (an honest 15 per cent alcohol, the highest we've found on the islands) at the excellent **Da Nicola** on the Lungomare Vespucci in Sant' Antioco (tel (0781) 83 286; L25 000) or the **Tre Archi di Augusto** on Via Colombo in Carloforte for about the same price. The **Rocca 'Ia** in Carloforte, Via Sedini, offers pizza and specialities *alle brace* (on the grill) for around L25 000 for a full meal. In general it will be fish along the coasts and modest Sard dishes like *mallorreddus* inland; the inexpensive **El Trocodero** in Pula, Via Sant' Efisio, is worth a stop on your way to the ruins at Nora.

In Santadi, 20 km north of Teulada and 3 km off the N293, an inexpensive and charming little trattoria, the **Mauritiana**, Via Veneto 11 (tel (0781) 955 455, closed Mon), serves full meals with excellent wines in the L20 000 range. Especially recommended are the *tagliatelle* with hare sauce, and the lamb speciality *agnello alla Mauritiana*. A hot contender for Sardinia's finest restaurant, along with Cagliari's Dal Corsara, is **Dell'Hotel Is Morus** in S. Margherita di Pula (tel (070) 921424), not only for its splendid position on the sea, but also for the dedication of its staff who have worked to make it such a fine establishment. Some specialities include crab and pepper salad in American sauce, avocado and shrimp cocktail, artichoke soufflé and excellent desserts (around L40 000; closed Nov–Mar). After a round of Golf at Is Molas, 30 km from Cagliari, you can dine at the **Is Molas Clubhouse** by the pool for L30–35 000; for those eager to get back on the green there's a lunchtime buffet service (tel (070) 920 9062).

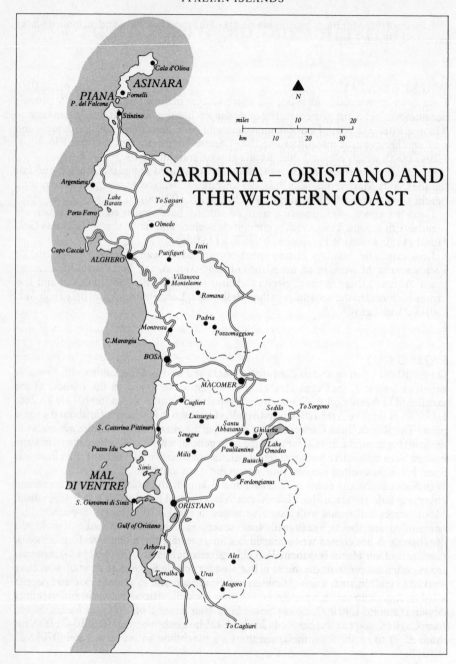

SARDINIA – ORISTANO AND THE WESTERN COAST

Cala d'Oliva

ASINARA

PIANA

Fornelli

P. del Falcone

Stintino

N

miles   10   20

km   10   20   30

Argentiera

Lake Baratz

To Sassari

Porto Ferro

Olmedo

Capo Caccia

ALGHERO

Putifigari

Ittiri

Villanova Monteleone

Romana

Padria

Montresta

Pozzomaggiore

C.Marargiu

BOSA

MACOMER

Cuglieri

Sedilo

To Sorgono

Lussurgiu

Santu Abbasanta

Ghilarsa

S. Catterina Pittinuri

Senegne

Lake Omodeo

Putzu Idu

Milis

Paulilantino

Busachi

MAL DI VENTRE

Sinis

Fordongianus

S. Giovanni di Sinis

ORISTANO

Gulf of Oristano

Arborea

Ales

Terralba

Uras

Mogoro

To Cagliari

Oristano and the Western Coast

The old Giudicato of Arborea has been reborn since 1975 in the province of Oristano. Cut from parts of Cagliari and Nuoro, it is the smallest of the four Sardinian provinces. Even so, few parts of the island have so much natural and historical interest. The modestly beautiful city of Oristano, and the Sinis peninsula, are two destinations that no traveller in Sardinia should miss, while the province's interior offers nuraghic, Classical, or medieval monuments in nearly every village.

The province of Oristano, facing west across the Mediterranean, has always played a major role because of its strategic position, and has witnessed the mingling of diverse cultures. An ideal place to settle with its mild climate, abundance of food from the sea and the large, fertile plain, this part of the world has been inhabited since Neolithic times.

To head north from Oristano the N131, a rather characterless road, runs to Nuoro; you can branch off before Ghilarza to reach Macomer and beyond that Sassari. A much pleasanter way to reach the northern coast, however, is to take the coastal N292 to Bosa Marina. From here (stay with the coast, not the N292), the 40 km of coastline that runs up to Alghero is one of the most impressive and unspoilt in Sardinia. The road winds round one spectacular bend after another, and there are a hundred little coves to swim from if you can find your way down the steep cliffs. The telltale sign of a good swimming spot is a group of cars parked by the side of the road (especially if they have German number plates). Do likewise and look for the path. It's a good idea to fill up your car and stomach before you tackle this road—there isn't a garage or restaurant in sight.

South of Oristano

The swampy plain south of the city, facing the Gulf of Oristano, was good farmland in ancient times, but almost entirely deserted when its reconstruction was begun in 1919. A system of dams was built all along the Tirso, Sardinia's longest river; irrigation canals were dug and swamps drained. The centre of this new land is tidy, prosperous Arborea, founded by Mussolini in 1928. The town boasts a dairy and wine industry, and a fishing cooperative. The Municipio houses a small archaeological collection of finds from Roman times discovered in the surrounding area.

Further inland, route 442 branches off the main Sardinian highway at Uras, where the last Arborean resistance was stamped out in 1470 by the Spaniards, to a string of mountain villages on its way to the Barbagia. **Morgongiori** has what is reputed to be one of the only working obsidian mines in the Mediterranean; it seems to have been worked since the Neolithic era. Today Morgongiori, situated on the south side of Monte Arci, is a compact little town with houses built closely together, separated by narrow winding streets. Nearby **Mogoro** is an important handicraft centre, especially for tapestries and carpets in traditional brilliant colours. **Ales**, an ancient bishopric, has a cathedral originally erected in 1100 and later rebuilt in the 16th century by the architect Salvatore Spotorno.

Oristano

Oristano today is a city of many qualities, and much subtlety. Its quiet and dignified air, and the orderliness and simplicity of its streets and buildings, make it seem an almost otherworldly place. Of the four provincial capitals, Oristano is perhaps the most Sardinian in character, even more so than Nuoro. Like many of the small cities of the Mediterranean islands, it is a lesson to all of us accustomed to life in the metropolis in how much urbanity can be concentrated in a town of 20,000 or less.

When ancient Tharros, on the Sinis peninsula, became too unsafe in the early Middle Ages, the population retreated to this defensible site, surrounded by marshes. The city was founded in 1070, and soon became the seat of the bishop and of the Giudicato. For 400 years the Giudicati maintained this independence by a continually shifting foreign policy, at times allied with the Pisans, the Genoese, and for a time even with Aragon. Imperialist Aragon, in the end, was to prove their greatest enemy.

In the 14th century—the great age of Mariano IV and his daughter, the Giudichessa Eleonora—Oristano attained its greatest prosperity and influence; Arborea's leaders spoke for all Sardinia in the struggle against the invaders. After 1410, when the city was finally taken, a period of decline set in that lasted until the present century. The irrigation and reclamation schemes of the Kings of Sardinia, Mussolini, and the post-war Republic have re-established Oristano, both as a capital and as the centre of a flourishing agricultural region.

GETTING AROUND
In the city of Oristano, small as it is, both the railway station (Piazza Ungheria) and the bus station (Via Cagliari) are a good walk from the centre. If you take a train through the province, keep an eye out for nuraghes; the tracks follow a natural route of communication, and on the stretch from Oristano north to Chilivani at least a dozen of the most important sites in Sardinia, including nuraghes Losa and Sant' Antine, can be seen from the train.

Unfortunately there is no public transport into Sinis—though that probably helps keep it unspoiled and beautiful. The buses can take you almost anywhere else mentioned in the text, though as always plan the trip out well in advance.

TOURIST INFORMATION
In Oristano, the EPT office is at Via Cagliari 276, near the bus station (tel (0783) 74 191).

WHAT TO SEE
Oristano's walls were torn down long ago, and a circle of broad avenues surrounding the old town has replaced them: Via Mazzini, Via Solferini, Via Cagliari. In the Piazza Mariano part of the fortifications remain, the Portixeddu ('little tower'). Another tower, the Porta Mannu or St Christopher's Tower, stands on the edge of Piazza Roma, the modern centre of Oristano. Behind the tower the Corso Umberto, a pedestrian-only shopping street, extends towards the Piazza Eleonora with a statue of the great Giudichessa. Oristano is still very much Eleonora's city; her house can be seen at 4 Via Parpaglia and her tomb at the Santa Chiara church.

Just behind this square, set in a small garden, is the Cathedral. Though begun in the 11th century, most of what exists today, including the lovely, slightly leaning octagonal campanile with its leering faces near the top, dates from the 1700s. Across from the cathedral is the 18th-century Seminary; also here is the Church of San Francesco. The building itself is 19th-century neo-classical, but inside is a striking medieval crucifix called 'Di Nicodemo', and a statue of San Basilio by Nino Pisano. There is a small museum in Oristano, the Antiquarium Arborense on Via Vittorio Emanuele (open 9–12 and 3–5; closed Sun), with a collection of Punic and Roman objects from Tharros and elsewhere.

Following Via Cagliari, 3 km south of Oristano is the suburb of Santa Giusta with the 12th-century church of the same name; built by the Pisans, this is one of the outstanding medieval monuments on the island. Some of the columns in the nave were taken from Roman ruins at Tharros.

Around Oristano Province

On route 388, running up the Tirso valley, **Villanova Truscheddu** has an important nuraghe nearby. **Fordongianus** is an ancient Roman settlement—Forum Traianus. Roman piers still carry a bridge over the Tirso, and there are ruins of an ancient spa, the *Aquae Hypoitanae*, with a modern establishment just across the river. The 13th-century Church of San Lussorio, site of that saint's martyrdom, is 1.6 km west of Fordongianus. There are catacombs underneath. Many *domus de janas* can be seen at **Busachi**.

Directly north of Oristano is **San Vero Milis** with the Nuraghe Surachi to the west of it, near Sinis. **Milis** and **Bonarcado** have 13th-century churches; the area around **Seneghe** is renowned for its many natural springs.

Near **Paulilatino** are many nuraghi and some giants' tombs. Nearby, a major nu-raghic site has recently been discovered at **Santa Cristina** with a temple, a sacred well and many tombs. These sacred wells are a fascinating relic of the nuraghe culture. Many, like this one, are triangular holes in the ground with steps leading down under a corbelled roof. Archaeologists are fond of reading them as symbols of the female principle. The builders saved their best work for them; their perfectly squared stonework is better than anything in the nuraghes. **Abbasanta**, on its plateau, is a large agricultural town; just south of it is the great defensive complex of **Nuraghe Losa** with a three-storey central tower (only the first and second storeys remain). The Carthaginians did not succeed in capturing Losa until the 6th century BC. West of Abbasanta, a cluster of villages on the heights surrounds **Lake Omodeo**, where a huge dam holds back the Tirso. The lake is named after the engineer who designed the dam, and is well stocked for the enjoyment of fishermen. One of the villages is **Ghilarza** where you can visit the home of the famous socialist philosopher Antonio Gramsci. At the far end of the lake is the old and very traditional village of **Sedilo** with still more prehistoric remains nearby.

Sinis

This is a true wonderland, one of the best-kept secrets in Sardinia, but it may not remain so for long; it's a favourite spot on Sunday morning for the gathering of the Oristano set, and the occasional German car. (There are no buses to Sinis; as with so many other of the island's sights, you'll need your own transport.) Sinis is a low, flat peninsula northwest of Oristano, covered mainly with heather. Just the same it is indeed a poetic landscape, as the Sards claim, with a wealth of interesting things to see. Sinis is separated from the rest of the island by the Stagno di Cabras, a lagoon full of fish and eels, near the town of Cabras. The road from Oristano passes over a narrow strip of land between the lagoon and the sea, passing the popular lido at Torregrande.

Where the road splits there is a nuraghe, and to the right the **Sanctuary of San Salvatore**, surrounded by a festival village; deserted for most of the year, it springs to life in September when families from all over the island move in for a week of celebrations. The church is built on an ancient religious site; a trapdoor in the floor leads to a 4th-century sanctuary dedicated to Hercules Soter, with Roman frescoes portraying Venus and Cupid, and Hercules slaying a serpent.

At the southern tip of the peninsula is the fishing village of **San Giovanni in Sinis**, a place where the 20th century is only a dim rumour. The village consists of a long row of huts made of rushes along the shore, built according to an age-old highly aesthetic design. The fishermen also use the rushes to build their boats. The parish church of San Giovanni is, after San Saturnino in Cagliari, the oldest in Sardinia, dating from the 5th century. Like San Saturnino and all the early Christian monuments in Sardinia, it is in the form of a Greek cross with a dome over the centre. There is an original baptismal font, carved with a fish at the bottom.

Close to the village are the excavations of **Tharros**. As in Nora, part of the city is under water. On the hill overlooking the town are the Punic necropolis and *tophet*, a Spanish tower of the 15th century and the remains of a synagogue. There is still a near perfect sewage system from Carthaginian–Roman times, and a maze of little back streets. Several beaches are in the vicinity, one of the most spectacular being **Is Arutus** of tiny white quartz. Here you can swim in the cleanest sea in all of Italy, and the long deserted stretches of beach are an unbelievable bonus to this pretty area. The western coast of Sinis produces some spectacular sheer cliffs which climb 25 m above the crystal clear sea; the beaches scattered along the coastline here are accessible only by boat. A large beach of multicoloured pebbles looks out to the island mysteriously known as **Mal di Ventre** (stomach ache), uninhabited except for some bold rabbits and bored seagulls. The island is geologically distinct from the mainland, being formed of granite. If you can get out there you'll be rewarded by the turquoise water fringed by exquisite little beaches. At Capo Mannu, on the northern end, is the small resort of **Putzu Idu**. A small lagoon nearby, the Stagno di Sale Porcus, is one of the last summer homes of the European crane (*fenicotteri* in Italian). They are a wonderful sight, but try not to disturb them.

North of Sinis

Along the coast north of Sinis, a beach resort is developing around **Santa Caterina di Pittinuri**, with its coastline of great variety and beauty. To the north the rocks are volcanic and forbidding, whereas further south the bleached white crags separate numerous beaches. Nearby is a magnificent natural bridge, one of the biggest in Sardinia, called the 'Archetto' (little arch), and the ruins of another ancient city, Cornus. Further north, around the slopes of Monte Ferru, a not-quite-extinct volcano, is

Cuglieri in a pretty wooded setting, with the 15th-century church of Santa Maria della Neve. The Pro Loco has a small archaeological collection of objects from Cornus. South of the town is an interesting decorated Neolithic hypogeum. In the hills just to the north, near Scano di Montiferro, are a number of nuraghi.

To the east of Cuglieri is **San Leonardo** with a 13th-century church and some radioactive springs. Near Santa Lussurgiu is the beautiful waterfall known as **Sos Molinos**.

Macomer and Santa Sabina

Macomer is an agricultural market town, and the most important road and rail junction on the island. Travelling in Sardinia, sooner or later you'll end up in Macomer. The numerous nuraghi in the neighbourhood include Nuraghe Santa Barbara northeast of the town. South of Macomer, at Borore, is one of the best of the 'giant's tombs'.

If you take Route 129 inland towards Nuoro (all this territory, including Macomer and Bosa, is part of Nuoro province), you'll pass **Silanus**, in the foothills south of Monte Lameddari. Here, visible from the road, a large nuraghe and the 11th-century church of Santa Sabina, resembling an early Christian or Byzantine work with its Greek-cross plan, stand facing each other in an open field. The area from here to Macomer is lined with nuraghi; then as now, this was the principal route across the island, and the nuraghe-builders took great pains to defend it.

Bosa

The little River Temo has the distinction of being the only navigable one in Sardinia— for all of 6 km. It stops being navigable at the ancient city of Bosa, founded by the Carthaginians. This town, which shows much Spanish influence in its buildings, is famous for its handmade lace and Malvasia wine. From the riverfront promenade, Bosa climbs upwards to the half-ruined Serravalle Castle built by the Pisans in the 12th

Chiesetta di Santa Sabrina, Silanus

century. In between is the peculiar Cathedral and the Piazza Umberto with its fountain. Outside the town is one of the earliest and best Romanesque churches, the 11th-century San Pietro Extramuros, along with ruins of another medieval castle, the Malaspina.

Bosa Marina on the coast, an old port with a 17th-century watchtower, has a good beach, and is developing into a resort. A small island called Isola Rossa is joined to the port by a causeway.

WHERE TO STAY   (tel prefix 0783)
Oristano city has five middle-range hotels which are all about the same, the least expensive of which is the **Piccolo, Via Martignano 19 (tel 71 500; L45 000 with bath). The only four star hotel is the ****Mistral (tel 212 505; L70 000). Near the beaches at Cuglieri–S'Archittu is the *Columbaris (tel 38 032), where rooms are L30–40 000 with bath. An inexpensive stay at the beach can also be spent at *Su Pallosu, at Su Pallosu (tel 52 021; L35 000) or *Da Cesare at Putzu Idu (tel 52 015; L32 000) or else at the Torregrande Marina near Oristano: the ***Del Sole (tel 22 000; L58–80 000). In Santa Caterina the tourist board owns ***La Scogliera (tel 38 231), where service and rates are good (L45–60 000 with bath). The ***Ala Birdi, Strada N. 24 (tel 800 512) in Arborea is a comfortable hotel with all facilities (L90 000). In Cabras there are two hotels in the L95 000 range, **El Sombrero (tel 290 659) and **Summertime (tel 290 837). Terralba offers one small but comfortable place, the *Mura (tel 81 912; L33 000).

In Bosa Marina there are a number of reasonably priced hotels: ***Al Gabbiano, Viale Mediterraneo (tel (0785) 374 123; L50 000 with bath); **Turas, Loc. Turas (tel (0785) 373 473; L45 000 with bath) and *Miramare, Via Colombo (tel (0785)373 400; L36 000 with bath); Roma (tel 373 065; L35 000).

Modest accommodation can be found in Ales, Ghilarza, Bauladu and Abbasanta.

EATING OUT
Oristano, like Cagliari, is a good city for restaurants and is famous for a speciality called *bottarga* (the roe of a fish called the *muggine* that lives in the Stagno di Cabras), smoked and served as antipasto or with spaghetti. You can try it at Il Faro on Via Bellini 25 in Oristano (tel 70 002), which also has no shortage of good meat dishes too (L40–50 000; closed Sun and 1st two weeks of Jan & July). La Forchetta d'Oro on Via Giovanni XXIII (tel 70 462) and La Ruota, Via Tharros 72 (tel 72 992) both specialize in Sard regional cooking in the L20 000 range.

Don't let the name put you off, the OK Corral is an excellent, unpretentious restaurant conveniently situated on the N537, 35 km from Oristano, 46 km from Nuoro. The speciality here is fish, but don't overlook the wild boar (L25–30 000; tel (0785) 54 188, closed Mon). In Cabras Il Caminetto, Via C. Battisti 8 (tel 0783) 291 139), also has seafood specialities and good Sardinian wines (L20–25 000; closed Mon and first 15 days of Dec). On the lovely Sinis peninsula, once again seafood is the first choice, and the mixed grill at the Casas hotel in San Giovanni di Sinis is one of the best places to try it. Mussels and shrimp are a speciality (L25–30 000; closed Fri, tel 290871). Similarly, in Su Pallosu the hotel of the same name has excellent food and service, particularly good are the pork and lamb (L20–30 000). In Ghilarza, 38 km from Oristano, drop into Su Cantam, Via Monsignor Zuccam (tel (0785) 54664, closed Fri). It's a lovely little restaurant and has *risotto* and spaghetti with shrimp and oyster sauce. In winter they serve excellent soups.

Alghero

Alghero is a beautiful city in a beautiful setting, one of the prime tourist centres of the island. The British, in particular, favour it; they have been coming here for decades, and their numbers are increasing.

In a sense, Alghero isn't a Sardinian town at all. Founded by the Arabs, and controlled by Genoa in the early Middle Ages, the Aragonese found it a valuable and strategic site, beginning their Sardinian conquest with Alghero's annexation in 1355. The Algherese did not prove to be very docile subjects; after two fierce rebellions the Aragonese solved their problem by deporting the entire population to the interior and replacing them with Catalans. Thus did Alghero become a kind of foreign concession on the island, as Bastia was under the rule of the Genoese in Corsica. Sards were forbidden to remain within its walls after dark, under severe penalty, and no more than ten at a time were allowed in during the day.

In Alghero today, the town's past is readily visible. It has all the appearances of a town built for noblemen ('You are all knights', Emperor Charles V said on his visit in 1542—the Algherese still recall this with pride), and this of course suits Alghero perfectly for its modern role—as a town built for tourists.

GETTING AROUND
Alghero's airport lies 10 km out of town. There are daily flights from here to major Italian cities including Cagliari; also charter flights from Britain. Buses run to Porto Torres (for sea connections to France and northern Italy) and Sassari, where you'll have to change for other destinations, likewise with the train.

TOURIST INFORMATION
AAST, Piazza Porta Terra 9 (tel (079) 979 054).

Around Alghero's Harbour
The old town has most of its fortifications still intact. On the seaward side, the top of the walls makes a promenade with views of the town and its gulf. Five towers remain on the landward side: Torre dello Sperone, the southernmost, is also called the Torre di Sulis after the Sardinian revolutionary who was imprisoned there following Angioy's rebellion, and the Torre di Porta Terra marks the old main gate. Across from it is the tourist information office (AAST). Through the Bastione della Maddalena is the small harbour with excursions by sea to the Grotta di Nettuno on Capo Caccia.

Alghero still has a marked Catalan flavour; until recently, everyone spoke the language. The older ones still do. Street names in the old part of town are in both Italian and Catalan. The city's landmark is the 16th-century Cathedral on Via Manno. Unlike most churches in Sardinia, the interior is more interesting than the plain façade. The real attraction, however, is the lovely, typically Catalan campanile that dominates Alghero's skyline. You'll need to go around the back to appreciate it best (on Via Roma); there is a finely sculptured portal at its base.

Across the street from the Cathedral is the Palazzo d'Albis, where Emperor Charles stayed during his visit. Two blocks east, Via Carlo Alberto has most of the city's shops. Also in the old town are the Casa Doria, a fine 16th-century palace on the Via Principe Umberto; the Municipio with Alghero's historical archive, on the Piazza Municipio; and two churches on Via Carlo Alberto: San Michele (17th century) with its multicoloured tile dome, and San Francesco (14th century). Both have beautiful interiors. Just outside the old town, across from the Torre di Porta Terra, is the Giardino Pubblico, a pretty park patrolled throughout the summer by a horde of pretty but audacious caterpillars.

The Coral Riviera and Neptune's Cave

Alghero is the centre of a big resort area, now being promoted as the 'Riviera del Corallo'—since the success of the Costa Smeralda every strip of Sardinian coast has acquired a similar name. This one, however, may be the most attractive of all. North of Alghero there is a huge sandy beach that runs for several miles, all the way to Fertilia, a town founded by Mussolini as the centre of a big agricultural reclamation area, the Nurra. On the stream just before Fertilia are the remains of a Roman bridge. Beyond the town is another beach, Le Bombarde, and the Palmavera Nuraghe: then comes a bay, Porto Conte, with some small undeveloped beaches.

The western side of this bay is another of Sardinia's natural wonders: **Capo Caccia** with its dramatic cliffs and views of Alghero and the two great rocks in the sea, Isola Piana and Isola Foradada. Near the cape the cliffs are several hundred feet high, forcing the visitor to walk down 650 steps to visit the **Grotta di Nettuno**. It's more than worth the trouble; this is one of the most beautiful caves in the world. Only a few hundred yards of it have been fully explored, but what has been opened out is now a big tourist attraction, with guided tours and electric lighting. The sea surges against the narrow entrance, but inside calm reigns. Neptune's Grotto is special not only for the subterranean lagoons and delicate stalactites—they look like a forest drawn by Antonio Gaudi—but for the colours. There's another cave, reached by another set of stairs, just to the north, the Grotta Verde, but it is not nearly as spectacular.

North of Capo Caccia, the Coral Riviera continues with more small resorts: at Porto Ferro, Argentiera and Nurra near Capo Mannu. Just inland from Porto Ferro is tiny Lake Baratz, which has the distinction of being the only natural lake on the island.

North of Alghero, off the road for Porto Torres, is the great Neolithic necropolis of **Angelu Ruiu**, the largest in Sardinia. The 36 *domus de janas* contain interesting decorations, mostly of bulls' heads; the statuettes and ornaments found here are housed in the Sanna Museum in Sassari. Near the necropolis is Fertilia Airport, which serves Sassari, Alghero and Porto Torres.

WHERE TO STAY (tel prefix 079)

Alghero has a tremendously wide choice of hotels. On the Lungomare Valencia there's the elegant ******Villa Las Trovas**, at No. 1 (tel 975 390; L110–140 000), in an old palace with private beach, pool and garden; and the *****Carlos V** (tel 979 501; L85–120 000); alongside more modest places like the ****Eleonora** (tel 979 236; L35–50 000 with bath) and even cheaper hotels a block or two from the beaches. The pensione ***Sardegna**, Via S. Agostino 1 (tel 975 247), for example, has rooms with bath for L30 000. In the quieter area of Porto Conte and Fertilia north of town, there are others like the ***Bellavista, Lungomare Rovigno (tel 930 124; L45–60 000 with bath) and the ***Porto Conte (tel 942 036; L65–90 000, from April–Oct), on the lovely peninsula around Capo Caccia.

EATING OUT

Alghero is blessed with some excellent restaurants, some not so good, and some cover-all-options at fast-food places. You can crunch happily into a lobster while up the road someone else is chewing on chicken 'n' chips. The local speciality is *aragosta alla Catalana*, lobster cooked with tomato, onion and herbs. It's on the menu at **Diecimetri**, Vicolo Adami (tel 979 023), in the heart of the old town, which specializes in seafood, although occasionally they have *porcheddu*, and always good steak. One of their unusual pasta dishes is *ravioli di pesce*, in a clam, caper and anchovy sauce (L30 000). Lobster also makes a grand appearance at **La Lepanto**, Via Carlo Alberto 135 (tel 979 116), where it's done in a variety of ways, and other traditional Algherese dishes (L40 000). **Il Pavone**, Piazza Sulis 3 (tel 979 584), has some tasty antipasti, including sea-snails and crab, *risotto allo scoglio*, similar to *paella*, pasta with caviar and shrimp, and fish soup (L35 000). Also in the old town **Da Uccio**, Via Minerva 16 (tel 979 238), offers *paella* (L25 000) and **Don Juan**, Via Santa Barbara 4 despite the name, serves traditional Italian–Sard food for L25–30 000. You can get a good pizza meal at **Da Marcheddu** for L10 000.

For homesick Britons there are a number of 'pubs' dotted around the old town: **The Dubliner**, Via Zaccaria 12, **The Piccadilly**, Via La Marmora 48, and so on, and the **Jamaica Inn**, Via Pr. Umberto 57, where you can get chicken and chips, but peas are extra.

Sassari and the North

Sassari is the largest province in Italy (Nuoro, incidentally, is second, and Cagliari fourth). Predictably, its wide open spaces can show you a wide variety of landscapes: green, intensively farmed valleys, rocky badlands, and scrubby, pleasant hills that probably seem like heaven to the Sardinian sheep. Among them are hundreds of villages, each with some venerable attraction (plenty of lovely medieval Pisan country churches) or some small claim to fame, but the real action is along the coasts. The north attracts most of the tourists in Sardinia to its many beaches.

Sassari

The first recorded mention of the village of Sassari (pronounced Tha-thari) is in a register of 1131. At this time the ancient town of Torres, capital of the region since the Carthaginians founded it, was beginning its long decline. Pirates and disease ravaged the coasts, and the population was gradually moving inland. Sassari grew rapidly; though originally under the protection of Pisa, and later of Genoa, the town developed as a free city—the only one on all the Italian islands—with its own code of laws administered by the Council of Anziani (elders).

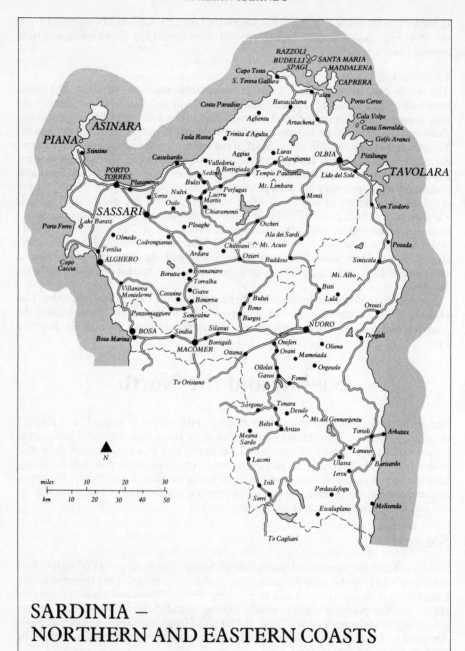

RAZZOLI
BUDELLI
SPAGI
SANTA MARIA
MADDALENA
Capo Testa
S. Teresa Gallura
CAPRERA
Costa Paradiso
Bassacultena
Palau
Porto Cervo
Aglientu
Cala Volpe
Arzachena
Costa Smeralda
Isola Rossa
Trinita d'Agulta
Golfo Aranci
PIANA
ASINARA
Aggius
Luras
OLBIA
Pittulungu
Stintino
Valledoria
Calangianus
Castelsardo
Sedini
Bortigiada
Tempio Pausania
Lido del Sole
TAVOLARA
PORTO
TORRES
Platamona
Bulzi
Perfugas
Mt. Limbara
Sorso
Nulvi
Laerru
Monti
Osilo
Martis
San Teodoro
SASSARI
Chiaramonti
Lake Baratz
Ploaghe
Oschiri
Porto Ferro
Olmedo
Ala dei Sardi
Posada
Codrongianus
Chilvani
Mt. Acuto
Fertilia
Ardara
Ozieri
Buddoso
Siniscola
Capo
ALGHERO
Caccia
Borutta
Bonnanaro
Mt. Albo
Villanova
Torralba
Bitti
Monteleone
Cossoine
Giave
Lula
Orosei
Pozzomaggiore
Bonorva
Bultei
Semestene
Bono
Orani
Silanus
Burgos
NUORO
Dorgali
Bosa Marina
BOSA
Sindia
Bortigali
Oniferi
Oliena
MACOMER
Ottana
Orani
Mamoiada
Ollolai
Orgosolo
To Oristano
Gavoi
Fonni
Sorgono
Tonara
Desulo
Belvi
Aritzo
Mt. del Gennargentu
Tortoli
Arbatax
Meana
Sardo
Lanusei
Laconi
Ulassa
Barisardo
Isili
Ierzu
Serri
Perdasdefogu
Melisenda
Escalaplano
To Cagliari

N

miles 10 20 30
km 10 20 30 40 50

SARDINIA –
NORTHERN AND EASTERN COASTS

Under the Spaniards Sassari's privileges were taken away, but the town continued to prosper. The archepiscopal see was moved from Torres in 1438, and the University, founded in 1558, was the first on the island. During the War of the Spanish Succession, Sassari was occupied for a short time by the Austrians.

One thing has been constant throughout Sassari's history—a contentious passion for liberty that stands behind the city's frequent revolts. Already in the 13th century Michele Zanche (whom Dante placed in the fifth circle of the Inferno) was leading a democratic rebellion; Sassari fought the Spanish, Austrians and Savoy kings with equal stubbornness. Always more attuned to the currents of European thought than the rest of the island, the Sassarese warmly embraced the ideals of the Enlightenment and played a role in the various Sardinian insurrections of the Napoleonic era. In 1848 they finally succeeded in booting the Jesuits out of town, and afterwards destroyed the old Aragonese Castello as a 'symbol of oppression'.

GETTING AROUND
Sassari's station (at Piazza Stazione on the western edge of the old town) is the centre for rail connections in the province. FS trains for Porto Torres, Olbia, Oristano and the south leave from here, as well as the SFS (Strade Ferrate Sarde) narrow-gauge trains for the Alghero–Tempio Pausanio–Palau route. This line, whose trains are more like trams than real trains, passes through some wonderful scenery, and provides a delightful excursion through the Gallura region.

Sassari city does not have a bus station as such; buses depart from a piazza, the Emiciclo Garibaldi, next to the Giardino Pubblico. Olbia and Alghero are other centres for bus transport, with connections to most of their neighbouring villages.

TOURIST INFORMATION
EPT, Viale Caprera 36 (tel (079) 233 729).
AAST, Via Brigata Sassari 19 (tel (079) 233 534).

WHAT TO SEE
Sassari today has over 100,000 people, the second largest city on the island. Its rivalry with Cagliari holds perhaps a modicum of disdain, for the Sassarese take a great deal of pride in their town. Sassari somehow manages the clever trick of being a place very Sardinian in character, yet different from anywhere else on the island. There is still very much the air of a medieval free city here: the civic spirit is reflected for example in the 'Festival of the Candlesticks' (organized each year by the ancient guilds) as well as in the buildings themselves, and in the jewel of a medieval town that is the historical centre. The newer parts of the city fit harmoniously with the old, and the whole is beautiful and alive and one of the finest cities to be found anywhere on these islands.

Three almost contiguous squares connect the old town with the new. **Piazza Italia** is a 19th-century creation, with the obligatory statue of Vittorio Emanuele. The stately sandstone building houses the offices of the provincial government; its assembly hall is more worthy of a great nation than a mere province. Across the square is the **Giordano Palace**; not a palace at all, or very old either, it is a splendid work of what must be the Mediterranean version of Victorian Gothic. A bank and the tourist information office share the ornate interior.

293

Next, to the north, comes the **Piazza Cavallino de Honestis** often referred to by its old name, Piazza Castello. Here was the grim fortress that offended the 19th-century Sassarese; for 300 years it had been the local headquarters of the Spanish Inquisition. Today the square holds Sassari's two skycrapers and many cafés. Before the walls were demolished, this had been the main gate. We continue northwards into the old town through the pretty triangular Piazza Azuni, a busy shopping area, and down the Corso Vittorio Emanuele, main thoroughfare of the medieval town, with the Civic Theatre and two fine buildings from the 15th century at Nos. 42 and 47.

North of the Corso is another fine square, the **Piazza Tola** named after two brothers, Sardinian patriots of the 19th century. At its southern end is the 16th-century Palazzetto Usini. On Corso Trinita can be seen parts of the old wall and a tower.

Sassari now is quite a sophisticated place (would you expect, for example, a Sardinian town to name a street after Martin Luther King?) but it hasn't lost touch with the countryside. Two bridges off the Corso Trinita carry the city over to its northern extension, but beneath them, in a narrow valley, farmers still tend their vines and orchards. Down here, accessible by steps from the Rosello Bridge, is the **Rosello Fountain**, symbol of Sassari. This Renaissance fantasy, looking more like a stage-set than a fountain, is decorated with figures representing the four seasons, dolphins and gargoyles.

South of the Corso, in a puzzle of narrow winding streets, is the **Cathedral**. Originally a 13th-century structure, of which only the campanile remains, the church was completely rebuilt in the 15th century. Then, in the 1700s, the famous Baroque façade was added, a work of rare beauty, a confection in stone unique in Sardinia, but having much in common with the Southern Baroque styles of Apulia; unlike so many other contemporary works, the underlying simplicity and sense of proportion of this one makes the profuse decoration become part of the building, not just tacked on for decoration's sake. Inside there is a Cathedral Museum with liturgical bric-à-brac and some paintings.

Around the corner, on Via Santa Caterina, is another fine building, the 18th-century **Ducal Palace**, now the Municipio. The reception rooms are an informal museum with works of art and Sard costume dolls. The **University** (17th century, though rebuilt), with a large library, is on the Piazza Università. The western limit of the old town is the Corso Vico, with the railway station—a copy of the one in Trapani and several others; the Ferrovie dello Stato planted these all over Italy in the 19th century. At the end of Corso Vico is the 13th-century church of **Santa Maria de Betlem** with carved wooden altars. The giant 'candlesticks' are kept here between festivals.

Just behind the University is the pleasant **Giardino Pubblico** with its modern Handicrafts Pavilion, with exhibits of Sard handicrafts most of which are for sale. On Via Roma, main street of the modern part of town (a block from the squat, unlovely Palazzo Giustizia—Mussolini's contribution to Sassari), is the **Museo Archeologico Sanna**. The archaeological collection here is not quite as rich as that of Cagliari, but this is a 'progressive' museum, with a wealth of explanatory pictures and notes, extremely helpful and informative—but only in Italian. The art and artefacts from all periods of early Sardinian history are represented; especially interesting are the exhibits on the shadowy Neolithic people who preceded the nuraghic builders, with finds from their important religious site, Anghelu Ruiu near Sassari. There are some nuraghic bronzes and ceramics, and a trepanned skull, testifying to Bronze Age surgical skill, as well as Punic and Roman relics.

Part of the museum is a separate collection, the Museo Gavino Clemente, a wonderful exhibition of Sardinian costumes, crafts and folk art. The attendant will probably play some Sard music on a phonograph to entertain you during your visit.

WHERE TO STAY AND EAT   (tel prefix 079)
Sassari town has not a long listing of hotels. The most luxurious is the ****Grazia Deledda, Viale Dante 47 (tel 271 235; L130 000), named after the Nobel prizewinner, of whom there are memorabilia within; the ***Marini Due, on Via Chironi (tel 277 282; L60 000), is perfectly comfortable and in the heart of things, such as they are, the *Rosita, Via Pigliaru 10 (tel 241 325; L27 000 with bath, L23 000 without).

Returning after some years of experience in Milan, two young Sards have opened the restaurant Da Gianni & Amedeo, Via Dante 31 (tel 274 598), which has rapidly shot to fame for its excellent antipasti and the house speciality, *tagliatelle di manzo* (L30–35 000, closed Sun and Aug). One of the most popular trattorias in town is Migali, Via Turitana 31 (tel 236 540), where traditional and homemade food is served in a charming and unpretentious atmosphere, and you can still pay less than L20 000. It has delicious lamb, pork and fried shrimps. If you are around this part of the world in autumn or winter, then a whole array of gastronomic delights will be available to you at Da Tomasso, Via Ospizio dei Cappucini (tel 23 504), where onion soup, wild boar and beans with lard make their appearance out of the summer months, when the menu is somewhat lighter but just as good. Here again, you can eat well for L18 000.

South of Sassari

This region, the Logudoro, once formed the greater part of the old Giudicato of Torres. Route 597 runs southwest out of Sassari towards Olbia. This road is sometimes called the 'way of the churches'; before Chilivani it passes near three of Sardinia's greatest medieval monuments. Of these, the best known is the 12th-century SS. Trinita di Saccargia in open country near Ploaghe and gloriously decorated with green-and-white stone stripes. The façade and a campanile are a Sard masterpiece in stone. Ploaghe's parish church, not impressive outside, has a big surprise inside: a fine collection of about 40 paintings, including one by Filippino Lippi, given to the church by a Sardinian historian named Spano who was born in the village.

In the Middle Ages, Ardara was an important centre, a rival to Sassari. Before the Spanish occupation it was the capital of the Giudicato. Still a pleasant town, it is worth visiting for the 12th-century Santa Maria del Regno. Inside this church is a beautiful wooden altarpiece of the 15th century, containing a number of paintings by Martin Torner and Giovanni Ruiu, a Sardinian. The third of these 12th-century churches is Sant' Antioco di Biscarcio which, like SS. Trinita, stands in open country.

Route 131, south from Sassari, is the main highway of Sardinia. It is still sometimes called the 'Carlo Felice' after the king who built it, connecting Sassari with Cagliari. Near the turn-off from Ardara is another 12th-century church the 'Mesumundo', built over the remains of a Roman thermal spa. Further south the road passes Bonnanaro, where some of the most ancient Neolithic remains on the island have been found. In **Borutta** yet another Pisan Romanesque church testifies to the prosperity of the Logu-doro in the Middle Ages; this one, San Pietro de Sorres, is perhaps the most beautiful of them all, isolated on a plateau overlooking the town with a fine view.

South of Borutta, on the plain around Torralba, is the **Sant' Antine** nuraghe, with Barumini one of the two largest and best preserved in Sardinia. It seems to have been an important religious site as well as a fortress. Inside the walls are a sacred well, two small towers and the great three-storey central tower. All over this plain are scattered other nuraghi; this site may possibly have served as a northern capital for the nuraghe-builders, situated square in the centre of the region most densely populated by them—the northwest corner of Sardinia from the River Tirso to the northern coast.

From Torralba a second road (route 131 bis) travels to Alghero past the artificial Lake Bidighinza and the villages of Thiesi and Ittiri. The latter has another 12th-century church, hidden behind a very peculiar modern façade; of the original work, a fine, tall campanile remains. On the 'Carlo Felice' south of Torralba are **Giave**, with a panoramic view from the ruins of its medieval castle, and **Bonorva** with the 'Tres Nuraghes' nearby and some *domus de janas*. Further south is a vast barren plateau, the Altopiano Campeda, which forms the southern boundary of the province. The circle of small villages west of Bonorva includes Semestene (with another 12th-century church) and Pozzomaggiore, known for its embroideries.

East of Bonorva is a picturesque region of hills and forests called the Goceano. Bono, a pretty town, is the main centre; to the north, near Bultei, is the thermal spa of San Saturnino. **Burgos**, south of Bono, was settled first by Spaniards, as its name implies. Its well-preserved castle was the scene of many a conflict in the days of the Giudicati.

East of Sassari

There are remains of several castles in Sardinia built by the noble Malaspina family; one of them is at Osilo in the mountains just east of Sassari, with a fine view over the northern coast and Corsica. Between Osilo and the River Coghinas are a number of villages: Nulvi is known for its devotion to the old customs. Just west of Martis there is a small petrified forest. Perfugas and Sedini have Aragonese Gothic churches: near the latter is a big *domus de janas* and many limestone caves, the largest of which is the Grotta della Conca Bulia.

To the south, in the centre of Sassari province, **Chilivani** is the rail junction where the track divides for Sassari and Olbia. The town's name, seeming to be typically exotic Sardinian, actually honours the Indian wife of Benjamin Pierce, the English engineer who built the railway. East of Chilivani the distinguished-looking town of **Ozieri** occupies a natural amphitheatre on a hillside. Its cathedral, rebuilt in the 19th century, contains works by the 'Master of Ozieri' along with some by the 'Master of Castelsardo', one of the two great anonymous Sardinian artists of the 11th century. The town has many fine small palaces with loggias, and there is a beautiful fountain in the Piazza Grixoni. This corner of Sardinia, best known for the breeding of horses (there are occasional races near Chilivani), has recently begun to take a very active interest in its ancient patrimony. Ozieri has a new Archaeology Museum with nuraghic finds from the many sites in the neighbourhood as well as Punic and Roman items. Another new museum is just to the southwest in the hamlet of Ittireddu; here the star exhibit is a famous ancient bronze work—a model of a nuraghic castle.

Some of these artefacts were found at the nuraghic castle at **Burghidu**, north of Ozieri just off the Sassari–Nuoro road, with a sacred well and remains of a town.

East of Ozieri rises Monte Acuto, a 'patch' of mountains like the Gennargentu, only smaller. Around it, towards Olbia, is one of the most sparsely populated and lonely regions of Sardinia, the bare mountains and dry valleys of southern Gallura. In all of it there are only a handful of villages: Budduso, a mountain resort; Monti, with a famous festival; and Oschiri. **Budduso** is known for the skill of its craftsmen in woodcarving. Another village nearby, **Pattada**, is equally famous for handmade knives. Three miles west of this village, near the big dam and lake on the Coghinas, is a site with ruins of a medieval church and castle, a Roman fort, and a nuraghe all very near each other.

To the north, on the opposite slopes of Monte Limbara (highest mountain in the province), is a greener and pleasanter side of Gallura, around **Tempio Pausania**. This is of Roman foundation, but like Sassari it became an important place when the coasts became unhealthy and unsafe in the early Middle Ages. Today it is a mountain resort, with a famous medicinal spring called Fonte Renaggiu south of the town, and the surrounding countryside produces, conveniently enough, both wine and cork. The use of grey granite in the buildings makes Tempio, like many towns in the Gallura, reminiscent of Corsica. Indeed, many Corsicans have migrated to this corner of the island over the centuries; their influence is felt in many of the region's villages, some of which are almost entirely Corsican.

Piazza Gallura is the centre; the **Cathedral** (15th century, rebuilt 19th century) is on the nearby Piazza San Pietro. An Oratorio, also on Piazza San Pietro, was built by the Aragonese, rebuilt in the 18th century, and incorporates some Roman remains—combining all into a pretty façade. West of Tempio is Bortigiada with many nuraghi and Aggius; to the east is Calangianus, centre of the cork industry and renowned for its boar-meat salami.

The Northern Coast

The northwestern corner of Sardinia is a narrow peninsula dotted with lagoons. Near the tip is **Stintino**, a fishing village that is in the process of becoming an important resort. Off Punta del Falcone lies the uninhabited islet of Piana, and beyond it the island of **Asinara**. Asinara is a big island, and looks very picturesque from across the strait, but you can't visit it; it suffers from the curse of so many Italian islands, being the home of a penal colony. Its natural inhabitants were evicted in the last century, and now make up the population of Stintino. (They catch tuna in the spring and summer, performing the *Mattanzas* as in San Pietro.) Asinara's claim to fame is that it's the only place in the world where albino donkeys are bred.

East of the peninsula is **Porto Torres**, which flourished under the Carthaginians and Romans as *Turris Libyssonis* and again in the Middle Ages as capital of the Giudicato of

Torres. The city's long decline began in the 14th century, and only recently has Porto Torres come back to life as a port (boats to Toulon, Genoa and Leghorn) and industrial centre.

The effects of the decline can still be seen in the old town, half-abandoned and decrepit; modern Porto Torres has gravitated back down to the port area, with its main street, Corso Vittorio Emanuele, connecting the old and new. In the old town is the largest medieval church in Sardinia, the Basilica di San Gavino. It is a simple and beautiful work, but somewhat idiosyncratic—there's no façade at all, but apses at both ends. There may have been an ancient temple on the site; the basilica incorporates 28 Roman columns in its interior.

West of the Corso, next to the railway station, excavations continue in the remains of old Turris. This is the romantically but deceptively named Palazzo di Re Barbaro (Palace of the Barbarian King—really a Roman governor named Barbarus), with ruins of various structures, a temple and baths. A new museum, the Antiquarium Turritano has recently been opened to show off the finds. Nearby, a Roman bridge still in use crosses the River Turritano. Where the Corso meets the waterfront is the Piazza Cristoforo Colombo with a Roman column marking the end of the road from Karalis (Cagliari). The old Roman road followed the course of the modern 'Carlo Felice'.

There are beaches near the town at Marinella and Platamona, a lido popular with the Sassarese. On the road to Sassari are many nuraghi and a Neolithic sanctuary at Monte Accodi with tombs, remains of temples, two menhirs and a great altar.

East of Porto Torres, near Sorso is the 11th-century church of San Michele di Plaiano. Further east, route 200 will take you to **Castelsardo**. Originally called *Castelgenovese*, this great fortress defended the coast of the Giudicato of Logudoro. The castle is on the height of a narrow promontory, with the village on the slopes around it; on a clear day, Corsica and much of northern Sardinia is visible from here. The Cathedral houses a wonderful painting, the *Madonna with the Angels* by an unknown artist called the Master of Castelsardo. Other examples of his work can be seen in the small picture collections around Sardinia (as in the Cagliari Museum). Castelsardo today is famous for its basketwork, made from palm branches.

The coast around Castelsardo has many unexploited beaches. South of the town is the 12th-century church of Nostra Signora di Tergu and on the side of the road east to Tempio is a peculiar rock formation, typical of the weird eroded forms on the northern coast, called the **Elephant Rock**. The early Sards chiselled two small *domus de janas* into it. **Valledoria** is an agricultural village near the mouth of the largest river of the north, the Coghinas. Just south of it is the thermal spa of **Casteldoria** with ruins of a medieval castle.

For lack of anything more original, the local tourist boosters have begun calling the northern coast of Sardinia the 'Costa Paradiso', an area stretching from Isola Rossa (the name of both an islet and a village on the coast near it) to Porto di Li Francesi. In between are a few beaches, but not many hotels. Most of the coast is dotted with villas managed by private associations, as on the Costa Smeralda.

More resorts adorn the northern tip of Sardinia, sharing in the current fame of the Costa Smeralda, not far to the south: among these Baja Sardinia, Palau and Porto Pozzo. **Palau** is the terminus of the narrow-gauge railway from Sassari, and the point of departure for the island of La Maddalena. The coast in this area, even more than the rest of Gallura, is marked by bizarre forms in granite eroded by the strong winds. One, near Palau, is unmistakably 'The Bear', and the rest, like the nearby Les Calanches on the western coast of Corsica, will put your imagination to the test.

Santa Teresa

The northernmost town in Sardinia, and a growing resort in its own right, is Santa Teresa di Gallura. In the Middle Ages this town was known as *Porto Longone*; after a long decline, it had to be refounded in 1808 by King Victor Emanuele, who resettled it with Piedmontese and named it after his wife Teresa. The port, with connections to Corsica and La Maddalena, is an inlet 0.8 km east of the town centre; this was the site of the medieval town. There is an excellent beach at Rena Bianca, guarded by a Spanish watchtower, and impressive views of Corsica from the heights at Punto Falcone and Capo Testa. The latter has been a quarry since ancient times; you can still see some Roman columns lying about, and stone from here was used in the famous medieval baptistry in Pisa.

LA MADDALENA AND CAPRERA

Off the coast between Santa Teresa and the Costa Smeralda, a small archipelago straggles north towards the southern tip of Corsica. Two of the islands are part of Corsica, though all the largest ones are Italian. La Maddalena is the only inhabited island, joined to nearby Caprera by a causeway. Of the others—and there are about 60 of them—the vast majority are tiny chunks that serve only to decorate the coastline. Razzoli, Spagi, Budelli, Santa Maria and Santo Stefano are each about 2.6 square km in size, but offer nothing to see (Santo Stefano and Budelli have beaches, and Santo Stefano a campsite). During the season excursions run from La Maddalena around the archipelago.

The islands' only brushes with history came in the 19th century. During the Napoleonic Wars, Nelson and his fleet spent a few months cruising the area while waiting for the French to come out and be sunk at Trafalgar. The King of Sardinia's official neutrality prevented Nelson from ever actually landing, but the admiral sent regular reports to London explaining what a lovely base Sardinia would make and how he thought it could be had, at the time, for a song. London was not impressed, and chose Malta instead. Caprera, as every Italian schoolboy knows, is the burial place of Garibaldi, who spent the later years of his life there.

GETTING AROUND

Four different companies handle the Palau–La Maddalena ferry service, and between them there are several runs a day. Some call at Santa Teresa. For another fascinating excursion, consider a quick trip to Corsica. The Tirrenia Line (Via Porto, in Santa Teresa; tel (0789) 754 156) runs a regular ferry service to Bonifacio, surely one of the most unusual and distinctive cities in the Mediterranean, with its medieval granite houses perched on the edge of lofty cliffs over the sea.

La Maddalena

La Maddalena, the town, is a prosperous and charming place. Some of that prosperity comes from tourism, but the Americans you'll see everywhere in town aren't tourists at all; they are sailors from the huge NATO base on the island. (American servicemen never wear their uniforms while on leave, but you'll recognize them by the bulky portable radios they carry.) La Maddalena is renowned as the softest station in the Mediterranean, and most of them never want to leave.

There are two small harbours, with the ferry dock in between. That on the left is the Cala Gavetta, where excursions to the other islands depart, also the buses for Caprera and the rest of La Maddalena. Two blocks north of the port is the Piazza Garibaldi, from which runs the Via Garibaldi, the main shopping street. La Maddalena's church of Santa Maria still has a pair of silver candlesticks, a gift from Nelson.

From this town a 'Via Panoramica' circumnavigates the island's coast. Beaches are everywhere, notably at Spalmatore and Cala Maiore on the northern side. West of town the road passes over the long causeway and onto Caprera, most of which is beautifully planted with pines. The road leads directly to Garibaldi's house, the Casa Bianca, now a national museum. The 'hero of two worlds' arrived here after his sojourn in America, and the house is built in South American style. Living in this rustic idyll, pottering around the house and garden, Garibaldi spent the last 33 years of his life—that is, when he wasn't campaigning through Sicily and the peninsula and scaring the daylights out of Italy's ruling classes. His tomb, the pine tree he planted for his daughter Clelia, his bed (in a big glass case), and the other memorabilia are explained on the guided tour.

WHERE TO STAY   (tel prefix 079)
At Castelsardo there are hotels on the shore in town, such as the ***Riviera, Lungomare Angiona 1 (tel 470 143; L50 000), but the beaches are about 3 km away at Cala Ostiva and Lu Bagnu; at the latter is the ***Costa Doria, Corso Italia 73 (tel 474 043; L40–50 000 with bath) and **Ampurias, via Imperia 1 (tel 474 008; L38 000 with bath).

(tel prefix 0789)
Similarly, at La Maddalena you'll have a choice between places in town or on the beaches, like the quiet ***Cala Lunga, at Porto Massimo (tel 737 389; L80–140 000) with private beach and pool, or the very reasonable but small (7 rooms, all with bath) locanda *Da Raffaele, at La Ricciolina (tel 738 759; L30–35 000). Santa Teresa and its environs also have a wide range, among them the ***Bellavista (which, of course, has a view), Via Sonnino (tel 754 162; L35–45 000 with bath), and many at Capo Testa: the ***Large Hotel Mirage, which describes itself adequately (tel. 754 207; L65–90 000) or the small 7-roomed **Bocche di Bonifacio (tel 754 202; L33–40 000 with bath), with a restaurant.

EATING OUT
In Castelsardo, in Piazza Bastione (tel (079) 470 428), near the castello is La Guardiola with a terrace and a kitchen devoted to seafood marvels, notably shellfish antipasti, *risotto alla marinara* and the house special *rigatoni alla Benito* (with a variety of cheeses and caviar), presumably named after the owner and not Mussolini (L30–35 000). Down by the sea fish is also on the menu at Riviera da Fofo, Lungomare Angrone 1 (tel (079) 470

143), with spaghetti in a lobster sauce, fish soup and a mixed platter from the oven (L30 000). On the Costa Paradiso the culinary treats are to be had in the hotels and seafood is the main staple, naturally—try the **Corallo**, Via Lungomare 36 (tel (079) 694 055; L25 000). There's more choice in Santa Teresa Gallura, with the **Vittoria Riva**, Via del Porto (tel (0789) 754 392), but meat lovers will be disappointed. Among the house specialities are *spaghetti alle aragostine* and *zuppa di cozze* (L25–30 000). On Via Nazionale 23 **Canne al Vento** has a range of seafood delights and, in season, roast lamb and pork (tel (0789) 754 219; L25–35 000).

Eastern Sardinia

Its coast is the Sardinian playground, the greatest concentration of resorts on the island. Olbia and Golfo Aranci are the major centres, just south of the tepid Babylon of the Costa Smeralda. Though full of beaches, and probably the most familiar corner of Sardinia among foreigners, paradoxically this is the last place on the island to consider for a vacation. The prices are the highest, the beaches and scenery nothing special compared to the rest of the island, and most of Sardinia's genuine attractions are far away.

The Costa Smeralda

Twenty years ago, were you to ask the average citizen about Sardinia, you would get a blank stare in reply. Today, the chances are that he would say 'Ah yes, the Costa Smeralda!' In the early sixties, when this strip of coastline between Arzachena and Golfo Aranci was one of the emptiest corners of the island, the Aga Khan, Muslim nabob and international playboy, and some friends started buying up the land.

What they had in mind was a little principality devoted entirely to luxury vacations, and it has become just that, one of the great successes of the modern tourist industry. In a way, the Costa Smeralda is the suburban dream applied to tourism. The consortium begun by the founders exercises strict planning controls and regulations over architecture and land use; the effect is tidy, tasteful, and all of a piece. Unfortunately, however, it has almost nothing to do with Sardinia. The hotels and villas, in a phony 'traditional' style, are the epitome of contemporary tourist architecture, closer in spirit to Disneyland than to Gallura.

A frequent complaint from the Sards is that all the land and hotels are owned by foreigners; very little, if any, of the money that tourists bring in ever stays in Sardinia. Today, while prices continue sky-high—absolutely the highest in all Italy, in fact—for the Costa the crest of the wave seems to have passed. The coastline itself is pleasant, but there is little to see. The only centre (everything is spread out in suburban style) is Porto Cervo whose recently built Stella Maris church has a painting by El Greco, the *Mater Dolorosa*.

Arzachena

Arzachena the old town inland from the Costa Smeralda, has been changed as much as Olbia by the tourist tide. In the vicinity are some unique nuraghic sites. An unusual necropolis at Li Muri, just to the south where the road turns east for Luogosarto, consists of a long, paved trench-like grave, closed at one end by a row of enormous dolmens. At Li Macciunitta there's a circle of standing stones with a tomb at its centre, and other curiosities at the sites of Malchettu, Caddi Vecchiu and Li Lolghi, all little-known and recently excavated.

Olbia

Olbia is an ancient city; it was the first Carthaginian settlement on the east coast and, with its harbour, the best on the island, *Olvia* knew prosperity through the periods of Punic and Roman rule. Like Porto Torres, it declined greatly after Rome's fall. Until 1939, when Mussolini restored the old name in the 'Imperial Revival', Olbia was known as *Terranova Pausania*. Now, thanks to DDT and tourism, Olbia is prosperous again, an unpleasant and very un-Sardinian town of overpriced restaurants and overdressed youths. The only sights are the plain 11th-century church of San Simplicio, ruins of the Roman baths and a necropolis.

The coast around the Gulf of Olbia is especially scenic, and has many big resorts. Lido del Sole to the south and Lido Pittilungu to the north are the most popular. Everywhere the view is dominated by the fantastic bulk of the Isola Tavolara, one of the uninhabited islands in the bay. North of Olbia, off route 125, is a nuraghic sanctuary with a view at Cabu Abbas, and on a long promontory at Capo Figari, the fishing village of Golfo Aranci—the name comes from *granchi* (crabs), not *aranci* (oranges)—which is becoming a popular resort.

WHERE TO STAY   (tel prefix 0789)
On the Costa Smeralda, the best (and most expensive) is the *****Pitrizza, Loc. Liscia di Vacca (tel 91 500) with cottages in a secluded forest setting, but prepare yourself for its rates, they are in the L750–1 000 000 range. The *****Cala di Volpe (tel 96 083) and*****Romazzino, Loc. Porto Cervo (tel 96 020) are similarly exclusive and exhorbitant (but you don't get silk sheets, however de-luxe are the facilities and prices), but you can get by cheaper at the apartment-hotel complex ***Residenza Capriccioli, Loc. Capriccioli (tel 96 016) where the rates hover around L1 400 000 for the week, which is the minimum you can stay. In the same place, and with the same name (don't confuse them, it could be a very expensive mistake) is a hotel for shallower pockets, the ***Capriccioli (tel 96 004; L75–100 000). Resorts at Baja Sardinia and Porto Rotondo take advantage of their proximity to the Costa Smeralda to charge more than they ought; one that doesn't on the Baja Sardinia is the ***Ringo, Loc. Cala Bitta (tel 99 024), with its own pool and rooms at L70–90 000, and you'll find nothing cheaper in this area.

Comfortable and inexpensive in Olbia is the **Centrale, Corso Umberto 85 (tel 23 017; L55 000 with bath, and the *Mastino, Via A. Vespucci 5 (tel 21 320; L45 000). There are, of course, more luxurious places to stay, but if you pay their prices you might just as well move up to Porto Rotondo, the poor man's Costa Smeralda and check into, for example, the ***Nuraghe, Loc. Punta Nuraghe (tel 34 436) and pay L85–130 000.

EATING OUT
On the Costa Smeralda the best places to eat are the hotels, which is to be expected considering their rates. Should you fancy dropping in and hobnobbing you will, of

course, pay for the privilege, so expect to drop anything from L70 000 up, up, up. One of the famous names in Baia Sardinia is the originally titled **Casablanca** (tel 99 006) Belonging to the Club Hotel, it claims to serve the best in *nouvelle cuisine méditerranée*, particularly delicately herbed and spiced fish. Its name demands a piano bar, which of course it has (at least L70 000). On the road to Porto Cervo **Le Tre Botti** (tel 99 150) is a hotel–restaurant, where you can choose your own lobster, or settle for spaghetti in lobster sauce *ravioli di ricotta*, straightforward fish and meat dishes, or opt for a pizza (L35–50 000, more for lobster).

After a round of golf at the **Del Pevero Golf Club** (tel 96 210) (much favoured by the Aga Khan and considered one of the best three in the world), you might like to try their buffet lunch served at the poolside (L30–35 000). This elegant restaurant is extremely popular; the sumptuous dinner of seafood will cost at least L60 000 (closed Nov–Apr). Two more modest establishments, serving good Sardinian fare, are **Il Pulcino**, Loc. Piccolo Pevero (tel 92 529), and **La Regata**, Marina di Porto Cervo (tel 91 312), where you can eat for less than L30 000. In Porto Rotondo, **La Ghinghetta** has immaculate service, crystal glassware and superb cuisine, with many surprises (Via Cavour 26, tel 508 143; L45 000). The best-known eating place in Olbia is **Dell'Hotel Gallura**, Corso Umberto 145 (tel 24 648); if you want to try something special you won't do better than the large seafood mix, a mouth-watering mixture of fish, shrimp and lobster. The superb soups and pasta (especially spaghetti with crab sauce) make up a faultless menu (L45 000, closed Fri & Christmas).

The Nuorese Coast

The northern limits of Nuoro province border on the Costa Smeralda. Its coast is in many ways just as attractive, but less developed, and it is hardly surprising that one can discern a certain bemusement from the locals who see the tourist hordes in the Costa Smeralda paying double or more for everything, while Italians in the know have just as good a time at growing resorts like San Teodoro and nearby Budoni. An extraordinary number of beautiful beaches stretch for miles down the coast. One of the loveliest spots is the peninsula of **Monte Pedrosu**, where without doubt the most attractive of beaches is to be found at **Capo Coda Cavallo**. The transparent water and beautiful views across to the islands of **Tavolara** and **Molara** leave an unforgettable impression. Just to the south of Capo Cavallo the enormous, spectacular beach of **Brandinchi** stretches around the gulf, with sand as fine as flour.

It is not, however, always easy to find your way to the sea by car—signposting is erratic and some of the tracks which leave the N125, the main road from Olbia down to Cagliari, are rather hostile to anything that's not a jeep. Fifty km south of here at Posada, on the mouth of the river of the same name, is the ruined medieval **Castello della Fava**. **Siniscola** is an old agricultural town, famous for its women's costumes, but it is becoming the centre of a big vacation area, with a broad sandy beach at **La Caletta** and another by the old fishing village of **Santa Lucia**. Further to the south is a headland, **Capo Comino**, with the Nuraghe Artora, and further south another resort, **Cala Liberotto**, with another nuraghe in the hills above it.

Further south on the N125 **Orosei**, on the mouth of the river Cedrino, is a Roman foundation, *Fanum Carisii*, that was important in the Middle Ages; it has a ruined castle. Of interest is the church of **San Giacomo**, with its domes, buttresses and impressive bell tower. This is in the middle of another agricultural reclamation area, on a narrow plain under the mountains. The 3-km-long beach at **Marina di Orosei** has alluvial dunes formed by the outlet of the Cedrino river. The water couldn't be cleaner and the beach, framed by pines, is seldom crowded. To the south, the N125 curves inland to **Dorgali**, an important handicraft centre that produces leather, ceramics, rugs and jewellery. In the neighbourhood there are many nuraghi, some of the best-preserved in Sardinia, and the nuraghic village of **Serra Orrio**, typical of its kind, the buildings designed in circular fashion with low walls. On the edge of the village are the remains of two rare temples. At **Cala Gonone** is another growing resort in one of the prettiest places in Sardinia, with a view across the Gulf of Orosei. From here, excursions by sea are available to the **Grotta del Bue Marino**, the largest of the many caves on this part of the coast. The 'Bue Marino' (sea-ox) is the Mediterranean monk seal; this cave is one of the last hiding places of these large animals, though you would be lucky to see one. Just inland from Dorgali the River Cedrino is dammed to create a large lake.

A long empty stretch of highway runs south of Dorgali, under the peaks of the **Sopramonte**. The coast is mountainous and inaccessible as far as **Arbatax** on Capo Bellavista, the centre of a resort area that stretches from **Santa Maria Navarrese** to **Lido Orri**. The dramatic coastline includes the red rocks of **Cala Morescu** and the rock of **Ogliastro** in the sea just off Santa Maria. **Tortoli** is an agricultural centre; this reclaimed area is largely devoted to subtropical fruits: oranges, persimmons and even bananas grow here.

Further south, nuraghi pop up like toadstools in the area around **Barisardo**, along with some *domus de janas* on the hillsides. There is a beach by a medieval watchtower on the coast at **Torre di Bari**, with fine sand and shady woods. South of here the landscape once again becomes rather empty, as the road follows a valley between two mountains. There are embryonic resorts, hard to reach, at **Sa Foxi Marina** and **Melisenda** on the coast.

WHERE TO STAY   (tel prefix 0784)
Along the east coast, beach hotels are almost all recent additions, modern and up-to-date if somewhat simple. In many of the resorts, as at San Teodoro, they are spread out all along the coast—peaceful, but not convenient unless you have a car. Of these, the most luxurious is ******Due Lune**, Loc. Punta Aldia (tel 864 075) with its own beach, pool, tennis courts and seclusion (L180–250 000). Lower down the price scale is ****La Palma**, Via del Tirreno (tel 865 962; L45 000 with bath) also on the beach and with a restaurant. On the shore near Budoni is *****Agrustos**, Fraz. Agrustos (tel 846 005) also with pool and garden, and reasonably priced at L55–70 000 with bath. About 20 km south of Siniscola off the N125 is Cala Liberotto, where the *****Cala Ginepro**, Loc. Cala Ginepro (tel 91 047) has rooms for L65 000. Cala Gonone, on the shore near Dorgali, has a large selection: *****Nettuno**, Via Vasco de Gama (tel 93 310; L62 000) and ****La Favorita**, Via Lungomare (tel 93 169; L50 000 with bath).

In Arbatax (tel prefix 0782) the *****Villagio Saraceno**, Loc. San Gemiliano (tel 667318) is sports-orientated, with everything from water-skiing to *bocce* (L80 000), and the *Supersonic, Loc. Porto Frailis (tel 623 512) has super low rates—L35 000 with bath.

EATING OUT
At irregular intervals down the coast there are places to eat on the N125, and wherever you stop, you can't really go wrong. In Cala Gonone **Su Recreu** (tel (0784) 93 053) prepares a menu with a little difference—shrimp salad with sea snails, shellfish soup and shellfish lasagna, *polenta con sepia* (a rather heavy cornmeal pasta with inkfish, or a type of squid) and rich suckling pig (L30 000). Also in Cala Gonone, in Piazza Madonna del Mare is **Tre Ruote** (tel (0784) 93 201) with a terrace; it preserves a happy medium, mixing food from the sea and the mountains: shellfish risotto, lobster salad and crayfish (jumbo shrimp) in white wine, contrasted to the roast **porchetto**, lamb and kid, with local Dorgali wine (L25–30 000). Don't forget that any supermarket or trattoria will make up sandwiches, rolls or *pannini* for you for a measly L2500 to help you on your way.

Nuoro and the Gennargentu

The triangular-shaped province of Nuoro runs from the east to the west coast of Sardinia, and is bordered to the north and south by the other provinces of Sassari, Oristano and Cagliari. The rocky mountainous roof of the island, the Gennargentu, a wild land of shepherds and bandits, retains many of Sardinia's ancient customs and folk-life. Grazia Deledda, the island's best-known novelist, wrote that Nuoro is the real heart of Sardinia; only because of the harshness of the terrain has it managed to retain its originality. The climate is Mediterranean, but in the mountains the winters can be very chilly with heavy snowfalls. In Roman times the story was much the same. For this, and for being unable to extend their control here, the Romans dubbed this part of the island *Barbaria*. The name lives on as Barbagia for the areas below the Gennargentu. A striking and unique flora and fauna, dotted with crystal-clear lakes and long sandy beaches, makes this a visitor's paradise, where the economy is based mainly on sheep rearing, handicrafts, a few minor industries and tourism. Despite the rocky landscape, an efficient network of major and minor roads allows accessibility to almost every corner.

The numerous and remote villages, set among the extraordinary shapes of the mountains, are an instant reminder of a troubled history and consequential need for defence. Almost as if not wanting to be discovered or seen, a new village will suddenly appear in front of you, often with a spectacular backdrop of unfriendly peaks, thick green forest and the occasional gushing waterfall. The narrow-gauge railway, which runs north from Cagliari through Mandas, where it branches off for Belvi and terminates at Sorgono is an unusual and memorable, if slow, way of witnessing these sights.

GETTING AROUND
A spur of the main railway line of Sardinia connects Nuoro city with Bosa on the west coast; it crosses the main line at Macomer. Bus connections may be difficult, not from any deficiency in the service, but simply because the system is so complex, connecting the innumerable villages with the capital and with each other. Nuoro's bus station is on the Piazza Vittorio Emanuele. It's a madhouse; consult the enormous schedule board and

then start asking everyone for further information. Try to reach a consensus, but meanwhile keep an eye on the buses.

If you're driving, expect some treacherous but wildly scenic mountain roads—particularly in the southern Barbagia. Remember that snow and ice can be a problem any time during the winter or spring. The villages are close together though, and there should be little problem with services.

TOURIST INFORMATION
In Nuoro the EPT is in Piazza Italia 19 (tel (0784) 30 083 or 32 307). The Pro Loco organizations may be helpful in Oliena (Piazza Palach), and Belvi (Viale Kennedy 26), but don't count on finding anyone about.

Nuoro

When the Barbagia became a province of Italy, it didn't have a city to use as a provincial capital, so it was necessary to invent one. Nuoro, or Nugoro, is really an overgrown village. In existence only since the Middle Ages, it began to achieve some importance in the 18th century when it became a bishopric. In 1926 Nuoro became the capital of the province, and it has grown steadily since. Despite its new urban development, the town still has an attractive old quarter, and Nuoro itself is situated beautifully at the foot of Monte Ortobene. A 16-km round trip to this mountain will reward you with a spectacular panorama over this city of 30,000 inhabitants, whose reputation for hospitality is well known throughout Sardinia. Though its citizens are among the most ardent students and practitioners of the old Sard ways and arts, the town also has a reputation in the mountain villages as a place where people stamp papers for a living. Nuoro, as you will soon learn if you visit there, gave Italy two of its greatest writers of this century, Grazia Deledda, who won the Nobel Prize for literature in 1926 and whose novels are evocations of Sardinian life, and the poet Sebastiano Satta.

WHAT TO SEE
There isn't much; the old town is at the eastern end, on a height with occasional wonderful views over the countryside below. The **Cathedral** on the Piazza Santa Maria della Neve, dates from the 19th century. The quarter of San Pietro, with its winding old streets, houses a museum at the birthplace of Grazia Deledda, Via Chironi 28. The main streets, Via Lamarmora and Corso Garibaldi, are thronged with shoppers, many of them tourists in search of terracotta, lace, ceramics and wood-carvings. The Corso Garibaldi runs past the newly opened **Sardinian Handicraft Exhibition** and terminates in the Piazza Vittorio Emanuele, a pretty park where it seems to be the hour of the *passeggiata* all day.

One of Nuoro's two museums, the **Museo Regionale del Costume** (open 9–1 and 3.30–7, closed Mon), is in a modern building recreating the traditional architecture, just south of the town on the Viale San Francesco; the building also houses an institute dedicated to Sard folklore. In the museum's collection are costumes of the various villages with explanatory notes, jewellery, handicrafts and photographs. At Via Leonardo da Vinci 5 is the often overlooked Museo Civico Speleo (open 8.30–12.30, holidays 9.30–1, closed Mon). Though small, it is one of the best organized and most informative museums on the island. Besides exhibits of objects from the local nuraghi and from Punic and Roman sites, it is the best introduction to the many caves around Nuoro and on the coast.

East of Nuoro, **Monte Ortobene** is capped with a giant statue of Christ the Redeemer. The mountain, with its fine views, has become a small summer resort with two hotels. Nearby is the church of Nostra Signora della Solitudine where Grazia Deledda is buried.

North of Nuoro

There is a nuraghic village with a sacred well, just north of Nuoro at **Noddule**. This little village is well known throughout Sardinia and beyond for its brightly coloured carpets in traditional design. The geometric patterns are known as flames and are produced on vertical looms. There is a carpet weavers' cooperative which also trains young people in the craft. *Bitti* is a large village, based on a dairy economy. There's an interesting church, the **Chiesa del Miracolo**. If you are here between 1 and 10 May, **Lula**, a small farming village nearby, is of particular interest for its San Francesco celebrations, when there's a huge feast, flowing wine and dancing in traditional costume. The valley of the River Posada, not traversed by any road, and Monte Albo to the south, really a chain of rugged peaks, are haunts of shepherds, wild boar and *muflone*.

South of Nuoro

This is the Barbagia, a land of intricate geography, with hills, mountains and valleys thrown down on the map seemingly at random. At its centre is **Gennargentu** ('silver gate')—a collection of the highest peaks on the island. Mountain villages surround it on three sides: in the Barbagia Ollolai to the north, the Barbagia Mandrolisai to the west, the Barbagia di Belvi to the southwest, and Barbagia Seulo to the south.

Just a few miles south of Nuoro is **Oliena**, one of the most typical of Nuorese villages, with a splendid tradition of folk craftsmanship, especially in coral and gold, but producing very fine embroidery and traditional costumes too. The village is also famous for its wine and cheese, and local attractions include potholing in its limestone caves or birdwatching, as this is the home of many vultures and eagles. The village is surrounded by vineyards and olive groves, and of historical interest is the 15th-century church of Santa Maria. Outside the town are two sanctuaries, those of **Nostra Signora di Monserrato** and **San Giovanni**, near the latter is a natural spring with a waterfall at **Su Gologone**.

South of Oliena stretch the scattered peaks of the **Sopramonte** of which the tallest is Punta Corrasi (1449 m). This is one of the most mysterious parts of the island, a stretch of mountains and valleys with hardly any roads and hundreds of caves, great and small, the perfect hideout for bandits. Deep inside it a remarkable nuraghic village has recently been discovered at **Tiscali**, hidden inside a deep, round grotto, partially open to the sky and with a huge crag sticking up in the centre like a menhir. The site is almost inaccessible—the ancient Sards built it that way, in the last years of their freedom when they were constantly faced with Roman attacks—but if you really want to see it the Pro Loco in Oliena can provide directions.

Orgosolo, like Oliena, is a shepherd village, renowned as the centre of Sardinia's sheep-rustling activity, as it has been for many centuries. It's very much in the public eye in Sardinia at present for a longstanding family feud which has cost many untimely deaths—the busiest man in town is the one who posts the death notices, and this town certainly seems to have more than its fair share of them on display. The walls of the streets are also adorned with some very impressive murals depicting various scenes of rural life and many strong political allegories; the town is an ideal base for picnics and excursions to the nearby Sopramonte and neighbouring grottoes, gorges and oak forests. **Mamoiada**, in a lovely wooded setting, is famous as the home of the *Mamuthones* (see Festivals), stars of the pagan pre-Lenten festival. The highest town in Sardinia is **Fonni**, with its distinctive costume. Fonni lies on the slopes of Monte Spada (1582 m) and has Sardinia's only ski-resort. Route 389 from here passes west of Gennargentu, past the sources of the Flumendosa (one of which is a big artificial lake), and on over a stretch of 30 miles to Lanusei without passing a single village; it is a very scenic road.

North of Fonni, some moderately difficult driving can take you around another artificial lake, Lago Gusanno; Gavoi, a mountain resort; Ollolai, the big shepherd town that gives the region its name; and Orani, a mining town near which is the mountain sanctuary of Nostra Signora di Gonari. Near Oruferi are some *domus de janas*. **Ottana**—it's hard not to get confused by the fifteen villages in this region that begin with O—is the site of a modest effort to industrialize the Barbagia. Nevertheless, it is still a traditional village, with ancient pagan rites at the Carnival which are similar to those of Mamoiada, though not as well known. The church of San Nicola is a beautiful 12th-century work—Pisan architecture at its best, with all the familiar motifs of false arches, diamonds and stripes of different coloured stone.

South of Fonni, the Mandrolisai region contains many forests of holm-oak, ilex and walnut. The centre of the region is **Sorgono**, a mountain resort and a very pretty one. Sorgono is the terminus of the secondary railway from Cagliari. Nearby at **San Mauro** is a fine 16th-century church with a big rose window. **Aritzo**, on the western slopes of the Gennargentu, has become one of the most popular centres for mountain vacations. Another place of great natural beauty, if you are willing to take the trouble to get there, is **Desulo**, almost in the centre of Gennargentu, and close to the island's two highest mountains, Punta la Marmora (1817 m) and Brancu Spina (1812 m).

South of Sorgono, in a heavily forested area, **Meana Sardo** has a 16th-century church and many nearby nuraghi. **Laconi** proudly proclaims itself the home of the utterly obscure St Ignatius of Laconi (18th century); here you'll find the ruins of the Aymerich Castle (11th–17th centuries), a fortress of the Giudicati of Arborea. **Isili** is a famous centre for handicrafts. South of here, on the borders of Cagliari Province, are the two striking plateaux, the Giara di Gesturi with its wild horses (see *North of Cagliari*) and the Giara di Serri. Near Serri are several nuraghi including the well-preserved Is Paras with the remains of a village around it.

The upper valley of the Flumendosa lies to the west, with two of Sardinia's largest artificial lakes, Lago di Flumendosa and Lago Mulargia. North of these, route 189 passes the southern borders of the Gennargentu through a number of tiny villages to **Lanusei**, a mountain resort very near the beach resorts at Arbatax on the coast. Lanusei is the largest town of a small region called the Ogliastro; to the south, near the towns of Ulassai and Ierzu, are odd limestone formations called *toneri* and a large number of limestone caves, most of which have yet to be explored. The land south of Ierzu is an almost barren plateau, a perfect site for the Italian rocket-launching station near Perdasdefogu. South of Escalaplano, near the border of Cagliari Province, is a sacred well of the nuraghic Sards called Fontana Coperta.

WHERE TO STAY   (tel prefix 0784)
Nuoro city's hotels range from four stars to one; the ****Grazia Deledda, near Piazza Sardegna at Via Lamarmora 175 (tel 31 257), is very reasonably priced at L75 000. Also near the centre are ***Grillo, Via Mons. Melas (tel 38 678; L60 000) and **Da Giovanni, Via IV Novembre (tel 30 562; L30 000 without bath). High above the city on Monte Ortobene is the ***Fratelli Sacchi, Loc. M. Ortobene (tel 31 200; L42 000 with bath).

In the mountains, several towns and villages are now making a living by entertaining tourists. Fonni, Aritzo, Oliena, and Gavoi are perhaps best equipped. The ****Sporting Club, 5 km from Fonni on Monte Spada (tel 57 285), keeps its visitors busy with skiing and Land Rover excursions into the wilds, and will be reopen with a new look and new prices for 1989, but count on around L90–120 000 for a room. While at Oliena, the ***Su Gologone, 8 km from Oliena (tel 287 512; L60 000), has a fine restaurant and riding tours (lessons also offered). More modest accommodation is available in most of the larger villages, such as the pleasant **Moderno in Aritzo, 6 Via Kennedy (tel 629229; L50 000). Far from being the forbidding mountain wilderness it often seems to outsiders, the Barbagia can be explored quite comfortably. Just don't expect to find a room without advance notice during any of the village festivals.

EATING OUT
As Nuoro is the city of Grazia Deledda, it is only to be expected that a restaurant take the name of one of her novels, which is the case with Canne al Vento, Viale Repubblica 66 (tel 35 641; closed Sun, except in summer). The speciality here is the pasta, canne al vento, with a sauce concocted from local sausages, cream, tomatoes and pecorino cheese; there's also the usual seafood dishes, including lobster (L20–30 000, much, much more if you opt for a full lobster dinner). If you are peckish after a shopping expedition or museum visit, try Del Grillo Via Mons. Melas 14 (tel 32 005) for lunch. Above all savour the home-cured prosciutto and sausages, which like the owner hail from Arzana, and if you're tiring of seafood, try the fresh water variety, such as trout or eel, with good local wine (L20–25 000).

In a traditional region like this, it isn't surprising that most of the restaurants are in hotels, like the Fratelli Sacchi in Nuoro, mentioned above, where if you are in the mood for some barbaric pasta (alla Barbaricina) the Sacchi brothers will be happy to oblige (but forks, not fingers, please) followed by a mixed meat plate of pork, lamb and veal or some fish delicacies such as lobster (L25–30 000, without the lobster, naturally; closed Mon from Oct–May).

At the Su Gologone outside Oliena (tel 287 512), meat is on the menu in a big way; pork and lamb done over the open fire, and some tasty antipasti with pecorino cheese and prosciutto ham (L25 000). Ai Monte del Gennargentu in Orgosolo is now run as a cooperative by an enthusiastic group of youngsters, the previous owner having decided to emigrate to the Costa Smeralda where he has introduced his Barbarian cooking to the civilized international jet set. The new management has maintained the high standard of cooking, and particularly good are the bean soup, ravioli and mixed grill of pork, lamb and kid. The house wine they make themselves—a *Cannonau* red and **Vermentino** white (tel 402 374; L20–30 000). These, and most of the rest throughout the province of course specialize in Sard cuisine. In fact, you should probably avoid anything which is not Sard; you can find sorry pizzas towards the coast, and very peculiar hamburgers in Nuoro.

ARCHITECTURAL, ARTISTIC, GEOGRAPHICAL AND HISTORICAL TERMS

Acropolis: the highest point of an ancient city, usually site of its most sacred temples

Agora: ancient Greek marketplace, the central square of a city

Ambones: twin pulpits in some early churches (singular: *ambo*), often elaborately decorated

Antefix: decorative protrusion on the corner of the roof of a Greek or Roman temple

Architrave: lower part of a temple's entablature

Atrium: entrance court of a Roman house or early church

Badia: *Abbazia*, an abbey or abbey church

Baldacchino: baldachin, a columned stone canopy above the altar of a church

Basilica: a rectangular building, usually divided into three aisles by rows of columns. In Rome this was the common form for lawcourts and other public buildings, and Roman Christians adapted it for their early churches.

Campanile: a bell-tower

Camposanto: a cemetery

Cardo: or *cardus*, the traverse street of a Roman *castrum*-shaped city

Caryatid: supporting pillar or column carved into a standing female form

Castrum: a Roman military camp, always neatly rectangular, with straight streets and gates at the cardinal points. Later the Romans founded or refounded cities in this form, hundreds of which survive today

Capital: top of a column

Cavalcata: cavalcade

Cavea: the semicircle of seats in a classic theatre

Cala: a small cove or inlet

Cella: the enclosed sanctuary of a Greek or Roman temple

Certosa: Carthusian Charterhouse

Chthonic: of the underworld, of gods of fertility and death

Comune: commune, or commonwealth, referring to the governments of free cities in the Middle Ages. Today it denotes any local government, from the Comune di Palermo down to the smallest village

Conca: a wide valley, or basin

Confraternity: a religious lay brotherhood, often serving as a neighbourhood—mutual aid and burial society, or following some specific charitable work. In the South, confraternities are in charge of the various Holy Week processions

Corinthian Order: the latest and most elaborate of the three traditional Greek orders, with fluted columns and acanthus leaf capitals

Cupola: a dome

Cyclopean walls: fortifications built of enormous, irregularly polygonal blocks

Dammuso: typical domed house of Pantelleria

Decumanus: street of a Roman *castrum*-shaped city parallel to the longer axis, the central main avenue called the Decumanus Major

Domus di janas: Sardinian fairy houses, ancient rock-cut tombs of the Shardana

Doric Order: characterized by unfluted columns, fairly simple round capitals

Duomo: cathedral

Entablature: the architrave, frieze, and cornice of a Classical building

Ephebos: Greek youth undergoing training

Exedra: semicircular recess

Ex-voto: figurine, painting, or silver pendant given in expressing gratitude to a god or saint

Faraglione: a large rock or boulder in the sea

Faro: lighthouse

Forum: the central square of a Roman town, with its most important temples and buildings. The word means 'outside', as the original Roman forum was outside the first city walls.

Fossa: volcanic crater

Frigidarium: the cooling room in a Roman bath

Fresco: wall painting, the most important Italian medium of art since the Etruscans. It isn't easy: first the artist etches a *sinopia*, or outline on the wall. This is covered with plaster, but only a little at a time, as the paint must be on the plaster before it dries.

Fumarola: spurting outlet of volcanic steam

Giudicato: political division of Sardinia, governed by a popular-elected assembly

Ghibellines: one of the two great medieval parties, the supporters of the Holy Roman Emperor

Grotesques: carved or painted faces used in Etruscan and later Roman decoration; Raphael and other artists rediscovered them in the 'grotto' of Nero's Golden House in Rome.

Guelphs: the opposition party to the Ghibellines, supporters of the Pope

Hypogeum: underground burial chamber, usually of pre-Christian religions

Ionic Order: known for its elegant fluted columns and the distinctive curl of its capitals

Intarsia: work in inlaid wood or marble

Kore: a young girl

Kouros: a boy, or Archaic Greek male figure

Krater: conical, round based mixing bowl

Kylix: a wide shallow vase with two handles

Latomia: a tufa quarry, especially in Syracuse

Loggia: a covered gallery or balcony before a building

Lozenge: the diamond shape—along with stripes, one of the trademarks of Pisan architecture

Lunette: semicircular area over a door, in vault or ceiling, often decorated

Macchia: maquis, typical Mediterranean scrubland

Megaron: ancient Greek sanctuary

Metope: panel on the frieze of a temple

Misteri: floats or tableaux in Holy Week processions

Narthex: the enclosed porch of a church

Naumachia: a mock sea battle performed in a flooded amphitheatre

Nuraghe: prehistoric Sardinian castle-like structure

Nymphaeum: a temple of the Nymphs, usually near a spring; later a kind of summer gazebo

Opus reticulatum: Roman masonry consisting of diamond-shaped blocks

Palazzo: not just a palace, but any large, important building

Pantocrator: Christ 'ruler of all', a common subject for apse paintings and mosaics in areas influenced by Byzantine art

Pediment: gable on façade of ancient building

Peribolos: a temple precinct and immediate area

Peristyle: a garden court, surrounded by colonnade

Piscina: a Roman tank or pool

Pithos: large ceramic vessel

Polyptych: painting divided into more than three sections

Presepio: a Christmas crib

Punta: promontory

Putti: flocks of cherubs with rosy cheeks and bums that infested much of Italy in the Baroque era

Quattrocento: the 1400s—the Italian way of referring to centuries (*duecento, trecento, quattrocento, cinquecento*, etc.)

Rupe: escarpment

Scolgio: rock, cliff; plural, *scolgiere* is a reef

Sesi: early, nuraghe-type structures on Pantelleria

Stagno: lagoon

Stoa: porticoed shelter for merchants and city business

Stentinello: early Neolithic culture in Sicily that made pottery decorated with geometrical incisions or seashell imprints

Stylobate: base of a columned temple or other building

Telamones: male caryatid

Termae: baths

Tholos: a circular building, a form often used for Greek tombs

Tophet: Carthaginian cemetery for sacrificed infants

Trasenna: marble screen separating the altar area from the rest of an early Christian church

Triclinium: the main hall of a Roman house, used for dining and entertaining

Triptych: a painting divided into three sections

Trompe l'oeil: art that uses perspective effects to deceive the eye

Villa: a country house or garden

LANGUAGE

The fathers of modern Italian were Dante, Manzoni, and television. Each did its part in creating a national language from an infinity of regional and local dialects; the Florentine Dante, the first to write in the vernacular, did much to put the Tuscan dialect in the foreground of Italian literature. Manzoni's revolutionary novel, *I promessi sposi*, heightened national consciousness by using an everyday language all could understand in the 19th century. Television in the last few decades is performing an even more spectacular linguistic unification; although the majority of Italians still speak a dialect at home, school, and work, their TV idols insist on proper Italian.

Perhaps because they are so busy learning their own beautiful but grammatically complex language, Italians are not especially apt at learning others. English lessons, however, have been the rage for years, and at most hotels and restaurants there will be someone who speaks some English. In small towns and out-of-the-way places, finding an Anglophone may prove more difficult. The words and phrases below should help you out in most situations, but the ideal way to come to Italy is with some Italian under your belt; your visit will be richer, and you're much more likely to make some Italian friends.

Italian words are pronounced phonetically. Every vowel and consonant is sounded. Consonants are the same as in English, except the *c* which, when followed by an 'e' or 'i', is pronounced like the English 'ch' (*cinque* thus becomes cheenquay). Italian *g* is also soft before 'i' or 'e' as in *gira*, or jee-ra. *H* is never sounded; *z* is pronounced like 'ts'. The consonants *sc* before the vowels 'i' or 'e' become like the English 'sh' as in *sci*, pronounced shee; *ch* is pronouced like a 'k' as in *Chianti*, kee-an-tee; *gn* as 'ny' in English (*bagno*, pronounced ban-yo); while *gli* is pronounced like the middle of the word million (*Castiglione*, pronounced Ca-stee-lyon-ay).

Vowel pronunciation is: *a* as in English father; *e* when unstressed is pronounced like 'a' in fate as in *mele*, when stressed can be the same or like the 'e' in pet (*bello*); *i* is like the i in machine; *o* like 'e', has two sounds, 'o' as in hope when unstressed (*tacchino*), and usually 'o' as in rock when stressed (*morte*); *u* is pronounced like the 'u' in June.

The accent usually (but not always!) falls on the penultimate syllable. Also note that in the big northern cities, the informal way of addressing someone as you, *tu*, is widely used; the more formal *lei* or *voi* is commonly used in provincial districts.

Useful words and phrases

yes/no/maybe	si/no/forse
I don't know	Non lo so
I don't understand	Non capisco
(Italian).	(italiano).
Does someone here	C'è qualcuno qui
speak English?	chi parla inglese?
Speak slowly	Parla lentamente
Could you assist me?	Potrebbe mi aiutare?
Help!	Aiuto!
Please	Per favore

Thank you (very much)	(Molto) grazie
You're welcome	Prego
It doesn't matter	Non importa
All right	Va bene
Excuse me	Scusi
Be careful!	Attenzione!
Nothing	Niente
It is urgent!	E urgente!
How are you?	Come sta?
Well, and you?	Bene, e lei?
What is your name?	Come si chiama?
Hello	Salve *or* ciao (both informal)
Good morning	Buongiorno (formal hello)
Good afternoon, evening	Buona sera (also formal hello)
Good night	Buona notte
Goodbye	Arrivederla (formal), arrivederci, ciao (informal)
What do you call this in Italian?	Come si chiama questo in italiano?
What?	Che
Who?	Chi
Where?	Dove
When?	Quando
Why?	Perche
How?	Come
How much?	Quanto
I am lost	Mi sono smarrito
I am hungry	Ho fame
I am thirsty	Ho sete
I am sorry	Mi dispiace
I am tired	Sono stanco
I am sleepy	Ho sonno
I am ill	Mi sento male
Leave me alone	Lasciami in pace
good	buono/bravo
bad	male/cattivo
It's all the same	Fa lo stesso
slow	piano
fast	rapido
big	grande
small	piccolo
hot	caldo
cold	freddo
up	su
down	giu
here	qui
there	li

315

Shopping, service, sightseeing

I would like . . .	Vorrei . . .
Where is/are . . .	Dov'è/Dove sono . . .
How much is it?	Quanto viene questo?
open	aperto
closed	chiuso
cheap/expensive	a buon prezzo/caro
bank	banco
beach	spiaggia
bed	letto
church	chiesa
entrance	entrata
exit	uscita
hospital	ospedale
money	soldi
museum	museo
newspaper (foreign)	giornale (straniero)
pharmacy	farmacia
police station	commissariato
policeman	poliziotto
post office	ufficio postale
sea	mare
shop	negozio
telephone	telefono
tobacco shop	tabaccaio
WC	toilette/bagno
men	Signori/Uomini
women	Signore/Donne

TIME

What time is it?	Che ora sono?
month	mese
week	settimana
day	giorno
morning	mattina
afternoon	pomeriggio
evening	sera
today	oggi
yesterday	ieri
tomorrow	domani
soon	presto
later	dopo, più tarde
It is too early	E troppo presto
It is too late	E troppo tarde

DAYS

Monday	lunedi
Tuesday	martedi
Wednesday	mercoledi
Thursday	giovedi
Friday	venerdi
Saturday	sabato
Sunday	domenica

NUMBERS

one	uno/una
two	due
three	tre
four	quattro
five	cinque
six	sei
seven	sette
eight	otto
nine	nove
ten	dieci
eleven	undici
twelve	dodici
thirteen	tredici
fourteen	quattordici
fifteen	quindici
sixteen	seidici
seventeen	diciassette
eighteen	diciotto
nineteen	diciannove
twenty	venti
twenty-one	ventuno
twenty-two	ventidue
thirty	trenta
thirty-one	trentuno
forty	quaranta
fifty	cinquanta
sixty	sessanta
seventy	settanta
eighty	ottanta
ninety	novanta
hundred	cento
one hundred and one	cento uno
two hundred	duecento
thousand	mille
two thousand	due mille
million	millione
billion	miliardo

TRANSPORT

airport	aeroporto
bus stop	fermata
bus/coach	auto/pulmino
railway station	stazione ferroviaria
train	treno
track/platform	binario
port	porto
port station	stazione marittima
ship	nave
automobile	macchina
taxi	tassi
ticket	biglietto
customs	dogana
seat (reserved)	posto (prenotato)

TRAVEL DIRECTIONS

I want to go to . . .	Desidero andare a . . .
How can I get to . . . ?	Come posso andare a . . . ?
Do you stop at . . . ?	Ferma a . . . ?
Where is . . . ?	Dov'è . . . ?
How far is it to . . . ?	Quanto siamo lontani da . . . ?
When does the . . . leave?	A che ora parte . . . ?
What is the name of this station?	Come si chiama questa stazione?
When does the next . . . leave?	Quando parte il prossimo . . . ?
From where does it leave?	Da dove parte?
How long does the trip take . . . ?	Quanto tempo dura il viaggio?
How much is the fare?	Quant'è il biglietto?
Good trip!	Buon viaggio!
near	vicino
far	lontano
left	sinistra
right	destra
straight ahead	sempre diritto
forward	avanti
backward	in dietro
north	nord/settentrionale
south	sud/mezzogiorno
east	est/oriente
west	ovest/occidente
around the corner	dietro l'angolo
crossroads	bivio
street/road	strada
square	piazza

318

DRIVING

car hire	noleggio macchina
motorbike/scooter	motocicletta/Vespa
bicycle	bicicletta
petrol/diesel	benzina/gasolio
garage	garage
This doesn't work	Questo non funziona
mechanic	meccanico
map/town plan	carta/pianta
Where is the road to . . . ?	Dov'è la strada per . . . ?
breakdown	guasto *or* panne
driver's licence	patente di guida
driver	guidatore
speed	velocità
danger	pericolo
parking	parcheggio
no parking	sosta vietato
narrow	stretto
bridge	ponte
toll	pedaggio
slow down	rallentare

Italian menu vocabulary

Antipasti
These before-meal treats can include almost anything; among the most common are:

Antipasto misto	mixed antipasto
Bruschetto	garlic toast
Carciofi (sott'olio)	artichokes (in oil)
Crostini	liver paté on toast
Frutta di mare	seafood
Funghi (trifolati)	mushrooms (with anchovies, garlic, and lemon)
Gamberi al fagiolino	shrimp with white beans
Mozzarella (in carrozza)	buffalo cheese (fried with bread in batter)
Olive	olives
Prosciutto (con melone)	raw ham (with melon)
Salame	cured pork
Salsicce	dry sausage

Minestre e Pasta
These dishes are the principal typical, first courses (*primo*) served throughout Italy.

Agnolotti	ravioli with meat
Cacciucco	spiced fish soup
Cannelloni	meat and cheese rolled in pasta tubes
Cappelletti	small ravioli, often in broth

Crespelle	crepes
Fettuccine	long strips of pasta
Frittata	omelette
Gnocchi	potato dumplings
Lasagne	sheets of pasta baked with meat and cheese sauce
Minestre di verdura	thick vegetable soup
Minestrone	soup with meat, vegetables, and pasta
Orecchiette	ear-shaped pasta, usually served with turnip greens
Panzerotti	ravioli filled with mozzarella, anchovies, and egg
Pappardelle alla lepre	pasta with hare sauce
Pasta e fagioli	soup with beans, bacon, and tomatoes
Pastina in brodo	tiny pasta in broth
Penne all'arrabbiata	quill-shaped pasta in hot spicy sauce
Polenta	cake or pudding of corn semolina, prepared with meat or tomato sauce
Risotto (alla Milanese)	Italian rice (with saffron and wine)
Spaghetti all'Amatriciana	with spicy sauce of salt pork, tomatoes, onions, and hot pepper
Spaghetti alla Bolognese	with ground meat, ham, mushrooms, etc.
Spaghetti alla carbonara	with bacon, eggs, and black pepper
Spaghetti al pomodoro	with tomato sauce
Spaghetti al sugo/ragu	with meat sauce
Spaghetti alle vongole	with clam sauce
Stracciatella	broth with eggs and cheese
Tagliatelle	flat egg noodles
Tortellini al pomodoro/panna/in brodo	pasta caps filled with meat and cheese, served with tomato sauce, cream, or in broth
Vermicelli	very thin spaghetti

Second courses–Carne (Meat)

Abbacchio	milk-fed lamb
Agnello	lamb
Animelle	sweetbreads
Anatra	duck
Arista	pork loin
Arrosto misto	mixed roast meats
Bistecca alla fiorentina	Florentine beef steak
Bocconcini	veal mixed with ham and cheese and fried
Bollito misto	stew of boiled meats
Braciola	pork chop
Brasato di manzo	braised meat with vegetables
Bresaola	dried raw meat similar to ham

Capretto	kid
Capriolo	roe deer
Carne di castrato/suino	mutton/pork
Carpaccio	thin slices of raw beef in piquant sauce
Casoeula	winter stew with pork and cabbage
Cervello (al burro nero)	brains (in black butter sauce)
Cervo	venison
Cinghiale	boar
Coniglio	rabbit
Cotoletta (alla Milanese/alla Bolognese)	veal cutlet (fried in breadcrumbs/with ham and cheese)
Fagiano	pheasant
Faraono (alla creta)	guinea fowl (in earthenware pot)
Fegato alla veneziana	liver and onions
Involtini	rolled slices of veal with filling
Lepre (in salmi)	hare (marinated in wine)
Lombo di maiale	pork loin
Lumache	snails
Maiale (al latte)	pork (cooked in milk)
Manzo	beef
Osso buco	braised veal knuckle with herbs
Pancetta	rolled pork
Pernice	partridge
Petto di pollo (alla fiorentina/bolognese/sorpresa)	boned chicken breast (fried in butter/with ham and cheese/stuffed and deep fried)
Piccione	pigeon
Pizzaiola	beef steak with tomato and oregano sauce
Pollo (alla cacciatora/alla diavola/alla Marengo)	chicken (with tomatoes and mushrooms cooked in wine/grilled/ fried with tomatoes, garlic and wine)
Polpette	meatballs
Quaglie	quails
Rane	frogs
Rognoni	kidneys
Saltimbocca	veal scallop with prosciutto and sage, cooked in wine and butter
Scaloppine	thin slices of veal sautéed in butter
Spezzatino	pieces of beef or veal, usually stewed
Spiedino	meat on a skewer or stick
Stufato	beef braised in white wine with vegetables
Tacchino	turkey
Trippa	tripe
Uccelletti	small birds on a skewer
Vitello	veal

Pesce (Fish)

Acciughe or Alici	anchovies
Anguilla	eel
Aragosta	lobster
Aringa	herring
Baccalà	dried cod
Bonito	small tuna
Branzino	sea bass
Calamari	squid
Cappe sante	scallops
Cefalo	grey mullet
Coda di rospo	angler fish
Cozze	mussels
Datteri di mare	razor (or date) mussels
Dentice	dentex
Dorato	gilt head
Fritto misto	mixed fish fry, with squid and shrimp
Gamberetto	shrimp
Gamberi (di fiume)	prawns (crayfish)
Granchio	crab
Insalata di mare	seafood salad
Lampreda	lamprey
Merluzzo	cod
Nasello	hake
Orata	bream
Ostrice	oysters
Pesce spada	swordfish
Polipi	octopus
Pesce azzuro	various types of small fish
Pesce San Pietro	John Dory
Rombo	turbot
Sarde	sardines
Seppie	cuttlefish
Sgombro	mackerel
Sogliola	sole
Squadro	monkfish
Tonno	tuna
Triglia	red mullet (rouget)
Trota	trout
Trota salmonata	salmon trout
Vongole	small clams
Zuppa di pesce	mixed fish in sauce or stew

Contorni (side dishes, vegetables)

Asparagi (alla fiorentina)	asparagus (with fried eggs)
Broccoli (calabrese, romana)	broccoli (green, spiral)

Carciofi (alla giudia)	artichokes (deep fried)
Cardi	cardoons, thistles
Carote	carrots
Cavolfiore	cauliflower
Cavolo	cabbage
Ceci	chickpeas
Cetriolo	cucumber
Cipolla	onion
Fagioli	white beans
Fagiolini	French (green) beans
Fave	fava beans
Finocchio	fennel
Funghi (porcini)	mushroom (boletus)
Insalata (mista, verde)	salad (mixed, green)
Lattuga	lettuce
Lenticchie	lentils
Melanzana (al forno)	aubergine/eggplant (filled and baked)
Mirtilli	bilberries
Patate (fritte)	potatoes (fried)
Peperoni	sweet peppers
Peperonata	stewed peppers, onions, etc. similar to ratatouille
Piselli (al prosciutto)	peas (with ham)
Pomodoro	tomatoes
Porri	leeks
Radicchio	red chicory
Radice	radishes
Rapa	turnip
Sedano	celery
Spinaci	spinach
Verdure	greens
Zucca	pumpkin
Zucchini	courgettes (zucchini)

Formaggio (Cheese)

Bel Paese	a soft white cow's cheese
Cascio/Casciocavallo	pale yellow, often sharp cheese
Fontina	rich cow's milk cheese
Groviera	mild cheese
Gorgonzola	soft blue cheese
Parmigiano	Parmesan cheese
Pecorino	sharp sheep's cheese
Provalone	sharp, tangy cheese; *dolce* is more mild
Stracchino	soft white cheese

Frutta (Fruit, nuts)

Albicocche	apricot

Ananas	pineapple
Arance	oranges
Banane	banana
Cachi	persimmon
Ciliegie	cherries
Cocomero	watermelon
Composta di frutta	stewed fruit
Dattero	date
Fichi	figs
Fragole (con panna)	strawberries (with cream)
Frutta di stagione	fruit in season
Lampioni	raspberries
Macedonia di frutta	fruit salad
Mandarino	tangerine
Melagrana	pomegranite
Mele	apples
Melone	melon
More	blackberries
Nespola	medlar fruit
Pera	pear
Pesca	peach
Pesca noce	tangerine
Pompelmo	grapefruit
Prugne/susina	plum
Uve	grapes

Dolci (Desserts)

Amaretti	macaroons
Cannoli	crisp pastry tube filled with ricotta, cream, chocolate or fruit
Coppa gelato	assorted ice cream
Crema caramella	caramel topped custard
Crostata	fruit flan
Gelato (produzione propria)	ice cream (homemade)
Granita	flavoured ice, usually lemon or coffee
Monte Bianco	chestnut pudding with whipped cream
Panettone	sponge cake with candied fruit and raisins
Panforte	dense cake of chocolate, almonds, and preserved fruit
Saint Honoré	meringue cake
Semifreddo	refrigerated cake
Sorbetto	sherbet
Spumone	a soft ice cream
Tiramisù	cream, coffee, and chocolate dessert
Torrone	nougat
Torta	tart

Torta millefoglie	layered custard tart
Zabaglione	whipped eggs and Marsala wine, served hot
Zuppa inglese	trifle

Bevande/beverages

Acqua minerale con/senza gas	mineral water with/without fizz
Aranciata	orange soda
Birra (alla spina)	beer (draught)
Caffè (freddo)	coffee (iced)
Ciocolata (con panna)	chocolate (with cream)
Gassosa	lemon-flavoured soda
Latte	milk
Limonata	lemon soda
Sugo di frutta	fruit juice
Tè	tea
Vino (rosso, bianco, rosato)	wine (red, white, rosé)

Cooking terms, miscellaneous

Aceto (balsamico)	vinegar (balsam)
Affumicato	smoked
Aglio	garlic
Alla brace	braised
Bicchiere	glass
Burro	butter
Caccia	game
Conto	bill
Costoletta/Cotoletta	chop
Coltello	knife
Cotto adagio	braised
Cucchaio	spoon
Filetto	fillet
Forchetta	fork
Forno	oven
Fritto	fried
Ghiaccio	ice
Griglia	grill
Limone	lemon
Magro	lean meat/or pasta without meat
Mandorle	almonds
Marmellata	jam
Menta	mint
Miele	honey
Mostarda	candied mustard sauce
Nocciole	hazelnut
Noce	walnut

Olio	oil
Pane (tostato)	bread (toasted)
Panini	sandwiches
Panna	fresh cream
Pepe	pepper
Peperoncini	hot chili peppers
Piatto	plate
Pignoli	pine nuts
Prezzemolo	parsley
Ripieno	stuffed
Rosemarino	rosemary
Sale	salt
Salmi	wine marinade
Salsa	sauce
Salvia	sage
Senape	mustard
Tartufi	truffles
Tassa	cup
Tavola	table
Tovagliolo	napkin
Tramezzini	finder sandwiches
Umido	cooked in sauce
Uovo	egg
Zucchero	sugar

FURTHER READING

Tuscan Islands
Racheli, Gin, *Le Isole del Ferro*, Mursia, Milan, 1978.

Elba
Hoare, Sir Richard Cole, *A Tour through the Island of Elba*, W. Bulmen, London, 1814.
Pickthall, Rudolf, *The Comic Kingdom: Napoleon, The last phase but two*, John Lane, London & New York, 1914.

Ischia
Bret Harte, Geoffrey and Kit, *The Island in the Sun*, Little, Brown & Co, Boston, 1937.
Douglas, Norman, *Summer Islands*, Colophon Press, New York, 1931.
Lowrie, Walter, *Enchanted Island*, Philosophical Library, New York, 1953.

Procida
Lamartine, Alphonse de, *Graziella* (trans. James B. Runnion), A. C. McClurg, Chicago, 1911.

Capri
Cerio, Edwin, *That Capri Air*, Thomas Nelson, London, 1957
——, *The Masque of Capri*, Harper & Bros, New York, 1929.
Douglas, Norman, *Siren Island*, M. Secker, New York, 1929.

Tremiti Islands
Mancini, Enzo, *Isole Tremiti Sassi Diomede*, Mursia, Milan, 1979.

Sicily
Aziz, Ahmed, *A History of Islamic Sicily*, Edinburgh University Press, 1953.
Blok, Anton, *The Mafia of a Sicilian Village 1860–1960*, Polity Press, 1979.
Brea, Luigi Bernabo, *Sicily Before the Greeks*, Thames & Hudson, London, 1957.
Brydone, Patrick, *A Tour through Sicily and Malta*, London, 1776.
Campbell, Rodney, *The Luciano Project: The Secret Wartime Collaboration of the Mafia and the US Navy*, McGraw Hill, New York, 1977.
Cronin, Vincent, *The Golden Honeycomb*, Hart Davis, London; Dutton, New York, 1954.
Dolci, Danilo, *Outlaws* (trans. R. Munroe), Orion Press, New York, 1961.
Durrell, Lawrence, *Sicilian Carousel*, Viking Press, New York, 1977.
Fineley, Moses, *A History of Sicily: Ancient Sicily to the Arab Conquest*, published in a 3-volume set with Dennis Mack Smith's *Medieval Sicily, 800–1713* and *Modern Sicily, after 1713*, Viking Press, New York, 1968.
Goethe, J. W., *Italian Journey* (trans. W. H. Auden and Elizabeth Mayer), Penguin Classics, 1982.
Guido, Margaret, *Sicily: An Archaeological Guide*, Faber, London, 1977.
Lewis, Norman, *The Honoured Society*, Eland Books 1969.
Norwich, John Julius Cooper, *The Kingdom in the Sun, 1130–1194*, Harper & Row, New York, 1970; Faber, London, 1976.

Pirandello, Luigi, *The Old and the Young* (trans. C. K. Scott-Moncrieff), Dutton, New York, 1928.

Quennell, Peter, *Spring in Sicily*, Weidenfeld & Nicolson, London, 1952.

Randall MacIver, David, *Greek Cities in Italy and Sicily*, Clarendon Press, Oxford, 1931.

Runciman, Steven, *The Sicilian Vespers*, Cambridge University and Penguin Paperbacks.

Sciascia, Leonardo, *Salt in the Wound* (trans. Judith Green), Orion Press, New York, 1969.

Simeti, Mary Taylor, *On Persephone's Island*, Knopf, 1986

Tomasi di Lampedusa, Giuseppe, *The Leopard*, Harville, USA; Fontana, London, 1972.

Verga, Giovanni, *The House by the Medlar Tree* (trans. Eric Mosbacher), Dutton, New York, 1928.

——, *Mastro Don Gesualdo* (trans. D. H. Lawrence), Jonathan Cape, London, 1925.

Aeolian Islands

Racheli, Gin, *Eolie di Vento e di Fuoco*, Mursia, Milan, 1977.

Egadi Islands

Maxwell, Gavin, *The Ten Pains of Death*, Dutton, New York, 1959.

Racheli, Gin, *Egadi, Mare e Vita*, Mursia, Milan, 1979.

Pelagie Islands

Mancini, Enzo, *Le Isole del Sole*, Mursia, Milan, 1978

Sardinia

Balducci, Carolyn Feleppa, *A Selfmade Woman: Biography of Nobel Prize Winner Grazia Deledda*, Houghton Mifflin, Boston, 1975.

Boucher, Edmund Spenser, *Sardinia in Ancient Times*, Blackwell, Oxford; Longmans, Green & Co, New York, 1917.

Delane, M., *Sardinia: The Undefeated Island*, London, 1968.

Deledda, Grazia, *The Mother, The Woman and the Priest* (trans. Mary G. Steegman), Jonathan Cape, London, 1923.

Ferracuti, F., R. Lazzari and M. Wolfgang, *Violence in Sardinia*, Rome, 1971.

King, Russell, *Sardinia*, Stackpole Books, Newton Abbot, 1975.

Lawrence, D. H., *Sea and Sardinia*, Viking Press, New York, 1972.

Waite, Virginia, *Sardinia*, Batsford, London, 1977.

INDEX

The smaller islands are indexed both individually and within each group of islands. Places in Sardinia and Sicily are dispersed alphabetically throughout the index; 'Sa' = Sardinia, 'Si' = Sicily. Names of people are in italics.

INDEX

San Nicola 82, 84, 86–7
Troina (Si) 198

Ulassai (Sa) 308
Umile of Petralia, Fra 98, 178, 198
Uras (Sa) 283
Ustica 226–30
Uta (Sa) 277

Vaccano, D. A. 81
Vaccarini, Giovanni Biagio 99, 120, 122
Valledoria (Sa) 298
Vassallaggi (Si) 194
Vendicari (Si) 137
Ventotene 58–62
Verga, Giovanni 100, 124
Vico, Giambattista 65
Villa Casale (Si) 199–200
Villamar (Sa) 277
Villanova Truscheddu (Sa) 285
Villaputzu (Sa) 275
Villasimius (Sa) 274
Villaspeciosa (Sa) 277
Vinifrido, Paolo 84

Vittoria (Si) 142
Vittoria Colonna 63–5
Vittorio Emanuele II 96, 261
Vittorio Emanuele III 47
Vivara 70, 74
Vizzini (Si) 124
volcanoes 30
Vulcano 213–15

water sports 15
Waugh, Evelyn 115
Whitaker, Joseph 244
William I ('the Bad') of Sicily 94, 161, 165, 199, 200
William II ('the Good') of Sicily 94, 162, 165
wine 102, 177, 267
Woodhouse, John 177

yacht charter 10
youth hostels 22

Zafferana Etnea (Si) 116
Zanche, Michele 293
Zanone 58